GRACE

GRACE

The Life of Grace MacInnis

S.P. LEWIS

with a foreword by Alan Whitehorn

HARBOUR PUBLISHING
Madeira Park, British Columbia

HARBOUR PUBLISHING
P.O. Box 219
Madeira Park, BC Canada V0N 2H0

Published with the assistance of the Canada Council and the Government of British Columbia, Cultural Services Branch
Edited by Daniel Francis
Printed and bound in Canada
Front cover photograph: Grace makes her victory speech in Vancouver, BC after sweeping every poll in Vancouver–Kingsway in the October 30, 1972 federal election. [Ralph Bower/Vancouver Sun]
Back cover photograph : COMSTOCK/Yousuf Karsh
All photographs not otherwise credited are from the Grace MacInnis collection.

Canadian Cataloguing in Publication Data

Lewis, S.P. (Sunny P.)
    Grace

    Includes bibliographical references and index.
    ISBN 1-55017-094-5

    2. MacInnis, Grace, 1905–1991. 2. Legislators—Canada—
Biography. 3. Canada. Parliament. House of Commons—Biography.
4. Social reformers—Canada—Biography. I. Title.
FC626.M235L49 1993   328.71'092   C93-091644-1
F1034.3.M235L49 1993

This book is dedicated to my talented parents,
Charles E. "Chick" and Margie Lewis,
who encouraged me to write.

CONTENTS

Foreword

Grace MacInnis, the CCF-NDP
and the Quest for Social Justice

Alan Whitehorn

Alan Whitehorn is the former research director of the David Lewis memoirs, *The Good Fight* and author of *Canadian Socialism: Essays on the CCF–NDP* and co-author of *Canadian Trade Unions and the New Democratic Party*. He is professor of political science at the Royal Military College of Canada and a visiting professor (1994–96) holding the J.S. Woodsworth chair at the Institute for the Humanities at Simon Fraser University.

Grace MacInnis was one of those individuals whose remarkable character could leave a lasting impression even after a brief encounter. I can vividly recall my first meeting, in the mid-1970s, when Grace, increasingly immobilized by arthritis, invited her old colleagues David and Sophie Lewis, along with myself and my wife Suzanne, to her home for afternoon tea and conversation. While tea was served on fine bone china teacups, each a unique part of her late husband's collection, the talk inevitably turned to politics. She expressed growing concern about the direction of the NDP and social democracy, decrying the party's preoccupation with polling and the platitudes of public relations advisers. Instead, she called for a bolder vision based on a stronger dose of political philosophy and public policy. She urged more "ginger" and a more humanistic orientation. One could only marvel at the zeal and passion of the lifelong social activist, not in the least diminished by age and the debilitating effects of her illness.

A biography of this extraordinary Canadian is long overdue. Born in 1905, Winona Grace Woodsworth was the daughter of a no less extraordinary man. J.S. Woodsworth was a courageous voice for the poor and the downtrodden, first as a radical preacher and later as a founder of the CCF-NDP. Grace inevitably grew into a determined activist herself, a modern woman in a society still dominated by nineteenth-century attitudes governing the sexes. She was the eldest of Woodsworth's children; bright, well-educated and fluently bilingual. Had she been a son she would have been assured a relatively easy entry into the world of politics. As a woman she was forced to make a lengthy detour, starting with a stint in the traditional female role of schoolteacher, then serving long apprenticeships in support of her father's and husband's political careers. As S.P. Lewis makes plain, Canada's left-wing parties were no guarantee against the heavy male domination that characterized political life.

In 1932 a relatively young Grace Woodsworth married Angus MacInnis, a CCF MP almost twice her age. In 1941 she took advantage of the scarcity of wartime labour, which opened doors for women in industry and politics, to become one of the first female members of the BC legislature. After losing provincial and federal elections in 1945 and 1949 and sitting out the 1950s due to the failing health of her husband, Grace returned to the fray in 1965, when she became one of only four women MPs elected to the federal parliament. After the 1968 election she was the only female member. Even for a daughter and a wife of veteran parliamentarians, the role of solitary female in this male bastion was a daunting one, too often obstructed by reactionary attempts to thwart women's gains of any kind. Grace served ably as an NDP Member of Parliament from 1965 to 1974, continuing the socialist tradition of both her father and husband. But arthritis took its toll, and gradually she had to limit her political activities and travels. Even then, she encouraged others (former Vancouver MP Margaret Mitchell, for one) to follow her lead, and she remained active in Vancouver and British Columbia NDP circles right up to her death at the age of eighty-five in 1991.

As the author of this biography, S. P. Lewis has conducted extensive and painstaking archival research, undertaken a thorough reading of Hansard, and completed scores of interviews, including many with Grace MacInnis herself. The result is a well-researched, thoughtful and balanced biographical account. It does justice to its subject; as such, it is a welcome addition to the literature on Canadian socialism and the CCF-NDP.

Grace is no less valuable for the insight it provides into the early liberation struggles of Canadian women. By running for elected office at the municipal, provincial and federal levels and serving in major posts within the CCF-NDP itself, McInnis helped to break down the barriers so that others could follow.

Grace's legacy is multifold. She helped win a place on the national agenda for such issues as family planning, better conditions for homemakers, consumers' rights, greater justice and equality for women, and access to safe abortions. Her views sometimes seemed less radical to later activists, but contemporary feminists who have found strength in numbers will be moved to read about the lonely vigil of Grace MacInnis.

Among other things, the book provides a fresh view of J.S. Woodsworth. We see the day-to-day life of a man regarded as a saint in politics, but we also observe a very human Victorian father. We also get to know Grace's husband Angus MacInnis, one of the few manual workers who rose to the leadership ranks in the CCF. Despite their age and class differences, Grace and Angus established a prototype of the modern marriage. In an era when women were expected to be at home raising children, they opted to pursue careers, with all of the ensuing difficulties. In the early 1940s when Grace was an MLA in Victoria and her husband an MP in Ottawa, they must have been among the first first couples to juggle careers a continent apart.

A bonus of this biography is the detailed historical backdrop it provides showing the organization of social democracy both in British Columbia and Canada. Among the themes it follows are the clashes between idealism and realism, principles and electoral considerations, radicalism and moderation, social movement and party.

In the final analysis, *Grace* is a heroic tale of a determined individual who devoted her life to a political struggle defending the interests of the have-nots in a corporate-dominated capitalist society. It is also the moving story of one individual's indomitable courage in a battle with crippling arthritis.

Almost a decade after our first meeting, I saw Grace once more but under dramatically different circumstances. Instead of a small living room, it was a cavernous hall at the site of the 1983 NDP federal convention in Regina. The party had dropped in the polls, many members were openly critical of Ed Broadbent's leadership, and media were speculating about the demise of the NDP. During the day, the convention debates over a new Regina Manifesto revealed deep fissures within the party. It was not proving to be the unifying event for which party strategists had hoped. That evening, however, the turnaround in the party's fortunes commenced. A prairie-style home-cooked banquet had been organized for the thousand-plus delegates. It was a tribute both to the fiftieth anniversary of the Regina Manifesto and to retired party leader T.C. Douglas. But before Douglas spoke on his old home turf, he was introduced by another longtime CCFer, Grace MacInnis. By this time, her arthritis had become far worse. Every step to the podium was painful. Yet once she began, it was evident her passion was as vibrant as ever. She spoke with the resounding voice that emerges from moral conviction and a commitment to a better and more just world. Her powerful words left her audience profoundly moved, rank and file and leaders alike. Inspired, Tommy Douglas gave what many considered the speech of his life.

The one-two punch of the veteran CCFers was just the tonic dispirited party activists needed. An unforgettable standing ovation followed. The applause got louder and louder. It went on for an amazing twenty minutes.

Its crescendo marked an electrifying moment in the history of the CCF–NDP. Together these two old socialists had shown the path ahead, if only people dared to have the vision, the passion and the commitment.

Both of those eloquent voices have since been stilled, but at a time when her political heirs sorely need to hear it, Grace's continues in the pages of this book.

Preface

February 24, 1987 was the usual frantically busy day in the life of a Vancouver radio news reporter. I had two days to complete the current assignment, the creation of a twelve-part series on the fight to save the federal riding of Vancouver–Kingsway, threatened with elimination by redistribution. I had interviewed the current Member of Parliament for the riding, Ian Waddell, as well as Vancouver Mayor Gordon Campbell, a member of the three-person Electoral Boundaries Commission and people on the streets of the neighbourhood.

For historical perspective I called Grace Woodsworth MacInnis, who had represented Vancouver–Kingsway for the New Democratic Party from 1965 to 1974, the first woman ever elected to the House of Commons from British Columbia. Her husband, Angus MacInnis, was MP for the same area of Vancouver from 1930 to 1957, and I suspected she might have a few insights to contribute about this part of the city. I received far more than I expected.

I reached Grace as she was packing to move from her apartment to an intermediate care home on British Columbia's Sunshine Coast. The arthritis that forced her resignation from the House of Commons in 1974 had now become so painful that living alone was out of the question. Grace was in the midst of sorting through more than eighty years of memorabilia, correspondence, photographs and awards. Although up to her ears in boxes, she took the time to give me one of the most fascinating interviews it has ever been my privilege to record.

The twelve-part series was broadcast on deadline, and in due course the Vancouver–Kingsway riding was eliminated after a court challenge failed. Still, I was left with an overwhelming curiosity about the life of Grace MacInnis which was not submerged by my work on other stories. I wanted to know how one woman, born in 1905 before Canadian women had the vote or even were accorded legal status as persons, had managed to carve out a role for herself in the founding of the Co-operative Commonwealth

Federation/New Democratic Party, become a member of the BC Legislative Assembly during World War Two, and achieve significant changes in law and public opinion as an MP in opposition during the chaotic 1960s and 1970s. What had she accomplished to deserve an Order of Canada, eight honorary doctorate of laws degrees and the first Governor General's Persons Award given on the fiftieth anniversary of the declaration of legal status for women as "persons" in Canada? What battles had she fought and what scars did she bear? In her view, how far distant was her goal of equal rights and justice for all Canadians, and what could be done to realize this goal?

A few months later, after she had a chance to get settled, I visited Grace MacInnis at Shorncliffe, high on a hill overlooking the logging–fishing–tourist town of Sechelt, north of Vancouver on the Gulf of Georgia. It was the kind of day that gives the Sunshine Coast its name, all brilliant blue sky and crystalline air scented with cedar. Grace sat in a comfortable chair by the window. The gnarled hands and prominent bones of her fragile frame were evidence of the rheumatoid arthritis she had battled for more than twenty years. But her face, framed by a full crop of snow-white hair brushed back in a no-nonsense style, her famous face was strong and whole and full of light, bearing no trace of pain. Wisdom shone from her clear grey eyes.

The walls of the simple room were adorned by three photographs, images of the key people in Grace's life: her father, her mother and her husband. The stern yet loving countenance of James Shaver Woodsworth, founder of the CCF/NDP, was reflected in a photograph of a bust of her father, sculpted by a European artist and installed in the lobby of the new Woodsworth Building, a provincial government office tower in Winnipeg. The image of Grace's mother, teacher and peace activist Lucy Staples Woodsworth, showed her at sixty-five, a perceptive, kindly look in her eyes behind their spectacles. Grace's husband, Angus, appeared casually businesslike with one hand on his hip, in a 1953 photo he had taken especially for Grace on the occasion of the last of his many election victories.

Sunlight streamed through the open window, turning the leaves of the potted shamrock on Grace's table to translucent emerald. The story of this shamrock is entwined with the history of Grace's family. In the telling, Grace took me back to St. Patrick's Day 1904 when James was courting Lucy. "Because Mother came of Irish ancestors, Father gave her roses on St. Patrick's Day, and he had the florist put in a little branch of shamrock. They were married on September 7th of 1904. Mother had saved that little shamrock and planted it, and it became one of our travelling companions. Wherever we moved we had the little shamrock. It grew and thrived, and over the years Mother treasured it very much. We children got little slips of it here and there.

"Years later when Father was ill, Mother and Father were staying at Angus's and my suite in Vancouver, and Father died. He wanted his ashes strewn over the Gulf of Georgia, so we took my eldest brother's cabin cruiser, Mother carrying the urn. Mother strewed the ashes over the water, and we noticed she let float a little bit of the shamrock in with the ashes."

I was fascinated by the romance of her family's story, by the sense of history that brought an entire century to life, and by the political achievements of this remarkable woman. As Grace finished the poignant anecdote I felt inspired to write her larger story. Like so many other outstanding Canadian women, she had not yet been honoured with a biography to tell of her life. Since her retirement several other writers had approached Grace about working with her on a biography, but, Grace confided, she had discouraged them. Yet she saw in me, as a journalist and a woman, a person in whom she could place her trust. She decided to co-operate with me in this endeavour to chronicle her life so that the lessons she had learned would not be lost to future generations. I am grateful for the generous amount of time she set aside for our interviews, and for her introduction of the project to Howard White of Harbour Publishing.

As a biographer of Grace MacInnis, I have often felt like a detective, coaxing half-forgotten episodes from the memories of elders, and unearthing hidden anecdotes from dusty files of letters marked "confidential." I am thankful to Grace for retaining these files and donating them to the National Archives of Canada and to the Special Collections Division of the University of British Columbia's Main Library.

In writing her story, I have made a sincere attempt to achieve reportorial objectivity. It is fashionable among journalists today to hold that objectivity is impossible, that the best one can do is to state one's biases and try to be fair and balanced. I believe that although perfect objectivity cannot truly be attained, efforts toward that goal are possible. At the same time that I have undertaken to record accurately the facts of her life, I have also ventured to plumb the motives behind Grace's actions, and to understand the wellsprings of her emotions.

My research has revealed Grace's life to be full of illuminating adventures, tales of co-operation, clashes and risks, struggle and hard work, love and loss. It is the story of the roots of Canada's New Democratic Party and the striving of Canadian women toward greater liberty. In a wider sense it chronicles the social history of Canada as a nation from the turn of the century to the present.

Grace died in July 1991, a few days before her eighty-sixth birthday, yet her voice endures. Her legacy of sharing and co-operation, her great compassion for ordinary people and families, the courage to act on her convictions in the face of harsh criticism, and the steps she took to advance the status of women will live on.

My thanks to editors Mary Schendlinger and Dan Francis, who managed their cuts with sensitivity and patience.

I am much obliged to Alan Whitehorn for his detailed comments on the first draft of this book, and especially for his encouragement along the way. I would like to thank Charles Woodsworth for unstintingly sharing with me his unique viewpoint. My gratitude for his words of encouragement goes to the dean of biographers, Leon Edel, who took a special interest in this project because he knew J.S. Woodsworth and Frank Scott at McGill in the 1920s.

I gratefully acknowledge a grant of $1,500 from the Boag Foundation which allowed me to employ researcher Tracy Cohen. Researcher Stephen Phillips of the UBC Political Science Department contributed his competent investigative skills.

I am grateful to George Brandak and the staff at the University of British Columbia Library, Special Collections Division, who kindly allowed me the use of a research cubicle and handled innumerable requests for information cheerfully. Thanks are due also to the helpful staff in the Documents section of the UBC Main Library. A special thank-you belongs to the staff of the History and Government section of the Vancouver Public Library, who are quick with the facts by phone.

Staff members at all these libraries were co-operative in helping me to gain access to their unique materials, often going out of their way to send photocopies, pamphlets and books: the National Archives of Canada, University of Guelph Library, Carleton University Special Collections, Roosevelt Library, Hyde Park, New York, the Manitoba Historical Society, the City of Winnipeg Archives, the City of Vancouver Archives, the Simon Fraser University Institute for the Humanities, and G.F. Strong Rehabilitation Centre Clinical Information. Thank you to Elaine Bernard for generous loans from her private library. And, not least, thanks to the Permissions Division of Stoddart Publishing Co. Ltd. for their loan of a hard-to-find title.

No words can encompass my gratitude to my partner, Jim Crabtree, for his loving support.

S.P. LEWIS

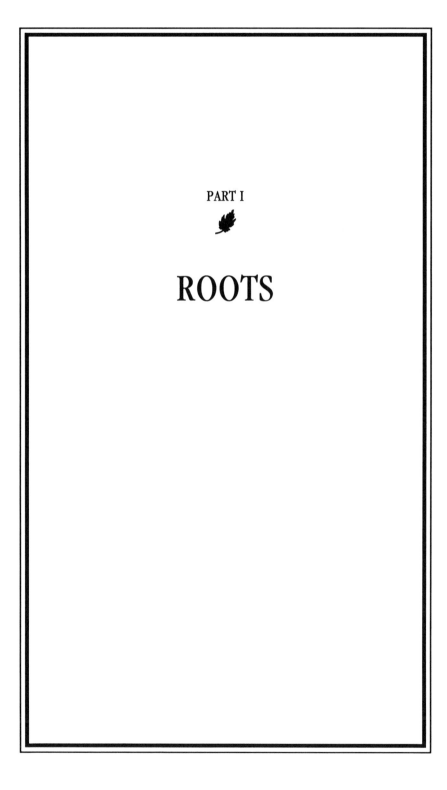

PART I

ROOTS

CHAPTER 1

A Prairie Lily

July 25, 1905 dawned clear and hot in Winnipeg, Manitoba, a city sprouting in Canada's abundant plains. An early breeze stirred a verdant shamrock plant by the bedroom window in the parsonage of Grace Church, but little air reached the great bed upon which Lucy Woodsworth strained in labour. Sequestered in a book-lined study down the hall, James, the church's junior pastor, prayed that his wife might deliver their first child safely and quickly. Hours passed as Dr. Popham's experienced hands encouraged Lucy. At last, success—a breath, the first cry—an infant girl was born.

All day family and friends came to the Methodist parsonage at 273 Ellice Avenue in the fashionable part of the city. James Woodsworth gingerly carried the baby about, happy and excited, proud to show her off to each caller. Dr. Popham departed, refusing to accept a fee for his services. And all the while beneath the surface of conversation James considered the important question of his daughter's name.

Around the evening fire the Woodsworths often read aloud the poems of Henry W. Longfellow. They loved the verse from *Hiawatha's Childhood* about the naming of Hiawatha's mother, a first-born daughter.

> In the moonlight and the starlight
> Fair Nokomis bore a daughter,
> And she called her name Wenonah,
> As the first-born of her daughters.
> And the daughter of Nokomis
> Grew up like the prairie lilies . . .

When Lucy had rested from her labour the new parents chose Wenonah, Anglicized as Winona, as the name for their own first-born daughter. The serious-minded young minister had been reading the novels of William Waverly as a rare indulgence in fiction. Tempted to write Winona Waverly

Woodsworth on the birth certificate, at the last minute James chose to honour the church in which he and Lucy began their work together. The little girl became Winona Grace Woodsworth. From the first she was called Grace.

Grace was born into a bustling, rapidly expanding city, gateway to the economic boom sweeping western Canada. In Winnipeg that Tuesday, July 25, 1905, the nation's mayors gathered for the convention of Canadian municipalities, and 30,000 people clicked through the turnstiles of the Dominion Industrial Fair. Its noisy midway, livestock exhibits, tractor hill climbs, racing and fireworks were but lures drawing people into the real business of Winnipeg real estate.

In 1870, when Manitoba entered the Dominion, Winnipeg's population was 241; by 1905 it was 100,000. From the United States and across Europe immigrants flooded into Winnipeg, tempted by offers of free homesteads or work on the railroads. Newcomers speaking dozens of languages poured into Winnipeg's North End: Russians, Austrians, Ruthenians, Galicians, Poles, Scandinavian peoples, Syrians, Bohemians, Germans, Catholics and Jews. All were crammed together in unsanitary hovels. In well-to-do homes telephones and gas lighting were standard amenities. Horse-drawn carriages and bicycles jostled the first automobiles on the city's newly paved streets.

Across Canada in 1905, Alberta and Saskatchewan entered the Dominion as the eighth and ninth provinces. A Liberal government was in power, led by the country's first French-Canadian Prime Minister, Sir Wilfrid Laurier, and opposed by the Conservatives under Robert Borden. Edward VII was on the throne of England, Lord Earl Grey, donor of the Grey Cup to Canadian football, was Governor General, and British troops were still stationed on Canadian soil. Of 5,371,000 Canadian residents, nearly one in six was a Methodist, making Methodism the second largest religious denomination in Canada. Only Catholics were more numerous.

The opening of Canada's first cinema, Marconi's new wireless transmission, and rail lines creeping across virgin prairie brought Canadians at the turn of the century great advances in technology and business. Social conditions for women lagged far behind. Grace, born female in 1905 Canada, faced a life of restrictions. Women were not yet considered persons before the law. Canadian women did not have the vote, married women were not permitted to own property in their own names, and women speaking in public were frowned upon. No woman belonged to a labour union, ran for public office, preached from a pulpit, served on a jury, sat as a judge or wore a skirt above her ankles. Work outside the home was discouraged by low wages and limited opportunities. If they could find employment, women laboured as domestics or as unskilled workers in factories. At best they could become nurses, teachers or office secretaries. Any other career was unheard of.

There were but three types of women, as *Life* magazine put it in 1903. "Women who want to be kissed. Women who do not want to be kissed. Women who look as though they would like to be kissed, but won't let men kiss them. The first men kiss, the second they do not kiss, the third they marry."

Globally it was an age of imperialism. The great European powers and Japan raced to secure far-flung colonies as markets and sources of raw materials. United States President Theodore Roosevelt presided over his country's western boom while mediating an end to the Russo-Japanese War. French bankers were funding industrial and rail expansion in Russia to counter the German alliance with Austria–Hungary. Kaiser Wilhelm II, claiming a "place in the sun" for Germany, was building ships to compete with the mighty British Navy. Britain had an entente with France.

Socialism of several varieties was spreading in Europe and across the English-speaking world. A 1905 report on poverty and ill health in British slums appalled the nation, confirming the warnings of Fabian socialists against the detrimental effects of capitalism. Early in 1906 a Liberal government took power in Britain, and the Labour party led by Keir Hardie won thirty seats, its first substantial parliamentary group.

Deep within semi-feudal Russia, a revolt was brewing that would profoundly alter world politics. In January 1905, the Tsar's forces fired on a peaceful demonstration triggering widespread strikes and revolts. Russians seeking freedom of speech and assembly, representative government, and the right to organize and strike had been active for twenty years in Russia and in exile. Some were inspired by German radical Karl Marx, especially by his 1847 Communist Manifesto; others drew ideas from earlier French revolutionary socialists. Amidst the radical fervour of 1832 in France the term socialism had been coined from the Latin *socius,* meaning companion, to describe the dream of a just distribution of property and equal rights for all social classes.

By the time Grace was born, Russian revolutionaries had divided into ideological camps. The Bolsheviks, led by Vladimir Ilich Lenin, initially in the minority, later became the largest group. They favoured armed insurrection, a closed party led by professional revolutionists and a dictatorship of industrial workers called the proletariat. The more moderate Mensheviks, led by Leon Trotsky, favoured a more open party membership policy. They formed the first *soviet* or representative council in 1905. Both wings called for the workers to come to power. A third group, the Social Revolutionaries, advocated individual acts of terror against landowners and members of the Tsar's family to motivate revolution.

Meanwhile, a less violent but equally influential socialist philosophy was taking shape in Germany, America and Britain. In 1884, the year the fledgling British Fabian Society published its first four-page tract, *Why Are the Many Poor?*, American socialist Laurence Gronlund wrote *The Cooperative Commonwealth*. The book detailed the structure and ideology of democratic socialism. By 1905 *The Cooperative Commonwealth* had been reprinted several times and had gained a wide audience in the United States, Canada and Europe. J.S. Woodsworth, deeply dissatisfied with the inequities of the current social order, most likely read Gronlund's work with great interest. Many of the ideas upon which Woodsworth founded Canada's third major party, the Co-operative Commonwealth Federation—most obviously the party's name—were first published in English by Gronlund.

Many of these ideas—the inevitability and gradual evolution of socialism, for instance—are also hallmarks of British Fabian socialism. Others are identical with the social gospel, particularly the notion of creating the Kingdom of Heaven on Earth.

Many British Methodists of this era equated holiness with concern for social welfare, an approach known as the social gospel. These Methodists were interpreting the New Testament as a method for setting up the Kingdom of God, an international social Utopia, on earth. To them salvation was no longer a purely personal matter. They believed one could save one's own soul only by service to humanity. When J.S. Woodsworth encountered these views during a turn-of-the-century study year at Oxford, they struck a sympathetic chord in him. A compassionate man, he believed that people usually awaken spiritually only after they are healthy, warm and fed.

The Socialist International was gaining strength around the world. In Winnipeg during the first decade of the century it took the form of increasing concern for human welfare. The Socialist International was created in 1889 when four hundred delegates from twenty countries met in Paris to create a new organization of socialist parties. The First International, 1864 to 1872, was a loose confederation of small political and trade union groups with Karl Marx as its dominant intellectual figure.

By 1905, when Grace appeared on the scene, her father was fervently seeking his true path in life. The young Canadian Methodist minister had acquainted himself with all these approaches to improving the human condition. Although the birth of the political party which he would inspire lay more than twenty-five years in the future, J.S. Woodsworth was already starting to forge an amalgam of Fabian socialism, the social gospel, and the co-operative commonwealth, together with his own spiritual and practical experiences. They would become a potent tool.

For the time being, James and Lucy Woodsworth saw their role as service within the bounds of organized religion. They pledged themselves to that vocation on September 7, 1904, by inscribing in the family Bible, "On this day of our marriage we desire unitedly to consecrate our lives to the work of the Christian ministry."

As yet the young couple had no home of their own. After their wedding on the lawn of the farm where Lucy was raised in Cavan, Ontario and their honeymoon at Muskoka Lake, they stayed with James's parents on Vaughan Street in Winnipeg. It was an arrangement marked by mutual tolerance and affection. During the summer of 1905, while the minister was on holidays, they lived at the Grace Church parsonage, and there Grace was born.

The house James and Lucy had rented was not ready when the minister returned; they had to board for several weeks. Baby Grace was growing quickly and known within the family for her astounding lung power, but Lucy was ill and weak for some months after the birth. They had no crib; at times Grace slept in a softly padded dresser drawer.

The new family finally moved into a house on Cumberland Street near the church and within walking distance of James's parents (James was called J.S. to distinguish him from his father, who bore the same name). In November, baby Grace was baptized in Grace Church. James, though loving with his wife and daughter, was frustrated by his seemingly comfortable position ministering to the well-to-do of Winnipeg, "who needed to purchase their souls once a Sunday and then forget about it," as Grace later described them. In the Grace Church congregation were some of the city's merchant princes, daily enriching themselves with grain and land speculation—in the young minister's opinion—at the expense of the working people crowded into squalid slums. He wanted to work with the people who truly needed help.

His sermons grew more pointedly critical of the rich. In one he warned, "money not only talks but rules," and in others he pointed out the vulgarity of conspicuous wealth. He attacked his audience for their indifference to the crying needs of the foreign-born. "A severe condemnation still rests upon indifference," he preached one Sunday. "Christianity stands for social righteousness as well as personal righteousness . . . . Indeed, my friend, you will save your own precious soul only as you give your life in the service of others . . . . We have tried to provide for the poor. Yet, have we tried to alter the social conditions that lead to poverty?" This was the essence of the humanitarian idealism called the social gospel, but his observations were deeply disturbing to Woodsworth's wealthy congregation. At the same time the young minister's recurrent doubts about the literal truth of some Methodist doctrines were resurfacing. He felt the need for spiritual refreshment, so he asked the Methodist Conference for a year off. James and Lucy planned a long visit to Europe, and then a solo journey for James to the Holy Land.

In June 1906 James and Lucy took Grace to her childhood home, the farm at Cavan, where the family would look after her until Lucy returned in October. On her first birthday, Grace played happily with Towzer the dog amidst chickens, cows and horses, while her parents explored Ireland.

Lucy was delighted to be revisiting the homeland of her ancestors. Born Lucy Lillian Staples in 1874 on the farm at Cavan, Ontario, sixteen miles west of Peterborough, Lucy was always proud of her Irish heritage. She told Grace, "I don't know exactly where our people came from in Ireland, but my mother often used to refer to a village called 'Tubberneara,' or at least it sounded like that. They took a wooden money box filled with gold sovereigns aboard the sailing ship. The voyage took three months."

It was Grace's great-great-grandfather, seventy-five-year-old Thomas Staples, and his second wife Jane Bell who set sail from Wexford, Ireland in 1823. Jane died just before the ship arrived. One story says she was buried at sea; another that the family managed to conceal the death, and brought the body ashore in a trunk for burial. Lucy descended from Thomas through a series of second marriages. Her father Richard, grandson of old Thomas by his first wife, was the son of a second-generation Thomas by his second wife. Hannah Staples, Lucy's mother, was Richard's second wife and his first cousin.

In Canada the Stapleses lived peaceful and productive lives. Of her mother's upbringing in a conservative Irish Protestant family Grace wrote, "She grew up in a home free from ideological struggle. A 'Marie a Chapdelaine' [sic] acceptance of the processes of nature—seedtime and harvest—sunshine and storm—plus the idea that the Lord planned the world and looks after his own. Struggle there was—but it was the struggle of the individual soul to live more in accordance with its best knowledge."

Lucy showed early evidence of a bright and eager intelligence. At seventeen she completed requirements for a teaching certificate at Lindsay, Ontario, near the family farm. Next fall she took her first teaching job in a high school a few miles away.

On school mornings for the next six years Lucy smoothed up her black hair, smiled at her grey eyes in the mirror, and took her place in various classrooms in Ontario and Quebec, either to teach or to upgrade her credentials. She stayed close to home and remained single. Then, in lieu of her share of the farm, her father financed Lucy's attendance at Victoria College at the University of Toronto where she studied history, French, and English language and literature. Grace later described Lucy as "one of the first women that was interested in a career outside marriage, and one of the first women graduates from Victoria College. She was the beginning of women's liberation."

It was while they were both attending Victoria College that J.S. Woodsworth first met Lucy, who was living in the same boarding house as her college friend Clare Woodsworth and Charlie Sissons, both first cousins to James. It was natural for him to board with them during his year as a divinity student. James completed the three-year Bachelor of Divinity course in one year, and at twenty-five sailed to England for a year of post-graduate work at Oxford. He was a new generation's standard-bearer of the proud tradition of Methodist Woodsworths.

James's father, Grace's paternal grandfather, was Reverend Dr. James Woodsworth, the first Superintendent of Methodist Missions for Western Canada. He married Esther Josephine Shaver, also a devoted Methodist. Josephine's family, United Empire Loyalists of Dutch ancestry, had built a comfortable colonial brick home at Applewood, a two-hundred-acre spread in Etobicoke, Ontario. There James and Josie were married; there their first child, Grace's father James Shaver Woodsworth, was born in 1874.

Eight years later the elder James moved his growing family from comfortable Ontario to the wilds of Brandon, Manitoba. As a pioneer missionary he drove a buckboard hundreds of miles across the western territories, often with his eldest son for company. The year Grace was born, he moved his home mission office from Brandon to Winnipeg and was named executive head of all Methodist missions from the Great Lakes to the Pacific Ocean.

This patriarch, a member of the first generation of Woodsworths born in Canada, was the seventh of twelve children of Richard Woodsworth and Mary Ann Watson, Grace's great-grandparents. In 1803 Richard was born Richard Wood in Sledmere, Yorkshire. When he emigrated to Canada he changed not only his country but his name. On a 1909 trip to Sledmere, Grace's uncle Joseph Woodsworth pinpointed the change of name. Blue tickets imprinted with Bible verses gave the proof. Joseph described them as "Wesleyan Methodist Quarterly tickets which do not indicate whether they were issued in England or in Canada, but on which the name Richard Wood occurs in 1826 and Richard Woodsworth in 1827. Grandfather told Father that he had taken the older form of the name." The tickets were carefully pasted in the Woodsworths' Commonplace Book.

Richard Woodsworth immigrated to Canada as a carpenter and became a well-to-do merchant builder with his own lumberyard at the corner of Yonge and Wellesley streets in Toronto. He was also a respected lay preacher who helped build the fledgling Methodist church in "Muddy York" as Toronto was called in the 1830s.

In 1831 Richard married Grace's great-grandmother, Mary Ann Watson, the Massachusetts-born daughter of an Empire Loyalist family. The Watsons moved to Canada after the War of 1812 when Mary Ann's father grew disgusted with anti-British attitudes in America. They too were devout Methodists, and the Woodsworth–Watson union was consecrated at the Watson home in "Muddy York."

When William Lyon Mackenzie and his band of rebels rose in arms against the government in 1837, Richard Woodsworth joined other Toronto Tories to defend the city. The sword he was given by the authorities to fight that battle later hung in a place of honour in J.S. Woodsworth's study. Grace remembers it as a source of inspiration. "Father was enormously proud of that sword. It reminded him that his forebears had been prepared to fight for their beliefs and it gave him a sense of family pride. He used to tell us that the only way he could be worthy of his grandfather was to fight for the new causes of today, even if that meant opposing the very things for which his grandfather had fought."

J.S. Woodsworth's year at Oxford in 1899–1900 changed his life dramatically. He had a plan "To study life . . . . To gain as many points of view as possible—more especially to see what may be helpful later. To get a fair idea of the principles of the religious and educational and social problems and work, and to try to understand the spirit which characterizes the whole system."

He was there at the time of the Boer War. As Grace explained in her award-winning biography of her father, the suffering he saw inflicted upon British families by a conflict in far-away Africa gave rise to ". . . a rooted hatred of war in any way shape or form which he maintained until the end of his life. It was probably the most deeply held of all his beliefs."

His Oxford studies, his social work in a London settlement house and his travels on the continent were fascinating. But when his year was over, the young minister returned to Canada, where he had an appointment to the Methodist church in the tiny prairie town of Carievale, Saskatchewan. After one year at Carievale and another at a church in Keewatin, Ontario, all James's doubts about his calling were back in force. From the isolation of these country parishes, James dreamed of carrying on city mission work of the kind he had seen in London. He was dispirited NS seriously considering resignation from the ministry when he was offered a year as junior pastor in Grace Church. It was an answer to his prayers. But more was needed to complete his life. Loneliness had left its mark on young James's heart.

When a letter from his university friend Lucy Staples reached him in Winnipeg, James longed to see her again. He visited Ontario, where she was teaching history at Lindsay Collegiate Institute. The two devout and serious people, both now nearing thirty, realized they were in love. They exchanged kisses and vows in a whirl of romance that left James breathless.

Now, back in the Old World and still deeply in love, James wanted to share with Lucy the insights of his voyage six years before, his dreams of creating a better life for humanity. One exalted day at the Grassmere Lake home of poet William Wordsworth they renewed their vows. Lucy wrote of that visit in the Commonplace Book, "We shall never forget the sacredness of this day's walk nor the inspiration it has brought us to seek only after the true, the beautiful, the good." On another page of their Commonplace Book, James inscribed his watchword for life, "Idealize the Real, Realize the Ideal."

Through Holland, Belgium, Germany and France the lovers explored cities and countryside together, cherishing their closeness, for they knew they would soon be separated. In October Lucy sailed for Canada, leaving James to journey on alone to Switzerland, Italy, Egypt and Palestine.

In the holy places of Jerusalem, James felt his faith renewed and rededicated himself to realizing his ideals. The young minister returned from the Holy Land with a crown of thorns that joined his grandfather's sword in his study as a reminder of how often victory is wrested painfully from defeat. This brown, dry circle of thorns was a sober inspiration to young Grace and her sister and brothers. Later, in his House of Commons office, it reinforced the image of James Shaver Woodsworth, MP as the "saint" of Canadian politics. It is now in the J.S. Woodsworth collection at the National Archives of Canada in Ottawa.

Lucy was again pregnant when she returned to Cavan to find baby Grace well and happy. James rejoined his family for Christmas on the Cavan farm, but he left almost at once for Revelstoke, a mining town in the mountains of British Columbia. Scandal had shattered the Methodist church there, and James was assigned to revitalize it. He quickly repaired the damage.

The Revelstoke church asked him to stay, but James was again struggling with spiritual doubts. He was not happy as a preacher; he wanted to help people in a practical way. He prepared to leave the ministry and wrote a letter of resignation. Meanwhile, at Cavan, Grace was discovering the joys and frustrations of living with her newborn sister Belva Elizabeth, born May 2, 1907.

James submitted his formal resignation to the Manitoba Methodist Conference in early June, but the special committee that interviewed him refused to accept it. Instead the Conference placed James in the position that would start him on the path to the House of Commons. He was put in charge of All People's Mission in Winnipeg, founded in 1898 to spread the Methodist faith and offer traditional charity. In the six years he would lead All People's Mission, James would broaden its work to serve the social as well as the spiritual needs of immigrants from more than forty countries jammed into the tenements of Winnipeg's North End.

Lucy travelled with Grace and the baby to a joyous reunion with James in Winnipeg June 20, 1907. Once again, they made their home with the senior Woodsworths on Vaughan Street. James took hold of his new job with vigour and imagination, drawing on the experience of social workers across North America to find ways of combating the alienation and ignorance which isolated the foreign-born from their Canadian neighbours.

Later that year all three generations of Woodsworths moved into a new home at 60 Maryland Street. The new eleven-room house seemed like a mansion with its broad verandah, beamed living-room ceiling and study with wooden sliding doors. Two-year-old Grace's life at 60 Maryland Street followed an orderly Christian routine of daily prayers after breakfast, church on Sunday in a white ruffled dress, and meals made ahead of time so there would be no work on the Sabbath. Wash Monday, ironing Tuesday: each day brought its tasks. Grandmother and Grandfather Woodsworth never varied the traditions of their own upbringing.

In April of 1909 Grace and Belva were joined by a brother, Charles. Later that year Grace's Grandfather Staples died on the Cavan farm. James and Lucy moved the family across the CPR tracks into the North End to establish the Stella Avenue Mission, another branch of All People's Mission. After five years of marriage the younger Woodsworths finally had their own home close to their work. A sturdy four-year-old when the family moved to 464 Stella Avenue, Grace long recalled the battle against the cockroaches as "something quite alien to our experience and very exciting." Their home became an integral part of the mission. One room was turned into an informal employment office, and English lessons went on continually.

One afternoon in a corner of the back garden at Stella Avenue, Grace made her public speaking debut. "I guess the reason I remember it is that one of the adults caught me at it. I had upended an old box and I was talking to an imaginary audience—I gather preaching at them, because you see the only thing that I would have as a model there would be my father. So while I wouldn't be preaching at them about Bible things, I'd be preaching at them about things that needed to be done. My father was at the social work stage then."

Lucy did not believe that a mother's duties were finished when she had fed the baby at one end and cleaned it up at the other. From the time Grace was very small, Lucy would teach morals with little stories and incidents from her own childhood. "The interesting thing," Grace reflected later, "is that you resented it in your teens, you were cold to it in your twenties or thirties, or forgot about it, but in your forties and fifties and sixties, seventies and eighties, the value of that teaching came to you."

Disciplining in the family was done by whoever was there when the offence occurred. There was never any recourse, no appealing the discipline of one parent to the other parent; they worked as one. "Sometimes my father would be quite irritated and angry; he was particularly so with a lie. If anybody ever told a lie, which was very seldom, he would punish with a slap or corporal punishment quickly. Mother's punishment was the other kind. We had cupboards there in the bedrooms and other places, and if the offence was great, Mother would put the child in the cupboard for a while and shut the door."

Grace retained vivid memories of the poverty that surrounded them. "Father took us for walks about the neighbourhood which was so different from the one we had left. Here the sights and sounds and smells were colourful and vivid. We got used to the bright kerchiefs of the women, the rough sheepskin coats of the men, and everywhere the queer talk we couldn't understand. We got used to the unpaved streets of North Winnipeg, to the

The Reverend James Shaver Woodsworth shortly after his return from Europe, c. 1900.

Lucy Lillian Staples, one of the first women to graduate from Victoria College, University of Toronto. She earned an honours degree in modern history in June 1901.

The Woodsworth children play with a toy lamb in the backyard of Stella Avenue Mission, the scene of Grace's first public address. Winnipeg, 1910. From left: Belva, Charles, Grace.

children playing about in the mud, and even to seeing pigs and chickens cluttering up the dooryards. We even became accustomed to the flies that swarmed around the garbage heaps in the back lanes or settled on the meat in the crowded little corner stores. Those pigs and chickens and flies worried my father; he was always indignant that the city authorities did nothing about them."

James published facts and organized like-minded people to fight the indifference of the wealthy and of the church establishment to the difficulties of the foreign-born workers. Two books were launched from his desk during the All People's Mission years, *Strangers Within Our Gates* in 1909, and *My Neighbour* in 1911. He drew together the leaders of all the diverse charitable groups in the city under one organization, the Associated Charities, formed in 1910.

James knew there was a great deal the "strangers within our gates" could contribute to their new country. Grace reflected, "He did his best to get the other Canadians to appreciate the beauty and the colour and variety of cultures that were coming in. He wanted the new immigrants woven into the tapestry of Canadian life." To foster cross-cultural under-standing, in 1909 James started a weekly lecture and concert series, the People's Forum, with the intention of creating a people's university. Held first in the auditorium of St. John's Technical Institute, the People's Forum moved in 1910 to the old Grand Theatre, and became a centrepiece of Winnipeg cultural life.

"We grew up in the midst of immigrants," Grace said. "That's where we got our general outlook over life which was that a human being is a human being underneath every superficial difference. We have never, never fallen for slurs or looking down on any race. We were taught then that the immigrant women's shawls of many colours were beautiful, intricate designs; the music that they made was lovely if it didn't get too strenuous. We were taught to see new things and good things in the people who came in."

James had been struggling to improve living conditions for working people since he had started with the All People's Mission, but he took his first formal seat at a labour table in 1909 when the church's Ministerial Association appointed him as its delegate to the Winnipeg Trades and Labour Council. There he came into closer contact with socialist thought. The Trades and Labour Council endorsed the socialist paper, *The Winnipeg Voice,* and in 1909 Woodsworth wrote a series of articles critical of the church establishment for the *Voice* under the name of Pastor Newbottle.

In 1910 Woodsworth took his first step into the socialist political arena. As a member of the Provincial Labour Representation Committee he sought support for Fred Dixon, the Social Democratic Party (SDP) candidate in provincial elections, who became a close friend. Formed in April 1909 in Vancouver as a breakaway group from the more doctrinaire Socialist Party of Canada, the SDP saw "socialism . . . as an evolutionary process," but nonetheless sought "the final overthrow of capitalism."

By 1911 the All People's Mission had become more than a vehicle for Christian teaching. It was an attempt to create a complete social settlement. There were Methodist Sunday schools and religious services, night school classes, English classes, exercises in self-government, a boys' police force, a baseball team, mothers' meetings, cooking and sewing classes, a gymnasium, hospital visitations, and direct relief for immigrants. At a time when there was no compulsory education or kindergarten, the All People's Mission had two kindergarten schools.

Grace wrote, "I remember the kindergarten, a sunny, happy place where the mothers brought their children, struggling at the same time with winter wrappings and the English language . . . . There was the library whose books had been donated by 'more fortunate' people in other parts of the city, that splendid room where I made the acquaintance of Alice in Wonderland, looking eagerly at the pictures and longing for the time when I could read the text."

There was a swimming pool in the basement of the Stella Avenue Mission, to the delight of the North End children, whose homes often had outdoor privies and no bathing facilities. There five-year-old Grace first met six-year-old Tommy Douglas, later her beloved political confederate, the future Co-operative Commonwealth Federation (CCF) premier of Saskatchewan and the first New Democratic Party national leader. But in 1910, at the mission pool, Tommy was a newly transplanted Scottish schoolboy, swimming and shouting with the rest despite repeated trouble with osteomyelitis. For wee Tommy swimming was more than a diversion; it was a welcome respite from his crutches, endured until a skillful surgeon saved the painful leg with a pioneering operation.

On Sunday nights James sometimes gave talks illustrated by lantern slides. It was a magic moment when the mysterious equipment was assembled, the coal-oil placed in the lamp and the lens focussed on the wall to show the hand-coloured slides. Grace recalls her father's enthusiasm for dramatic visuals. "From the 'magic lantern' he graduated to charts and diagrams and pictures, which he continued to use for most of his life."

One week before Christmas 1910 the fourth Woodsworth child, Ralph, was born. When he was a year and a half old, the flies in neighbourhood alleys became a personal problem for the Woodsworths. That summer, despite the urging of James and other concerned citizens, the civic authorities refused to clean up unsanitary conditions in the North End. A disease bred there, an intestinal infection called simply the "summer complaint," swept the city. Like many other North End babies, Ralph Woodsworth fell so ill that the doctor gave up hope. But Lucy would not give him up. She nursed Ralph back to health, and he survived to become a medical doctor.

Other babies were not so lucky, and James was furious with the apathy of well-to-do Winnipegers confronted with these infant deaths. "My father got very angry with people who said that this was the will of God. He felt that this was blasphemy of the worst type." Finally, on the insistence of Woodsworth and others, a clean-up effort was begun in the North End.

When James discovered that nearly one-third of Manitoba's children did not attend school of any kind, Woodsworth dinner table discussions often centred on their plight. From James's pen flowed a stream of newspaper articles successfully urging juvenile courts, playgrounds and compulsory school attendance.

For her first day of school in 1912 Grace simply walked across the street to Alexander School. Because she could already read, and all the new Canadian children there were still learning English as a second language, the family soon decided to send her across the CPR tracks to school in an English-speaking part of the city. But it was not her early lessons Grace remembered; it was the icy Winnipeg mornings as she crossed the Salter Street Bridge enveloped in great clouds of steam from the locomotives as they passed under the bridge.

"We had a lot of people to dinner," Grace recalled. "Father had the idea of bringing home a couple of guests without any particular notice, and Mother was always able to rise to the occasion." Despite the increased workload, Lucy enjoyed the intellectual stimulation provided by frequent visitors. "She kept abreast of modern affairs and saw to it that the older children always sat at the table, even when there was company. We were never encouraged to barge into the conversation at all; we listened. But as we got older, if we had the odd intelligent question to address to any of the guests, that was always encouraged. We heard conversation and information from the time we were little."

On Sunday afternoons heated discussions brought world events to life around the dining table. Over Lucy's luscious cream pie, Serbs, indignant over the annexation of Bosnia and Herzegovina by Turkey, argued their position. Other recent arrivals from Greece, Montenegro, Bulgaria, Rumania, and Albania refought all their territorial and cultural conflicts. Finally Lucy had to ask James to consider the backgrounds of their guests before inviting those from warring nations to tea at the same time. Grace, listening quietly, absorbed the excitement of intellectual challenge, the ferment of political change.

All the Woodsworth youngsters were brought up to be courageous and self-reliant, but one thing about walking through the Stella Avenue neighbourhood struck fear into Grace's heart: dogs. A fierce dog was kept chained all day across the back lane from the Mission House; its response to any stimulus was to rush out barking viciously. Grace was always terrified to go up that lane, afraid that the chain would break. It never did, but the fear of dogs stayed with her until after she was married.

Grace first heard the facts of life when she was six. "I remember picking blueberries one time, and I wasn't very big, at Keewatin, we went there for the summer. And Mother explaining how babies came into the world, not that she went into the last gruesome physical detail, but she made it explicit and clear. Then later when we got up to Gibsons in my early teens, I remember the girls indulging in sort of smutty speculative talk about this kind of thing, and I wasn't even remotely interested because I felt I knew the facts, and it wasn't very nice to speculate about those things anyway. Those were perfectly natural things and I wasn't going to get mixed up with that kind of talk. Mother was very, very wise. She taught us the things we needed to know and she trusted us." To help with housework at the mission, Lucy hired young women most in need of the work, those who were pregnant and unmarried. She explained their situation to her own little girls as soon as she felt they could understand. Lucy's practical, kindly outlook remained with Grace all her life and shaped her thinking as a legislator in the House of Commons during the 1960s and 1970s on issues of family planning, birth control and abortion.

Lucy was part of the earliest birth control movement in Winnipeg. She met regularly with a group of doctors' wives to discuss the controversial question and press for a change in public attitudes. This was a quasi-legal activity: until 1967 publication or exchange of birth control information was punishable by two years in prison. It was not until fifty-five years after her mother's work on family planning that Grace as a Member of Parliament was instrumental in changing this law.

Christmas was an enchanted time in the Woodsworth family. The holiday started early in December when Grace, Belva and Charles spent happy hours in Grandmother Woodsworth's fragrant kitchen helping with the mincemeat for pies. The meat grinder was fastened to the end of the kitchen table, and meat and suet were crammed in while the children helped turn the handle. The mincemeat recipe came from Grandmother Woodsworth's favourite cookbook, prepared by the women of the Brandon Methodist Church. The pale blue cover decorated with curlicues was inscribed with the motto, "Let me cook the meals of our nation, And I care not who makes her laws." These sentiments, so typical of the women of her grandmother's generation, Grace would quickly outgrow.

As December 25 approached, the Woodsworth children would write their wishes in letters to Santa and send them up the chimney in flames, confident they would be answered. Grace wrote, "On Christmas Eve the candles flickered on the tree and the stockings were filled. But I cannot remember a time when Santa Claus was presented as anyone other than a delightful fairytale figure. The recital of 'Twas the Night Before Christmas was a regular feature of our Christmas Eve. So was the reading of the Bible story of the Wise Men and the star over Bethlehem and the birth of Jesus. After Father had read the story to us, we would talk about the baby for whom there was no room in the inn and who grew up so full of love and concern for people—particularly the poor and sick and despised—that he wanted to change conditions to make their lives better. This got him into trouble with the rulers who didn't want change and they finally put him to death in a horribly cruel way."

In 1911, when Grace was six, Lucy and the children put together a little book that became a Woodsworth Christmas tradition. In Father's Book each member of the family would tell of a special event from the year just ended, and decorate the book with drawings for James to enjoy on Christmas morning. Even in those early days, James was carrying a heavy load of responsibility and was seldom home. Although sometimes stern and autocratic, he was still emotionally available to his wife and children, and he cherished these intimate records of family life. Later, as a parliamentarian and party leader, when he lived away from home for many months at a stretch, James valued Father's Book even more.

After Christmas breakfast the gifts under the tree were opened. Most were handmade treasures, and a few store presents bought with pennies carefully hoarded for weeks. Then the family crunched through the snowy streets to Grandpa and Grandma's house for the Christmas feast. With Grace's aunts, uncles, cousins and family friends they were twenty or more around the table, laughing at Grandpa's stories as he carved the turkey. "Then came plum pudding and mince pie and Japanese oranges and nuts, until everyone had filled every crevice in his innards," Grace recalled.

But James was not narrow in his religious understanding, and he wanted to ensure his children were also broad-minded. He took Grace with him to various religious services around the neighbourhood: Roman Catholic, Greek Orthodox and Jewish. "I remember all during my childhood we were living in my grandparents' home," Grace reflected. "They had regular religious observances, prayers at meals, regular days in the week for certain observances, including, of course, Sunday. But there was no attempt to institutionalize us. Consequently, there was no break for us when he left the church. I felt very strongly that he did the right thing. So I grew with a firm belief in the rightness of Christianity and Christian thinking without any of the formal church accoutrements."

James and Lucy had completely different personalities; what united them was a common view of their role toward humanity, which was to serve. Grace explained, "Father would determine the direction he was going to serve in and Mother followed that direction. My mother shared Father's ideas and values. Their upbringings were so much of a same kind, that the two of them had more or less the same shared ideals. Their companionship was never that of the man dictating to the woman at all; it was a case of two partners. Mother perfectly cheerfully and naturally adopted the role of bearing and nurturing the children, but at the same time she never surrendered her mental furniture that she had acquired in university."Others may have considered the Reverend J.S. Woodsworth a saintly figure, but Grace said the family did not. "Very early on our attitude was set and it was set by Mother. She knew Father's character and disposition very well. She realized that he was really quite high-strung, and that under pressure what happened was irritability and all the nervous things that go with it. She made us aware quite early that he was doing very fine work in the world and that these were necessary side-effects. She would shut us down completely when he would come home tired. We were forbidden to make noises and sent out to play and that kind of thing. We realized very early there was a great pride in what our father was doing. We weren't at all blind to his shortcomings, but they were a part of the whole scheme and so it didn't bother us.

"Father didn't have much of a sense of humour," Grace explained. "He had a sense of fun if a thing was really funny, but Mother saw the funny side of nearly everything that came along, and that stood her in excellent stead."

"He was frequently a stern parent," Grace's brother Charles remembered from the safe vantage point of adulthood. "The rigorousness of our upbringing, tempered by Mother's loving solicitude and her brighter disposition, was based on deep affection and a fundamental sense of justice. His sternness could be excused—if excuse were necessary—in some part by the inherent intensity of his nature . . . . From my uncles and aunts I have gathered that this trait of Father's character exhibited itself at an early age. He was the eldest in a large family, presided over by a father who was the essence of lovable geniality and a mother the soul of upright and self-respecting practicality . . . . To say that Father was not beloved by his younger brothers and sisters would be to exaggerate. But the truth is that they were afraid of him. He ran the household with a stern hand, and woe to him or her who failed to sweep the floor, carry out the ashes or perform what other household task was assigned." James's children were also somewhat afraid of him, but this feeling was tempered by the loving closeness of family life.

James himself needed this intimacy to balance the demands of public life. As Charles wrote of his father's beard—unfashionable at the time but traditional in the Methodist ministry, "It was a mixed blessing when, pyjama-clad, we tumbled romping into our parents' big bed in the early morning, and Father would playfully tickle us with it like a stiff scrubbing brush when he was supposed to be giving us an affectionate kiss. And for all our pride in him we were just a bit embarrassed when unruly youngsters would shout 'Beaver' as we walked by."

By the spring of 1913 James had established the All People's Mission on a firm basis, but he was by then certain the church would not lead the way toward the establishment of social justice in Canada. In May he resigned from the mission to become a full-time social service worker. James organized a new body, the Canadian Welfare League, and accepted the position of secretary. Launched at the mid-September meeting of the National Conference of Charities and Corrections in Winnipeg, the new privately funded league was to promote interest in all forms of social welfare. It would foster adult education, train social work leaders, send out educational materials and speakers and co-operate with universities, governments, religious groups and Canadian Clubs. At this time Canada had no government social welfare programs. The needy relied on private charities and religious groups for help.

Lucy and the four children went to live on the Cavan farm while James was changing his focus from the All People's Mission to the Welfare League. In the fall, Grace attended the local school and did her lessons on slates along with the other rural children. In November 1913 the family returned to Winnipeg and, nearly $1000 in debt and with heavy expenses ahead, moved into a house at 14 Cooper Street. Grace attended Mulvey School where paper and pencils, not chalk and slates, were the tools of education.

World War One began June 28, 1914, a month before Grace's ninth birthday, when the "shots that rang around the world" were fired in Sarajevo, killing the Archduke Ferdinand, heir to the throne of the Austro–Hungarian Empire, and his wife, Duchess Sophie of Hohenberg. The Balkan conflict, simmering since the turn of the century, had exploded into war. On August 4, 1914 Canada entered the war automatically as part of the British Empire when Britain declared war on Germany and Austria-Hungary. The War Measures Act gave emergency powers to the Conservative government of Robert Borden.

Amidst these turbulent conditions the Woodsworth family expanded once again. On November 24, 1914, Bruce was born. He was baptized Christmas Day at the elder Woodsworths' lovely home. Money was still tight, but the family found enough for Grace to start music lessons. James spent 1914 and 1915 giving hundreds of lectures across western Canada on behalf of the Canadian Welfare League, and spent months in Montreal lecturing to theological colleges and private groups and giving an extension course sponsored by McGill University. Her father's frequent absences put Grace, as eldest, in a position of greater responsibility. "As Father's occupation took him travelling more and more of the time, Mother got more the bringing up of the children," she recalled. "When Mother and Father would go out I would be left in charge of the others. I didn't have sufficient maturity to handle it quietly, and I'm afraid I was rather strenuous in my efforts to get obedience. But we were a close family."

Like her father Grace was the eldest child in a large family, and her caregiving role was parallel to James's relationship with his siblings. In this and many other ways she identified with her father, and she shared many of his traits. James was intense; Grace was intense. James was sometimes irritable when challenged; so was Grace. James was certain of his convictions and held them with great firmness. Grace too was convinced of the correctness of her views with the same kind of crusading fervour. Both became teachers—inspired to try to convert the world, to find overarching solutions for the world's problems.

James instilled in all his children the guiding ethic of his own life, sharing. All for one, one for all. Grace's personality crystallized around this nucleus—devotion to duty, the duty to uplift the needy of the world. James and Lucy as a team constantly taught this lesson, both by precept and by example.

Woodsworth's firmly held pacifist beliefs were strengthened as the war ground on. He believed that war created an ideal breeding ground for social injustice: not only was war inherently evil, but also ordinary working people would be exploited more than ever in the rush to churn out war supplies. He was a Methodist still, but a recruiting meeting at a Montreal church revolted him so much as a "damnable perversion of the teachings of Jesus" that he wrote Lucy of his impulse to quit the church then and there. "A deliberate attempt was made through a recital of the abominable acts of the Germans to stir up the spirit of hatred and retaliation. No! . . . Lucy, my love for institutional religion is well-nigh dead. How can one love what one cannot respect?"

By now James had no patience with imperialism either, and was revolted by what he believed to be an imperialist war. Because he condemned British imperialism equally with that of the Kaiser, James refused to sing "God Save the King" at his speaking engagements. This attitude was unpopular with some of his audiences, and James did not escape their wrath.

In the summer of 1915, as an eight-year-old, the critic and biographer Leon Edel witnessed an angry incident at a Woodsworth lecture in Yorkton, Saskatchewan, where most townspeople were of British origin. Woodsworth had come to speak "at a liberal public forum conducted by a Fabian named Knox, the registrar of local land titles." At age eighty-six, Edel could still remember clearly "going with our parents one Saturday or Sunday afternoon to a ceremony on the lawn of the Yorkton Town Hall. Mr. Woodsworth stood beside some temporary memorial. Suddenly, I was shocked to see an irate burly citizen grab Mr. Woodsworth and drag him across the lawn into the local police station. I couldn't understand why this was being done against Mr. Woodsworth, who seemed so quiet and peaceful. My brother recalled that Mr. Woodsworth refused to sing 'God Save The King,' singing rather 'God save our men' or 'our soldiers'."

Ten-year-old Grace may not have heard about the physical consequences her father endured for his beliefs, but she did recognize his sense of fearless righteousness and the aura of martyrdom surrounding him. This aura grew stronger as the war dragged on, and Woodsworth's stubborn opposition to it came to the attention of a wider public.

The war had a more positive effect on the political situation of Canadian women. Manitoba became the first Canadian province to grant women the vote in January 1916. Other provinces followed Manitoba's lead one by one, and in May 1918 the Canada Elections Act enfranchised all women for federal elections.

The necessities of war dried up funds for Woodsworth's Canadian Welfare League early in 1916. To fill the void the governments of Manitoba, Saskatchewan and Alberta jointly created the Bureau of Social Research with purposes and activities almost identical to those of the Canadian Welfare League. Woodsworth became secretary of the new organization.

The war—and a much heavier workload for James—increased tension within the Woodsworth family. Charles remembers an incident from 1916 when he was seven. "There was the memorable night when we moved into our rented summer cottage near Kenora on the Lake of the Woods. The screens had not been put up, and hordes of flesh-maddened mosquitos assailed us. Sleep was impossible, and soon the cottage was a bedlam of wailing children. While Mother sensibly fixed up drapes to protect the youngest child's face from being bitten by the merciless insects, Father completely lost his temper and laid about him, not at the mosquitoes, but at us, interspersing sound slaps with savage advice to go to sleep and forget the mosquitoes, something as much beyond his power as ours. That occasion was an exception and generally speaking Father was able to handle most situations effectively as well as firmly."

The youngest Woodsworth entered the war-torn world on September 30, 1916. Howard was baptized after the family moved again to 21 Dundurn Place, two blocks from the Assiniboine River, close to the elder Woodsworths' Maryland Street home. Now, with Grace, her sister Belva, and the four younger boys, the family was complete. That fall Grace and Belva learned to swim and to skate, and Lucy published in *Woman's Century* a lovingly written article, "The Children, Here's to Them at Bedtime." Telling the story of her own family snuggled around the fire, building a bedtime story in which each child furnished the next turn of plot, Lucy drew a quick sketch of Grace through a mother's eyes. "She was ten and a bundle of nerves. The heights and the depths were for her with also the need of a constant struggle for self-mastery."

Suddenly James's work at the Bureau was brought to a halt. In late December, a federal government circular arrived on his desk requesting help in making the National Service Registration a success. Signed by R.B. Bennett, chairman of the National Service Board and later Prime Minister of Canada, the circular inflamed James's passionate anti-war feelings. The new scheme was designed to have all men between sixteen and sixty-five register with the board.

The *Manitoba Free Press* published Woodsworth's letter of protest December 28. He objected that Canadian citizens had had no opportunity to vote on the registration scheme. He urged that conscription of material possessions precede conscription of manpower for the war effort. He questioned the methods of enforcement to be used, and the equality of enforcement in all regions of the country. He concluded, "This registration is no mere census. It seems to look in the direction of a measure of conscription. As some of us cannot conscientiously engage in military service, we are bound to resist what—if the war continues—will inevitably lead to forced service."

The governments of Manitoba, Saskatchewan and Alberta reacted quickly to this public pronouncement of pacifism by one of their senior employees. They cut off funds and closed the Bureau of Social Research, leaving the forty-four-year-old Woodsworth, his wife and six children without income. Many former friends and associates now pointedly avoided the Woodsworths because of their anti-war convictions.

Nor was the family's bitter time of loss over. January 30, 1917, the day before the Bureau closed, the Reverend Dr. James Woodsworth died peacefully at seventy-four. Her Grandpa Woodsworth lived on in Grace's memory as a devout, sincere man, quiet and kindly with a rich sense of humour.

CHAPTER 2

Political Awakening

Both James and Lucy needed to recuperate after the long years of exhausting work, but in the dark days of January 1917 rest was still a distant dream. James was suffering a breakdown in physical health, and Lucy was hard-pressed to keep up her calm cheerfulness. After much soul-searching, they decided to take their six hundred dollars in savings and make a fresh start in British Columbia.

"Mother never sought security," Grace wrote much later. "The idea of settling down permanently in any dwelling—if she ever held such an idea—must have been abandoned very early in her married life. We children grew up with the expectation that our lives would be spent moving about from house to house, from province to province, in accordance with the needs of Father's work. We never thought in terms of any other arrangement—a sure indication of Mother's attitude."

On an icy day in mid-April James and his family made their way to the Winnipeg train station, westward bound. J.S. Woodsworth was not yet ready to pronounce himself a socialist; still, he was deeply revolted by this seemingly endless war, which brought profit only to the makers of munitions and war supplies. That same week, on another train far across the world, Vladimir Ilich Lenin was travelling from exile in Switzerland to a tremendous reception by his fellow revolutionaries in St. Petersburg. Lenin too wanted an immediate end to what he saw as the "piratical imperialist war" to make way for "the worldwide Socialist revolution." The opposing visions of socialism espoused by these two leaders would bring their followers to repeated clashes in the years ahead. Grace would play her part in these battles.

Now James and Lucy, who had eased the settlement of so many immigrants to Winnipeg, became migrants themselves. James especially felt the anguish of uprooting the fruitful tree of his life's work, and his pain was intensified when not one of the hundreds of people the Woodsworths had worked with and entertained during their twelve years in Winnipeg came to see them off at the railway station. As Canadian soldiers died in Europe, the outspoken pacifist minister and his family were shunned, even by those people they had helped.

"Mother knew that Father's action in opposing the First World War would not be popular," Grace wrote later, "but it must have startled her to see the way in which friends of long standing fell away from them, following the publication of Father's anti-conscription letter in the Free Press at the end of 1916. But Mother accepted without repining." By the age of twelve, Grace too had accepted the position of being in the minority, of standing firmly on principle, alone if need be, but with a comfortable conscience.

For the children the ride west was a glorious adventure. When she had time off from tending her rambunctious little brothers, Grace pressed her nose to the train window to drink in her first views of the wind-swept plains, the resplendent Rocky Mountains, and the Fraser River cutting through gold-bearing cliffs and spreading into a broad valley below. The rail trip terminated at the hustling port of Vancouver, but the Woodsworths carried on to Victoria.

The contrast between the world they had left and their new surroundings was delightful. Lucy wrote, "We left a city of deep snow and ice on Thursday night. Sunday noon we reached a city where already the crocus was past, where gardens were gay with blooming hyacinths and budding tulips and spring, albeit with something of a chill for the marrow in your bones, was in the air."

For the next few weeks the Woodsworths stayed in the Foul Bay section of Victoria with the family of a Methodist minister they had known in Winnipeg, Reverend Abraham Osterhout. Their daughter Mildred had been Grace's childhood playmate, and the reunion pleased both girls.

At twelve, Grace had grown into a chunky youngster with straight brown hair cut even with the tip of her generous nose, a determined set to her lips, and piercing grey eyes that brightened with fun whenever responsibility was lifted.

In sunny, civilized Victoria, the Woodsworths prepared themselves to face the untamed wilderness of the mainland coast. The British Columbia Methodist Conference offered James the Howe Sound mission with a parsonage at Gibson's Landing (later renamed Gibsons) on the thickly forested mainland coast of Georgia Strait. James accepted this new challenge. In Vancouver on June 5, 1917 the family boarded the mail boat to the tiny settlement. When they disembarked at Gibson's Landing wharf, Grace took one look at her new home and fell in love with "the place specially made for us."

Gibson's Landing had been carved out of the wilderness just thirty-one years before. For the first time, apart from summer interludes, the family lived close to nature. Lucy wrote a lyric appreciation, "We have a beautiful view from our verandah. Across from us is Keats [Island]. Away down beyond this rises the Britannia Range, the northern half hidden from us by the dense evergreens just close at hand at the edge of the Indian Reserve. It's a wonderfully lovely view as one enters the road that runs through the Reserve and crosses the great high bridge over the ravine where now dashes and foams the wintry mountain torrent, and one looks up and up to the narrow lane of sky and cloud, bounded on either side by the tips of giant firs. We seem but pygmies wandering among the seats of the mighty."

In June 1917 there were only half a dozen Methodist families in the region, but James diligently visited almost all of the hundred and forty families in the Howe Sound Mission district. This took in a twenty-five-mile stretch of coast from Port Mellon to Sechelt and included three nearby islands, Bowen, Gambier and Keats. There were logging and shingle bolt camps, with separate ones for whites, Chinese, Japanese and Hindus. Port Mellon had a pulp mill; Sechelt had an Indian village, Catholic mission and school. People were constantly on the move: bachelors and families in search of work, summer tourists. Men were off fighting on the European front, leaving their wives to care for children, gardens and livestock. The church provided a twenty-five-foot gas boat with a cranky motor which James rechristened the *Good Will*. Lucy and all six children often went along on pastoral visits to outlying island families, singing the apt hymn "For Those In Peril on the Deep."

In a re-creation of his Winnipeg People's Forum, Woodsworth established Friday evening lecture-discussions at Gibson's Landing. They covered everything under the sun: agriculture, school matters, socialism and social reform, the printing press, the experiences of returned soldiers, the various nationalities in Canada, a permanent peace, the women's movement for suffrage, even sex hygiene. At election time each candidate was given an evening. Grace attended many of these meetings laughing as the rafters of the little schoolhouse rang with "accents and expletives amusing to younger ears."

"At Gibson's there is an unfortunate jealousy between 'the Landing' and the people 'on the hill,'" James reported to the Methodist Conference. "This sometimes narrows to English speaking people versus the Finns. There cuts across this division another which separates the local storekeeper and a little group who work with him from 'the community' which has found a one-sided expression in a co-operative store . . . . The Methodist Church is the only all-year round religious organization."

Monday afternoons at the parsonage were devoted to English classes for the Finnish women from the Hill. Over cups of tea James and Lucy tried to bridge the language gap, and the Finns "told them of the greed and corruption of the Russian church at home which had finally alienated them, made them Marxian socialists, and driven them to seek better living conditions in Canada." The Woodsworths welcomed the opportunity to learn more about the roots of the world-shaking Russian Revolution from people who had experienced at first hand the repressions and excesses of the Tsarist regime.

As the bloody military conflict dragged on, Woodsworth's own inner personal conflict was intense. He opposed the war as contrary to the teachings of Jesus, but he represented a church that supported it. He refused to read war bulletins from his pulpit and would not allow others to do so. Some believed he even refused to pray for the soldiers. His attitude polarized the people of Gibson's Landing. A few townspeople were also pacifists, but most pinned their faith on the conviction that Britain and Canada must win at all costs. The least tolerant of these became Woodsworth's enemies.

One prominent enemy was the storekeeper at the Landing, Mr. Winn. The Woodsworths riled him when they joined the co-operative store on the Hill. Winn was superintendent of the Sunday school, and he kept close watch on the church services. A British loyalist, Winn became angry at Woodsworth's refusal to read recruitment bulletins from the pulpit on Sunday mornings. But his patriotism apparently did not extend to business. "Draft evaders set up camp on Mount Elphinstone," Charles recalled. "The local storekeeper Winn was opposed to Father's pacifist views, but it was he who had been supplying the food to the draft evader camp."

In spite of Winn's influence, the new minister and his family earned the respect and friendship of most Gibson's Landing residents, pacifist or not. They formed an especially close relationship with the area's only doctor, Fredrick Inglis, who had built a comfortable, three-storey home overlooking the harbour. Dr. Inglis and his wife had six children—two elder girls and four younger boys—roughly parallel in age to the Woodsworths. Each child naturally formed an alliance with his or her "twin" in the other family.

Grace became best friends with the eldest Inglis girl, Kathleen. "Mother sent me over with a batch of biscuits for Mrs. Woodsworth when they arrived," Kathleen recalled. "There was Grace bathing her youngest brother; he must have been about eight months old. I had just acquired a new brother of my own about a month previously."

The girls, then twelve and thirteen, quickly compared notes on their parents. Dr. Fredrick Inglis "was my hero, just as J.S. was Grace's hero," Kathleen remembered. "We both adored our fathers. Dad was a much bigger man, six feet in his shoes, a hundred and eighty pounds. He was a medical missionary, Presbyterian. And they're very strict. You didn't read funnies on Sunday, you didn't play or sing songs on Sunday, you sang hymns only." Grace was not allowed to read the funnies either, an instant bond.

The two fathers were alike in some ways, very different in others. Kathleen said, "I knew that Mr. Woodsworth called himself a pacifist and my dad didn't call himself one. I figured Dad was more of a pacifist in the raising of his children than J.S. ever was. He was a real autocrat, but he wasn't home very much. It was Mrs. Woodsworth who kept him the head of the family;

he was the one they had to behave for. He would spank his children. That was all right with us. I was given permission to spank my youngest brother if I felt it was necessary, and I did once in a while."

Sunday mornings in the Methodist parsonage were not easy for the children, according Charles, who in 1918 was just nine. "Father carried over into our family Grandfather's custom of reading at length from the Bible as we sat around the table after breakfast. But whereas Grandfather had been content to stick to the text, which in itself is unquestionably beautiful, Father as an Oxford-trained Hebrew scholar could not refrain from annotating and paraphrasing almost every word and paragraph . . . . The result was distressing, not to say painful. Why Father felt constrained to explain on each separate occasion that 'Jehovah,' in the original Hebrew, was 'Jawe,' or 'Yaw-way,' or 'Ya-wee,' remained something of a mystery." When her father was away, Grace led a revolt against this practice of commenting on the Bible.

Bible readings aside, the summer of 1917 was an enchanted time for Grace and the other children. The two families hiked through the forest and up into the wilds of Mount Elphinstone. There were picnics on the beach and rides on Paddy, the patient horse who carried the minister and doctor from farm to isolated farm.

When night fell "there were walks or boat rides in the moonlight," Lucy wrote, "swims for the boys in just 'their birthday suits' and in the winter long evenings with violin and piano or reading by the roaring grate-fire with the gentlest of rains quietly dropping through the blackest nights I ever experienced."

But this happy time was not to last. Reverend Woodsworth could no longer reconcile his opposition to war with his service in a church that actively recruited men for military service. For the third time in his life he tendered his resignation to the Methodist Church. This time it was accepted.

J.S. Woodsworth can now be recognized as the father of the Canadian peace movement, but then his move seemed a personal one, the inevitable result of adhering to his evolving socialist principles rather than taking the expedient, socially acceptable path. In the Woodsworth family Bible dated June 15, 1918, James and Lucy wrote the companion statement to the one they had signed on their wedding day: "Having felt it our duty to resign from the ministry of the Methodist Church, we are venturing forth on unknown seas. We still feel the call to service and re-dedicate ourselves and our family to the cause of God and humanity. Justice, Peace and Goodwill."

As a child on the brink of adolescence, Grace was deeply impressed with her father's way of resolving the contradictions in his life. Between 1918 and 1921, as Grace grew from a sturdy girl of thirteen to a self-aware young woman of sixteen, Woodsworth went from preaching in his own pulpit to working the Vancouver waterfront to jail in Winnipeg to a House of

Commons seat. The note of unity in all these diverse roles was her father's strict adherence to the inner voice of his own truth and compassion.

Once again James was unemployed and the family had nowhere to live. The problem of lodging was solved when Dr. Inglis invited the Woodsworth family to move into the ground floor of his large home. Both Grace and Kathleen were delighted.

Grace's thirteenth summer, though touched with trouble, was wonderful for the two best friends. "We hunted birds' nests together," Kathleen recalled with pleasure years later. "We walked barefoot in the mud at the head of the Gibson's wharf, left-hand side. It was lovely, squishy mud while we were looking for these birds' nests. We had dozens of them up in our attic. Her side and my side. We went to school barefoot a lot of the time. People were poor; they didn't have shoes. We played basketball in bare feet on gravel courts. I could walk on barnacles without getting cut."

The two families ate their meals separately, but in other ways were very close. When the weather was warm the Inglis children bedded down on the third-storey sleeping porches. They threw their pillows from the arched windows down onto the "friendly enemies" below who never got anything high enough in return to hit a mark. After chores Grace and Kathleen studied together, entranced by the novels of Scott and Dickens. Grace read faster than Kathleen, but needed her friend's help with mathematics and sciences.

The Woodsworths shared the ground floor of the big house with Dr. Inglis's dispensary which was cluttered with strange and ancient objects. Kathleen and Grace alone had permission to enter this mysterious place. "One day," Kathleen chuckled, "we decided we'd clear up Dad's very messy shelf of instruments. We were [standing] on chairs and rearranged all his things until they looked as if they were in the right places. Poor Dad couldn't find anything for weeks."

Dr. Inglis became interested in the socialism of the Finns on the Hill and read a great deal of their literature. He was persuaded—far more than J.S. Woodsworth at the time—that socialism was the best method of pursuing freedom and justice in the world. The two friends agreed to disagree on the question.

The musically inclined doctor formed the children into an orchestra. Grace and Kathleen played four-hands piano, Charles sawed away on the violin, and the others joined in. From sheet music they played pop songs and opera hits. He held a contest to see which child could most quickly memorize the words to the socialist anthems, "The Red Flag" and "The Internationale." Charles proudly claimed the ten-cent prize.

A carpenter in his youth, Dr. Inglis built a house and some cottages, and the children all helped him build boats. He mastered the rough and muddy roads in exciting ways—first on the faithful horse Paddy, then on a bicycle. Then he started zooming about on a Triumph motorcycle. The crowning glory was when he bought the first car to come to Gibson's Landing, a Model T Ford.

James Woodsworth had to find paying work at once. He left the family at Gibson's Landing and headed for Vancouver. He stayed at a boardinghouse kept by a distant relative and trudged from interview to interview, but found no openings as a teacher. One night, in Dr. Inglis's company, he attended a committee meeting of the Labour Party, which inspired him to seek manual work. Soon after at the Longshoremen's Hall he met Ernie Winch, who helped him find work. Over the next sixty years Ernie and his son Harold would play significant roles in the political careers of both James and Grace.

Ernest Edward Winch, then secretary of the Longshoremen's Union, was also president of the Vancouver Trades and Labour Council. At forty-one the elder Winch was a striking, strong-jawed man with blue eyes flashing revolutionary fire. He was born in Britain into an upper-middle class family of building contractors who attended high Church of England masses. His social conscience was awakened at the age of twenty-two when he witnessed a police attack on a peaceful demonstration in his home town of Harlow, Essex. An interested bystander until police began to break up the rally, Winch then joined in on the side of free speech and collective action. The incident radicalized him, and he started to study the labour and socialist movements.

In 1910, on his second trip to Canada, Ernie Winch settled in British Columbia and soon became interested in the many shades of Canadian socialism. Though inspired by the thinking of Karl Marx, Winch was never a communist, but a Marxian socialist. His biographer, Dorothy Gretchen Steeves, later one of the first CCF members of the British Columbia Legislature, described his complex political nature. "Ernest loved the traditional revolutionary expressions of socialism and he insisted on using them until the day he died, even though during many of his later years all his thoughts were concentrated on the humane measures which he sought for the relief of pain and poverty. In fact, he had a foot in both camps—the camp of uncompromising socialism and the camp of gradualism and reform. In the early days and until he became a member of the Legislature the revolutionary character was predominant. He was a bit like Keir Hardie who is said to have remarked once that he didn't need to read Karl Marx in order to learn that the worker is robbed at the point of production."

When J.S. Woodsworth showed up, Winch welcomed the opportunity to debate socialism versus religion with the sky pilot, as some people called ministers behind their backs. He invited Woodsworth to join the bachelor home he and his son Harold shared in Vancouver (his wife and family were living in White Rock), and there the men's wall-shaking debates lasted into the early morning hours, when they usually came to a draw. The two strong-minded men concluded that religion and socialism had the same end in view; only the means were different.

Back in Gibson's Landing, Grace was amazed to read her father's first letter home describing his new job—an eight-hour day unloading a freight car full of two-hundred-pound boxes for sixty-five cents an hour. She wrote, "That letter shocked me because I had never thought of my father earning a living by doing manual work. Mentally, I recognized that men in overalls were just as worthy of respect as men in white collars; emotionally it was a shock when my father took off the collar and put on the overalls. His letter makes it apparent it was something of a shock to him as well."

In the converted church that served as the Longshoremen's Hall and on the Vancouver docks, this frail father of six learned the hard way the life of the wage slave; he earned barely enough to keep body and soul together long enough to make it to work the next day. Like the other casual labourers, sometimes he was not called for work and had to turn away into the rain. Yet he endured. His body hardened, never his heart. He absorbed socialist ethics—not just by reading, not just through hearing secondhand the experiences of others, but from the docks along with the sweat of his back and the ache of his muscles. J.S. Woodsworth was that rare longshoreman who brought a white-collar education to his work. After his time on the Vancouver waterfront, Woodsworth was forever on the side of the worker and against the owner.

Up the coast in Gibson's Landing, Lucy was struggling to feed and clothe six children. She applied to fill a teaching vacancy in the town's high school but ran into opposition from Winn, the storekeeper who had tangled with James over the reading of recruitment bulletins from the pulpit. "Mother was so outraged," Grace recalled with amusement. "She didn't outrage easily, but she was outraged when there was any question of accepting a University of Toronto graduate as the teacher in this little rural school.

"There was a big dust-up meeting. The head-and-forefront was there and his cronies and the rest of the Landing. It was soon established where the sympathy was, all on Mother's side. She was an excellent teacher. The opposition had about three children among them and the others had the rest of the children. Finally, the head-and-forefront left in a great huff. And as he went out the door one of Mother's supporters piped up, 'Goodbye, give us a lock of your hair'."

When school started at Gibson's Landing in fall 1918, Lucy was in her classroom with Grace and Kathleen among her students. Still, money was hard to come by. Family financial records show James earned $491.50 longshoring from August 15 to year's end, while Lucy made $177.00 teaching. These few dollars had to cover food as well as the salary of a housekeeper while Lucy was teaching. There was no money left over for clothing. Friends donated used things which Lucy patiently patched and darned. Grace was never ashamed of wearing hand-me-downs. She wrote, "I remember scandalizing my sister by a proud recital to the girls at school of a list of those who had given me each article of clothing I wore. The variety was so great as to be intriguing!" Her feet were protected that winter by black rubber boots with hinged metal catches, footwear outgrown by Ernest Winch's son Harold.

In Vancouver Woodsworth was gaining recognition and respect from his fellow workers. Membership in the Longshoremen's Union was strictly limited, but he was admitted after nursing the union's business agent, who was dying of influenza. He became famous on the docks as the man who refused to load a boat with munitions intended for use against Russian revolutionaries. He attended union meetings and urged political action at a time when many Canadian unionists believed they should play no political role at all. He wrote regular articles for the *Federationist,* the BC Federation of Labour newspaper.

Woodsworth was becoming convinced that socialism was the correct path to justice for people, but in choosing amongst the wide spectrum of meanings attached to the word "socialism," he was precise and discriminating. In her insightful biography of her father, Grace analyzed his political perceptions as they were in late 1918. "From the first he made it clear that the socialism he advocated was not the doctrinaire variety so dear to the hearts of the self-styled 'scientific socialists'. Rather, it was kin to the socialism of the British Labour Party, a movement which had been fed from religious, ethical, co-operative and Fabian streams. Into his conception of socialism J.S. Woodsworth poured his love for his fellow-men."

One line of socialist thinking that closely paralleled J.S. Woodsworth's emerging philosophy was articulated by Laurence Gronlund, an American socialist, in his influential 1884 book, *The Cooperative Commonwealth.* This new social order was to result inevitably from the natural tendency of all political systems toward social democracy, or constructive socialism. "We must believe that the movement is being guided, or is guiding itself to happy issues," Gronlund wrote. He expressed the "mother idea of socialism" as the value of labour, and denounced profit as robbery of half of everything workers produced. Gronlund saw the wage system as unfit for higher civilization. Trade unions and co-operative stores were to be the antidotes to the injustices of capitalism. His critique of capitalism predicted economic depressions brought on by overproduction. The co-operative commonwealth would create demand by creating full employment. The unions would set the value of labour based on what it cost to live and raise a family; the state would control prices. Private property would be confiscated. If the "plutocrats" gave up their property peacefully, they would be compensated, otherwise they would not.

Government would be by referendum, not by representation, with all bills submitted to the popular vote. A "common education" would create "common opinion" and the feeling of a "common duty." Individualism was equated with private enterprise, a mere phase preceding the co-operative commonwealth. Yet Gronlund saw state action as complementary to, not restrictive of, individual freedom. The sphere of the state was to work for the public good, the greatest good of every individual citizen. The "class state" would develop into a commonwealth, a state of classless, interdependent equality. The commonwealth would further the highest development of the individual, and every citizen would be entitled by virtue of citizenship to the use of all public institutions: libraries, schools and hospitals. Women in the co-operative commonwealth would be economically equal to men, but would not compete with men in the workplace; there would be "special vocations for the sexes." This type of socialism aimed to support, not destroy, the family.

This was distinctly not communism, Gronlund stressed. "In short, the motto of Socialism is: 'Everybody according to his deeds'; that of Communism is: 'Everybody according to his needs'." He was convinced that "this coming change is God's will; that the society to be ushered in is not a pig-sty, filled with well-fed hogs, but is, indeed, the Kingdom of Heaven on earth."

Gronlund, an American, pointed to the clear roots of these ideas in German socialism. "Socialism," he wrote in 1884, "modern socialism, German Socialism, which is fast becoming the Socialism the world over—holds that the impending reconstruction of Society will be brought about by the Logic of Events; teaches that *The Coming Revolution is strictly an Evolution* [emphasis in original]." Gronlund was aware of the influence of his work. In his preface to the 1890 edition he claimed it inspired Edward Bellamy's popular Utopian novel *Looking Backward,* a staple of most socialist reading lists.

Most of these core ideas were central to Woodsworth's political work, which came to fruition in the party he founded, the Co-operative Commonwealth Federation.

Even while he was separated from his family, James set the highest possible standards of ethics and achievement for his children, especially for Grace, the eldest. She valued his approval enormously and, rather than rebelling against her parents as many teenagers do, took her father as a primary role model. She adopted his views and his values and tried to be worthy of his infrequent praise. Grace patterned herself after her mother in many ways, too, and there was little conflict because the two parents functioned as different yet complementary parts of a whole. Although her husband was the patriarch whose needs came first, Lucy never accepted for herself the limits placed on women by Canadian society in the early decades of the twentieth century. She felt herself to be as intelligent, as worthy of being considered a full member of society, as any man. She encouraged her two daughters to develop

their capacities as whole people, rather than accept the limitations which
then circumscribed girls.

Lucy gave Grace concrete responsibilities and praised her accomplishments; she taught Grace to find security within herself, rather than in
outward circumstances of money or position. Grace absorbed Lucy's love of
words for their rhythm and sound, her joy in academic study, and her
appreciation of the value of humour. And always her mother's voice sounded
in Grace's inner ear, admonishing her to "make earnest with life."

Life was hell on earth for the Canadian men fighting in the trenches of France,
and Conservative Prime Minister Borden was trying to introduce conscription at home. The issue pitted Francophones against Anglophones, divided
Opposition Liberals, polarized public opinion and finally led to a bitter and
vicious election campaign in 1917.

By 1918, the labour movement across Canada was in a sweat over
conscription. The Vancouver Labour Council held a referendum and a large
majority voted for a general strike. But the decision was referred to the BC
Federation of Labour where the wisdom was not to strike but to run
candidates in the next federal election. So, in early 1918, the BC Federation
of Labour formed the Federated Labour Party (FLP). Its platform declared
the ultimate goal to be the socialist "collective ownership of the means of
wealth production." One of the FLP's charter members was a young member
of the Streetrailwaymen's Union, Angus MacInnis. Woodsworth met him at
an early meeting of the FLP, which he attended to support the new party's
anti-conscription stance.

But J.S. Woodsworth never changed his mind about his ideal political
party. In a series of articles in the *Western Labour News* published in 1918 and
1919, he laid out the plan for the kind of third party he wanted. He was not
to see it realized until the July 1933 creation of the Co-operative Commonwealth Federation, but as political scientist Norman Penner explains, "his
conception of a third party in these articles was not of a labour party but of
a people's party, as he called it, which would unite in its ranks workers,
farmers, veterans, small businessmen and other sections of the common
people. It would not be a Marxist party . . . . Its program would be socialist."

Woodsworth called for the socialization of industrial, commercial, transportation and distribution sectors of the economy, with due compensation
to the current owners. He concluded, "Our ultimate object must be a
complete turnover in the present economic and social system. In this we
recognize our solidarity with workers the world over . . . . We must attack
the enemy all along the line, using both political and industrial power, and
any other legitimate power at our disposal."

The fall and winter of 1918 brought profound changes to the world.
October saw an offer of armistice from the German government to United

States President Woodrow Wilson based on his 14 Points. One of those points was the establishment of a League of Nations, the world's first attempt at a global approach to problem-solving. In November revolutions in Munich and Berlin finally forced the abdication of the German ruler Wilhelm II and the crown prince; leaders of the Social Democratic Party of Germany proclaimed a republic. After a winter of peace negotiations, in June 1919 Germany signed the peace treaty in the Hall of Mirrors at the Palace of Versailles. Prime Minister Borden signed for Canada, marking a new independent status for the Dominion. It was the first time Canada acted on her own as an autonomous nation instead of as a part of the British Empire.

Canadian women were moving toward greater equality with men. In 1917 Canada's first woman judge, Helen MacGill, was appointed to the bench of the juvenile court in Vancouver. Louise McKinney made history the same year in Alberta as the first woman in Canada elected to a provincial legislature. And on May 24, 1918 the Canada Elections Act enfranchised all women for federal elections.

In Gibson's Landing Grace was becoming a young woman, fully aware of the great events sweeping the world. Under her mother's tutelage she was learning French and taking her first steps toward becoming an accomplished political writer. Early in 1919, in her lined school notebook, Grace recorded mirror images of her parents' attitudes. "For four years a World War had raged in Europe. Each year had come to find more and more of the rights of the people taken away from them. Freedom of the press, freedom of speech, freedom of thought had all gone and in their place had come censorship, conscription, banned literature, fear of truth and light.

"Each year had come to find more and more of the working class discontent. So that the Armistice did by no means settle unrest among the workers. In every country they were beginning to wake up, beginning to see how they had been sent out to the front not to save Democracy, but that the capitalist might use them for his own ends. Revolution in Russia and Germany, civil strife in Ireland, strikes in Britain, the U.S. and Canada, showed that workers all over the world were beginning to realize their position and to attempt to throw off the yoke of capitalism which compelled them to slave all their lives so that a few people might have so much money that they did not know what to do with it. The whole world was seething with unrest and discontent." This unrest was about to touch Grace's own life in a very personal way.

Canadian veterans were returning from Europe war-weary, yearning for a hero's welcome and above all for jobs. Work was easy to find as a devastated Europe needed enormous supplies of almost everything, but prices were quickly spiralling upward. Wages were squeezed by inflation, labour markets tightened, and unions enrolled thousands of new members and began making demands on their employers.

Woodsworth was impatient to escape from manual labour on the docks and return to his true vocation, the spreading of ideas. In the spring his opportunity came in the form of an invitation from Reverend William Ivens, head of the newly formed Labour Church, to make a speaking tour across Canada. He was to educate workers' organizations to the need for social change, but some Canadian workers were already demanding fundamental transformations in their working conditions.

When Woodsworth arrived in Winnipeg June 8, 1919, a general strike had been underway for three weeks. The atmosphere was as charged as in the tense yellow-grey hour before a lightning storm. It had started with building trades workers who wanted higher wages and machinists who demanded the right to union recognition and collective bargaining. More than twenty-two thousand workers walked out in sympathy, including seventy unions of the Winnipeg Trades and Labour Council. Canada's first general strike spread to include civic and government employees and even policemen. A Committee of One Thousand citizens representing business interests formed to oppose the strikers, who were pictured in the daily newspapers as Bolsheviks in the iron grip of Moscow, fomenting revolution and seeking to overturn the government by force.

Hon. Arthur Meighen, Minister of Justice, and Hon. Gideon Robertson, Minister of Labour, arrived in Winnipeg and declared "there is absolutely no justification for the general strike . . . ." In this atmosphere the Borden government wrote and passed, in less than an hour, oppressive measures that were to remain on Canada's statute books for decades despite Woodsworth's persistent efforts to remove them. An amendment to the Immigration Act allowed deportation as an undesirable of any immigrant, British or not, without trial by jury, regardless of the length of time he or she had lived in Canada. Section 98 of the Criminal Code permitted a person to be arrested on suspicion of belonging to an outlawed organization and placed the burden of proof on the accused, thus rejecting the tradition of British law.

Woodsworth believed in the justice of the strikers' cause. The man who had invited him to take the speaking tour, Reverend William Ivens, was also editor of the strike bulletin. Ivens had been arrested quickly under the new laws, and Woodsworth took over as editor, a position that lasted exactly one week.

On the Saturday of that week a committee of war veterans called a parade that turned into a crowd of strikers and bystanders. Hastily recruited deputy police on horseback, swinging as weapons wooden horse-yokes sawn in two, charged into the crowd. In front of Winnipeg City Hall the crowd was turned back by soldiers with machine guns and rifles, but not before a man and a boy were killed and a hundred more people were wounded.

Woodsworth arranged for publication of a full account of "Bloody Saturday" in the strike bulletin. He wrote an editorial in the following Monday's

Western Labour News accusing those who had ordered the assault of "Kaiserism in Canada." A warrant was issued immediately for Woodsworth's arrest on charges of seditious libel. He was accused on six counts, two of which were based on verses from the Bible—quoted in the charges without elaboration! When informed of this unpleasant but not unexpected development, Woodsworth immediately turned himself in to police. The former assistant pastor of the largest and most respectable church in Winnipeg was locked in jail like a common criminal. He was searched and forced to leave his clothes on a stool outside his cell. He was allowed books and a comb, which he broke in two, giving half to his fourteen cellmates to share so that they could appear decently before the judge.

In a letter from his cell to Lucy in Gibson's Landing, James sounded pleased with himself rather than despondent about his incarceration. "I have managed to get into things in Winnipeg in a comparatively short time," he wrote. "One week of speaking, speaking, speaking. Then Editor of a paper for a brief week. At the end of the week our action for libel threatened the suppression of the papers. And my arrest. That's going some! So now I'm one of the 'leaders' of the strike. If ever I get out my fortune will be made sure!"

Evidently Woodsworth understood the wellsprings of Winnipeg public opinion. People now in need of his moral courage forgot that they had given him the cold shoulder when he displayed equal courage protesting a war he could not countenance. A little more than two years after his arrest the people of Winnipeg North Centre would elect Woodsworth to the House of Commons.

Woodsworth's personal values were forever changed by his jail experience. "Well, this surely about finishes the old conventional ideals," he acknowledged to Lucy. "To be in jail is no longer the most terrible thing. 'Justice' is no longer enthroned. In practice it depends upon a dozen conflicting interests, political and commercial. But one is committed as never before to the cause of the poor and the helpless, particularly the foreigner. This is only the first round!"

During lunch hour at school Lucy got the news of James's arrest. She pulled Grace and Kathleen aside and sent them on an urgent errand. "At once Mother thought of Father's literature and papers," Grace told her diary. "What if a policeman had come up on the boat with orders to search the house! It might mean a ten-year sentence. Mother sent me home at once to look over Father's books and papers and to carefully weed out any with titles such as 'Socialism', 'Russia', 'Bolshevism' or 'Pacifism.' Why? These were dangerous books! They encouraged people to think along new lines. They were banned!!!

"How well I remember the scene! Mrs. L., our housekeeper and I searching the shelves, boxes and files, while Dr. Inglis mounted guard at the door ready to whistle to us if anyone should appear! At length our work was done. We had a large pile of books, papers, poems and even sermons collected. We placed them in a tin box, tied it and put a piece of oilcloth on top.

"Then Kathleen Inglis and I crept stealthily with it into the next lot. Stepping carefully so as not to break any bracken that might betray us, and watching to see that no one was near, we hid it under a log. The spot was a fine, good one for the purpose. Deep down, covered with bracken and blackberry vines, and hidden by trees and stumps, we were sure its hiding place would not easily be discovered. We carefully removed all traces of our work and came cautiously home. Of course our parents and the older children knew it was hidden, but they did not know where. We did not tell them, because if they were questioned they could answer more easily.

"For more than four months it stayed there. Once or twice we visited it to see that the damp and rain had not hurt the books. Kathleen and I called the spot the 'Secret Vault,' and we spoke of the S.V. between ourselves."

Co-conspirator Kathleen could picture the very spot. "The secret vault we called it, in a rotten log. They were enormous logs you know, original fir. We pulled away all the rotting wood, and stuffed in the box. It wasn't that far away, it was a vacant lot next door."

"Then one day," Grace exulted, "the glad news came that Father had been set free and was returning home. Of course there was no longer need for secrecy. We put back the books on their shelves and in their boxes. Again we sang the socialist songs and looked at the 'red' papers. But was this the end? No! It was only a lull in the great and ever increasing struggle between labour and capital—the struggle which must eventually end in the true triumph for the workers."

So Grace wrote at the impressionable age of fourteen. Her father's imprisonment and the threat of police oppression radicalized her. Called upon to protect him, her hero who had always been her protector, Grace began to see herself differently. No longer was she a mere childish spectator; now she was a worthy young soldier standing shoulder to shoulder with her warrior father in an historic battle against oppression. These values, forged on the anvil of experience and struck upon her heart with love for the father she lionized, grew as Grace grew. They formed the core of her personal definition of socialism. "The Winnipeg General Strike was a watershed for me," Grace mused at age eighty-two. "I saw society really was divided into those who had and those who would like to have and didn't have." The have-nots of the world became Grace's children—she never bore any of her own—and she felt responsible for all of them, as she had been responsible for her five younger siblings.

Her successful mission and ability to keep a secret like an adult greatly enhanced Grace's standing with her brothers and sisters. Charles, who had not been told of Grace's move to hide the dangerous books and papers, wrote later, "Police officials never arrived at Gibson's to seize them and although afterwards we laughed heartily over it we felt privately that here was a loyal henchman, good to have around in an emergency."

The RCMP could have relaxed their suspicions with regard to the Woodsworths. "We were never communist," Grace said much later, "we were too close to our church origin for that. Not only church but ethical values." She was to spend decades defining the difference between communism and socialism.

After her father's arrest, Grace gave more weight to the importance of freedom of speech and thought. Much later, as she struggled to define the limits of permissible dissent within the CCF and NDP, Grace often recalled the anxious winter of 1919–20 when the possession of a book covered with red cloth, if viewed with suspicion by the authorities, could have put her strict and righteous father in jail.

Woodsworth was never brought to trial on the charges of seditious libel which formed two of the six charges against him. They were dropped. The other four charges were stayed by the Crown and never raised again for obvious reasons. Two related to articles written by his close associate and friend Fred Dixon, who was also charged with sedition but conducted his own defence and won. Two other counts related to articles written by Woodsworth but not printed. One of these outlined the platform of the British Labour Party, a perfectly constitutional program; the other, entitled "Alas! the Poor Alien" protested the hastily drawn new amendment to the Immigration Act. The last two charges were the ones based on quotes from the Book of Isaiah, quoted on the charges without editorial comment.

In spring 1920, between two legs of a cross-Canada speaking tour, Woodsworth at last was able to return to the family at Gibson's Landing nearly a year after he had left for Winnipeg. The entire family and much of the community met him at the wharf. Lucy sketched the scene with a chuckle of appreciation at its irony. "My eldest son, Charles, was learning to play the violin at the time, making up in gusto what he lacked in repertoire . . . . As the boat drew in to the dock all heads turned to the sound of music approaching rapidly down the rough planking from the road. It was Charles, violin tucked under his chin, bow sawing purposefully, in his best rendition of 'God Save the King'!"

CHAPTER 3

Dreams and Discipline

At the height of the Canadian price boom in the postwar summer of 1920, James and Lucy moved to Vancouver and bought the only home they ever owned. Grace and all the children contributed to the purchase from their piggy banks. A few blocks from the curving white sands of Kitsilano Beach the tall frame house at 2147 West 3rd Avenue got a proud new coat of battleship grey from the conquering Woodsworths.

The family vigorously cleaned every corner of their wooden castle and washed out all the bedding. The neighbours had something to talk about when Lucy hung out sheets adorned with the words "In 1915 we buried 279 babies" and "Last year we buried 500 babies" in large black lettering. She had to explain that these were James's Sunday school and teaching charts, drawn on the family bedsheets for lack of better material in wartime. The children had become accustomed to sleeping on them and were not frightened by these statistics. They knew the deaths were caused by poverty and the neglect of careless landlords.

As a city Vancouver was an awkward adolescent in 1920: some streets were still just slashes through a virgin forest of gigantic firs and cedars. But by the time the Woodsworths settled in, Vancouver had acquired a thin patina of European culture. It had an Opera House where Sarah Bernhardt had performed, a library, movie theatres, a Board of Trade, active labour unions, long-distance telephone service and an electric streetcar system.

Vancouver's streetcar company, the BC Electric Railway, had an exceptional conductor, Angus MacInnis. In time he would marry Grace Woodsworth, but now it was her father who interested Angus as a fellow socialist thinker and political colleague. Angus, now thirty-six, had made his way to the West Coast from a skin-and-bones potato farm on Prince Edward Island. The middle son of Neil MacInnis and Flora MacDougall's nine children, he was born on September 2, 1884 at Glen William, PEI. His father and mother were both from Skye. Angus learned English at school, as Gaelic only was the rule in the strictly Presbyterian MacInnis home. The children were raised on the Bible and the hearty verses of Robbie Burns.

Angus was in grade eight when his eldest brother died; he left school to help on the farm. Then Neil died leaving sixteen-year-old Angus, the oldest male MacInnis, in charge of the farm. "The family was always poor—the farm was poor," Angus wrote later. "My education was somewhat neglected as there was always something to plant or something to pick . . . . In the spring there were potatoes to plant. In the fall there were potatoes to pick. In the summer we picked potato bugs. That job lasted nearly all summer because the bugs were prolific and healthy. The infant mortality was low. In fact, I have never heard of a potato bug in PEI dying a natural death at any age . . . . But the worst picking of all was picking stones. Our farm produced the best and most plentiful crop of stones on the Island, red rough sandstone. There may be more back breaking jobs for a boy than picking stones, but I have not heard of it."

The MacInnises are a Scottish clan of ancient origin. In Gaelic the name is MacAonghais, derived from Clan Aonghais, meaning unique choice. The clan motto, "Irid Ghibht Dhe Agus An Righ," is translated as "Through the Grace of God and the King." Angus felt his Highland heritage as an important part of his identity, and he later wrote of his "emotional Highland temperament."

When his younger brothers grew old enough to work the farm, Angus was free to travel. After a stint with a Boston ship chandler, he rode the harvest trains west to Manitoba in the fall of 1908. As soon as the crops were in, an opportunity to work on his uncle's dairy farm drew him to the Vancouver suburb of Lulu Island. Keenly aware of his lack of education and voraciously curious, Angus read economics, history, political science and literature, often burning the midnight oil. He dipped deeply into the socialist thought that was shaping current events: Marx, Lenin, British Fabian socialists Sidney and Beatrice Webb, and American Eugene Debs.

In 1910 he got a job as a streetcar motorman, then as a conductor. Angus soon became active politically as business agent for Division 101 of the street railway employees at a time when few unions saw politics as a suitable activity for their members, let alone in their best interest. He went to all of Vancouver's frequent theatre meetings, where socialist orators spoke vividly of vast changes to come in the world order.

Angus was physically unfit for military service and remained in Vancouver during World War One. A childhood diet composed mainly of potatoes with a touch of fish left him with many physical problems: he suffered from stomach and glandular troubles throughout his life, and was not a robust person in general.

In 1918 Angus joined the newly formed Federated Labour Party (FLP). It was a radical action—a clause in his union's constitution forbade political activity—but Angus wanted fundamental change and knew that job action was not enough. Without representation in Parliament, labour power would be limited.

As FLP secretary Angus signed the 1919 membership cards of both James and Lucy Woodsworth. When Woodsworth first became a political candidate in the British Columbia provincial election of October 1920, Angus began to work actively with him. Woodsworth ran on the Federated Labour Party ticket with Tom Richardson, a former Labour member of the British House of Commons and W.R. Trotter of the typographical union. Their platform was based on "securing industrial legislation and collective ownership of the means of wealth production." The ultimate object was "a complete change in the present economic and social system." Solidarity with workers all over the world was primary.

The provision of an equal share of wealth for all citizens drawn from their own common land and resources was a central theme in the evolving political thought of Woodsworth and MacInnis. They believed that the country's coal, oil, gas, forests, waters and minerals should be "retained and operated on behalf of and in the interests of the whole community. If in private hands, measures should be taken to secure the reversion to the State." This concept was crucial to Federated Labour Party thinking, was later a basic idea behind the Co-operative Commonwealth Federation and still underlies many policies of today's New Democratic Party.

Woodsworth, Richardson and Trotter were considered radical reformers for their advocacy of free medical and dental services, and a welfare state. "Citizens whether men, women or children who are unable through disability—economic, physical or mental—to provide for themselves, should be wards of the community by right of citizenship," the FLP platform stated.

Women had won the right to vote federally two years before, in 1918. FLP policy included equal rights for women, as Woodsworth's campaign leaflet stated. "Labour representatives have always been consistent advocates of equal suffrage for women, and though this is now on the statute books, there remains much to be done before equality, economically and before the law, is established."

When the provincial polls closed on the first of December 1920, Woodsworth, Trotter and Richardson were not elected, but they had garnered about 7500 votes apiece. James spent the winter and spring doing educational work and organizing for the labour movement.

During this period he wrote an essay on sex education for boys and girls published by the Winnipeg Labour Church. Called "Where the Baby Came From," it took the Woodsworths' matter-of-fact approach to sex, birth and family planning, the same attitude that Grace was to expound so vividly in the House of Commons forty-five years later. James started with a simple explanation of plant reproduction, and moved quickly up the scale of evolution to mammals. After giving children a chance to feel comfortable with this exciting topic, he began to explore human processes of sex and birthing, which then took place most often in homes, not hospitals, often within earshot of the older children. James dealt frankly with questions like "Why does Mother scream?" "Sometimes it is very painful for Mother when the baby comes, so the doctor is often called," he wrote.

He preached self-control to adolescents dealing with their "strange, new feelings . . . . This sex-hunger is natural and good, but we must control it . . . . That is what marriage is—the coming together of the man and the woman. Growing boys and girls are not ready to form a home," he warned. "Unfit parents produce miserable runts."

"The sex-hunger is good and clean," James told the young people, "but sometimes smutty stories and filthy practices make it rotten. Keep clean for the sake of the one who may one day be your body and soul . . . so that one day you can look your own little boy or girl in the eyes." With these precepts ringing in her mind, it is no wonder that Grace remained a virgin until her marriage at twenty-six.

J.S. Woodsworth's advanced ideas about the desirability of birth control were in accord with the attitudes of many European and American socialists. A meeting of the Socialist International in Paris at the turn of the century disputed the Marxist condemnation of contraception as bourgeois. The socialists argued that women's control over their reproduction was as important to socialist goals as workers' control over conditions of employment. American socialist birth control pioneer Margaret Sanger publicized this view before she opened her first birth control clinic in 1916.

On sexual matters Lucy was completely in accord with her husband. "Her wisdom was that things grow gradually, and a marriage grows gradually like a tree or a plant, and it strikes deep roots," Grace reflected. If Lucy ever disagreed with her husband, she kept her feelings for private talks between them. Before the children and in public Lucy always protected and defended James.

Dinner time at the Woodsworth home was as much an occasion for lessons in social service as it was a time for nourishment. The nightly meal opened with a grace James had composed which is still much quoted today.

> We are thankful for these and all the good things
> of life. We recognize that they are a part of our
> common heritage, and come to us through the efforts
> of our brothers and sisters the world over.
> What we desire for ourselves we wish for all.
> To this end may we take our share in the world's work
> and the world's struggles.

A favourite Woodsworth table game on the same theme was "Who Set the Dinner Table?" The answer was not "Mother." "Where did she get the bread?" James would ask, leading the children to understand that working men and women had coaxed wheat from the vast Canadian prairies, milled it into flour, baked it into loaves, and transported it to stores for sale beside Canadian milk, vegetables, fruit and meat—each step in the process accomplished by honourable labour. World geography was demystified painlessly and faraway places brought home in the plates from England, the tablecloth from Ireland, rice from Asia and pepper from the Malay States. The children were inspired, in Grace's words, to "set the world's dinner table, clothe the world's people or do something to help with the world's work."

As a high school senior Grace was intense and romantic yet judgmental, tending toward self-righteousness, as she confessed to her diary seven years later when she had attained some perspective. "Rather early in life, I fear, I became possessed of a certain sort of high seriousness. At the ridiculously early age of eleven I set about reforming the young rapscallions at school. And of all sorts of reform I chose the most absurd—manners! Funny for me, wasn't it?

"Well, then came the war, and for quite a while my ambition wavered between being shot as a martyr and going over to France to urge the contending parties to unite in a sort of glorified Sunday School picnic. About this time I became addicted to [Edgar] Guest, Alton Locke and Karl Marx. Such a queer melange as my brains must have held! War, religious scepticism, socialism, romance, a bit of mysticism, and above all a distrust and contempt for the rich and powerful.

"By the time we reached Vancouver I must have been a delightful specimen—quite unclassifiable, I imagine. I remember being set on fire by speeches on Ireland, Russia, Theosophy—good or bad it made no difference. At school I was a sulky little brute, flaring out suddenly in long-winded denunciations of everything in the Western Hemisphere. Then in the true spirit of the prophets of old I would ascend to the housetop and curse the port of Vancouver and its inhabitants."

In her youthful search for identity Grace followed in the footsteps of her beloved father as the eldest lion cub follows the leader of its pride. It would take Grace years before she could live up to her powerful father's example of sacred service to humanity, Father, but the attempt to do so shaped her entire life. Her performance would always be measured by his exacting standards.

When she entered as an arts freshman at the University of British Columbia in the fall of 1921, Grace joined an estimated 22,000 full-time undergraduate students in Canada; fewer than 4000 were women. Grace wanted to become a schoolteacher like Lucy, whose love of language and history was an inspiration. And although James and Lucy had taught their girls that they

Best friends Kathleen Inglis (Godwin) and Grace explore Shelter Island, one of the rocky islets dotting the Sunshine Coast of British Columbia. Summer 1922.

Grace at age seventeen, in the garden at Congregation de Notre Dame, where she immersed herself in the study of French language and culture. Ottawa, 1923.

Grace and Aunt Mary Woodsworth graduate together from the University of Manitoba, Winnipeg, June 1928.

could achieve anything in life regardless of their gender, at the time teaching and nursing were among the very few careers open to women.

Grace brought to university a disdain for her fellow students of which she was well aware. She confided to her diary, "By the time I got to university I was no longer able to call a spade a spade. Either attempting in impassioned language to turn the conservative from their evil courses, or listening in ill-veiled contempt to the senseless chatter of the human beings about me. How I loved to parade my book-learning."

Grace would have been very lonely but for the companionship of her best friend, Kathleen Inglis, who came down from Gibson's Landing to board with the Woodsworths. She attended the British Empire's first university degree program in nursing, established at UBC in 1919. At university Kathleen resumed her old role as Grace's tutor in mathematics and science, while Grace helped Kathleen with her English. "She wasn't interested in sciences at all," Kathleen mused. "I went on in sciences, she went on in languages. She had a wonderful vocabulary."

UBC was still housed in one stone building and a collection of wooden houses at Heather and 12th Avenue where Vancouver General Hospital stands today. Grace and Kathleen called them "the little chicken houses in Fairview," and suffered through drafty classrooms and chemistry classes held in tents. Grace had just turned sixteen, but neither she nor her best friend was yet interested in the opposite sex. "Oh, no," said Kathleen, "we were too young."

Initiation into university life was drastic. All the apprehensive "freshies" had to go through this ordeal at the hands of the "sophs" who, having survived the year before, took great glee in tormenting their hapless victims. That Christmas, Grace told the awful tale of initiation as her contribution to Father's Book.

"With a sinking heart I followed my conductor into a room lighted by flaring candles. There a horrible apparition seized me with shrill cries of 'Murder!' and 'Vengeance!' and daubed my face with brilliant red, green and blue paint. With a dreadful shriek another forced down my throat a nasty liquid tasting suspiciously like castor oil. Then my head was anointed with glycerine, and I was given a parting coat of shoe blacking . . . . In an instant we felt that something was being rubbed on our faces. It didn't take us long to recognize the odour of limburger cheese. Giving us no time to protest, they shoved a spoonful of half cooked spaghetti into our mouths, regaling us all the while with gentle murmurs of 'Just a wee worm, my angel.' . . . Blindfolded, we were now treated to an aeroplane ride on a board. Our heartless persecutors next led us into a room, and without uncovering our eyes ordered us to feed one another syrup. The result may be better imagined than described!"

Grace and the other freshettes stayed up until midnight washing their hair and nursing their injured pride but, harsh though it was, there was value in the experience. Bonding with her classmates through a shared experience of humiliation and pain, Grace no longer felt as isolated on her high plane of book-learning.

But her time at UBC was to be brief. Events in Ottawa would draw the entire Woodsworth family to the nation's capital before the end of 1922.

Conservative Prime Minister Arthur Meighen called an election for late in 1921. J.S. Woodsworth won the unanimous nomination of the Independent Labour Party for Winnipeg Centre, where he then faced Liberal and Conservative candidates. He took as a theme for his campaign speeches a review of the various functions of the Dominion government, and showed how they vitally affected the life of every Canadian citizen.

On December 6, 1921, Woodsworth was elected to Parliament, the first Independent Labour Party member elected in Canada. With this victory he reversed a position that had seemed hopeless only two years before. Denounced as a Bolshevik, jailed and charged with sedition, Woodsworth had lost his professional standing and had had to turn to manual labour. He had resigned from the Methodist ministry. He had been forced out of a government position on the conscription issue, denounced as unpatriotic and left friendless at the railway station. Yet the people of Winnipeg Centre, a working class riding, knew who they wanted representing them in Ottawa— a man who had proved he really cared about them.

At sixteen Grace was still too young to vote, but she devoured her father's newsy letters. He wrote of the wild excitement in Winnipeg Centre on election night when "Someone picked up a dray—hitched themselves to it and placing me in it dragged me in triumph, singing and shouting college-like yells: W-O-O-D-S-W-O-R-T-H. At the Free Press we halted and thousands cheered themselves hoarse."

It was an historic three-party election. Canadians elected the first Progressives to sit in the House of Commons, and one was a "first" twice over. Agnes Macphail, the first woman ever elected to the House of Commons, represented the Ontario riding of Grey South East, winning on a Progressive ticket in the first federal election in which women exercised their franchise. A farm woman born and raised, Macphail started as a campaigner for the United Farmers of Ontario. She was an asset as a speaker from platforms in drafty halls, in church basements, and around kitchen tables. Political ambition was considered not quite nice in men, and was still less acceptable for a woman. If Macphail had shown how much she wanted to be elected, her biographers say, the farmers would have been shocked and repelled. But she showed herself to be modest, retiring, capable and available for nomination.

When Parliament opened on March 8, 1922, Agnes Campbell Macphail joined sixty-four other Progressives in a House with a minority Liberal government led by William Lyon Mackenzie King, fifty Conservatives under Arthur Meighen, and two Labour men, William Irvine from Alberta and his leader J.S. Woodsworth from Manitoba.

Woodsworth may have been elevated to the grand status of an MP, but to his children he was still Father, a very human being. As he was getting ready for the opening of his first parliamentary session, Grace wrote a poem built on a first line by Kathleen's mother, here abridged.

> Come forth my dress suit from thy long repose
> Tonight I dance with Lady Maud.
> Where's back? Where's front? O goodness knows
> I would not be a clod.
>
> Come forth my silk hat from thy dusty box!
> She'll wear an egret fair
> My children filled it up with rocks
> O dear! What shall I wear?
>
> Come forth gloves, kerchief from where'ere you lie
> Her mouchoir's rarest lace
> I wish I knew the colour of this tie
> I'll ask my daughter Grace.
>
> Come forth my dress suit from thy long repose
> The hour approaches fast
> A chill come creeping up my toes
> And yet—the die is cast.

On a chilly West Coast evening, Tuesday December 12, 1922, the Woodsworths were again boarding a transcontinental train, leaving British Columbia after five and a half years, heading east. James had lived alone in Ottawa during his first year in the House, to avoid pulling the children out of school in mid-term, and he sorely missed his family.

In Toronto Grace learned how much her mother was respected. The Women's International League for Peace and Freedom gave a banquet in Lucy's honour. Later, at another reception for Lucy given by "university people," Grace told her diary, "Mother made an excellent speech on 'How I Became a Labour Man.' Really I don't see how she had the nerve to do it in such an audience, but it was splendid."

Then it was back on the train for a ride to the Cavan farm for Christmas. Grace wrote, "At length we reached Bethany and there with the big bob-tailed sleigh were Uncle Sandfield, Ralph and Gordon. Oh! it was glorious riding along the familiar road after nine years with the sleigh-bells and the frosty air! . . . Mother spoke at the village Sunday School and one man remarked afterwards, 'I think she's some sort of a Bolshevist'."

In early January the Woodsworths moved into their new home at 152 Osgoode Street near the Rideau River, about twelve blocks from the Parliament Buildings. A few days later Lucy, Grace and Belva received an invitation to attend the opening of Parliament. Belva was shy and Lucy unenthusiastic, but Grace was determined to see the ceremony. On January 31, 1923, at age seventeen, Grace entered the Parliament Buildings for the first time. She was more concerned about clothes on this occasion than she would ever be again.

"We set off for the House, Belva and I in our little silk dresses and Mother in her plain black velvet," Grace recorded in her diary. "We were shown into a handsome dressing room with several attendants. Then it was that my heart failed me. Such a sight as we saw! It was as if all the fashion catalogues had come to life! The room fairly glittered with dresses. All the colours of the rainbow were there—pinks, blues, whites, satins, silks, velvets, feather fans, iridescent beads, elaborate head-dresses etc. (There is such a thing as being conspicuous through being plainly dressed and among the youngest present.) We pulled on the old white gloves lent us by a friend, and followed the chattering crowd to the Senate Chamber which was already filled with society lights anxious to see and to be seen."

Later at the Speaker's reception Grace met the Prime Minister, Mackenzie King. Later she wrote, "For once, and for once only we were among the highest society people in Ottawa. Yet, apart from their dress, I failed to notice any reason why they should be considered any better than many people upon whom they profess to look down."

Her parents encouraged all their children to learn French, and for the next six months Grace was a day student at a convent school in Ottawa, Congregation de Notre Dame. In the real world she made friends and built upon the foundation of French grammar Lucy had taught her back in Gibson's Landing, but in her imagination Grace was not a school girl but an "heroic, world-worn martyr who sought refuge in the Congregation de Notre Dame."

In February she was invited to a luncheon at the House of Commons. "What was my dismay to find that both Mother and Father wished me to go!" Seated beside the daughter of Progressive leader Robert Forke, Grace found her "not at all artificial or stand-offish." The real treat of the day came after the party broke up when Grace took a seat in the gallery of the House to listen to the debates. She commented, "Mr. Meighan [sic] is a fluent speaker, but I cannot say that his biting sarcasm is as agreeable to me as is the humorous irony of Mr. Irvine."

In April 1923, Grandmother Staples died on the farm at Cavan, and although her end was, in Lucy's words, "gracious and peaceful," it was a sad event for the family. A few months later the Woodsworths moved several blocks west to 134 McLeod Street, and in the fall Grace entered Ottawa

Normal School, training to become a teacher. It was intolerably boring for a young woman (nearly eighteen) who for years had read philosophy and great literature to endure classes in cookery, dishwashing and the rural school lunch. But her romantic dreams could not be confined within the curriculum's narrow boundaries. Over a recipe for cream sauce, Grace pinned into her notebook small buff pages on which she recorded a revealing dream. "Seated on the crumbling stone steps near the house was a girl dreaming in the silence . . . . She breathed the rich fragrance of the warm air, and marvelled at the sweetness of life. Surely she was happy, serenely and perfectly happy. Into her musing stole the opening notes of a melody—an old love song familiar to her ear . . . . She knew who was playing that song, yet never before had she heard him play as he did that evening. Tenderly he drew his bow across the strings and they spoke of love in all its clinging sweetness . . . . Love? Why then did she tremble tonight as she listened to a simple melody? . . .

"Suddenly the music swelled out into the conflict between love and circumstance . . . . Tense with excitement she stood up. The blood was pounding at her heart and she felt suffocated . . . . Ah! she knew it all now. Never again would she feel peaceful contentment in life. Life was a struggle which vanquished all except love, and she must be ready to meet it valiantly. She would be ready."

Preoccupied until now with her ethical and intellectual development and her role within the family, Grace was to keep her passionate dreams sealed within the "secret vault" of her heart for years. She fought shy of physical or even social contact with men of her own age. She feared embarrassment if her "strange, new feelings" were to be exposed to any other human being. Privacy was her friend. Nor did she yet feel the need for real boys in her life. None of them could begin to compare with her beloved father, and the spirited antics of her four brothers left Grace with no illusions about what boys were really like.

1924 opened with Lenin's death. Russia was absorbed by the struggle between Stalin and Trotsky, which culminated in Trotsky's expulsion from the Communist Party in 1927. In January Britain's first Labour government took office under James Ramsay MacDonald which extended recognition to the Soviet Union. In the US President Calvin Coolidge won re-election on a prosperity platform, but times were not so prosperous in Canada.

Grace completed normal school courses and in September of 1924 took her first teaching job at Dunrobin, Ontario. She boarded with the family of one of her students in an old house with stone walls three feet thick. At this point Grace wanted to be a teacher like her mother, and dreamed of expanding the minds of her eight students far beyond their one-room school. For a salary of nine hundred dollars she instructed them in arithmetic, spelling, composition, grammar, geography, history, hygiene, music, art and nature. In her lined scribbler Grace did not record how successful her teaching was, but rather how much she herself had learned.

Overall, Grace was happy in Dunrobin, seeking with her students to "learn the truths of life." Far as she was from a cultural centre, Grace did not neglect her own education that year. Her reading list ranged from Helen Keller's *The Story of My Life,* to Sidney and Beatrice Webb's socialist classic, *The Decay of the Capitalist Civilization,* which she called "a careful, forceful indictment of capitalism." She read John Reed's *Ten Days That Shook the World,* and Henry David Thoreau's *Walden.* She read H.G. Wells, Anatole France, Jules Verne, and George Bernard Shaw. "If only we can contribute one stone in the foundation of the world that is to be," she wrote in her diary, "we shall share its beauty and triumph."

Soon after her twentieth birthday, Grace was back in her home town of Winnipeg, where the family had moved to be close to James's political base. Grace entered the University of Manitoba as a second-year arts student alongside her aunt, James's sister Mary Woodsworth.

In the federal election of October 29, 1925, Woodsworth won handily for the Independent Labour Party (ILP) in the newly redistricted riding of Winnipeg North Centre. The family was living at 76 Chestnut Street just over the boundary into the newly created riding of Winnipeg South Centre, depriving Lucy of the chance to vote for James. Grace could not vote at all in this second federal election for which women were enfranchised, as she was still nine months short of age twenty-one.

The Manifesto of the Independent Labour Party of Manitoba in 1925 advanced the concept of the co-operative commonwealth. It stated: "The Independent Labour Party of Manitoba is formed for the purpose of giving political expression to the aspirations of all workers regardless of industrial affiliation, who believe in the establishment of a Cooperative Commonwealth, with production for use and not for profit as its economic basis."

After election night in the ILP committee room Grace wrote in her diary, "In the little room, almost hidden by the grey cloud of tobacco smoke, a small group was listening in attentively at the radio where the Eastern results were beginning to arrive . . . . Men and women pressed forward to greet their candidate as he entered . . . . The group at the radio gradually increased. Figures were taken down and compared with feverish intensity. A favourable result came. Great excitement. Now a poor result. Depression. Then a period of absolute silence over the radio—jazz music. Ah! listen, all of you. 'Woodsworth elected!' A great shout bursts from the crowd . . . . For a moment they catch hands like children and laugh aloud in their pride and relief. Soon they recover themselves and surge forward to congratulate their new member. For this is the hour of their victory."

The Conservatives under Arthur Meighen won 116 seats. King lost his North York seat, and the Liberals captured only 101 ridings. In 1921, 65

Progressives had entered the House, but now Mackenzie King absorbed all but 24 into the Liberal ranks. This splinter group of 24 Progressives held the balance of power in that volatile fifteenth Parliament. They came to be known as the Ginger Group for their spicy, peppery political views. Woodsworth was one of four independents elected. He was beginning to meld these independent-minded people into a political force.

Mackenzie King arranged for his re-election in the riding of Prince Albert, Saskatchewan, then vowed to Governor General Lord Byng that he would meet Parliament as Prime Minister and win its confidence. To make good this vow, King counted on the support of the twenty-four Progressives and four independents. According to Byng's version of this celebrated interview, King had promised that if he could not govern with the support of the Progressives, he would hand the Government over to Meighen without another election. According to King's version, he had been given the Prime Minister's normal right to call another election at any time, once he had received a vote of confidence in Parliament.

This parliamentary impasse, with King attempting to control things from the gallery, grew more complex when the Conservatives presented to the House evidence of corruption in the Customs Department under the previous Liberal government. To win a vote of confidence King offered a budget of tax and tariff reductions. To get Woodsworth on his side he promised, in writing, to introduce Canada's first legislation on Old Age Pensions as Woodsworth had requested repeatedly. He also promised to repeal two repressive laws passed hastily during the Winnipeg Strike, Section 98 of the Criminal Code and a section of the Immigration Act allowing deportation without a hearing for those suspected of subversion.

Early in 1926 King invited Labour MPs Woodsworth and Abraham Heaps and Ottawa *Citizen* editor Charles Bowman to dinner at his residence, Laurier House. There King offered Woodsworth the position as Minister of Labour in his government. Woodsworth declined, nor did he mention the invitation even to most of his family. Heaps told the story publicly twenty-five years later. But James confided in Lucy, and Grace's diary records the event at the time it occurred. Once again her father's socialist principles took precedence over ambition or political expediency, no matter how high the position offered. Grace took the lesson to heart—principle was everything.

In June, King's government was forced to resign over the customs scandals. Governor General Lord Byng refused King's request for a new election, and Arthur Meighen became Prime Minister on June 29. Four days later the Meighen government was defeated in a non-confidence motion. Another election was called for September 14, 1926. Grace had turned twenty-one on July 25, 1926, and less than two months later, thanks to Canada's parliamentary turmoil, she was eligible to vote in her first federal election. As the family home was in the new riding of Winnipeg South

Centre, Grace did not have J.S. Woodsworth's name on her ballot. Her choice was between a Liberal and a Conservative. The incumbent was Major William Walker Kennedy, a Conservative World War I military hero. J.T. Thorson, a British citizen of Icelandic descent, dean of the Manitoba Law School and a Liberal, was the only other candidate. He got Grace's first vote. This time King and his Liberals won a majority.

When the Old Age Pension Bill was re-introduced in the 1927 session, it was again passed by the House of Commons. Later that year after much wordy opposition, senators—secure in their own generous pensions—also permitted ordinary Canadians to receive at public expense twenty dollars a month at age seventy, if a means test proved they were truly in need.

In the 1920s, when Grace was attending the University of Manitoba, most Canadians believed that a woman's place was in the home. For generations many women had been taught to put their own needs last. It was an attitude consonant with the socialist dictum to help oneself by helping others. Lucy's example as a teacher and peace activist authorized and inspired Grace to create a career for herself, but this freedom existed within the limits of general social attitudes shared by female university students, most of whom thought no further than marriage soon after graduation, if not before.

Grace was earning a reputation as a brilliant scholar at university. She took classes in psychology, zoology, English literature, botany and history, but her specialty was French, in which she got the highest marks possible and won several scholarships over three years. She joined the Debating Union and trained herself in public speaking by representing the university in interprovincial and international debates. Still, Grace envisioned herself as a teacher, not a politician. But while she was a high achiever academically, she was struggling socially. Defensive in the face of criticism of her father's socialist and pacifist politics, Grace at first assumed a superior attitude toward other students that did not win her many friends.

Self-analysis and self-improvement consumed Grace's thoughts during that first Winnipeg winter of 1925–26. "It is of medium height," she wrote of her body, "broad-shouldered, and of well-nourished appearance, a particularly irritating feature. Short straight hair, ordinary hazel eyes, a snub nose and a wide grin set in a cheerful looking round face all add to my annoyance." Regardless of valiant attempts to base her estimation of herself solely on intellectual achievement, Grace wanted to look striking, and was impatient with what she saw as her ordinary appearance. Her "mental furniture" came under equally intense scrutiny. She was torn between peer group pressure for sameness and private pride in her individuality, especially in her high grades, her scholarships and her distinguished status as the eldest daughter of a Member of Parliament.

Grace was experiencing mood swings from the lowest depths to the highest peaks with little in between. "Indeed I've seen the poor thing weep with vexation when its will was crossed," she wrote. "Conceit is generally mixed with a sort of timidity called awkwardness. The horrid creature plagues me from daylight till dark with its queer mixtures and 'Bull in the China Shop' performances. Dreaming is one of its favourite occupations, and it doesn't wait till bed-time either."

She raised self-criticism to a fine art that winter. "Once there lived a girl who had the following faults," Grace wrote in her diary. At the top of the list was selfishness, then egoism, next cowardice of people, life and dogs. Irritability displayed morning, noon and night with brothers, sister and parents was followed by hypocrisy with regard to general culture, society, hatred of dress and modern youth. She faulted herself for carelessness toward friends and family and slowness in growing up, music and doing work.

At the same time Grace felt stirring within her a formless, powerful yearning for high goals and accomplishments, but she had no idea as yet how she would achieve them. In a diary entry titled "Uncertainty," she wrote, "Ever since I became conscious of my identity and began that process of self-analysis which acts as 'a goad of discontent' I have been aware, more or less definitely, of a feeling that I am destined to play some part in the history of mankind."

"But how to find my life's work," she continued in her diary. "Ideas and inspirations surge within me clamouring for an outlet." Instead of clear-cut goals and straightforward movement toward them, Grace described her mind at that time as "a rag-bag, odds and ends of knowledge and thought gleaned from various sources . . . a confused tangle of patches." She longed for something or someone to step in and organize her, but for the time being no one did.

Love did make its appearance in Grace's life during her first year at the University of Manitoba in a form more substantial than dreams. "The worst has happened!" she confided to her trusty diary. "Mr. [Ralph] Bird has asked me to go to a toboggan party on Wednesday evening. And a dance after! and I consented! I'm sure I don't know why. Why do my peaceful habits of study have to be so rudely upset after these years? It's positively tragic!!"

As it turned out Grace enjoyed knowing Ralph Bird. She attended plays with him and shared confidences over ice cream. But his attempts at physical intimacy were unsuccessful. Proud of maintaining her "puritanical independence," Grace wrote, "Ralph made a slight attempt to hold my hand, but I forestalled him!! He goes on Monday. I'll be relieved, for I do hate to have him get too sentimental."

Early that spring Grace experienced her first touch of the trouble that was to make an agony of her later years. She had pains in her shoulders, called neuralgia by the doctors, that were so severe she was in bed for days at a time and kept up with her studies only with Lucy's help. "I've had it ever since I was about fifteen," she recalled, "twinges in this shoulder. Then in university Mother had to read to me to get through the year. I wasn't able to read any more because of the pain. That year I managed a scholarship, so I was very pleased to be helped that way."

In May 1926, after finishing classes, Grace earned part of her tuition with a two-month teaching job at Dehowa School in the farming town of Poplarfield, Manitoba. "Evening alone in the little cottage," she mused. "It is queer to be the only English person within miles. To have thirty little Ruthenians half of whom understand half you say and the other half nothing at all is hard work. This is going to be a stiff pull. Well, I will try it. I don't want to be a coward."

At Poplarfield Grace learned she had won a scholarship for the 1926–27 school year. With light heart she set off with her father on a westbound train for a summer holiday. Their destination was Gibson's Landing to see old friends and revive old memories. Grace's spirits were high, "all pulsing with life and movement and the joy of being young." After fun with old friends at Gibson's Landing, Grace visited the remote northern British Columbia community of Burns Lake where her best friend, Kathleen, had settled with her new husband, Sidney Godwin, publisher of the only newspaper in town, the *Observer*. Kathleen was the proofreader and printer. Pioneer-fashion the two women cooked up great quantities of white wash in a big copper boiler and strung it out on lines while they filled each other in on recent events. For fun they took a motor boat up one of the nearby lakes to picnic and explore a lead-silver mine.

Too soon the carefree summer was over and Grace plunged back into university. This year she was less defensive and enjoyed more of a social life. She had the French Club, debates on issues of the day, and class suppers to organize. Still, she gave everything harsh criticism, especially professors who lectured merely on the facts without presenting ideas. Grace told her diary, "Principles we must have—principles to explain the facts of life—principles with which to build up a philosophy . . . . But perhaps this year may have helped to hasten the process of learning—to give a key to the secret of power."

Grace the bookworm and dreamer got a jolt of reality in the summer of 1927. She and Belva took waitress jobs at the Chateau Lake Louise, an elegant resort hotel in Alberta's Rocky Mountains. There was no time for daydreams or fantasies: Grace served meals all day and sometimes danced all night. She started to use makeup, and to take a less critical view of girls who cared more about boys and clothes than about books and principles.

But back in Winnipeg for her final year of university, Grace took horrified stock of herself. She wrote, "Well, in another year or so I would be just a cog in the machine . . . . I would become standardized in my ideas and lose all my boasted puritanical independence. And, Oh horror of horrors! I already like the university girls, and worse still I had a sneaking suspicion that in time I might come to tolerate the men."

Lucy had a talk with her eldest about her "standoffishness," and Grace took her mother's encouraging words to heart. The next day at a tea, she wrote, "I found that suddenly I had lost my inferiority complex dating from Dunrobin days. I was able to chatter away quite unconcernedly without caring what sort of impression I made. It was fun! Since then everything seems different. Somehow I think I've found out that you've got to be human to get anywhere in this world . . . just now I feel really emancipated."

The "inferiority complex" Grace took from her teaching experience at Dunrobin was the result of testing her incomplete teaching skills against her ambitious desire to bring these rural children out of ignorance into the light of civilization. As educators, her father and mother were both highly skilled; Grace had by then thoroughly internalized their standards of excellence. She felt self-conscious and inadequate in comparison. The feelings had become pervasive.

One dark night between her studies and her dreams Grace wrote a poem expressing grave doubts about her essential worth. She pictured her doubts, jealousies and fears as filthy, slimy parasites, choking the life out of healthy creative thoughts.

FUTILITY

Slimy things slip coiling through the darkness of the mind
Frozen hateful things
Slinking among the roots of living thoughts
Poor, feeble stems that struggle towards the light
Of reason, far beyond
Their pitiful, blind gropings.
Curving among their roots unceasingly
Sapping their strength in odious embrace
The sinuous ones twine in their filth
In baleful jealousy of those who seek the sun
Undaunted by their mediocrity.
Why this eternal struggle? Why the worms that twist
The life from thought ere yet it once can live?
Why the whole mad jungle?
Need there be a why?

Yet Grace still cherished some faith in her own genius. When she had exorcised her misgivings by writing them out, she tucked the poem inside a notebook she had covered with tan suede and inscribed in flowing script, "Genius Burns."

At last the spring of 1928 arrived and with it graduation day for Grace and her Aunt Mary. The University of Manitoba yearbook complimented her capability and dependability. Though it was impossible to guess from the level gaze under square-cut bangs in her graduation picture, Grace was anything but confident about her future. She whispered to her diary, "Here it is a mere ten days till graduation and I'm scared stiff. Honestly I'm afraid I'm going to make a mess of things . . . . Oh well."

But she had won a French government scholarship for a year of study at the Sorbonne University in Paris. Adventure was awaiting her across the Atlantic.

It was a wild, wet trip across the Atlantic Ocean for Grace and the group of teachers from Canada with whom she sailed on the Canadian Pacific liner, *Empress of Australia*. Early July storms tossed the ship like a cork upon the ocean, but finally Grace got her first glimpse of England, Southampton Harbour at sunrise.

She fell in love with the city of London. She was dazzled by the kaleidoscopic bustle of the market in Petticoat Lane: the weight-guesser, the artist, the palmist, the African herbalist, the hunchback selling silk stockings, the brilliantine lady. Each huckster appeared unique and mysterious. She visited Hyde Park just in time to hear a friend of her father's give a speech on co-operation to the crowd sprawled on the grass. The British Parliament was a revelation, a shrine peopled by famous legislators of the past.

France, homeland of one of Canada's other founding cultures, was of enormous interest to Grace. She and her shipmate friend Isobel investigated every corner of Paris. They rose at dawn to visit Les Halles market with its mountains of vegetables and banks of flowers, ranks of fish and live lobsters. Shivering with reverence and delight, they climbed the tower of Notre Dame cathedral, up the same worn stone steps climbed by the hunchback Quasimodo, to view the city stretching to the horizon. The Château de Versailles where Napoleon executed his coup d'état appeared a "heap of gilt and debris."

France was aviation-crazy. The record-breaking achievements of aviators seemed to embody the hopes of people on both sides of Atlantic for unprecedented prosperity, freedom and fun. In this golden age artistic expression too stretched its wings and took flight. It was the Paris of cubist painters Picasso and Matisse, Braque and Magritte. There were performances of the Ballet Russe, Sergei Prokofiev and Heitor Villa-Lobos. Grace attended as many concerts and plays as she could afford.

The sculptures of Rodin made a deep impression on Grace. She told her diary, "From the moment when I saw the Thinker surrounded by the trees in the garden, I had a feeling absolutely different from that with which I had looked at the other works of art. I found a message in these statues of bronze: to struggle is the great thing in life."

At the end of August, Grace and Isobel travelled to the town of Cinq Mars

Grace in her room on rue Cler in Paris, where she lived while attending classes at the Sorbonne, winter 1929. Much to her amusement, she was often mistaken for a Parisienne.

on the Loire River and stayed with a French couple with whom Grace practised her French and her self-control. She wrote, "M. Fuchs and I walked together talking politics. We were on dangerous ground for he hates socialism of all kinds with a hatred born of complete ignorance. It's no use to argue with him, so I try not to quarrel even if I do feel like a bull in the presence of a red rag!"

The two young women bathed in the chilly river, washed their clothes and cut each other's hair. They visited the castle where Catherine de Medici had schemed, and they marvelled at her boudoir walls with the secret cupboards where she had kept her poisons.

All was not play. One day Isobel, Mme. Fuchs and Grace set out for the vineyards to pick grapes alongside the other *vendangeurs*. "I took the skin off my first finger during the first hour, but a little thing like that wasn't going to stop me," Grace told her diary, *en français*. "They began to look upon us with respect. 12:30 came at last and we stopped for lunch. My! we were tired! Hips, back, arms and legs! The lunch was very good: stewed rabbit with potatoes (kept warm by being wrapped in shawls on the way to the field), bread, cheese and an excellent red wine made from M. Garnier's grapes.

"The peasants asked us questions about Canada . . . . It's quite a triumph to be able to interest the French peasant. But the afternoon! I believe I've never done anything so hard," she went on. "I was encouraged to hear a man talking to his neighbour, 'Canadians are a strong race, you know.' Our pride was the only thing that kept us going."

Soon after that day in the vineyard Grace returned to Paris for the opening of classes at the Sorbonne. She took the course for foreigners covering the history, literature and geography of France, modes of dress and social customs, all in French naturally, as well as a diction course to improve her accent. She chose to compress this course into four months instead of the usual eight, so the other four months could be free for exploration.

To find lodgings she put an ad in the newspaper, and found a room in the rue Cler with a "rather patrician" old lady, her daughter and granddaughter, and a tiny dog. Food was scarce and luxuries like butter carefully doled out.

Grace had to safeguard her reputation as a respectable young woman even though she was living on her own in Paris. "In those days in France there were just two kinds of girls," she explained. "There were the kind that were chaperoned carefully by an elderly woman, nice, careful girls, and there were the other kind that were anybody's game. I soon ran into those, of course. I remember taking pains on several occasions, in my halting French, to explain to them that we weren't a bit like French girls, that we had our own ideas of what we would do and what we wouldn't do. People just couldn't believe it, but they had to. People would say to Mother, 'What did you mean by letting your daughter go over at twenty-three to France. You know that nice young girls don't go around unchaperoned in Paris.' Mother would say, 'My daughter, she's of age now. She knows all that I know about living anyway, and I trust her to use her own judgment'."

In the depths of that Paris winter Grace met Richard de Kiewiet, a young Dutchman from South Africa, brilliant and thoughtful. They roamed the city, charted the book stores, walked in the Bois, and attended concerts and lectures. It was fun, but they had no serious intentions toward one another. Grace always went home alone. She was proud to know Richard, and believed he was destined to become a great man, but Grace was not ready to pledge her heart. At Easter they travelled together to Germany, but at the last minute avoided making any change in their friendship. Grace sensed that Richard was not prepared for a permanent commitment; both training and inclination made her draw back from a temporary alliance. She was content to save herself for marriage in accord with the moral code of the Woodsworth family and of the times. She was not ready to give up dreams of doing something worthwhile in Canada without knowing that her love for this man was the strongest hope and dream of all. She parted company with Richard in Germany. Instead she visited Heidelberg and sailed down the Rhine with brother Charles, who was free on a study break.

It was a Germany in which Adolf Hitler was gathering power for his National Socialist Party, the Nazis. The German Social Democrats, strengthened by the election of 1928, headed the Weimar Republic, but by the time Grace sailed the Rhine in 1929 trouble was brewing. Unemployment was rising, and all Germans wanted French troops out of the occupied Rhineland.

Later that spring Belva sailed over from Canada, and the two sisters travelled to the south of France. Through fragrant, flower-blown Avignon they rolled in a third-class rail carriage, then on to Nîmes, where they listened to the glorious music of Lohengrin seated on the steps of an ancient Roman amphitheatre.

Swimming in the Mediterranean Sea near the Italian border, Grace nearly drowned; she had never seen such heavy surf. Fear swept over her with the waves. "Suddenly to be just lifted and banged down and unable to get your feet, I was just frightened silly," she recalled. "Fortunately there were a couple of young fellows there who came along and hauled me out, but it gave me a feeling of the power of the sea."

Just before her return to Canada in October 1929, Grace shared her impressions of France with an audience at the French language school Alliance Française in Paris. She spoke on the personality of the nation, which she called her adopted homeland. The speech was reviewed kindly in one of the Paris daily newspapers. Complimenting her on speaking without manuscript or notes, the reporter commented on the perfection of Grace's accent and grammar and labelled the speech "vraiment délicieuse." It was an honourable finish to an adventurous study year.

PART II

FLOWERING

CHAPTER 4

Back Home and Broke

Grace returned from Europe to a joyous family reunion in Winnipeg, and found that her legal status as a Canadian woman had changed just a week earlier on October 18, 1929: she was now a "person" before the law. The British Privy Council, then the final court of appeal in Canadian law, overruled a Canadian Supreme Court decision that women were not "qualified persons."

The Persons Case was the culmination of a long struggle: requests by women's groups for the appointment of a woman to the Senate had fallen on deaf ears in both Conservative and Liberal governments since 1919. Finally, legal action was brought by five women: Judge Emily Murphy, Nellie McClung, Louise McKinney, Irene Parlby and Henrietta Muir Edwards. They used a section of the Supreme Court Act to ask the Liberal government of Mackenzie King for an Order in Council directing the Supreme Court to rule on the constitutional question of whether the term "qualified persons" in Section 24 of the British North America Act included women. English common law of the time stated that "Women are persons in matters of pains and penalties, but are not persons in matters of rights and privileges." When Canada's highest court turned them down, the five persistent petitioners asked the government for leave to appeal to the Privy Council. Prime Minister Mackenzie King agreed. The women obtained from Britain what their own country would not grant them—the status of "persons."

No sooner had Grace absorbed this news than the stock market crash of October 29 plunged the world into financial turmoil. At first Grace considered herself fortunate to be hired as a French teacher in a Winnipeg junior high school. She had six rooms of students, some of them repeaters, to drill on the basics of the French language. "I tried to teach every student individually, and it just drove me up the wall," Grace recalled. "About Christmas I was getting in a bad state nervously and they gave me a primary class and that was OK." It seemed dreary after the excitement and intellectual stimulation of Paris, but at least she was working at a time when many were losing their jobs.

The Woodsworths celebrated Christmas of 1929 together at 60 Maryland Street in Winnipeg, with all its precious memories of happy times with Grandpa and Grandma Woodsworth. The family had moved back there from Chestnut Street in November. James was confined to bed with high blood pressure, so the Christmas tree was set up in his room. Lucy wrote in Father's Book, "Last year with Grace and Charles far from us, the realization that we cannot always count upon the family circle being complete as we did in those old days was so sharp as to heighten the joy of the all togetherness of this Christmas."

Grace finished the school year and went to northern British Columbia for a welcome holiday with Kathleen and Sidney Godwin. Back in Winnipeg in the fall she took another job teaching French, this time at Ralph Brown School in the city's North End. An even greater number of students than the year before led to more problems. Grace had just over a year's teaching experience and, in her own estimation, did not know enough to teach for "a mythical average." Instead she tried to teach each individual separately. It was not the right technique.

One can only imagine what the classroom was like the day Grace finally reached the boiling point. The young rowdies hated French. Many of them were repeaters, restless with empty bellies; they must have heckled her unbearably. And as soon as the bell rang, in came another of her six classes, rowdier or more apathetic than the last. Suddenly Grace's motivation to be the perfect success her father expected vaporized in a blaze of rage. She simply quit on the spot. She left the school in a taxi and went home to bed where she remained for several weeks. "I didn't have the brains to break down in a mild sort of way," she said. She never taught school again.

Classroom teaching was a dead end for Grace, a truth she had felt more keenly each day as she stood at the front of her French classes. Still, she blamed herself for the breakdown. Her contribution to Father's Book of Christmas 1930 is a revealing apology to him for what she considered a shameful loss of creative momentum. She traced her love of writing from the poetry of Gibson's Landing days, through the political writing of Vancouver and Ottawa, "meetings described with feverish gusto—personalities thrown on the screen in noisy confusion—the whole molten mass struggling in the white heat of passionate emotions—hate and hero worship." Then in Winnipeg, she wrote, "The rising star of Ambition—no particular ambition, but just pure unadulterated AMBITION, blazoned in capitals.

"Europe—and the full revelation of one's amusing naiveté and utter uselessness. That year saw the beginning of a marked reluctance to pose as an authority on science, religion, philosophy and the rest . . . . And then finally came the first sobering touch of work—spelled in little, hard, angular letters, that in certain lights seem to become tentacles alive with destruction," she lamented.

Grace's self-esteem hit rock bottom. She was propelled into a period of disillusion, frustration and perplexity, but even so she was better off than thousands of other young women without employment that winter of 1930–31. She lived with Lucy and her younger brothers at 60 Maryland Street, and watched enviously while James travelled the country weaving the fabric of a new Canadian political consciousness out of private meetings, and speeches, conferences and dinners.

Just at this difficult juncture, James invited Grace to Ottawa to volunteer in his parliamentary office. She would take care of routine clerical and secretarial tasks, keep his appointments book and greet visitors to the office. Grace jumped at the opportunity to be with her beloved father at the hub of the country's political action. She took a small room close to the Parliament Buildings and near her father's modest lodgings and took to her new life like a duck to water.

Woodsworth's office had become the centre of his existence, and he filled it with reminders of home and family. Five photographs on the walls were wellsprings of her father's inspiration: Keir Hardie, the first British socialist MP; Eugene Debs, the American socialist who had gone to prison for his beliefs; E.D. Morel, the British writer; Ramsay MacDonald, Britain's first Labour Prime Minister; and Agnes Macphail, Canada's first woman MP.

Charles, his father's secretary in 1930, vividly described the office decorations, each treasured object a lesson in socialism. "There was the little bronze bust of Savonarola, the fifteenth-century martyr burned at the stake for refusing to retract his reformist preachings. On a metal filing cabinet rested three huge scrapbooks in which Father religiously had pasted every item from the early social welfare days onward . . . . [There] was a short steel bill hook with a wooden handle which he had used as a stevedore on Vancouver's waterfront, [and] a sturdy piece of oak, two feet long, round and tapered, which Father never wearied of explaining was half a neck-yoke issued as a club to the auxiliary police sworn in to maintain order during the turbulent days of the Winnipeg strike.

"In a corner near the door were some less grim souvenirs which Father collected and framed with great delight—four or five original cartoons by Arch Dale, Racey and Jack Boothe, depicting him, beard and all, in situations representing highlights of his life in Parliament."

Grace placed a small desk in the corner beneath the cartoons and settled in to help her father deal with his voluminous flood of correspondence. This same office, halfway down the sixth floor corridor known as "socialist alley," now numbered Room 639C, would be her base of operations for more than thirty years, from 1931 through 1974—except for the nine years between Angus's retirement in 1957 and her own election to the House of Commons in 1965. She was right in the centre of things, listening and learning from the best speakers, organizers and thinkers of the day. Best of all, her father really needed her help.

Feeling there was so little time to accomplish the great task before him, Woodsworth worked incessantly. He was usually up at five in the morning, if he slept at all. In those days sessions of the House went on all night until some exhausted Member called a halt; Woodsworth sometimes stayed up several nights running. He spent no money on himself, carrying his bag onto trains, eating in all-night places to save money. But when it came to his children, Woodsworth was open-handed. Music, university, travel abroad— he was happy to give his children anything he could. Now he would give Grace an opportunity to put her excellent education to good use.

The seventeenth Parliament wore a Conservative face. In the election of July 1930 the Conservatives, under Calgary lawyer Richard Bedford Bennett, soundly defeated King's Liberals 137 to 88, with twenty seats going to independents and smaller parties. The unemployed and hungry country had turned to the right in hopes of stable financial management to pull them out of the Depression crisis. The wealthy Bennett, owner of the large E.B. Eddy Match Company, had promised during the 1930 campaign to end unemployment "or perish in the attempt."

Labour MPs Woodsworth and Abraham Heaps, both of Winnipeg, had the parliamentary support of the Ginger Group, the few Progressives remaining of the 65 elected in 1921 who had not been drawn into the Liberal Party. At the opening of the 1931 session the group included Robert Gardiner, Ted Garland, Henry Spencer, George Coote, William Lucas, Donald Kennedy, Alfred Speakman, Michael Luchkovich and William Irvine, all of the United Farmers of Alberta; Archibald Carmichael and Milton Campbell of Saskatchewan; and Agnes Macphail of the United Farmers of Ontario. Most were old parliamentary hands, but joining them for the first time was Woodsworth's old friend from Vancouver, Angus MacInnis, elected in Vancouver South on the Independent Labour Party (ILP) ticket.

MacInnis had long been convinced that working people needed political as well as union representation. He began his political activity by presenting grievances of the unemployed to the Vancouver City Council, then ran for school trustee in 1921 and came fourth of nine candidates for three seats. The following year, when the school board added a seat, Angus tried again and was elected for 1922–23, quite an achievement for a man whose formal education had ended at grade eight.

Angus's aim was higher than his reach in his next few electoral attempts. In the 1924 provincial election he ran unsuccessfully as a candidate for the Federated Labour Party. A columnist for Vancouver's *Province* wrote, "Mr. MacInnis is spare of frame and spare of words. But such words as he's got he uses to good effect."

In 1925 the fragmentation of socialist groups in British Columbia reached a peak. It was part of the worldwide splintering of socialist groups following the formation of the Comintern in 1921 and the announcement of its twenty-one conditions. One BC journalist of socialist ideals described it sadly: "So many contending socialist factions, the One Big Union, the Workers' Party, the Socialist Labour Party, the Federated Labour Party, the Socialist Party of Canada—hurling epithets, expletives, jibes and sneers upon each others' revolutionary heads with a venom and hatred they never exhibited towards the capitalist class."

Topping the list of the Comintern's twenty-one conditions was the command to "systematically and mercilessly remove from all responsible posts in the labour movement . . . all reformists and followers of the 'center'." This command divided labour activists into two camps: revolutionists and reformers. The Comintern declared "a decisive war against the entire bourgeois world and all the yellow, social democratic parties." The model for communist parties worldwide was to be small local cells absolutely obedient to the Comintern in Moscow. As a key member of the labour movement who was not a communist, Angus was to be a prime target of this command.

Angus helped to form, in 1925, the Independent Labour Party (ILP) in British Columbia, the immediate ancestor of the Co-operative Commonwealth Federation. A streetcar conductor, Angus played the role of conductor in his political life as well, guiding would-be rebels through the perplexing maze of splintering groups toward his vision of evolutionary, not revolutionary, socialism. Angus served as its president for most of its short life. The BC ILP was a younger brother to the Manitoba ILP represented in Parliament by J.S. Woodsworth. Both Canadian branches were descendants of the ILP in Britain, born in 1893 of provincial labour and urban socialist parents. Its platform stated, in part, "Collective ownership of the means of production; social appropriation of that which is socially produced, is the only means to end exploitation." This was Angus's political lineage.

He unsuccessfully contested the Ward 8 seat on Vancouver City Council for the 1925–26 term, but persisted and won it the following year. Angus was re-elected in 1927, having made a name for himself as a man of integrity. In 1928 Vancouver was reorganized in a system of twelve wards with two-year terms for aldermen. Angus contested Ward 7 and won by a wide margin. Busy with political work in addition to his job on the streetcars, Angus had little time for romance. He purchased a small house in Chinatown not far from the waterfront, where he lived with his sister Christine, his mother, who still spoke only Gaelic, and his niece Violet.

On July 28, 1930, shortly before his forty-sixth birthday, Angus won a seat in the House of Commons representing Vancouver South. Stretching from Burrard Inlet to the Fraser River, the sprawling riding had been held since 1921 by Conservative Leon Ladner. "The Liberals were very anxious to unseat him," Grace later explained, "so they approached Angus. By this time he had built himself up quite a little reputation because he was very forthright with what he had to say and had good judgment. And to everybody's surprise he won the election. The reason he did so well and stood so high in the opinion of the people who knew him is that he was a very straight shooter."

Angus's victory as an ILP candidate over his Conservative opponent went against the prevailing vote in 1930. He was one of only twenty MPs from small farm and labour parties, most lining up informally with J.S. Woodsworth. Angus never shrank from identifying himself as a socialist, but he was not an old-line Marxian socialist. In September, en route to Ottawa for a special session of Parliament called to deal with unemployment, Angus spoke to a Socialist Party of Canada meeting. He wrote, "I answered one question to my own satisfaction if not that of the questioner, an old time socialist who commented, 'Evidently you don't agree with Karl Marx.' I replied, 'When Marx and I disagree, Marx is most likely to be wrong. I've had the opportunity of knowing everything Marx knew and a lot more because a lot has happened since Marx's time. Marx hadn't the opportunity to know the things I know.' The fellow left the hall, muttering, 'You don't think much of yourself, do you'."

While in Vancouver during the winter parliamentary recess, Angus felt the first bite of his communist opposition. One freezing February afternoon he was heckled by a crowd of unemployed workers. A reporter observed, "While all the other spokesmen received a respectful hearing, the freshman federal member for Vancouver South faced a barrage of epithets, samples of which were 'Yellow rat' and 'Yellow Socialist.' The heckling was led by those in the crowd, which numbered several thousand, who were distributing or rather selling Communistic literature . . . . A resolution demanding the right of free speech was endorsed by the big majority of those at the meeting."

Free speech was an incendiary issue for dissenters from the left who criticized government policy. Criminal Code Section 98, passed during the 1919 Winnipeg Strike, and not yet repealed as King had promised, allowed a person to be presumed guilty as a member of an unlawful association unless he or she could prove otherwise. Across the country police were breaking up meetings of desperate unemployed workers who were all seen as possible subversives, and in 1931, Section 98 was used for the first time to imprison eight communists, including Communist Party of Canada leader Tim Buck.

Communists were not the only dissenters to be denied freedom of speech in the early 1930s. Other left-wing speakers were denied the use of halls in Toronto, among them the first woman MP, Agnes Macphail, Progressive MP for a rural Ontario riding since 1921. Macphail, a dignified and hardworking former schoolteacher, was insulted to find herself labelled as a "dangerous person."

After membership in the Communist Party was outlawed—even attendance at a meeting was illegal—the social vacuum left by the ban allowed a new party of the left to coalesce. Just eighteen months after Angus was heckled as a yellow rat, he would be a key figure in the formation of the Co-operative Commonwealth Federation (CCF). The creation of the CCF blocked communism from ever becoming a mass movement of the left in Canada.

Angus arrived in Ottawa early in March 1931 for the opening of the second session of the seventeenth Parliament. In preparation for his important maiden speech in the House, he went to consult with J.S. Woodsworth, leader of the small labour contingent in Parliament and his colleague from Vancouver FLP days. Grace had come to Ottawa a few weeks earlier and was ensconced at her small desk in the corner of her father's office. The tall, angular, fresh-faced older man with the piercing grey eyes attracted her interest at once.

"What impressed me first of all and continuously as I knew him was that he seemed to be one of the few people who had real, original thinking going on. You had the impression of a quiet, resourceful person who would wait until a strategic time in the discussion to put in the bit of originality that he had. His judgment was very solid. I felt that in any group of people there was nothing flashy about him at all. Occasionally a rather ironic bit of humour would creep out. He was very good-humoured, but very terse and to the point."

In his maiden speech March 20 Angus jumped into the debate raging across the country about Canada's freshly imposed embargo of Russian commodities. Canada had resumed diplomatic relations with Russia in 1929 under King's Liberal government, but an Order in Council just passed by the Bennett government prohibited the import of coal, pulp, lumber, timber, asbestos and furs. Angus criticized the Bennett government for cutting off trade with communist Russia at a time when so many Canadians were unemployed.

Angus deftly distinguished his position as a socialist from that of the communists, while championing the needs of the unemployed and the working poor. Demonstrating that he could turn heckling aside with the best of them, Angus declared, "We are told that in Russia there is forced labour. In this country we have forced idleness. Which is worse? Many of these men would be glad to have the opportunity of being forced to work but they cannot get it."

Watching from the press section of the gallery, Grace was impressed. She had taken over her father's job of writing a weekly roundup of parliamentary news for a dozen labour, farmer and socialist newspapers across the country headlined "The Week at Ottawa," or "Parliament From the Gallery." Grace was not the only journalist in the gallery who saw value in the remarks of the freshman member from Vancouver South. T.C. Bullock, Ottawa correspondent for the *Vancouver Sun,* wrote about a month later that Angus was "recognized in Eastern Canada as one of the strongest men in the Labour Party in the Dominion" and noted his "fearless thinking, plain speaking and personal integrity."

Bullock wrote the earliest characterization of Angus in Ottawa. "In private life (Angus) is a quiet, studious, almost painfully diffident individual. He makes friends slowly and carefully. He is the very reverse of flamboyant.

"But on the floor of the House he is a giant. His methodical marshalling of logic, his ready command of homely expressions, his harsh, honest voice, and his tall, gaunt, Lincoln-like figure make him a commanding personality when he rises to address Mr. Speaker . . . . It is prophesied freely in the Capital," wrote Bullock, "that if the Labour Party in Canada ever approximates the strength of the Labour Party in England, Angus MacInnis will hold one of the most important positions in public life in the Dominion."

As weak spring sunlight melted the ice on the Rideau River, Grace fell in love, seriously, for the first time in her life. She was unconcerned that her beloved was nearly twenty-one years her senior, just ten years younger than her father. Here was a man who was as principled as her father, as trustworthy, as strong—they shared the same ideals and worked for the same ends. As Bullock had observed, Angus was very cautious in private life. On first meeting he was friendly and warm but reserved, while he took his time assessing the person before him. If that person met his high standards, as Grace soon did, his hard shell of reserve would melt, and he would tell funny jokes, one after the other, and put aside his habit of thrift, disclosing the generous nature underneath.

After the House closed and office work was done, Grace and Angus would go walking together. "At first it was a very platonic arrangement," she recalled. "We were never intimate or physically concerned at that stage at all. We were interested in ideas. This was the thing that held us always together, our common interest in ideas, and the fact that we differed on them too, to some extent."

In addition to writing her columns and serving as personal secretary to her father, Grace also began to take notes as members of the Ginger Group, Labour and other co-operating members met informally in one or another of the offices along their sixth floor hallway. She was taking on more responsibility, but was still not certain of her future direction, as she confided to Angus during their evening walks.

"I used to say that I would just have to find some kind of job, I'd made a mess of teaching and so on. I think he was really kidding me along, knowing that I'd already got the job I wanted which was working with the group and with my father, and probably also being interested in him. It just gradually came to . . . we felt we wanted to get married."

In the House Woodsworth and Abe Heaps, Labour MP for Winnipeg

North, pressed the government for "a Federal system of insurance against Unemployment, Sickness and Invalidity." In one of her "Week at Ottawa" columns Grace wrote, "Often from the Farmer–Labour corner come suggestions regarded at the time as utterly impractical by the Government. A few years later these self-same suggestions re-appear as highly respectable legislation introduced by the government with all the pride of a fond parent." Canada's first Unemployment Insurance Act was not passed until 1940.

Some of Grace's articles marked the outlook of the co-operating groups as international with a pronounced admiration for the Soviet model. She, like many others at the time, was likely unaware of the immense suffering that the Soviet people were living through as Stalin killed millions of *kulaks*, the so-called rich peasants, and appropriated their land for the creation of collectivized farms. Grace held up the Soviet Union as a model of successful state planning. "Russia, of course, is the outstanding example of a country where the various units of industry are being fitted into the whole pattern harmoniously," she wrote. "Co-operation, carried out by governmental authority, is proving infinitely more efficient than organized competition."

Woodsworth pressed his case for unemployment insurance during the summer of 1931 with a clear warning that it was a choice between peace and war of one kind or another. "This system of unregulated competition is breaking down before our very eyes," he told the House. "Not only in our own country, but in almost every other country in the world we have vast armies of unemployed men and women almost on the verge of starvation, while at the same time the nations are rolling in wealth . . . it would seem as if only a great war could be again looked forward to as a means of solving international difficulties, can we say that the system is not breaking down? . . . But those of us who would like to have a peaceful transition to a new social order are under obligation to do our best to bring about that change by peaceful methods, and this is one method which I venture to advocate."

Bennett's budget of 1931 had little relief for the unemployed. In the budget debate, Woodsworth defined his and Grace's type of socialism, assuring Canadians that he would never collectivize personal property. "Socialism . . . has often been misunderstood and misinterpreted . . . we must so change the system that this great organization will in some way come under collective control, will in some way come under the administration of the people themselves and will be used not merely to pile up profits for a few but used rather in the interests of the great majority of the people."

The 1931 session closed with no system of unemployment insurance in place, only patchwork relief funds to support provinces and municipalities too broke to offer any relief at all to hordes of angry, desperate poor. The government also proposed to establish work camps for single, unemployed men under military supervision. Woodsworth advised against them. "I believe if camps are established under anything like military control, they may become schools of bolshevism," he warned. Instead he advocated the government create more currency to finance public works as it had done to finance the Canadian National Railway, but his advice was not accepted.

In August, Grace returned to Winnipeg to look after her brothers at 60 Maryland Street while James and Lucy travelled in Europe. Angus went home to Vancouver via a string of meetings with industrial workers across the country, and included a stop in Winnipeg. The lovers were by now firm in their intention to wed, but Grace was apprehensive about her father's reaction. Before James and Lucy went away, she prevailed upon Angus to break the news.

James's only reservation was the idea of his cultured eldest daughter marrying a streetcar conductor with only a grade eight education. Grace recalled, "Father was concerned not about the difference in years, he was concerned about the difference in cultural background. That didn't worry me, but it did worry him and some of our friends." Grace's mother and brother Charles had absolutely no objections.

Grace's father may have been experiencing a touch of the jealousy many fathers feel when a beloved daughter becomes engaged to be married, especially an eldest daughter. Until she met Angus, Grace's heart belonged completely to her father, and she had declined to open it for casual suitors of her own age.

James had long cherished the dream that one or more of the offspring he had taught so diligently might follow him into politics, as he had followed his father into the ministry. His eldest son Charles was never seriously interested in becoming active in politics. He was a writer, more comfortable with the role of spectator-commentator. James's next oldest son, Ralph, was already leaning toward medicine. The other two boys were still teenagers; Grace's shyer sister Belva was not passionate about politics. So, although Grace was the wrong sex in the eyes of 1930s Canadian society, James was grooming her for politics.

Most significantly, Grace did everything within her power to pattern herself after her father, her primary role model. In his parliamentary office she worked not for money, but to win his approval and to advance his cause, which she had made her own. She put just as much work into the position of honorary caucus secretary as if she were paid. There were those within the CCF and NDP who said much later that if Grace had been a man, she might easily have been party leader.

Even at age eighty-three, considering whether she could have led the party at any stage, Grace could not free her thinking completely from the restrictions of her gender. "No, I think I would have been crushed between two millstones, my husband and my father. I would have been a poor second to either one of them. As it is they didn't compare me, nobody ever thought of comparing me to either my father or my husband. In the early days I was a freak so I had a freedom that I wouldn't otherwise have enjoyed. Mind you, you knew perfectly well that you were responsible for setting a trend."

Grace often opened her early speeches with the self-deprecating comment, "I begin with two disadvantages tonight, my father and my husband." Colleagues too were aware that she had sublimated her own talents and capacities to being first her father's daughter and then Angus's wife.

Although within the Woodsworth family boys and girls had always enjoyed equality, in the wider world women who exercised intelligence, determination and ambition were considered overly masculine. Grace never wrote, "I wish I were a man," but she always wore her hair very short in a style often described by political colleagues as mannish. She avoided frills in favour of plain styles; she often wore a tailored suit jacket with a white shirt and a man's tie. In head-and-shoulders photographs from the 1930s and 1940s she could have been mistaken for a young man. Slender rather than full-figured, Grace never flaunted her female nature. Instead, throughout her life, Grace de-emphasized gender with such statements as, "I don't think that as long as you are clinging to your masculinity or your femininity that you are making progress toward becoming a full human being."

James may subconsciously have been unwilling to accept his eldest child fully as a woman, preferring to concentrate on the non-sexual aspect of her nature as a human being. But when Grace announced she would be married, he could no longer cherish any illusions. Whatever the reason, James put up some preliminary resistance to the wedding arrangements. At first he even refused to attend the ceremony. Grace recalled that she and Angus "decided that we would get married and go right to the session in January, and those days the only way you travelled was by train. Then my father was going to go on some kind of trip north to talk to some little meetings and so on, a trip that would keep him out of town. He said, 'I'm not sure if I would be back for the twenty-third of January or not.' I said, 'All right, Father, that's quite understandable. We're just going ahead with the wedding anyway.' He was back."

While her parents were still abroad Grace addressed a political crowd for the first time. Orange newsprint flyers dated September 10, 1931 advertised a branch meeting of the Independent Labour Party at Norberry School in Winnipeg. Grace was to take the platform second, after her father's longtime colleague, MP Abe Heaps, an upholsterer and labour leader turned politician. In the chair was the venerable Reverend William Ivens, who had invited Woodsworth to visit Winnipeg for the Labour Church, the trip which brought him to the Winnipeg Strike.

Grace used her political speaking debut to go after the top of the Canadian capitalist pyramid, the wealthy Prime Minister. "When Prime Minister Bennett talked glibly before his election for unemployment," she told the crowd, "he did not know what he was saying. He did not know his economics." Not a particularly novel idea, especially before such a receptive audience, but still, these remarks received coverage in the local newspaper, unusual notice to be taken of a twenty-six-year-old woman.

Lucy and James arrived home in Winnipeg on December 19. With just over a month to plan for Grace's wedding and celebrate Christmas, it was a hectic time.

Grace had a bad case of the jitters when Saturday, January 23, 1932 arrived at last. "On my wedding day I suddenly discovered that I knew very little about the procedure of the ceremony—where to stand, what to say and so on. I directed a multitude of questions at Mother, who I suspect, was almost as much at a loss in such matters as I was myself. Further, she had a great many things on her mind that day. In the midst of my questioning she turned to me and in the richest accents of her Irish forbears, she exclaimed, 'To hear you today a body would think you'd never been married before!'"

It was Grace's first and last wedding, and the only one ever held in the Woodsworth home at 60 Maryland Street. A friend of Lucy's made the neat white travelling suit Grace wore for the ceremony. She carried a bouquet of golden roses, symbol of grace and fidelity. Family and friends, mostly on the Woodsworth side, filled the dark-panelled parlour and overflowed into the dining room. Angus's aged mother, who still spoke only Gaelic, stayed in Vancouver, with his sister Christine to care for her.

The daughter and granddaughter of two of Canada's foremost Methodist ministers was married outside any church, as she and Angus wished. "We both felt this wasn't a religious matter at all. It was a social gathering, a solemn occasion, but in our minds it was a civil thing rather than a religious one." James had no objections to the civil ceremony, as he had long since severed any connection with the Methodist church. It was one of the first civil marriages ever solemnized in Manitoba, where civil ceremonies had been legal for less than a year. Judge Lewis St. George Stubbs officiated, in the first ceremony he had conducted outside a courthouse. A well-known socialist, Stubbs was later removed from the bench for his political views. On that joyous day he was appreciated by people of like mind.

With a kiss, Lucy bestowed upon her first-born and first-married child a slip of the shamrock she had nurtured since 1904 when James had given it to her as a love token during their courtship.

The *Victoria Daily Times* covered the wedding with the observation that the bride was "expected to prove a real asset to the Labour party in the Coast province. In private life she is a modest little lady, respected alike by political friend and opponent." It was the kind of patronizing comment Grace hated most. And in the headline her new name was spelled incorrectly on the very first day she adopted it as her own. It was printed "McInnis," the most common of the misspellings—among them McGinness, MacGinness, Mac-

Guinness, Mcinnis, Macinnis, Mcinnes, McInnes, and McKinnis—that would appear frequently in newspaper articles and books throughout Grace's life.

As planned, Grace and Angus spent their wedding night aboard a train rolling across the snowy hills for Ottawa. Then they enjoyed a few private honeymoon days at the old Bytown Inn before the next session of Parliament began. They moved into a furnished room at 319 Frank Street, and on the hall table placed a brand new guest book. The first visitor to sign, on February 7, was J.S. Woodsworth.

The spring of 1932 was fertile for the political growth of farmer–labour–socialist co-operation in the House of Commons and across the country. Labour representatives from the four western provinces had met together in annual conferences since 1929. In July 1931 they "heartily welcomed" eastern labour political parties and western farmers' organizations to a conference in Winnipeg. To its January convention the United Farmers of Alberta invited others interested in forming a co-operative commonwealth in Canada.

William Irvine's sixth-floor office in the Centre Block had become the favourite meeting place for members of the co-operating groups. The big Albertan MP for Wetaskiwin was British, originally recruited to Canada as a Methodist preacher by J.S. Woodsworth's father. A violin reposed in his office, and when discussions became heated Irvine would snatch it up to play "Ave Maria" or a melody he felt expressed the thrust and parry of competing views.

On May 26, 1932 a germinal meeting took place in Irvine's office—a meeting to form a national political organization tentatively called "the Commonwealth party." Many experienced co-operators were there: Woodsworth and Abe Heaps of Winnipeg and Ontario's Agnes Macphail, who had served the past eleven years as the lone woman in Parliament. The Albertans were Irvine, Robert Gardiner from Acadia, Ted Garland from Bow River, monetary theorist George Coote from Fort Macleod, and Donald Kennedy from Peace River. Henry Spencer from Battle River, Saskatchewan was there; so was Angus MacInnis along with another trade union man, Humphrey Mitchell of Hamilton East. Also present, though not elected members, were future CCF leader M.J. Coldwell, then president of the Saskatchewan Labour Party, and several people from the League for Social Reconstruction (LSR), a new group of academics and intellectuals formed along Fabian socialist lines. Grace was present in her role as secretary to the independent caucus. Those present agreed to take concrete steps toward constructing a nation-wide political party that would give Canadian voters a socialist choice.

Although broad consensus was achieved at that meeting, the path ahead was still rocky. "The CCF nucleus was quite a while getting formed in the caucus because it was divided into the people who thought monetary reform was enough as a first step and those who wanted to get after the economic side," recalled Grace with a grin. "Some of us used to call them the non-co-operating groups because the caucus meetings were quite stormy." When people got prickly, Grace would call them "cactus" meetings.

When the House recessed at the end of May, Grace and Angus travelled west to campaign in the Manitoba provincial elections. Grace spoke at several meetings, mostly to women and to French-speaking audiences in St. Boniface. Angus proudly credited Grace with helping inspire the voters of St. Boniface to elect their first ILP candidate during that election.

As they travelled west through Saskatchewan and Alberta, Grace was the principal speaker at larger meetings. She grew increasingly confident on the platform as she picked up skills from Angus, who, as hecklers often learned the hard way, was very quick on the draw. A prime example occurred at a small hall in Saskatchewan: as Angus extolled the efforts of his father-in-law to secure a better life for Canadian people, a large fellow rose and shouted, "I don't like J.S. Woodsworth! He's got no guts." "Well, that depends," MacInnis answered mildly, "on whether you refer to quality or quantity." And he cast a thoughtful eye on the big man's paunch.

By the end of July Grace and Angus were in Vancouver, settled in the first of the suites they rented over the years at the Montrose Apartments, a block-long three-storey building that still stands at 1190 West 12th Avenue. Visiting the MacInnis family home on Prince Edward Street, Grace became acquainted with Angus's mother, his sister Christine and niece Violet. She made friends with the family dog, a collie with a sweet disposition. Clinker helped Grace get past her childhood fear of dogs.

In 1932 Angus went to Calgary for the now-famous meeting at which the Co-operative Commonwealth Federation (CCF) was formally created. Grace remained in Vancouver. So many conferences were scheduled that summer, Grace explained, she failed to realize the importance of that particular meeting. There, in Calgary's Labour Temple, 105 delegates agreed on a program roughly equivalent to the first eight sections of the Regina Manifesto, adopted the following year at the party's founding convention. The first principle was "the establishment of a planned system of social economy for the production, distribution and exchange of goods and services." The program included socialization of banking and credit; security of tenure for the farmer on "use-land" and for the worker in his home; equal opportunity regardless of sex, nationality or religion; encouragement of co-operative enterprises; socialization of health services; and federal government responsibility to provide either "suitable work or adequate maintenance."

They also came up with the name Co-operative Commonwealth Federation (Farmer–Labour–Socialist) selected from among many others including Socialist Party of Canada, National Workers' Federation, and Canadian Commonwealth Federation, the name favoured by Woodsworth.

The creation of the CCF was only part of a general urge to try a collective approach to the overwhelming financial problems facing Canadians in that perilous year of 1932. Even the Conservative government nationalized radio, set up marketing boards for farm produce, and—partly due to the urging of members of the Ginger Group in Parliament—created a Canadian Central Bank. The Depression brought continuous cuts for Canadian business people: prices, wages, the work force, dividends, costs and corners, even personal expenses. Business efforts to hold or restore price levels led to an upsurge of price manipulation. Cartels and trade associations struggled to set floors on domestic prices, fix export prices and work with producers in other countries to set world commodity prices. Competition was a suspect term, invariably preceded by the adjectives "cutthroat" or "wasteful." Still, prices for wheat and other Canadian commodities continued to slip. Increasing numbers of business people saw greater government spending as the road to recovery.

The cities and provinces remained responsible for relief of close to half a million unemployed Canadians. Too slowly the Dominion government began to deal with unemployment. In addition to contributing close to one-third of relief funds paid out by all three levels of government, Bennett set up work camps for single men. Just as Woodsworth had warned, these camps became the breeding ground for revolt, which came to a head in the 1935 On To Ottawa Trek. Dissatisfaction with the measly pay of twenty cents a day, callous treatment and overcrowded conditions in the camps, provided an ideal organizing milieu for communist activists to agitate for revolution. The fatal error of the federal government was in placing the camps under the control of the Department of National Defence. Confrontation was inevitable.

Meanwhile, in Vancouver, Grace began to establish her own political base. She had lived in Angus's home town for only two years in 1920–22. First she reconnected with a childhood friend, Mildred Osterhout, who had just completed her studies at the London School of Economics. Mildred had been inspired by contact with British Fabian socialists Harold Laski and the Webbs, and was especially moved by meeting Mahatma Gandhi, who stayed at the London settlement house where she worked while he negotiated with the British government. That summer of 1932, Grace and Mildred Osterhout and Gretchen Steeves, a lawyer of Dutch origin, formed a socialist study group which became the Vancouver branch of the League for Social Reconstruction.

Canada's LSR paralleled the British Fabian Society. It originated in the summer of 1931 when history professor Frank Underhill from the University of Toronto met McGill law professor Frank Scott at a conference in Williamstown, Massachusetts. During a hike in the nearby mountains, they agreed that the time was ripe for formation of a Canadian organization devoted to critical social and economic analysis. The LSR did not consider itself solely a political group, but included painters, poets, lawyers, students and business people. J.S. Woodsworth was made honorary president; Angus MacInnis spoke to an early meeting. By the end of 1932, Woodsworth had asked Scott and Underhill to help write a program for a socialist political party. In effect the LSR became an intellectual think tank for the new party.

Grace began working closely with two Socialist Party of Canada colleagues, Frances Moren and Dr. Lyle Telford. A noted medical doctor, Dr. Telford was even better known as a radio broadcaster of socialist commentary on CKMO, CJOR and CRCV four nights a week. A person walking through Vancouver residential neighbourhoods that summer would never miss a word of the broadcast as it came floating through open windows, across porches and over rosebushes to the street. A diminutive ball of energy with a silvery mane, Dr. Telford found time to edit of one of three small socialist newspapers in British Columbia, *The Challenge*.

Frances Moren was Dr. Telford's assistant editor and managed his radio show; she was also his longtime mistress. She was a social worker and a socialist speaker who had just been chosen as an SPC candidate for the upcoming provincial election. That summer Grace and Frances were writing educational materials for the LSR and the SPC, when Grace found herself the intimate witness to her friend's love triangle with the doctor and his wife, Florence Telford—a triangle with political overtones.

Lyle Telford was an outspoken advocate of "companionate marriage," the then controversial belief that a marriage would be strengthened if a couple used birth control for their first two years together. If they found themselves to be incompatible, they could divorce without serious emotional damage to themselves, and there would be no children to suffer. In April of 1932 he and Frances had opened Canada's second birth control clinic in the fashionable new Marine Building at the foot of Burrard Street. The first had opened a few weeks earlier in Hamilton, Ontario. Birth control was then against the law and Suite 1030–31 was the only establishment in western Canada where women could obtain condoms, diaphragms and contraceptive jelly. Dr. Telford's clinic was intended to serve married people only, or couples about to be married. It had nothing to do with abortion. Yet these pioneers were committing a crime which carried a maximum penalty of two years in prison for distribution of birth control information or devices. Several other doctors referred patients to the clinic, which was conducted by a nurse with the assistance of Frances Moren.

Grace championed the work of the clinic, believing it provided services which "Vancouver needs terribly." In this she was carrying on the Woodsworth family conviction which both James and Lucy had fought for. As early as 1919 her father told a Vancouver audience, "in the new social order the prospective mother should be allowed to say whether she wished her child to be brought into the world or not."

A few days before she left Vancouver for Ottawa, Grace was invited to the Telford home, not by Kyke but by his wife. Florence wished to unburden her troubled heart: she had discovered that for the past nine years her husband had been involved in an intimate affair with Frances Moren. She asked Grace to withdraw her support for Frances as a socialist politician.

At first Grace thought of the love triangle as "a purely personal matter," but in Ottawa she changed her mind. With Florence's permission, she wrote Frances to say she could no longer support her as a CCF candidate for the 1933 provincial election. "On personal grounds there is no reason for change," wrote Grace tolerantly. "I might very easily find myself in exactly the same sort of situation and should very properly feel that I had no right to be looking after your ideas of right and wrong." But, she continued, "The lives of both you and Dr. Telford are so intimately connected with public affairs in the province of British Columbia that your personal affairs must of necessity become intertwined with the public affairs in which you work."

Grace feared the adultery would become public knowledge. "Suppose that you are a member of the provincial legislature when the facts become known," she wrote to Frances. "You cannot fail to become completely discredited . . . . Your activities in the Birth Control Clinic will become the topic of scathing criticism . . . . No party is more carefully watched for flaws than ours. The slightest personal failing means incalculable harm done to the cause." Naively, Grace used Stalin's Russia as a model of upright behaviour. "I have heard that in Russia members of the Communist party are almost ascetic in their lives, realizing as they do, that as the leaders of the nation their conduct must be above reproach." She apparently did not realize that Communist Party members feared for their lives, should they draw the notice of Stalin to their activities.

Still, Grace was broad-minded about her friends' love affair. "You can see that the conventional morality of the thing does not concern me," she wrote in a second letter to Frances. "'Bad' and 'Good' do not seem to count in love." She stressed it was the public side of the situation that made her continued support impossible and foresaw that public opinion might someday be different. "In some future state of society when woman finds herself upon a footing equal with man—economically speaking—it might be quite possible for you and Dr. Telford to do what you are doing today. But, as we find things today, Mrs. Telford has the prior claim. Society recognizes this and I think you must recognize it as well." She complimented Frances as a speaker and urged her to break off the affair and concentrate on her political career.

But Frances did not heed Grace's advice. She continued the affair with Lyle Telford, and bore him a daughter out of wedlock. Florence Telford did make the infidelity public. The Telfords were divorced and Lyle Telford married Frances, but they later divorced, and Lyle married a third time. Frances withdrew from the political picture, but the revelation of his amorous adventures did not hurt Lyle's political career. The CCF provincial executive committee decided in 1934 that "the personal affairs of Dr. Telford are of no concern to the CCF." In 1937 he was elected to the BC Legislature as a CCF member from Vancouver East. During his term as an MLA from 1938 to 1940 Dr. Telford was elected mayor of Vancouver, but the party would not allow any member to hold two elective positions simultaneously. Dr. Telford resigned his CCF membership in 1939, and finished the legislative term as an independent.

The birth control clinic continued to operate in various Vancouver locations without Frances's assistance until 1955. Although authorities were aware of its existence—it was listed in the 1932 Vancouver phone book—it was never raided by police. When Ontario nurse Dorothea Palmer was acquitted in 1936 on charges of distributing birth control information, authorities unofficially stopped arresting people for the offence, although the law remained on the books until 1969. As a Member of Parliament Grace was to play a crucial part in changing this archaic and sexist law.

When Parliament resumed in February 1933, the first debate of the session was on Woodsworth's motion for "the setting up of a co-operative commonwealth in which all natural resources and the socially necessary machinery of production will be used in the interests of the people and not for the benefit of the few." He had introduced the same motion the year before but then, as Grace reported in her column, the House was poorly filled and attention was half-hearted. The motion was considered hopelessly visionary, entirely outside the sphere of practical politics. But now the Depression was one year deeper and heavily stamped into Canadian lives. This time almost every member was seated. The Conservatives kept up a noisy barrage of comment and interruption, while the Liberals listened in silence.

Woodsworth took care in this speech to clarify the difference between the socialist vision of the co-operative commonwealth and communism: "It is quite true that both believe in a changed social order, in a new economic system. The Communists are convinced that this can be brought about only by violence . . . . We believe that it may come in Canada by peaceful methods and in an orderly fashion, and that is the purpose of this organization."

Newspaper reaction to Woodsworth's proposal was to be the template by which newspapers cut their pattern of CCF coverage for nearly thirty years. In her column the following week Grace outlined this pattern of misleading press coverage. "In the main these statements are warnings to the people of Canada to have nothing to do with the CCF. This new organization, we are told, would take away our liberty, smash our industry, seize our homes and farms, scrap our constitution and introduce a reign of terror. For the CCF, they assure us, is communism; BOLSHEVISM!! R-U-S-S-I-A!!! For all of these assertions they give not the slightest scrap of proof; they are confident that people will not demand proof; they rely upon frightening people so thoroughly that they will refuse to think. In spite of all these warnings, people seem to be attracted by the ideas which the CCF is advocating; consequently, efforts to scare them are being redoubled."

It was indeed difficult for most Canadians to distinguish between social democrats, Marxian socialists and communists. Reflecting in later life, Grace drew a simple distinction. "A Communist believes in change by violence, or that it will arise at some stage. He also believes that if a lie will serve you better than the truth, you always use the lie . . . . Your social democrat honestly believes, like the Fabians in Britain did, that the thing to do is to build slowly, begin with your local environment and build on material security for ordinary people. Get their eyes open as you go along gradually, and get wider and wider circles until you get the whole.

"The Marxian socialists scorn that approach. They say the thing to do is to build self-consciousness and the psychology of confrontation in the working class. Well, unfortunately for them the working class doesn't know it is working class. They think they're middle class and entitled to all the amenities and good things the middle class has and nobody will tell them differently."

These distinctions were clearly drawn later and Grace never flirted with communism, but in the early 1930s she brushed very close to Marxism. She was a member of the Socialist Party of Canada (SPC), a doctrinaire Marxist group. She worked with Frances Moren and Lyle Telford, whose Vancouver newspaper *The Challenge* was at first unashamedly communist. The March 1931 issue carried a page one article headlined, "Let Us Take Communism From the Communists." The anonymous author, almost certainly Lyle Telford, wrote: "The profit system must be abolished first and foremost. We must have common ownership and control. But this is Communism . . . . Let us consider Communism, here in Canada . . . . Canadian Communism. Let us take Communism from the Communists, and use it intelligently."

The Communist Party (CPC) was outlawed in 1931, and that may have had something to do with the fact that as 1932 unfolded *The Challenge* became less communist and more socialist in outlook. It began to support the Independent Labour Party, which J.S. Woodsworth and Angus represented in Parliament.

By May 1932 Lyle Telford had turned against Canadian communists with all the bitterness of a lover betrayed. In a box on the front page of *The Challenge* he wrote: "I Accuse . . . . Certain so-called members of the Communist Party of . . . being agents provocateurs and leading our unemployed citizens into disrepute by means of 'frame-ups' and ill-considered demonstrations . . . of preaching class hatred instead of class struggle; . . . and lastly of misleading the people as to the true meaning of the greatest social and economic discovery of all time." At this point in the evolution of Telford and Moren's thinking, Grace began to work closely with them.

Disappointed that she had missed the CCF founding conference in Calgary, Grace was determined to be a delegate to the first CCF national convention, planned for July 1933 in Regina, but she ran into an immediate setback. "I was down with Angus at the time in Ottawa, and I learned that the Socialist Party wouldn't have me as a delegate. In those days there wasn't any way of getting there [to Regina] unless you had an old beat-up car or could ride the rods." Grace, as the spouse of an MP, had the advantage of a complimentary rail pass. "So I learned that the matter had come up and Ernie [Winch] had said, 'Oh, no, we can't send Grace because her father's a parson sky pilot, and we can't be sure that she would be advocating the straight goods'."

"Winch was always afraid of bourgeois penetration, that's always been the thing the socialists have been afraid of," Grace explained. As a Marxian socialist, though not a communist, Winch saw the preacher's daughter as a member of the petite bourgeoisie, not serious enough about effecting socialist change.

Grace had been exposed to the Marxist philosophy of class struggle since her teenage contact with the Finns in Gibson's Landing. "Basically," she observed, "I didn't swallow anything whole, but I thought that working class people would gradually rise to power. I knew that from the Magna Carta on, one layer after another of British people had been enfranchised until they got Parliament to support total male suffrage. That was, I suppose, the basis for my being basically social democratic in my approach rather than Marxist, but there were a lot of things about Marxism that I liked. Of course, when you're young and vigorous, you think—why work through Parliament if there's quick ways of doing it. Well, later on you learn there are no quick ways of doing it."

With or without the support of Ernie Winch and the Socialist Party of Canada, Grace was resolved not to miss the first convention of the political party her father had worked so tirelessly to build. Through the League for Social Reconstruction she saw a way. Members were middle class professional people and academics, some of whom Grace had helped recruit during the summer of 1932. Because only groups, not individuals, could join the CCF, these Reconstruction Party members formed CCF Clubs as a way of joining the new party. Grace offered herself as their delegate. "So they were very charmed. They couldn't fill out their quota, no travelling possibilities, and so I got down there."

Around the world the summer of 1933 was a time of deep despair. In January Adolf Hitler became Chancellor of a Germany with more than 5.5 million unemployed. By June German trade unions were broken up, and all political parties except the National Socialists—the Nazis—were suppressed.

Imprisonment without trial was prescribed for social democrats, Jews and communists. In Spain a disastrous civil war was brewing. Britain had a coalition national government headed by Ramsay MacDonald; 2.8 million Britons were unemployed. Stalin had just completed the first Five Year Plan, industrializing the Soviet Union at the cost of millions of lives.

US President Franklin D. Roosevelt inspired public confidence during his first inaugural address, saying, "The only thing we have to fear is fear itself." By July he had put in place five hundred million dollars' worth of Federal Emergency Relief, and a National Industrial Recovery Act which stipulated "codes of fair competition" and collective bargaining. He appointed the first female member of a US cabinet, Frances Perkins, as Secretary of Labor.

Canadians and Americans were singing, "Brother, Can You Spare A Dime?" and movies were big business. Public morals were in flux; Sally Rand drew crowds to the 1933 Chicago World's Fair to watch her dance clad only in ostrich plume fans. Modern amenities—polyethylene, vitamin B2, stereo recording, FM radio—were all introduced in 1933. In Canada close to twenty percent of the labour force was unemployed, and 1.5 million men, women and children were on direct public relief. But not everyone was suffering. Miners prospered when gold and uranium were discovered in northern Saskatchewan. Canadian distillers built new plants south of the border to profit from the US repeal of prohibition. In May the Canadian Radio Broadcasting Commission began transmitting in English and French from Montreal, opening possibilities for a more unified national awareness.

On July 18, 1933 a bus with Manitoba licence plates, bedecked with red, white and blue bunting and a big CCF banner, rolled into Regina loaded with delegates to the first national CCF convention. Startled Regina residents had CCF pamphlets thrust into their hands proclaiming the dawn of a new social order. A huge tented city sprang up on the shores of Wascana Lake as delegates and visitors from every province streamed into the city. Cars packed with delegates pulled in from BC, Alberta and Ontario. Two young men hitchhiked from Toronto. A prairie farm family too poor to buy gasoline creaked into town in a Bennett buggy, a car drawn by horses.

The next day at Regina City Hall, a kaleidoscopic spectrum of 131 delegates gathered at long tables to agree, if they could, on a common vision for Canada and the correct means to achieve it. The delegates included cautious Ontario farmers, more socialistic farmers from Saskatchewan and Manitoba, monetary theorist farmers from Alberta, Marxist urban socialists from Vancouver and Toronto, journalists, former Liberals, housewives, teachers, lawyers, representatives of urban industrial labour, and elected federal, provincial and municipal politicians. Roughly one-third were women. Grace broke them down into three broad groups—middle class white-collar workers, farmers, and organized labour—and likened them to three legs of a stool. Without all three legs a stool cannot stand. The brutal Depression was the common enemy against which these people with widely divergent beliefs joined in battle.

Very few of the people generally considered CCF and NDP pioneers attended this founding convention. Tommy Douglas was in Weyburn, Saskatchewan. Stanley Knowles a recently ordained Methodist–United minister was serving at Central United Church in Winnipeg that summer. Harold Winch was in Vancouver, and David Lewis was travelling in France.

Woodsworth had to counter constant attacks by those who believed the CCF was anti-religious and a communist organization funded by Moscow. Speaking to more than a thousand at the Regina City Hall auditorium on the eve of the convention, Woodsworth flatly denied any connection between the CCF and Moscow, and repudiated stories of payment of Russian gold to the movement. The former minister called charges that the party was anti-religious "absolutely absurd." In fact the ardent socialism of many CCF delegates was evangelistic in tone and sprang from Christian ethical roots. The fervour of Woodsworth's socialist preaching had attracted them; they stayed to find practical applications of his ideas to their own lives. As Vancouver delegate Mildred Osterhout said later, "We CCFers were evangelists, out to build a new world order, out to build the Kingdom . . . and we felt it could be done!"

Canadian public opinion was shifting: during that agonized summer, even the Toronto Conference of the United Church passed a resolution opposing the existing capitalist system, advocating a "Christian Social Order," and endorsing socialization of banking, transportation and other essential industries. Grace saw that "The great body of men and women at Regina had faith in themselves. There was an atmosphere almost of religious rising. I thought of covenanters in Scotland."

Some may have seen the Marxist delegates as the other end of the spectrum, but to Grace the Christians and the Marxists were two sides of the same coin. Later, characterizing Ernest Winch, she observed, "He was raised in a straitlaced church home against which he rebelled. He rushed from one church, Christian, into another, Marxism. Exactly the same kind of orthodoxy."

Winch and a few others, such as Bert Robinson and William Moriarty, an executive member of the Communist Party of Canada, had hopes of using the Regina convention to create a united front between the communists and the CCF to defeat the old-line capitalist parties. "The united front was a long established policy of the Communist Party under orders from the Comintern, to use and coalesce with radical and progressive-minded groups," explained Socialist Party of Canada president Arthur Turner. The CCF was to remain a target of highly organized united front actions until the late 1950s.

When she arrived in Regina, Grace was immediately pressured by Winch to vote for a united front resolution. Grace and a few others told Winch they would not vote for it, and Grace recalled that Ernie Winch said, "'You know what will happen to you when you get back to the coast.' And we said, 'We will just take our chances on that, but we are not going to support it.'"

The trigger for the united front resolution appeared July 17, two days before the convention opened, in the form of a telegram from the Canadian Labour Defense League, a communist organization. The CLDL wanted the CCF to participate in joint mass meetings and demonstrations aimed at the release of communist leader Tim Buck imprisoned in Kingston Penitentiary for violating Section 98 of the Criminal Code.

A majority of CCF delegates joined Grace in her refusal to vote for the united front resolution. The convention wired a reply to the CLDL upholding the rights of free speech and assembly for "all workers regardless of political affiliation," and emphasizing Woodsworth's battle to remove Section 98 from the Criminal Code "which has been used as a weapon of political oppression by a panic-stricken capitalist government." But the telegram continued, "We believe in constitutional methods to attain this result. On that point there is fundamental cleavage between us and the leaders of your organization."

As unanimously chosen president of the new party, Woodsworth made his position on other brands of socialism abundantly clear in his presidential address. Delegates and visitors sprang to their feet and burst into the song "Woodsworth is our leader" as he took the podium. "There are those who would frighten us with the horrible examples of failure in England or Germany or captivate us by idealizing the experiments in Russia," Woodsworth declared. "Undoubtedly we should profit by the experience of other nations and other times, but personally I believe that we in Canada must work out our own salvation in our own way. Socialism has so many variations that we hesitate to use the class name. Utopian Socialism and Christian Socialism, Marxian Socialism and Fabianism, the Latin type, the German type, the Russian type—why not a Canadian type?

"The CCF advocates peaceful and orderly methods. In this we distinguish ourselves sharply from the Communist Party which envisages the new social order as being ushered in by violent upheaval and the establishment of a dictatorship. The decision as to how Capitalism will be overthrown may of course not lie in our hands. Continued bungling and exploitation, callous disregard of the needs and sufferings of the people, and the exercise of repressive measures may bring either a collapse, or riots, or both. But in Canada we believe it possible to avoid chaos and bloodshed which in some countries have characterized economic and social revolutions."

The convention was remarkably united on most issues. But Woodsworth's clear statement against violence was not universally approved. William Moriarty, and Winch, moved that in the original draft of the Regina Manifesto the phrase "We do not believe in violent change," and the phrase stating that the CCF seeks "to achieve its ends solely by constitutional methods," be struck from the preamble. Moriarty argued that "the methods of capitalism are those of force," and declared: "If the ruling forces attempt to oppose the will of the people, we should go to the mat in a manner suitable to the occasion."

Stubbs warned that acceptance of the need for violence would be a fatal mistake. Grace, Angus and the majority of delegates agreed, and after some hot debate the Marxist resolution was defeated.

The fledgling party had every intention of soon becoming Canada's government. Plans for taking private property under public control after assuming power created the hottest debate of the convention. Should property owners be compensated? The manifesto as originally drafted said they should. Moriarty moved that this clause be struck.

Grace at first supported Moriarty on this point, entirely unaware that he was a member of the CPC executive. "I see no reason why we should compensate the present owners of industry," she argued. "If they never had any right to these things I don't see why they should be compensated." Her position for outright confiscation was shared by Thomas Cruden, President of the Socialist Party of Canada, and by Angus, Winch, and Robert Skinner of BC, soon to be elected the first CCF leader in the BC Legislature. George Stirling of Salmon Arm, BC, pointed out that "as the law is today the state can confiscate through taxation." The farmers understood this point; many were losing their land through inability to pay back taxes. Winch himself told the convention he had lost three houses to the taxman.

But to the farmer delegates with their insistence on security of land tenure, confiscation of private property without compensation was far too radical a stand. Agnes Macphail threatened to walk out of the convention and take the United Farmers of Ontario with her. She hated the word socialism. "I've heard nothing else but 'socialism' and 'socialization' since I came to Regina, and I'm sick and tired of it," she told an audience that week, and continued her speech using the word "nationalization" to describe CCF aims. Irvine, Priestley and many other CCF executive council members also believed it was important to provide compensation.

To resolve the conflict a committee was struck during lunch. Frank Scott, King Gordon and Eugene Forsey sat in a Regina restaurant booth scribbling on a cigarette box, drafting a paragraph allowing for flexible compensation. Next day it was presented to the convention. "We do not propose any policy of outright confiscation," it read in part. The welfare of the community was given priority over the claims of private property owners. The principle of conscription of wealth would be applied if economic circumstances justified this extreme action. Compensation would be paid to individuals and institutions during the transition period before the planned economy was operational. "But a CCF government will not play the role of rescuing bankrupt private concerns for the benefit of promoters and stock and bond holders," the resolution firmly stated.

Grace surrendered to this point of view. "If the interest of the people demands compensation we'll give it—otherwise not," she told delegates that day. "We intend a peaceful revolution if such a thing is possible." This change of position was an early instance of the type of pragmatic compromise Grace would make throughout her political career.

The Regina Manifesto as finally approved opted for a mixed economy: public ownership, private ownership and co-operative ownership. Despite the fights, all delegates stood and cheered enthusiastically as the fourteen points were read. The core of the document was democratic socialism. The preamble declared: "We aim to replace the present capitalist system, with its inherent injustice and inhumanity, by a social order from which the domination and exploitation of one class by another will be eliminated, in which economic planning will supersede unregulated private enterprise and competition, and in which genuine democratic self-government, based upon economic equality will be possible."

Comprehensive social planning was the primary goal to be accomplished, through socialization of finance; social ownership of transportation, communications, electric power and other essential industries; security of tenure for the farmer and encouragement of co-operatives; import and export boards for external trade; a labour code covering health and accident insurance, old age and unemployment insurance; freedom of association and participation of workers in management; socialized medicine; amendment of the BNA Act to give the federal government power over Canada's constitution; abolition of the Senate; a foreign policy of world peace and disarmament; a graduated income tax according to ability to pay; freedom of speech and assembly; repeal of Section 98 of the Criminal Code; amendment of the Immigration Act to prevent deportation; equality before the law irrespective of race, nationality, religious or political beliefs; and finally the establishment of a commission of psychiatrists, psychologists, socially minded jurists and social workers to humanize the law. An emergency program was included to provide for unemployment relief or provision of "suitable work or adequate maintenance" by the federal government, to be financed by "the issue of credit based on the national wealth."

The manifesto ended with a flourish. "No CCF Government will rest content until it has eradicated capitalism and put into operation the full programme of socialized planning which will lead to the establishment in Canada of the Co-operative Commonwealth." It was a statement that would be misunderstood often and turned as a weapon against the CCF.

Today many reform measures in the Regina Manifesto have been accomplished without eradicating capitalism. Canada is a mixed economy, composed of private enterprises operating alongside government-owned Crown corporations and many co-operatives. Government-funded medical care is well established; health and accident insurance are in place. Transport and power companies are publicly owned; the Constitution has been patriated; the Charter of Rights and Freedoms provides for freedom of speech and assembly. But for its day the manifesto was a radical program, although much of what it set forth had been clearly articulated in 1884 in Laurence Gronlund's book, *The Cooperative Commonwealth*. The manifesto immediately drew criticism from all sides, and the CCF delegates fanned out across the country to advocate and defend it.

Grace started at once. The convention ended Saturday afternoon; that night she was one of the keynote speakers at a huge meeting at the Regina Labour Temple. She told the overflow crowd the CCF was a political movement with a new idea and a new deal, using the phrase popularized earlier that year by newly elected US President Franklin D. Roosevelt. "Three alternatives," she said, "were all that many children growing up would have: of becoming a parasite and not caring whether they worked or not, of drifting and wasting, and a life of crime." Of the two hundred thousand students graduating from Canadian schools and colleges this year, she warned, "only one out of ten will get a job."

Her primary point that night was one she would make over and over during the coming years: ninety percent of the wealth of Canada was owned by five percent of the people. She explained that the CCF plan to assume power depended on securing a majority of the people's votes, and then the CCF government would plan for the needs of the people. Natural resources had been given away by government, she said, so "why cannot laws be made to take those things back again?"

It was just two days before her twenty-eighth birthday. The youngest member of the CCF leadership, Grace was only on the fringes of power, but—by virtue of her natural talents and family connections—she had been welcomed into the inner councils of the party. There she would remain throughout her life.

CHAPTER 5

Advance and Defend

The CCF was immediately hit from all sides with the most vicious criticism. "CCF Revolutionary, Will Destroy Liberty, Says Mackenzie King," was the headline of a Canadian Press dispatch the day after the Regina convention ended. Did the CCF propose to buy the industries and organizations of Canada? King asked his Winnipeg audience. If so a great increase in taxation would be inevitable. If the plan was not to buy but to seize them then it meant communism, nothing else.

The previous November Prime Minister Bennett had declaimed, "The 'swing to the left' behind Mr. Woodsworth is toward a government Soviet in its character." Recognizing that "the new doctrine is to share all things in common," Bennett threatened to "put the iron heel of ruthlessness against a thing of that kind." Now he thundered against the emerging socialist party with all his oratorical might.

The *Canadian Labour Press,* official newspaper of the Allied Trades and Labour Council of Ottawa, rejected the CCF as a "group of Fanatics . . . expounding the adoption of the communist Russian system in Canada." The Trades and Labour Congress (TLC) was more moderate. Its 1933 convention refused to endorse the CCF, but adopted a resolution "in favour of the co-operative ownership of the machinery of production and distribution . . . . By a system of planned economy and progressive absorption of industrial enterprises etc. this can be peacefully accomplished."

The communist response was harsh. A scathing critique appeared in the communist weekly *The Worker.* Early in 1934 a booklet, *Socialism and the CCF,* came out accusing Woodsworth and his fledgling party of being "social fascists." Author G. Pierce stated: "There is no fundamental difference between the capitalist democracy of Canada and the Fascist dictatorship of Germany. They are both dictatorships of the same ruling class, the capitalist class," and reasoned that social reformism was the "twin of Fascism" and the CCF was "the main bulwark against Communism . . . counterposing capitalist 'peace' to 'Communist bloody revolution.' Thus it . . . aids the fundamental class interests of capitalism."

G. Pierce was a pseudonym for Stewart Smith, then acting as CPC leader in place of the imprisoned Tim Buck. He ridiculed Woodsworth's concept of a Canadian type of socialism, attacked the name "Co-operative Commonwealth" as meaningless, mocked democracy as a means to socialism, and called the "peaceful revolution" which Grace advocated in Regina a fallacy.

Despite a hostile press, the CCF was making gains among voters in British Columbia. In the November 2, 1933 provincial election the CCF won sixty-five thousand votes—thirty-three percent—which returned seven MLAs, enough for the CCF to form the official opposition to the Liberals under Thomas Dufferin Pattullo. Ernie Winch was elected and so was his son Harold, then an unemployed electrician, whose dark handsomeness and debonair black moustache earned him the nickname "Clark Gable of the CCF." A columnist in the *Vancouver Sun* commented two days after the polling, "Without doubt—and I was no CCF supporter myself—it was the greatest triumph for the principles of economic socialism that this continent has ever seen." The following July, Gretchen Steeves won the North Vancouver by-election to become the first CCF woman elected to a Canadian legislature.

Grace had done her part to unify the British Columbia CCF. At the end of August, the CCF Clubs and the Reconstruction Party joined forces. At their unity conference in Stanley Park, Grace used her favourite story of harmonious co-operation, featuring the adventures of two mules, each representing a segment of the CCF. "A team of two mules was drawing a load along a road on either side of which were stacks of hay," she told the delegates. "Each mule, in straining away from his fellow in the endeavour to reach the hay on his side, not only for all his effort failed to reach the hay, but impeded the progress of the vehicle of which he was the motive power. Finally, both stopped and looked at each other. Then after a kind of mutual reading of each other's thoughts, they both together made straight for the hay on the right of the road. Having cleaned that up, they jointly made for that on the left. Thus, what by individual and dis-united effort neither could attain, was attained with ease by combined effort."

As the Depression ground on and on, Karl Marx's predictions of the inevitable collapse of the capitalist system appeared to be coming true. Marx had foreseen that industry under capitalism would concentrate into fewer and fewer hands; the working class would increase in misery; economic crises would become ever more extensive; and the industrial order would finally collapse and give way to a co-operative order. Grace and Angus perceived evidence of this pattern everywhere across Canada.

Grace led off her weekly column March 23, 1934 with the question, "Who Owns Canada?" The excessive concentration of wealth had been seen as the root of social problems since 1913 when the Grain Growers' Guide published research showing that forty-two men controlled one-third of the country's wealth, facts confirmed the following year by Gustavus Myers's book *History of Canadian Wealth*. Grace based her piece on figures given by MP Ted Garland: three men presided over approximately one-fifth of Canada's total wealth—six billion dollars. "Sir Herbert Holt has a controlling interest in almost three billion dollars," wrote Grace. "The other two are Sir Charles Gordon and Mr. W.A. Black, president and director respectively of the Bank of Montreal and dividing fairly evenly between them the controlling interest in about three billion dollars worth of Canada's wealth." Holt was president of the Royal Bank and a director of over forty corporations including: Montreal Light, Heat and Power Consolidated, Montreal Trust, Royal Victoria Hospital, Dominion Textile, CPR, Anglo-Canadian Pulp and Paper, Sun Life Assurance and Simpson's.

Early in the 1934 session of Parliament, Bennett's Trade and Commerce Minister, Henry Herbert Stevens of Kootenay East, BC, made a speech in Toronto detailing abuses of the system by capitalists out to make fortunes by cutting wages and firing workers while piling up vast profits. In response the government set up a committee of inquiry, the Special Select Committee of the House of Commons on Price Spreads and Mass Buying, with Stevens in the chair. After some sensational testimony which Grace detailed week by week in her columns, Stevens put out a report in July that was resisted by the Prime Minister.

The report, headlined "The Book That Bennett Banned," was reprinted widely in cheap editions. The cover screamed in capital letters, "WAGES CUT WHEN FABULOUS PROFITS MADE—Minister of Trade and Commerce issues warning of gravity of outrageous situation and danger to our constitutional structure."

Stevens detailed how the owners of the giant retailer, Simpson's, persuaded its employees to buy two million dollars' worth of Class B stock and sold ten million dollars' worth to the general public, then took that money out of the company, leaving twelve million dollars' worth of mortgage bonds, not even secured by company assets, in the hands of the working poor. At the same time the company was cutting wages. Stevens uncovered similar outrages in the needle trades, the livestock business, the pulp and paper industry, and especially in tobacco, where the Imperial Tobacco Company was the villain.

Here was proof from a Commons committee conducted by a minister of the government that confirmed what the CCF and the Marxists had been saying. Wealth was being concentrated in fewer and fewer hands while ordinary Canadians could not find money for shoes and decent clothing to send their children to school. Prime Minister Bennett, unable to put out the fire, turned the investigation into a royal commission.

Occasionally Grace had accompanied her father to act as translator on his speaking trips to Montreal. Apprehensively, she came face to face with the problems of promoting socialism in Quebec. She recalled, "Father would go down there often for big rallies, the St. James Market and the Atwater, and he would take me with him and usually have me try stumbling to do a few sentences in French of what he was saying . . . . I used to be terribly tense, both before and after because I knew how bad my French was and how fragmentary. But he would have me do it, and then we would meet the people. I could get on better in small groups."

Grace felt inadequate in the face of the pressure to perform applied by her father. He hoped that she could translate not only the literal words of his speeches, but also communicate his evangelistic fervour in a way that would convert his listeners into true socialists. Even had these personal anxieties been absent, social attitudes in Quebec created formidable barriers to the socialist message.

"Those were the days of pro-fascist groups down there, Italian and French protagonists," Grace recalled. "The trouble with getting the French-speaking people is that the church was dead set against us, and on several occasions that I know about refused to rent halls to us for our meetings. We were just blacklisted as the great enemy of civilization in every possible way."

In June 1934 Grace had an "intensely interesting" week organizing on her own in Montreal, an experience that helped build her self-esteem. At the invitation of "a few of our French-Canadian women," she stayed at the home of a widow with twelve children, "aged by care and work, but almost desperate in her eagerness to get the CCF into power." Every night of that week Grace held meetings in the homes of French-Canadian women, and on Friday night she organized the first women's section of the CCF in Montreal.

"It will be a long time before I forget that memorable evening," she wrote. "Every bit of space in the little dining-room and kitchen was taken up by chairs. Some twenty-eight women came—French-Canadian, English and Jewish. In the background were the husbands of some of them, much interested in the unusual proceedings. The excitement was running high; English, French and Yiddish were being spoken all at once as suggestions were made as to the constitution and personnel of the new organization. Finally, I seized the lid of a pot from the stove and used it as a gavel to restore order.

"The most outstanding thing about the election of the officers was the wish of all present to have women of the three nationalities fairly represented on the new executive. One after the other the women gave it as their belief that race, language and religion had been used as barriers to keep people apart for centuries. Now they proposed to break these barriers and to use the CCF as the means of doing so. All proceedings had to be carried on in the two languages, English and French, for there were many women present who understood only the one.

"It was a thrilling evening. Barriers of race, of sex, of religion, all were powerless before the goodwill of these men and women who foresaw the dawn of a new day. Life will be so much richer and happier when social justice becomes a living reality. Success to the pioneers!"

Grace spent the summer in British Columbia where the latest CCF development was the establishment of a summer camp on Saltspring Island. In 1935 the camp moved to a glorious site on nearby Gabriola Island known as Camp Woodsworth, where it remained for many years. "In those days," Grace recalled, "a lot of people, their whole lives were wrapped up in the party. They knew people went to summer camps, and they couldn't afford to go to any summer camps. So they thought it would be nice to have one for families where, above all, there would be socialist teaching and debating."

There was always plenty of lively debate, as the camp attracted socialists of all stripes. Grace's childhood friend Mildred Osterhout was now director of the BC CCF educational committee. Sometimes called "Christian Mildred" behind her back, the idealistic young woman nursed the camp through its early years, but Marxian socialists like George Weaver and lawyer Wallis Lefeaux were also early organizers and speakers. Grace and Angus led many discussion groups over the years. There were skits and plays, sometimes recorded by amateur filmmakers, sports, swimming and clamdigging, and lots of time for beachcombing. The summer camp was an experiment in co-operative living. Everyone took an equal part in the chores; even J.S. Woodsworth was occasionally seen washing dishes or scrubbing floors.

The CCF summer camp in BC was the oldest, but by 1945 the idea had caught on and similar camps were flowering across Canada. During the 1930s and 1940s discussion groups were led by such CCF notables as Professor Eugene Forsey, M.J. Coldwell, Dr. Lyle Telford, David Lewis and Helena Gutteridge, who in 1937 became the first woman elected to Vancouver City Council. Most of the CCF MLAs from BC visited, and as many MPs as could fit a relaxing week on Gabriola Island into their summer schedules.

In Ottawa in October 1934, a disgusted H.H. Stevens resigned from the Bennett government to start his own Reconstruction Party to reform capitalism.

In the midst of the price spreads hearings, Grace was joined in Woodsworth's office by her brother Charles who was taking a break from the Fabian-founded London School of Economics. Brother and sister collaborated on a pamphlet, *Canada Through CCF Glasses.* Designed as a handbook for platform speakers and study groups, it explained the various sections of the Regina Manifesto in detail and included a strong dose of "shocking" facts and figures from Stevens's committee.

For example, a shoe plant in rural Quebec was paying female employees a dollar fifty a week for a seventy-five-hour week; heads of families in Toronto were getting five to ten dollars per week for seventy-two hours of work. At the same time, Grace and Charles pointed out, Gray Miller, president of Imperial Tobacco, received a salary of twenty-five thousand dollars per year with an additional bonus of at least thirty-two thousand dollars in each Depression year.

As an antidote they outlined an ideal federal labour code. Many provisions of their labour code have now been implemented, but some are still what Grace termed "unfinished business." It called for: government regulation of all wages, with equal opportunity and equal reward for equal work; the right to work or adequate maintenance; unemployment, health and accident insurance; old age pensions; limitation of hours of work; protection of health and safety in industry; freedom of association and government encouragement and assistance in the formation of workers' organizations; and active participation of workers in the control of their industries by means of collective agreements and works-councils.

In *Canada Through CCF Glasses* Grace and Charles advanced a "Long Run Peace Policy" in which the League of Nations would function as a world government "given more powers to deal with the economic causes of war."

The 1934 convention in Winnipeg pronounced the party "unalterably opposed to war." It called for a declaration of Canadian neutrality, with no Canadian troops to be sent overseas. In line with this policy, *Canada Through CCF Glasses* denounced the armament makers "concerned only with profits" for supplying machine guns, planes and poison gas to armies on both sides of various conflicts, "whoever will buy." Disapprovingly Grace and Charles noted that "stockholders in armament firms include cabinet ministers, government officials, professional people and ministers of the gospel" and concluded, "Capitalism and peace are incompatible. Wars are fought today to make the world safe for capitalism . . . . THE PROFIT MUST BE TAKEN OUT OF WAR."

In the section on Women and the CCF, Grace noted that with labour-saving machinery women had more leisure time, and for many women, short on food for their families, "politics may be the key to the kitchen cupboard." Grace pointed out: "While babies need milk it is being thrown away. Apples are rotting in British Columbia orchards. Wheat is stored up in prairie elevators. Clothing is waiting unused in department stores" for lack of purchasing power by ordinary Canadians who were quite willing to work.

Grace and Charles's effort might not have been the bible of the socialist movement, but at its February 1935 meeting the CCF national council endorsed their "valuable new pamphlet," and recommended that it be used as a basis for short, snappy election pamphlets. In fact, achieving what she had outlined in *Canada Through CCF Glasses* proved to be the touchstone of Grace's work throughout her political career.

Five years into his mandate in 1935 Prime Minister Bennett startled the battered Dominion by announcing his version of a New Deal in five radio broadcasts modelled on those of US President Roosevelt. "The old order is gone. It will not return . . . . I am for reform! And in my mind reform means government intervention," Bennett declaimed. There would be unemployment insurance, regulation of wages and working hours, and control of prices, marketing, mortgage foreclosures and banking. But this Canadian New Deal attempt to turn the Depression around was a failure. It was far too late, and looked suspiciously like re-election image making. The plan was never implemented; because the federal government lacked jurisdiction under the BNA Act to handle matters of social security, Bennett's moves were later declared unconstitutional by the Privy Council.

In April, when the weather warmed in British Columbia, close to four thousand disgruntled men from the relief camps which they described as "slave camps" began to converge on Vancouver for a general strike. Demanding real work for decent wages, coverage under the Workmen's Compensation Act, removal from Department of National Defence jurisdiction, improved food and sanitary conditions, and the repeal of Section 98 of the Criminal Code, they elected as their leader communist Arthur "Slim" Evans. During April and May and early June the On To Ottawa Trek was organized.

Meanwhile Grace and Angus were on a speaking tour in May through New Brunswick, Nova Scotia and Prince Edward Island. They extolled the virtues of the CCF to capacity crowds in large theatres and halls. Wearing a black slouch hat set stylishly to one side, Grace spoke first on her favourite theme, "Who Owns Canada?" using the material she had developed for *Canada Through CCF Glasses.* She had obviously developed confidence over the past several years. The *Chatham Gazette*'s reporter found her "a bright, animated presence on the platform" whose "charm won her hearers at once." Her first point was always that as socialists they were not communists or Reds, but were opposed by communists.

Most news reports devoted more space to Grace than to Angus, partly because of her status as the daughter of J.S. Woodsworth, partly because a young woman on the speaker's platform was still a novelty, but also because she had a way with words that brought lofty theories down to earth and made them relevant to the lives of ordinary women and men. Grace had begun to master her father's impressive methods of marshalling facts to back her points. She was in the process of absorbing Angus's way of putting a sharp point on the end of a comment that left a lasting impression on his audience. She called it "putting a sting in the tail" and later learned to use the technique with devastating effect.

By this time Grace had realized that her father's apprehensions about her marriage to Angus were not fully misplaced. The difference in their educational backgrounds was causing friction. "I was much better educated than Angus," Grace recalled. "Sometimes I would make a careless remark and he would just clam up. He'd be silent for days and nothing I would do could bring him out of it. You see, he had a brilliant mind, but no chance to develop it because of the schooling situation. I had had everything the way I wanted schooling-wise: a proper home background, lots of reading, lots of conversation. Problems of composition and grammar just didn't exist. I was in the position where I could help him tremendously with his correspondence, his speeches, not the content of them, just the form. Well, it was quite a little problem for me to know how to do that without seeming officious and dictatorial, without wounding his pride about it. And these Highlanders are a pretty proud people. I think he was very pleased to be helped, but I could very well have ruined it with carelessness.

"Then finally I discovered how to reach him. I remembered to get the frame of mind of helping him get over it, not being irritating. There was no good of saying, 'Oh, I didn't mean any harm,' because the answer to that is, well, after all the harm was done. The interesting thing was, he was devoted to his mother, and she lived to be about ninety. She was fond of both of us, although I never could talk to her because she had no English. After she died I noticed we hardly had any of these spells. I think just gradually he had matured out of them."

Grace's sunny, optimistic nature pleasurably warmed her husband most of the time, but her enthusiasms sometimes foundered on his cool reserve. Her nature demanded that she be the centre of attention in the marriage and, while her older husband plainly adored her, sometimes he failed to notice her needs for affection. In time, she learned not to press him but to nourish herself emotionally until he was ready to give.

As they travelled, Angus fed his need for beauty by collecting elegant china, especially teapots and ornate cup and saucer sets. He had developed the passion for porcelain as a child on the PEI potato farm, when a broken shard of pottery was the only pretty thing he could get his hands on. Now the possession of exquisite china gave him aesthetic pleasure and was also a way of demonstrating that he had developed into a cultured person.

Back in Ottawa in early June, the House watched apprehensively as trainloads of relief camp strikers moved east. Two thousand reached Regina on June 14, while Evans and other leaders continued on to Ottawa to meet with the Prime Minister.

The House heard Angus defend the strikers and press their demands, enduring catcalls of "communist" from the Tories across the floor. "The relief camp workers' march on Ottawa was organized by the communists, but the CCF helped unofficially to a great extent," Grace recollected. "Even Angus, though he disliked the communists. One of the marchers' leaders was stricken with illness on the last lap of the trip. Angus and I took breakfast to him every morning in a private home where he was staying. With Angus the point was that in a humanitarian way that didn't jeopardize your own standing, you could work with them as human beings."

Angus believed that one of the objectives of Evans and his communist colleagues was to put the socialist CCF in a bad light. They told the newspapers of trying to contact Labour MPs, but no MPs reported communication with them. Angus went to Evans's hotel but was put off, and Evans broke two later appointments, even after Angus cancelled an out-of-town speech to meet with the trek leader.

"As far as Evans was concerned it was not at all necessary to consult us in the matter," Angus wrote Grant MacNeil in BC. "All that it was necessary to do was to instruct us as to what they had decided . . . . The idea was for the delegation to avoid the CCF members while making it appear that they were seeking our assistance and being refused or ignored."

Prime Minister Bennett rejected the strikers' demands and the trek ended in a pool of blood on Dominion Day in Regina. In the riot a Regina city detective was killed, a dozen police injured, half a dozen civilians shot and more than a hundred injured by police clubs or rocks thrown by strikers. In addition to the eight trek leaders, police arrested seventy-six people.

With the backbone of the trek broken and his New Deal safely—he thought—in place, Prime Minister Bennett called an election for October 14. It was the first electoral test for the CCF as a national party, and Grace threw herself into campaigning. Angus travelled back to Vancouver to campaign in his constituency, while Grace stopped with her father and mother in Winnipeg.

One day while at the 60 Maryland Street house, Grace witnessed a confrontation between her father and communist Party leader Tim Buck that reinforced the hostility between the two groups. According to Buck's account Woodsworth invited him for tea at the house. "I went over," Buck wrote. "He came to the door and shook hands with me. His wife and daughter were in the room when I walked in. Mrs. Woodsworth handed me a cup of tea. "Jim said, 'Is it true, Buck, that you're going to accept nomination in Winnipeg North?' 'I think so. Personally, I'd much rather run in Toronto, but the Party seems to feel that Winnipeg North is the center of the country and the constituency where I should run to focus attention. Also, they are of the opinion that I might possibly win.' 'Don't you know that that's Abraham Heaps's constituency?' 'Yes, I know that Abe Heaps runs there, although he is not sitting now, Mr. Woodsworth.' By the tone of his voice, I realized that this was no time to call him 'Jimmy.' 'You know, Mr. Woodsworth, I am very anxious that this whole question of constituencies should be discussed, and that the nine candidates that we have decided to run should run in constituencies on which your national committee agree, so that there is no conflict between us . . .' He got up and said, 'You get out of this house! To come here straight from Kingston [Penitentiary] and tell me that you will decide where you run, without consideration for the fact that a national party is contesting these elections . . . . I won't listen.' . . . He never spoke to me again as long as he lived."

Grace recalled different elements of the conversation that day. "I remember the two sticky points where Father took very strong issue. One was the necessity or otherwise for violence and taking account of violence as being a necessary part of the class struggle. The other one was on the necessity or otherwise of always telling the truth, which is part of my father's belief very firmly, and the CCF and NDP, but is not part of communist strategy, at least according to evidence." Grace recalled the conversation: "'Mr. Woodsworth,' Buck said, 'you're the leader of the party.' 'Yes.' 'You believe you can get these things by parliamentary means and by social change of that kind.' 'Yes.' 'And you don't believe that it's necessary to overthrow these things in a physical way.' 'NO.' 'Well then, as leader of the CCF, Mr. Woodsworth, you must go,' declared Buck.

"Well, Tim Buck was courteously ushered out the door, but J.S. Woodsworth stayed where he was."

By election day, October 14, 1935, Mackenzie King had turned the Depression to his electoral advantage. On the slogan, "It's King or Chaos," he led the Liberals to a landslide victory over Bennett, winning 171 seats to the Conservatives' thirty-nine. Social Credit, based on the monetary theories of Major Douglas, leaped into third place in Parliament. The CCF took just seven seats, a disappointing fourth-place non-showing, although they earned twice the popular vote of the Socreds. Woodsworth held his seat in Winnipeg North Centre, while Angus was re-elected in the new riding of Vancouver East, established in 1933. In BC the CCF candidates far outpolled the Tories, yet again won fewer seats. Stevens's new Reconstruction Party failed except for the one seat held by its leader in Kootenay East.

Grace knew that CCF insistence on extension of the vote to Japanese Canadians was a strong factor in the party's defeats, especially in British Columbia ridings. The Liberals placed a racist ad in a Vancouver daily newspaper warning voters that "a vote for any CCF candidate is a vote to give the Chinaman and the Japanese the same voting right that you have." Angus was fond of telling audiences after that election, "I got the largest majority west of the lakes, despite the fact that my Liberal opponent had spent a year talking about nothing but the Oriental franchise."

Campaign gatherings were lively with Grace on the platform. She devoted much of her attention to campaigning for J. King Gordon in Victoria. The LSR founding member and former Professor of Christian Ethics at United Theological College in Montreal had lost his teaching chair ostensibly for

Grace and Angus relax on Lover's Walk beneath the Parliament Buildings near the Rideau River, May 1935. Grace was inspired by these strolls to write love poetry during their courtship.

A cartoon showing fun and games at the CCF Summer School, Camp Woodsworth, at Fisherman's Cove. Galiano Island, BC, summer 1935.

budget considerations, but at least partly because of his outspoken socialist views. He had then become a travelling speaker for the newly formed Fellowship for a Christian Social Order (FCSO) which believed that "the capitalist economic system is fundamentally at variance with Christian principles."

During the campaign Victoria newspapers usually reported Grace's remarks at the top of the story, with Gordon's at the foot of the article. She opened her speeches with an attack on the capitalist system, and relied on straight facts and issues placed squarely before the voting public much as she had outlined them in *Canada Through CCF Glasses*. She would usually end by saying she liked to think of the letters CCF as meaning "Comfort, Culture and Freedom."

Then, less than two weeks before the election, Mussolini's Italy invaded Abyssinia (now Ethiopia). The League of Nations promptly voted to impose economic sanctions on the aggressor. Woodsworth, as a confirmed pacifist and socialist, was not very enthusiastic about the action of the league of capitalist nations. Grace explained her father believed that "we shouldn't be putting sanctions around the world because that would lead to war with Italy, so Father was scared of that, you see."

Grace agreed with her father. At that time she was a pacifist in general, and in particular opposed the placement of economic sanctions on Italy. Angus, while not a belligerent, was no longer the pacifist he had been during World War One. He believed that Canada had a duty to intervene to stop a dictator from imposing his will on another sovereign nation.

"Angus and I came to public disagreement over Ethiopia," Grace admitted ruefully. "I was speaking in favour of not putting any embargo on oil, and Angus was out there urging an embargo on oil; each of us out on platforms taking a different stand. That would never happen with Mother and Father. They never publicly disagreed." As Mussolini tightened his grip on Abyssinia and Hitler extended his dictatorship in Europe, debate over the consequences of a pacifist policy produced much conflict within the CCF.

Grace's attitude toward war and peace was not only a question of political policy, it was the first important moral issue she had to think through for herself. All her life Grace had followed her father's political prescription. She married a man whose ideas were for the most part the same as her father's. But when Angus moved from Woodsworth's pacifist stand, Grace was caught in the middle. She had to choose between supporting her husband or her father, a decision that was made in the full glare of national publicity. For the next twenty years, left-wing CCF members would criticize her severely for abandoning Woodsworth's pacifism.

All the conflicts that would shape the next decade seemed to crystallize in 1936. Grace called it the watershed year. "I've seen it over and over again," she reflected. "1936 was the year we stopped looking back to World War One and began to look forward to World War Two."

That June Grace was back in Victoria, stumping once again for King Gordon, this time in a federal by-election, one of the stiffest election battles on record. Conservative Dr. S.F. Tolmie defeated Gordon by a mere ninety votes with the Liberal running a close third. Grace made the treatment of Orientals in British Columbia an election issue, although she knew the CCF position on this issue had helped defeat them the year before. Taking a page from Angus's book, she challenged the Conservative and Liberal candidates to introduce a resolution in the House calling for exclusion of any Oriental from Canada who was not granted the franchise. She claimed the interests they represented were responsible for bringing Orientals into Canada as cheap labour.

In 1936 Angus was responsible for getting a team of four Japanese Canadians in front of the Franchise Committee in Ottawa. There, Grace recalled, they astounded the MPs from east of the Rockies who had thought they would be meeting coolies with poles over their shoulders speaking broken English. The delegation was headed by Dr. S.I. Hiyakawa, later a US senator, then head of the semantics department of a Wisconsin university. He made a flawless presentation. Committee members included Ian MacKenzie, MP for Vancouver Centre, Senator Tom Reid and a number of others, all Scottish-born and carrying a prejudice against Japanese Canadians. How amazed they were when Hiyakawa ended his speech by saying, "We Canadians are proud to say with Robbie Burns, 'A man's a man for a' that.'" Grace, watching from the sidelines, chuckled at that, and enjoyed the joke for the next fifty years.

It took until 1948, three years after the end of World War Two, before the Canadian government came around to the MacInnis' point of view and granted the full franchise to Japanese Canadians.

"Your Russian visas have not yet arrived." This disappointing news greeted Grace and Angus when they reached Liverpool August 14, 1936 after a week relaxing aboard a CPR ocean liner. Their first trip to Europe as a couple was a reconnaissance mission to assess for the CCF the progress of socialism in Scandinavia, the state of the British Labour Party at its annual conference, and the changes in Germany after more than three years of Hitler's rule. Angus, on his first trip to the continent, was looking forward to visiting the land of his ancestors, the Scottish island of Skye.

At the CCF annual convention in Toronto just before they sailed, the party had defeated eighty-eight to seven a resolution to work in a united front with the Communist Party of Canada (CPC). Grace and Angus had voted against the united front. Nevertheless, they wanted a firsthand glimpse of Stalin's Russia. This plan, however, was proving difficult to carry out.

Angus was not favourably impressed with his first look at the British Isles. Walking around Liverpool he and Grace came to the terra-cotta cathedral "only a stone's throw from the dirt and squalor of the slums." Angus felt the money and labour spent to build it could have been put to better use. "I wished they had built huge public baths in which the thousands of dirty little children we saw on the streets could enjoy the luxury of a bath and then the delicious feeling of being clean," he commented in the diary he and Grace kept together, each writing on alternate days.

In Norway, Sweden and Denmark they visited the offices of labour newspapers, trade unions and co-operatives, talking about the CCF and gleaning insights into the workings of social democracy in these fortunate countries which had remained neutral and largely untouched by World War One.

Grace appreciated the attitude toward family planning in Norway. "Parents are advised to have only a few children so that they may be well cared for and well educated," she wrote approvingly in the diary. "Birth control information is readily available. Health insurance makes it possible for expectant mothers to receive every attention during pregnancy and to go to a hospital where the baby is born in the best possible surroundings."

It was a working holiday, but Grace and Angus did not neglect the fun part. In Oslo they were dinner guests at the home of Gunvor Pettersen, a friend Grace had made during her student days in Paris. It was a convivial group. "After a merry evening we were driven home to bed," Grace wrote with satisfaction, "but not to sleep!"

The next day, Grace and Angus visited the office of *Arbeiderbladet,* the labour newspaper in Oslo, where they spoke with an editor who had just interviewed exiled communist leader Leon Trotsky, then living in a village near Oslo. "Trotsky is now implicated in the trials in Moscow of Zinoviev, Kamenev, Rykov, Radek, Tomsky and Bukharin," Grace wrote. "According to Trotsky, there is growing discontent in the USSR over the rising standard of living enjoyed by the ruling clique. In an attempt to divert the discontent of the masses. Stahlin (sic) is staking everything on these trials."

A group of "Old Bolsheviks" were on trial for the assassination of party star Sergei Kirov in 1934, and an alleged conspiracy to kill Stalin. It was the first of the great purge trials. The accused all confessed to the trumped-up charges, and were convicted and put to death. Not only political leaders perished in this wave of Stalinist persecution, but writers, artists, bureaucrats and army leaders were executed or died in prison camps.

But that sunny August day Grace and Angus were far from Stalin's terrors at a speedboat race and stunt plane demonstration with Gunvor. Later they toured large modern apartments built by the city of Oslo as slum-clearing projects to house unemployed as well as working people.

Then they took a train across Sweden where Grace noted "a few details which showed we were not in Canada. We saw no neglected buildings or unpainted houses . . . . Not once in the whole day did we see a burnt-over patch of woodland or a barren, denuded hillside. In Norway and Sweden they take care to conserve their forest wealth and to make provision for replacing such of it as they use."

Grace and Angus were impressed by the city of Stockholm and its people. They visited new apartments built by co-operative housing societies and by the city, some complete with kindergartens. Grace learned about the work of Swedish Social Demokratic Party (SDP) women's organizations toward improved health services. They came away from efficient factories with impressions of steel, glass and concrete cleanliness.

Norway, Sweden and Denmark were all in the throes of election campaigns while Grace and Angus were there. They attended a SDP election campaign meeting in Spanga, a town near Stockholm. There they found the hall "well-filled by the very sort of people who attend CCF meetings at home—an orderly crowd of ordinary working men, women and children," Grace wrote. They learned political propaganda techniques, Swedish style, from a campaign film. A love story was woven into a recital of what the SDP had done for Sweden during its past three years in power. A comical shoemaker stoutly defended social ownership. The conversion of a worker to socialist ideals was shown. "We came home feeling that we had learned something very useful," Grace wrote.

Still anxious, Grace and Angus tried in Stockholm to find out if their Russian visas had been issued, but found they must wait until they got to the Soviet consulate in Helsingfors (now Helsinki). Bound for Finland on a tiny ship loaded with tourists, Grace and Angus puzzled over the delay. They arrived in Helsingfors on Angus's birthday, September 4, an occasion they celebrated with a glass of sherry at lunch. Immediately they went to the Russian consulate, and the Intourist office, but even after many frustrating visits no one could find their visas.

Temporarily they gave up and began to explore the extensive Finnish co-operative movement. Finland was a social democratic republic with more than half the population organized into co-operatives, which carried on about thirty percent of the country's retail trade. Recalling the sweatshop conditions in Canadian garment factories, Grace and Angus visited a Finnish garment factory. "One entered by a courtyard so spotless a twig lying on the cement was conspicuous," Angus wrote. "Grace asked if there were many nervous breakdowns. Mr. T. was at first unwilling to believe that such things were possible among clothing workers. There were no nervous breakdowns in that factory."

Back at their hotel, Grace and Angus received a phone call from the Soviet consul informing them that their visas were refused. Indignantly Grace wrote, "We decided to leave Helsingfors by the afternoon train—'the Retreat from Russia.' We went to the CPR office to get accommodation. On hearing our story the agent laughed, 'They think you are spies.' He told us that only one other CPR passenger had been refused entrance into the USSR during the entire season."

Social democrats, especially those holding elected office, were now persona non grata in Soviet Russia. This should have come as no surprise by the time of Stalin's purge trials of 1936, ironic as it may seem given the Comintern's call for a united front. Socialism in Russia meant anything Stalin said it meant, and he viewed social democrats as bourgeois enemies of the dictatorship of the proletariat.

In Copenhagen Grace and Angus entered a society where co-operatives existed as early as 1866 and one in every three Danes was a co-op member. They spent a week touring co-op farms, factories and schools, and sightseeing at castles complete with dungeons. On a lighter note they indulged in a night of gaiety at the famous Tivoli Gardens with its orchestras, side-shows and restaurants. "Everywhere," wrote Grace, "was the laughter and jostling of a crowd." Later they went to nightclubs. It was the first time Angus had been inside a nightclub in all his fifty-two years. He enjoyed himself that night, but it was not an experience he wished to repeat.

Grace and Angus documented the inner workings of the Danish Social Democratic Party in some detail. In company with a Danish journalist, on election day they interviewed the Danish Prime Minister, Thorvald Stauning. In 1929 Stauning had forged a coalition government of Social Democrats and Radicals. By 1933 he had in place a comprehensive program of social and economic reform with unemployment insurance, old age pensions, sickness and disability insurance, public and child welfare services.

That evening in company with several journalists, Grace and Angus visited six of fifty SDP meetings assembled in Copenhagen to listen to the results. "We met the Minister of Commerce, listened to the Minister of Social Services, met the Prime Minister coming out of the 'Social Demokraten,' drove around for part of the evening in the car of the Minister for War. At one meeting we both made short speeches," Grace wrote.

On their last night in Copenhagen Angus wrote, "We felt that we were one people, [with the Danes] as I am sure we actually are," he wrote. "There are two crimes: War and Poverty. War is a crime because the peoples of the world have nothing to fight about. Poverty is a crime because we have learned how to produce an abundance for all. If the nations of the world will learn how to distribute that abundance equitably among their people, they will at the same time abolish poverty and remove the ultimate source of all modern wars. The Scandinavian countries are making substantial progress in this direction." But instead Europe was increasingly locked in a struggle between two totalitarian ideologies, communism and fascism, personified by two strong dictators, Stalin and Hitler.

Grace and Angus boarded a train for Hitler's Germany. They spent only three days in Germany, long enough to feel "that aggressiveness which means a desire to assert one's superiority." They were struck by the isolation of Germany from the rest of the world. In Hamburg Grace noted "a dull, expressionless look on most of the faces, a very different look from the cheerful gaiety of the Danes . . . we felt all the time an ominous undercurrent as of forces being dammed back, an unfriendly outlook on the world outside Germany's borders." They wondered if this feeling was a product of their imaginations. It was not.

By autumn 1936 Hitler had been in power for three and a half years. In that time he had reduced unemployment from nearly six million to just over one million. He had suppressed Communist and Social Democratic parties, and established a one-party Nazi elected assembly. He had eliminated all but Nazi newspapers, radio, books, art and films. He had abolished trade unions, collective bargaining and the right to strike, Nazified the education system, reorganized the courts, regimented the Christian churches, issued anti-Jewish laws, created an air force, begun intensive rearmament in defiance of the hated Treaty of Versailles, re-occupied the Rhineland without French resistance, and established an understanding with Italy's fascist dictator Mussolini.

Grace and Angus stopped next in for the first session of the League of Nations in its gleaming new six million dollar palace. Despite its pretentious exterior, the League had been unable to halt the takeover of Haile Selassie's Ethiopia by Mussolini's troops. On May 2, 1936 Italian forces entered Addis Ababa and on July 4 the League called off sanctions against Italy. Two weeks later in Spain, Franco staged a military revolt against the weak republican government and civil war broke out.

Grace and Angus heard British Foreign Secretary Anthony Eden address the League Assembly on "ways and means of avoiding war—first to strengthen the League machinery, second to strengthen the will to use it." Neither objective was to be fulfilled. Then Spain's Foreign Minister Alvarez Del Vayo presented evidence to the Assembly that non-intervention in practice meant that General Francisco Franco could obtain arms from Hitler and Mussolini, while the legitimately elected Spanish government was prevented from buying any armaments. He called for League help to drive back Franco's forces.

From their seats in the gallery, Grace and Angus could see Canadian Prime Minister Mackenzie King, and other members of the Canadian delegation. The next day Grace and Angus were guests of King for tea in his hotel sitting room. There they had what Grace termed a "pleasant conversation" about Canada's responsibility in the international situation. King believed, as did Grace's father, that sanctions against aggressor nations would produce war, and that war could be avoided without them. Angus was in favour of sanctions, but the Canadian government was not ready to adopt this course of action. Grace and Angus left Geneva for Paris without hearing Prime Minister King's speech to the League, but they were well aware that his position was generally supported by the Scandinavian countries, Switzerland, the Netherlands and Australia.

Grace was delighted to introduce Angus to the pleasures of Paris, her favourite continental city. They took a hotel room in the Latin Quarter near Sorbonne University, viewed the old Masters at the Louvre and visited Grace's old friends from 1929, M. and Mme. Fuchs. That very day the French government had devalued the franc, and civil service pensioners like the elderly Fuchses were badly hurt.

The Canadian Minister to France, Phillipe Roy, received them cordially at Canada House and arranged a visit to the French Parliament. Seated in the box of the president of the republic, Grace and Angus heard debate on the franc devaluation bill of the recently elected Popular Front government led by Leon Blum.

On a visit to the socialist newspaper *Le Populaire* a few days later, they asked secretary of the party, Comrade Lagorgette, about the United Front. "Was it stable? Did he think that socialists and communists could work together permanently? No, he did not. But the United Front—socialists, communists and Radicals—had been formed as an emergency measure. Frankly, the communists wanted war in Europe. They believed war between communist Russia and fascist Germany to be inevitable."

When they arrived in London Grace and Angus found a small bed and breakfast hotel near Whitehall and set out to explore the city. It was a London in which turmoil was simmering just under the smooth surface of society. "This is Black Sunday," Grace wrote on October 4. "This afternoon the [Nazi] Blackshirts are to fill the East End with trouble and chaos and the newspapers with heated controversy over the question of free speech." But all was quiet as they strolled through Saint James Park, and past Buckingham Palace to check out the soapbox orators in Hyde Park. After window shopping and a tour of the National Gallery, Angus and Grace took a bus back to the hotel. "On the way," she wrote, "we saw the remnants of [Nazi leader Oswald] Mosley's parade—the remnant which re-formed ranks after having been disbanded by the police. Young men and women for the most part, dressed in black shirts with the fascist swastika as an armband. Most of them looked like ordinary working class people," she observed.

Then they entrained for Edinburgh and the British Labour Party conference, the primary destination of their voyage. All hotels were jammed with delegates, but Grace and Angus found a place to sleep in the drawing room of the Chimes Hotel. Angus was in such heaven in this museum-like chamber, with its exquisite china in elaborate carved cabinets, that he did not even mind squeezing his lanky frame onto a davenport for the night.

Next day at the conference, Angus and Grace were seated on the platform with fraternal delegates from Spain, Holland, Belgium, Norway and the Socialist International. The party was debating its position with regard to the Spanish conflict. The national executive and the Trades Union Congress had announced support for the British government's policy of non-intervention by which the Spanish government would be denied the legal right to buy arms. But a large section of the movement, including the Socialist League of which Sir Stafford Cripps was chairman, disapproved. Many socialists felt that their leaders should support the Spanish republican government in its effort to survive. The executive proposal was carried 1,836,000 to 519,000, with an unusually large vote in opposition.

The next day the Spanish delegates addressed the conference. "Senor Asua spoke in French," noted Grace. "His hearers, not being able to understand him, applauded whenever he became particularly worked up. It was amusing to watch some of the pro-communist element in the gallery applauding the following: 'We do not want to establish a communist government in Spain. We are Liberals. We want to preserve democracy.' Madame de Palencia made a great, emotional appeal to the audience." This Spanish woman, called La Passionaria, roused a vigorous passion for justice and peace in the hearts of this audience. At the close of her moving speech the entire conference rose spontaneously to sing "The Red Flag."

On the last day the conference unanimously approved a Cripps resolution in support of the Spanish government recognizing that "the Fascist Powers have broken their pledges of non-intervention." But despite Attlee's vow that if the pact failed the Labour Party would press for the lifting of the arms embargo, many delegates were disappointed in their party's position.

That night Grace and Angus attended the Labour Party rally at Ussher Hall. Among the speakers were Attlee, who was not a particularly brilliant speaker but knew how to marshal his arguments, Grace observed; Ernest Bevin, who "expressed faith in the ILO and the idea behind the League of Nations;" and Herbert Morrison, MP who gave "a clear exposition of the implication of a new social order."

"The audience rose to sing 'The Red Flag.' The great organ pealed out the familiar music and the people sang with feeling. And then they streamed out into the misty air of the old city whose castle hung in golden light against a misty sky," wrote Grace, profoundly moved by feelings of fellowship.

On the last day of the conference a United Front proposal was "overwhelmingly defeated," Grace noted with satisfaction. After the usual thanks was voted all round, Grace and Angus were free of official obligations.

Old people were speaking Gaelic on the train to Mallaig on Scotland's west coast as they set off for a sunny five-hour sail to the isle of Skye aboard a trim little steamer threading its way amongst small islands. Once in Skye's main town of Portree, they decided to stay "in the town's best for once."

The next day Angus took Grace on a ride across moor and fen to search for his father's people at Kilmuir near Dunvegan, the point farthest west on the narrow road. After many attempts to find anyone with information,

Angus had to give up the hunt. But the trip was delightful. Grace and Angus fell in love with Skye and delighted in tourist pleasures: a history lesson at Dunvegan Castle, a Gaelic language book for Grace, and a Scottish woollen knee-rug for each of their mothers. In his diary Angus wondered "if automobiles, buses, electric lights, running water hot and cold at the turning of the wrist, the radio, the talkies would drive the ghosts, the witches and fairies out of Skye."

Back in London, the magic of Skye already distant, Grace and Angus were welcomed by Charles at King's Cross Station. Their two weeks in London were relaxed. They took in a staging of Jane Austen's *Pride and Prejudice* at St. James Theatre, and had tea with Hugh Inglis, one of the "friendly enemies upstairs" from Gibson's Landing days. Angus's passion for beautiful china was satisfied by a handsome red Mikado coffee pot for his favourite beverage directly from the Royal Crown Derby showrooms.

They picked up the latest in Fabian socialist thought at two lectures by pillars of the Fabian Society. G.D.H. Cole spoke on the question "Can Capitalism Survive?" He was, wrote Grace, "convinced that in such countries as England, France and the United States capitalism could stand several such shocks as it received in the last depression." He was not in favour of the British Labour Party forming a coalition with either the Liberal Party on the right or the communists on the left. Later they heard another famous Fabian socialist, Sydney Webb, speak on the future of Soviet communism.

After a final week of relaxation aboard the CPR liner *Duchess of York,* Grace and Angus saw the Montreal Harbour Bridge pass overhead. It signalled the end of their European adventure.

CHAPTER 6

World at War

Grace, along with the rest of Canada, looked on with growing apprehension as the late 1930s unfolded: as Hitler and Mussolini strengthened their bonds and tightened the net of fascism around Europe and across Africa, as Japan invaded China. Forewarned by her European experiences that her father's noble philosophy of pacifism was no protection if freedom and democracy were threatened by dictators, Grace now threw herself into building social democracy as a bulwark against totalitarianism. Armed with her observations of successful socialism in Scandinavia, Grace went to work to educate, persuade and organize Canadians.

The ongoing debate intensified between Grace and Angus over how the CCF should respond to the growing menace in Europe. At the British Labour Party conference Angus had realized that Britain should not uphold the non-intervention pact in Spain. "He came back saying we just had to take sides; we couldn't stand aloof," Grace explained. "I hadn't got that far. I was doing a little thinking in spite of my pacifist childhood, but I was slower than Angus had been, quite a lot slower."

The argument they had had in public before their European trip, over the imposition of an oil embargo on Italy, surfaced again after they returned. This time the issue was the more general moral question of using military force to halt totalitarian aggression. "We came back to Vancouver and were reporting around about what we had seen and heard [in Europe]. After one of the meetings where we were both speaking Angus said, 'Well, the divorce courts are going to have a very interesting time in British Columbia when they have our petition for divorce, yours and mine, on grounds of incompatibility on foreign policy.'" Grace enjoyed the joke later, but at the time the issue struck sparks between them.

In January 1937 Woodsworth had introduced a resolution in the House that clearly stated the CCF policy on war, then a reflection of his own pacifist belief. It proposed "In the event of war, Canada should be strictly neutral

125

regardless of who the belligerents may be . . . at no time should Canadian citizens be permitted to make profits out of supplying war munitions or materials," and the government should "discover and remove the causes of international friction and social injustice." Woodsworth called on French-Canadian Liberals to join the CCF in questioning the government's increased spending on defense.

Other members of the CCF, such as Angus and Tommy Douglas, now MP for Weyburn, Saskatchewan, were already convinced that the time had come either to work collectively to build world peace or be inexorably drawn into a world war. After much soul-searching Grace came to the reluctant conclusion that Angus and Tommy were right. She put her pacifist convictions aside in view of the imminent danger.

At the 1937 CCF national convention in Winnipeg, the split over foreign policy became apparent with just one crucial word. The Regina Manifesto declared unequivocally, "We stand resolutely against all participation in imperialist wars." The 1936 national convention had removed the word "imperialist." Now in 1937 the party's foreign policy resolution was amended by re-inserting the word "imperialist." This one word changed the policy from Woodsworth's insistence on no Canadian participation in any war, to that of non-participation in any imperialist war, leaving the door open for the party to support Canada's participation in wars it did not consider "imperialist."

The CCF had to look no further than its own doorstep for evidence of trouble. Canadian Nazis were active right there in Winnipeg, which had a large German population. On the Sunday after Dominion Day, just a few weeks before the CCF convention, there was a parade of Nazi strength. "It was a shocker," an eyewitness reported. "That parade took forever to pass and there must have been ten thousand marchers, all Germans, all smug and smiling, men, women and children. Singing. It was damn well organized, in groups like platoons and companies with German flags, the Nazi emblems on their sleeves."

At the 1937 national convention, Woodsworth was re-elected CCF president, but some of his responsibilities were assigned to the new position of national chairman, filled by M.J. Coldwell, then a first-term Saskatchewan MP. Grace too was relieved, concerned as she was about her beloved father's health and vitality.

In November 1937 Grace campaigned a third time for King Gordon in Victoria, in yet another federal by-election. With her complete support, Gordon argued for an "immediate embargo against the export of war materials to Japan." In a rare platform appearance with a communist, Grace spoke at a Gordon campaign rally chaired by Nigel Morgan. On election day Gordon lost again, this time to the Liberal.

Immoral profit from the sale of nickel was the subject of a scathing column

CCF Members of Parliament, 1937. From left: Tommy Douglas, Angus MacInnis, Abraham A. Heaps, J.S. Woodsworth, M.J. Coldwell, Grace, Grant MacNeil. Grace was honorary secretary to the caucus from 1931 until her election to the BC Legislature in 1941. {COMSTOCK/Yousuf Karsh}

Wearing a gold locket owned by her mother since 1882, Grace stands at the entrance to the Memorial Chamber in the Peace Tower, Parliament Buildings, Ottawa, 1938.

Grace wrote for the *Federationist* in January 1938. "Canadians are accustomed to regard themselves as peace-loving people. Yet from the mines of this country are being drawn today the materials which are arming the nations of the world. Yesterday it was the turn of defenceless Ethiopians to be torn to pieces by Canadian metal; today Spanish and Chinese peoples are writhing beneath the hail of death from Canada; tomorrow the arms boom, changing to boomerang, may destroy us in the general conflagration." Canada had ninety-nine percent of the world's supply of nickel, the one material essential for the manufacture of armaments. The nickel industry was owned and controlled by a single company, Grace informed her readers, the International Nickel Company of Canada (INCO) of Sudbury, Ontario. She took double-barrelled aim at monopoly and aggression.

Although Canada claimed a strictly neutral position in the Sino-Japanese conflict, Canadian exports of metals to Japan, especially nickel, had risen sharply in 1936 and 1937. Woodsworth, Coldwell and Heaps protested in the House, joined by Social Credit and Conservative members. A boycott of Japanese goods developed, especially in the West, where placards reading "Boycott Japanese Oranges" appeared in shop windows at Christmas. There were increasing demands for the defence of Canada's Pacific coast and calls to end the immigration of the 150 Japanese still permitted to enter Canada each year.

In March 1938, to "protect" the ten million Germans living in Austria, Hitler annexed the country, then engineered a higher than ninety-nine percent approval in a plebiscite on Austrian union with the Third Reich. Britain and France protested but appeased Hitler six months later when he grabbed the Sudeten section of Czechoslovakia, with its three million Germans. Neville Chamberlain travelled to Germany to meet with Hitler three times that fateful September, each time ceding more of Czechoslovakia on easier terms than Hitler demanded. At the final meeting in Munich the Czechs were not even at the table. In Canada, as in Britain, the Munich settlement was greeted with enthusiasm and heartfelt relief. Critics were seen almost as traitors.

The primary objective of the King government's foreign policy was to maintain a good trade relationship with Britain and the United States. In 1938 this strategy yielded a three-way agreement which reduced tariffs. Yet Canada was still in the straitjacket of Depression, hundreds of thousands were on relief, and dry topsoil continued to blow in clouds across the prairies. To make matters worse during the sweltering summer of 1936, when Grace and Angus were in Europe, the first epidemic of polio struck, leaving hundreds of children paralyzed.

The worst dust storm ever recorded blew across southern Saskatchewan in June 1937, devastating millions of acres of cropland. The next year prairie farmers fought hail, rust, more drought, and swarms of grasshoppers that devoured the wheat crop. In Regina grasshoppers coated the streets, buildings, telephone and rail lines. Finally, winged salvation: gulls arrived at Lake Wascana to feast until the insects vanished.

Across the country, CCF provincial councils were dealing with an equally devastating attack of communists by isolating, suspending and expelling them. In Ontario internal dissension had split the fledgling party repeatedly even after 1934 when Woodsworth stepped in, restructuring the provincial organization to get rid of communists. In 1936 agitators for the united front in BC had been so successful tactically that neither Grace nor Angus were able to address even a CCF Club meeting anywhere. Following Lenin's line, the communists saw social democrats, rather than capitalists, as their primary enemy in the struggle for control of the working class.

By 1937 Grace and Angus found a more receptive atmosphere in BC now that the provincial executive was convinced of the danger of associating with communists. A communist member of the Vancouver Centre CCF Club, Rodney Young, received a one-year suspension from membership in July of 1937 on grounds that he was a disruptive force and not the unsophisticated youth he appeared. The incident was but a prelude to the long struggle between Young and the BC provincial CCF.

Most troubling to Grace and Angus was a statement signed in April 1937 by nineteen prominent British Columbia CCFers, including MLA Gretchen Steeves, criticizing the party and demanding negotiations toward a "popular" front, another variant of the united front idea. Grace and Angus were able to turn back this attempt at closer relations with the communists, but their conflict with Steeves over the issue was only beginning.

Ironically, while leading members of the CCF were repeatedly accused of communism both in the House and by the press, the mainstream of CCF thinking as represented by Grace, Angus and J.S. Woodsworth disagreed strongly with the communists and for decades resisted an alliance with them. "We were closer always to the party that was in opposition basically over the years," Grace reflected. "Personally, I think most of us liked some of the Tories better [than the Liberals]."

Both Angus and Grace respected their long-time adversary, former Prime Minister Bennett. When Bennett announced in March 1938 his decision to retire from leadership of the Conservative party, Angus wrote in a note of regret, "It was your misfortune to be head of the Government of Canada in, perhaps, the most difficult period in Canadian history . . . . The task was undoubtedly a hard one but it was undertaken with courage and industry, and whether we can agree with all the things attempted and the things done, we all admired the faith and the determination with which you carried on."

Grace's workload increased as the 1930s drew to a close. She continued as secretary to the CCF national caucus, served continuously on the national council from its earliest years, and was still writing weekly columns for labour, farm and CCF papers when Parliament was in session. Grace worked to develop the fledgling CCF Youth Movement, the CCYM, and took over as CCYM president in 1938. Also, she was directly responsible for much of the educational material distributed to provincial councils for platform speakers and study groups.

She was always available to help her husband whenever he needed her, but from the beginning both Angus and Grace felt that she was essentially on her own. "I remember him saying to me, 'For heaven's sake, don't make a doormat of yourself. I want you to be a person in your own right.' That was always his position. A very unusual relationship, particularly given his background and his age," Grace remarked later.

In 1937 she collaborated with her brother Charles on another pamphlet aimed at exposing the evils of monopoly capitalism in Canada. *Jungle Tales Retold* used the nursery rhyme "The House That Jack Built" as an allegory to illustrate the socialist maxim that people working together in co-operation would produce a more just and equitable society than individuals locked in competition. In their view competition led inevitably to destructive monopolies. They tried to show how a few men heading huge monopolies held Canada in thrall.

"Monopolies operate at tremendous cost to the community," they wrote. "Smashing forward along the road to profits these gigantic steam-rollers leave in their wake the evidences of their crushing force . . . that wreckage is the consumer . . . . But in its heedless passage along the road, the steam-roller of monopoly has destroyed them. Through high profits, unplanned production and wasteful methods of distribution it has robbed them of the purchasing power which alone can keep them going. In so doing, private monopoly is inevitably destroying itself." As solutions, *Jungle Tales Retold* offered public ownership, also called social ownership, and a strong network of producer and consumer co-operatives.

Grace was to maintain this view of monopoly capitalism during her entire career. She often headed CCF committees at the national council level to develop strategies for the co-operative movement. Her concern for Canadian consumers would motivate much of her work in the BC Legislature and her activities as a Member of Parliament in the 1960s and 1970s.

Charles had been honing his skills as a news reporter and writer on both domestic and international affairs. In 1935 for the *Winnipeg Tribune* he covered the On To Ottawa Trek of the relief camp strikers by riding the rods with them. In 1938 he completed a study of the relations between Canada and Asian nations entitled *Canada and the Orient,* issued in 1941 under the auspices of the Canadian Institute of International Affairs. By the time it was published he was a reporter for *The Province* newspaper in Vancouver.

Grace and Charles were close, but had important differences in outlook. "It's a good thing we didn't try to make a permanent partnership because I was pretty rigid, I guess, and he was pretty impatient of my limited vision on a lot of things," Grace observed. "I've always felt Charles has been more interested in people than he is in policy . . . . You see, everything I did, the leaflets and pamphlets, they weren't just for the sake of putting things down on paper, but it was to be used to make converts or reinforce people's thinking or give them ammunition. And I think Charles had not that missionary spirit at all. But I have no doubt much the best of the humour and the aliveness of the writing came from Charles."

In spring 1938 provincial elections were called in Saskatchewan. From the middle of May Grace campaigned for CCF candidates across the parched province. With one candidate after another she travelled roads drifted deep with dust, speaking at large and small meetings and calling on individual voters. "In those days," she mused, "the great joy was that you could campaign or work with a group in any part of Canada and you felt just as much at home as you did at home because you had the common philosophy."

Her month-long campaign trip was epitomized by an hour on a Gull Lake farm. "As we drove up there was a farmer unhitching his horses, just walking skeletons, and I made some remark and the man who was with me said, 'Be careful, he feels terrible about it.' The young woman had been from the East and had come and married on the prairies. To get lunch she went to her root cellar and brought up a jar of prairie chicken which was just like she was entertaining royalty. And you know I could hardly bring myself to eat it. On the other hand I have never forgotten it.

"Yet those people came through and they were vigorous about it. They seem to keep their hearts and their minds active. As we drove around those roads in between meetings the farmer with me knew exactly how everybody was standing. The [local CCF] would work them like you'd weed a garden. That's how they got elected, just good hard work and nothing but their bare hands really to worth with, but they had dedication and devotion and belief."

Very much in love, Grace and Angus were lonesome for one another while Grace spent the late spring in Saskatchewan and he worked in his Vancouver constituency. She teased him from Regina, "I'm glad you are missing me. If I could find anyone here to make love to I'd be tempted to do so because I'm missing you. But they're all old or dumb or—something. Only one had possibilities, but I wasn't long enough in the riding to make a thoroughly artistic job of it. Now are you curious?!!"

When election day came Grace's efforts in Saskatchewan helped the CCF win eleven seats in the provincial legislature. The party now held the status of official opposition to the Liberal government of William Paterson.

By this time Woodsworth's health was worsening. Nearly blind in one eye due to high blood pressure, he too had been campaigning across Saskatchewan on a different circuit from Grace's. Father and daughter arrived home in Ottawa the same day but on separate trains. The next day at breakfast Grace asked, "Well, how did the campaign go for you, Father?" She sadly recalled, "He looked perfectly blankly at me and said, 'What campaign?' My mother was there too, and she had to talk to him for hours before she got him back into understanding what it was all about."

At the CCF national convention in July 1938 at Edmonton, Grace presented the national council resolution on co-operatives to unanimous approval. She had taken responsibility for fostering the party's links with the co-operative movement, believing that co-operatives could be an antidote to capitalism, a positive path by which people could "escape from economic bondage." But in a world rapidly being pushed to the brink of war, co-operatives were pushed into the background.

Displaying her lifelong opposition to a special place for women in politics simply because they were females, Grace told a reporter at the Edmonton national convention that Parliament needed women not as women, but as qualified persons. "There is no division between men and women as far as intellectual ability is concerned, and the sexes are equally fitted to do the same work if they apply themselves," she stressed. "Women have a capacity for detail and practical work that is invaluable in the business of procuring reform legislation." By now reform, not the "peaceful revolution" she had demanded at the 1933 Regina convention, was Grace's goal.

Hitler's overriding goal to create a larger Germany and unify all ethnic Germans in one great Fatherland was absorbing more world attention every day. Canada heard the thudding of Nazi jackboots with apprehension. In the House Woodsworth warned of the growing assumption in business circles that Canada was to become an arsenal for Britain. He feared that as Canadian firms invested in the manufacture of war material, hired workers, and built plants, these vested interests would draw the Dominion directly into the looming war.

But this opinion brought him into increasing conflict with most of his own party. Coldwell, Douglas, MacNeil and MacInnis headed a larger group within the CCF for collective action against totalitarian aggression. Grace understood her father's philosophy but stood with the larger group; the split over war and peace was dividing the Woodsworth family. "Mrs. W. is a pacifist," Angus wrote in 1939. "I am not. At the same time I am not a militarist. We both believe that the capitalist system breeds war, but we had war before we had capitalism. Mrs. W. is an anarchist when it comes to matters of peace and war. She accepts force as a means of keeping the peace in the community, but she rejects force as a means of keeping peace in the world. I believe that we must first have order in our international affairs before we can have peace. Aggressor nations must be stopped by those nations which believe in international order . . . we must try and choose that course which will extend the power of the people and curb the power of individuals."

As 1938 gave way to 1939, Grace reflected soberly on the progress of Canada's socialists. Lacking leadership, the CCF was in the doldrums in Ontario. It was riddled by communists in British Columbia and had lost much ground to Social Credit in Alberta. The party was practically comatose in the Maritimes, despite its first union affiliation by the United Mine Workers in October 1938. They were won over by Angus and David Lewis who spoke at every mining centre in Nova Scotia that summer, once they were convinced the UMW's interest in political affiliation was not sponsored by the communists. In Quebec the church had denounced the CCF, and the party was practically nonexistent. It was strongest in Saskatchewan and Manitoba, but even there was divided.

In the first week of 1939 Angus was asked to speak to a conference of the League for Social Reconstruction on the crisis in socialist policy. "Why do college-trained people almost invariably think of human progress in terms of violent jerks ahead, succeeded by periods of complete inertia?" Grace reflected. "They think in terms of crises. They are the ones who fall victims to the fear psychology used by the communists to prevent constructive action . . . . To me, there is no substitute for the steady process of education by doing. One cannot build a socialist movement on the shifting sands of fear. War and fascism are great evils. They can be combatted only by the intelligent creation of a society in which community ownership and democratic control will supersede the present tooth and claw struggle. To me, there is no present crisis in socialist policy."

Grace and Angus enjoyed a marvellous seventh anniversary on January 23, 1939. "We started off to work on the coldest morning of the winter so far—fifteen degrees below zero. Angus spent the morning preparing his speech on the Address—his first speech in the House this session.

"About eleven o'clock there came roses for me—lovely Talisman buds with their rosy saffron petals enclosing a deep rose heart. Angus never forgets those roses on our anniversary. Sometimes they are of one colour, sometimes of another, but always they remind me of that first 23rd of January. They were golden that time.

"We had lunch and hurried back to the House. Angus was in great trim and went down to speak with one of the roses in his buttonhole. He made a fine speech—clear, logical and forceful. I heard it from the Ladies' Gallery. He finished just before six and went down to correct the proofs while I typed an account of the speech for four of the CCF papers and got the letters away Air Mail.

"Just before eight we caught a street car and went over to Hull for the next part of our anniversary ritual. At Henri Berger's we found a table for two and had a really elegant meal . . . . Then at nine-thirty we slipped into the Cartier Theatre in Hull to see Bette Davis and Errol Flynn in The Sisters . . . . The weather being much milder, we walked home across the bridge. We had had a day so happy that we shall long remember it. Most of our days are minor celebrations; just being together fills us with deep contentment."

Conflict over the role of David Lewis surfaced at a CCF caucus meeting two days later. Angus's diary comment hints at the problem. "J.S.W. does not like having Lewis sitting in at caucus meetings. I think he has taken a prejudice to Lewis. I wish I were absolutely sure of Lewis myself. One suggestion in regard to an aspect of our movement made by him recently has disturbed me greatly. Yet it seems almost impossible to me that he should be playing a double game." Lewis believed the CCF could be strengthened by working closely with the trade unions, some of which were controlled by communists. Angus and Grace were entirely opposed to any hint of a united front.

The issue arose a few weeks later at an informal meeting called by Charles Millard, regional director of the United Auto Workers of America, attended by Angus and David Lewis, and two other Ontario CCF leaders. The influence of the communists versus the lack of CCF influence in the trade unions was the main topic, with auto, steel and mineworkers' unions as prime examples. Lewis noted: "This situation is of importance not only from the trade union angle but also politically. The communists are likely to make a strong attempt to control the CIO in Canada should a separate organization eventually be formed as a result of expulsions from the Trades and Labour Congress. The communists in the unions are likely to do everything possible to prevent the unions from identifying themselves with the CCF under present circumstances. This is of the greatest importance in Ontario." This was to be a crucial issue throughout the 1940s and 1950s. Twenty years would elapse before the issue would be sufficiently resolved for the CCF and Canadian trade unions to join forces, creating the New Democratic Party.

As key members of the CCF inner circle who decided party policy and direction, Grace and Angus worked not only through formal avenues such as council meetings and conventions, but also through informal socializing. To a dinner one January night they invited Hugh Keenleyside of the Department of External Affairs and his wife; M.J. Coldwell and his frail wife Nora; and red-haired Grant MacNeil, MP for Vancouver North. MacNeil, a World War One veteran, was the CCF military critic. This intelligent man with shrewd, kind eyes was realistic about Canada's preparation for war. As early as 1937 he predicted Canadian armed forces would fight at Britain's side. A few weeks later Grace and Angus entertained Sophie and David Lewis; Islay Johnston, from the Department of Agriculture; Kathleen Willsher, a secretary in the British High Commissioner's Office; teacher Muriel Kerr; Bob Inch, secretary of the League of Nations; and Jack Pickersgill, secretary to Prime Minister Mackenzie King, who had known Grace when they were undergraduates at the University of Manitoba. Conversation was on foreign policy, and all three viewpoints then prevailing in Canada were represented. "Jack Pickersgill is an isolationist, pure and simple," wrote Grace in her diary. "There were plenty of collective security advocates present to ensure an invigorating evening. Muriel Kerr has probably some Empire leanings. Anyway the entire field was well covered."

Woodsworth's health was deteriorating daily. In February Grace was in Toronto at a national conference on housing when Angus became worried about his failing father-in-law. "He had a complete loss of memory for a short while this morning," Angus wrote. "He seemed all right when he came into the living room, and we sat down to breakfast and talked about various things. He asked me when Grace was coming home. A few minutes afterwards he asked me, 'Where is Grace?' He realized himself that his mind was all confused. He said he felt as if he were still dreaming. He waited for me to walk to the buildings with him, something he had not done before this session." Grant MacNeil, noting these changes, feared that Woodsworth might "do something thing that may embarrass the group."

At the housing conference in the newly completed Royal York Hotel, Grace represented the Vancouver Housing Association and also, unofficially, the Vancouver City Council; her CCF colleague Helena Gutteridge was its Building, Civic Planning and Parks Committee chairperson. As the only woman on the steering committee, Grace was expected to pour the tea, a role she noted caustically in her diary.

Conflict at the conference arose over the need for low-cost housing versus the need to maintain union wage standards. In a steering committee meeting, Grace noted: "Mr. [F.W.] Nichols, National Director of Housing, expressed the opinion, 'that the sooner the present union standards were broken down the better. Builders couldn't afford them.' I was indignant and so, fortunately, were two others." In the end the conference passed a resolution on the need to maintain union standards, and another to make the National Housing Act (1938) operational.

When the conference closed, Grace slipped into her role as national president of the CCYM and embarked on a week-long tour of Montreal and Ontario cities organizing young people and generating enthusiasm for the party. In Windsor she addressed the annual CCF banquet, where she embraced two ideas that other people saw as conflicting—a policy of collective security through the League of Nations, and a policy of putting Canada first. "I believe that until Canadians have a real Canada-first policy we're not going to get very far in our social change," she said. "There have been far too many people spending their time and energy passing resolutions for Spain and China, and leaving none for the one country where they can make some social change, Canada. Until we have a real functioning League of Nations we won't have international law or justice either."

She dismissed as a "pipe dream" hopes of securing social advance through parades, mass meetings and agitation. "The human animal hates new things,"

Grace told the crowd, a refrain she would repeat often through the years. "The old socialist doctrine of waiting for the people to sink to the depths of hunger and despair until a desperate populace turns to the party has been found faulty. That only breeds fascist tendencies such as arose in postwar Germany." She concluded with a ringing plea for a CCF coalition of all groups and classes with anything to gain from a new social order: trade unions, co-operatives, educational institutions, farmers, small business and professional people, manual labourers, young people and the unemployed.

Grace returned to Ottawa with a touch of the flu and spent a week in bed. To spur her energy she went back to drinking coffee after four months of abstinence. She told their diary: "Angus says that's how religious sects get many converts—wait till they're weak in body and in will. The coffee was just as comforting as the religion and a deal more stimulating . . . . We still regard each other's company as the supreme luxury."

At the end of April, Senator Cairine Wilson selected Grace as her substitute to present a speech on the issue of refugees, to a meeting of the Smiths Falls, Ontario Council of Women. Cairine Wilson of Montreal, founder of the National Federation of Liberal Women, was the first woman appointed to the Senate in 1930, the year after the landmark Privy Council decision that Canadian women were persons before the law, and so eligible to sit in the Senate. Grace told the Smiths Falls women she did not favour any wholesale movement of refugees into Canada but did support admittance of a carefully selected group. She felt that unemployment would be helped, not hindered, by admitting them; most refugees had some capital and could create jobs. Distinguished doctors, scientists, musicians, artists, artisans and men of special skill were among the refugees. She stressed that of the million and a half people driven from greater Germany less than half were Jewish. This emphasis on the capital possessions and non-Jewishness of most refugees was quite uncharacteristic of Grace's attitudes in general, and may perhaps reflect the fact she was pinch-hitting for the far more conservative Senator Wilson.

In contrast to the more than a quarter-million immigrants entering Canada annually when Grace was born, only sixteen thousand were admitted in 1938. Under the impact of the Depression, the government had adopted drastic orders in council to minimize immigration. After the Depression eased, labour and farmers opposed immigration because they believed it would present severe economic competition. The CCF was the one party in the House which supported admitting even the most agonized refugees.

Of more concern to Grace and Angus was the 1937 sale of huge timber and mining properties on Vancouver Island and the Queen Charlotte Islands to Japanese interests. Press reports indicated that more than a billion board feet of timber and ten million tons of iron ore were involved in the deal, consummated under Premier Duff Pattullo's Liberal government. In an article for the *Federationist* Angus commented on "the hypocrisy of those who for personal and party advantage stir up race hatred and race prejudices."

By this time Grace and Angus were well known within the Japanese community as two of the precious few politicians without prejudice, and hypocrisy on the issue was intolerable to them. "Don't you remember," Angus wrote, "how we were told that if we gave the vote to Canadians of Oriental origin there was grave danger that some day we would have 'One Duck Lung' for Premier? How they made cold shivers run down our spines with stories of the danger of a Japanese invasion of this province! That was just before the election. Less than three weeks after electing a Liberal government to protect us from the wiles of the Oriental we read in our papers that a large slice of our natural resources has been handed over, not to Canadian born Orientals, but to aliens. To Japanese living in Japan, not Japanese born and living in BC."

All of Canada spruced up to welcome King George VI and Queen Mary on May 17, 1939. Designed to reassure the Commonwealth about the stability of the British monarchy after the abdication of the Duke of Windsor and to ensure support in the Dominions in case of war, the tour was a spectacular success. Grace was not a monarchist, but she took a spectator's pleasure in the visit.

That same month, Grace and Angus led the first CCF school for organizers in Ontario. Grace taught methods of tactful approach, how to organize a constituency for elections and how to conduct club activities. Angus led discussion on work with trade unions, and Woodsworth, Coldwell, Douglas and MacNeil showed budding organizers how to teach various aspects of the CCF program.

Grace and Angus returned to Vancouver in time for the June 1939 provincial CCF convention and took a downtown office in the Holden Building that would serve as CCF headquarters for years. Grace concentrated on organizing for the CCYM and especially on activities for Gabriola Island where the CCF summer camp was in its sixth year.

Grace celebrated her thirty-fourth birthday at the summer camp. She marked the occasion with a short essay, "Stocktaking at 34," a personal appraisal of uncompromising frankness. She began by comparing herself with the inventory of herself written when she was twenty. Her health was improved, she noted, "due mainly to dietary improvements and a happy marriage . . . . My disposition and general outlook on life have altered for the better as well. Many irritating features of character remain, stubbornness and a desire to have my own way being outstanding."

In Grace's eyes her achievements to date—the political and educational speeches, the articles, the CCYM organizing, the pamphlets—were unsatisfactory and petty, and she questioned her future direction. She saw two likely options: work with people or writing. Her work with people would continue to be organization of small study or discussion groups, she surmised. Her only interest in writing would be "to produce something of value in the achievement of socialism in Canada." She wanted to respond to the need of CCF clubs and study groups "clamouring for something to study," but felt the party had "nothing suitable to give them."

For the time being Grace concentrated on building the CCYM, which had elected Tommy Douglas leader in 1934 at its convention in Winnipeg. There Grace met Tommy for the first time since they were kids at the All People's Mission swimming pool. "The young people were delighted with him," she said. But Douglas was elected to Parliament in 1935, and the CCYM remained a collection of scattered groups of enthusiastic young socialists with no firm leadership until Grace took charge in 1938. She established the first regular channels of contact from province to province, and in 1939 set up the first CCYM national headquarters in Toronto.

Her strategy for attracting and involving young people was twofold. First she planned plenty of social affairs, dances and parties as well as sports events like ski trips to Grouse Mountain, both to raise money and to maintain contacts. Then she trained emerging leaders to spot other young people with leadership potential. The leader "gets them into study groups, speakers' classes, debating teams, dramatic groups. These are the future speakers, writers and organizers of the CCYM and later of the CCF. They are the backbone of the socialist movement," Grace wrote in the 1939 Alberta Labour Annual.

Grace wrote snappy, attractive CCYM flyers like the one issued by the CCYM national office during the winter of 1939–40, *What's In It For Me?*, in which she appealed to young people's need for a sense of achievement, the pleasure of companionship and opportunities to develop as leaders. Finally, she wrote, "Socialism has to offer a new way of life, a planned, intelligent economic and social system, a life in which there is a job for everyone who wants it, a life that guarantees comfort and security as well as mere existence, joy and satisfaction in every working day."

On August 23, 1939 Hitler and Stalin shocked the world by signing a German–Soviet non-aggression pact. In secret protocols attached to the pact Germany and Russia agreed to partition Poland, and Hitler agreed to keep out of Russian business in the eastern Baltic. Then, on September 1, 1939, Hitler's Army invaded Poland. In retaliation, on September 3, Britain and France declared war on Germany. Prime Minister King summoned Parliament to meet September 7, and meanwhile issued a proclamation declaring that "a state of apprehended war exists, and has existed as of August 25." Canada's neutrality was now a lost cause, but the exact extent and nature of Canada's participation in war was still in question.

On September 6, the CCF national council met in a long committee room in the Parliament buildings. Twenty-nine voting delegates and fifteen visitors from every province except Prince Edward Island, supplemented by provincial CCF officials, had gathered to decide a single wartime policy on which the divided party could agree. Grace and her mother were among the invited visitors. Woodsworth headed the meeting, although he had suffered a slight stroke a few days earlier.

National secretary David Lewis identified six differing strands of thought in the group. At one end of the spectrum were Angus MacInnis, Tommy Douglas, Abe Heaps and George Williams of Saskatchewan, who believed that the defeat of Hitler must be accomplished as a matter of survival for simple human decency. Many did not go that far, but objected to a position that would obligate Canada automatically to follow Britain to war. Some, especially from Quebec, objected to conscription of manpower and opposed sending forces to fight outside the country.

Others, such as Lewis, saw it as a war of mixed motives, "the common people against Hitler's aggression and the governments of Britain and France for the usual imperialist reasons." Canada's future autonomy was important to these realists as was the preservation of some semblance of unity within the CCF. From British Columbia a group of doctrinaire socialists, such as MLA Gretchen Steeves, saw the conflict strictly as an imperialist war; by their definition war was a product of imperialism. At the other end of the spectrum from Angus and Tommy was Woodsworth, whose small group of pacifist followers included the young Winnipeg preacher Stanley Knowles and fellow Manitobans Beatrice Brigden and S.J. Farmer.

Grace had come to accept the necessity of Canada's participation in the war but had grave reservations, as she wrote to a colleague in the anxious week before the council meeting: "My own desire would definitely be to keep Canadians here in Canada rather than to put even more human sacrifices on the altar of stupidity erected over so many years and in spite of the warnings of our movement and others."

Grace described her father's pivotal role in this decisive meeting. "As to his own stand there was no doubt. His voice gathered strength, his gestures became energetic, as he made a strong plea for keeping Canada out of the war or, failing that, for devoting the energies of the CCF to protesting against participation of any kind.

"The delegates listened, profoundly moved. Here was their national President, their leader whom they had loved and revered ever since they had known him, a man whose whole life had been one passionate protest against evil, pleading with them to take their stand beside him and denounce the ultimate evil, war. Every one of these men and women loathed war and feared its consequences; most of them had devoted active years to the task of trying to make sure that never would there be another war. Some of them would still take the pacifist position. But most had reached the slow conviction, along with socialists in other parts of the world, that the fascist and Nazi aggression meant inevitable war, and that the longer this was postponed, the more dreadful would grow the record of inhuman brutality and the less hope there would be for eventual democracy and peace."

Woodsworth submitted his resignation. It was refused. Then the council agreed that Woodsworth would make a separate statement expressing his own views in the emergency debate even then underway in the House.

A committee including Angus, David Lewis and Frank Scott drafted a CCF majority statement which Coldwell would deliver in the House. Reversing previous party policy, this majority statement called for qualified support of the war effort only to the extent of economic assistance, defence of Canadian shores, no military participation overseas and the preservation of democracy at home. Grace supported this national council statement which her husband, not her father, had written. No longer a pacifist, she had become a pragmatist.

Angus believed his position in favour of limited participation in the war had saved the party. "If I had opposed participation in September 1939," he wrote the following year, "the national council meeting would have broken up either without coming to a decision or by issuing a statement opposed to Canada taking a part. Either decision would have spelled the end of the CCF."

The House was hushed and solemn as Woodsworth rose to speak Friday night, September 8. The recent stroke had left his vision impaired and one side partly paralyzed. The night before Lucy had taken a few notes at his dictation and put them on cue cards in big letters. Tommy Douglas sat beside him and handed the cards up one by one to the Conscience of the Commons, the leader he loved and admired and would shortly vote against.

"While we are urged to fight for freedom and democracy," Woodsworth declared, "it should be remembered that war is the very negation of both. The victor may win; but if he does, it is by adopting the self-same tactics which he condemns in his enemy . . . it is only as we adopt new policies that this world will be at all a livable place for our children who follow us. We laud the courage of those who go to the front; yes, I have boys of my own, and I hope they are not cowards, but if any one of those boys, not from cowardice but really through belief, is willing to take his stand on this matter and, if necessary, to face a concentration camp or a firing squad, I shall be more proud of that boy than if he enlisted for the war."

His very last words in the Parliament he had served for nearly twenty years were in support of civil liberties. "I would hope that through all the restrictions and privations which necessarily must come in a war, the principles of liberty, the principles of free speech and the principles of a free Parliament . . . may be upheld to the very end of the war—however long it may last."

The father of the Canadian peace movement had spoken. Although he represented only a small minority of opinion in the country, he succeeded to this extent: Grace and his other children absorbed, honoured and lived his values if not his absolute pacifism. They lived his pride in the courage of standing for one's heartfelt convictions, no matter if one stands alone against the world, the party and the family. Yet he had taught his children not to adhere mindlessly to yesterday's wisdom. Grace remembered how he told her as a little girl, "What was good enough for my father is *not* good enough for me."

"We agreed to differ," Grace recalled lovingly. "He never gave up on me. He spent the last winter of his life in our place in Vancouver, and I remember him trying very hard to work on me, to get the pacifist position. I gave him my position and the way it had evolved. He was disappointed; it was his most cherished thing, and nobody would follow him. Among my mother, my father and Angus and myself there was absolutely no bitterness or recrimination. We each believed in the other's sincerity."

A large part of the CCF youth movement agreed with Woodsworth's pacifist stance. As national president of the CCYM, Grace received urgent letters from provincial CCYM people asking, "Is it considered a capitalist war?" and "If conscription is put into force, how should members of the CCYM act?" The party went on record opposing conscription.

By the end of April 1940 Hitler had overtaken Denmark and Norway. He took Belgium and the Netherlands in May. The world was aghast when France fell in June and Hitler set up the Vichy collaborationist government under General Petain.

The pacifism of the Regina Manifesto, which had become "conscription of wealth rather than manpower" in September 1939, soon changed to "no conscription of manpower without the conscription of wealth." By 1942 it became "conscription of wealth as well as manpower." When the King government introduced conscription in the House in 1942, the CCF supported it. Grace found herself defending the national council statement against attacks from CCYM members disillusioned that the absolute pacifism of their beloved idealistic leader had been repudiated.

Canadian communists did an about-face on the signing of the German–Soviet non-aggression pact. No longer were they pushing a united front against Nazism; now they were operating in sympathy with the fascists.

When the British Columbia legislature met in November 1939, CCF member Gretchen Steeves made a speech "questioning the nature of Canada's war aims and denouncing the capitalist imperialism of many countries which had helped destroy the League of Nations and had laid the foundations for the present conflict." Grace believed the speech did "considerable damage to our cause both within and outside the movement," because it deepened the existing impression that the CCF was divided on the war issue. Grace asked why Steeves did not present the national council policy she helped to form in Ottawa. Grace had warned Steeves "not to take this line" before the Victoria session. She respected Steeves, a Dutch national and lawyer who had married a World War One prisoner of war, but this was neither the first nor the last time they were at odds.

In January Angus went to Ottawa for a short emergency session of Parliament, leaving Grace to manage the Vancouver CCF office. She remembered constantly taking criticism for supporting the national council's position on the war. "People attacking Angus's stand, you see. They weren't attacking Father's stand but attacking Angus's stand and my stand. And I remember feeling sort of sad that it had to be so divisive, but I wasn't in any way either frightened or apologetic. I just simply said, 'Well, that's the way it is. That's the way it has to be.'"

Prime Minister King called a federal election for March 26, 1940. The CCF election program emphasized the supremacy of Parliament and civil liberties, the need to plan now for security for war industry workers and returning soldiers, and opposition to war profiteering, unfair taxes and high interest rates. Planning for postwar peacetime was high on the CCF agenda.

CCF peace aims were based on those declared by the British Labour Party. Peace should be negotiated and not dictated. Great and small nations must all recognize an international authority superior to individual states. Aggression and national armaments must be abandoned by agreement. All peoples must have the right to develop their own civilization, and the rights of national, racial and religious minorities must be respected. Imperialism must be renounced, and provision made for economic co-operation and equal access to raw materials and markets.

Grace campaigned on this platform for CCF candidates in Victoria, Kamloops, Vancouver and the Fraser Valley. When the votes were counted, the CCF had won eight seats, an increase of one. Angus had held Vancouver East, Woodsworth was re-elected by a slim margin, winning because he had captured enough of the overseas service vote. Although he had opposed the war, the soldiers trusted him. Coldwell and Douglas were back to sit beside three new Saskatchewan members: Percy Wright, Sandy Nicholson, and Hugh Castleden. For the first time Nova Scotia returned a CCF member, Clarence Gillis from Cape Breton. Grant MacNeil and Abe Heaps were defeated.

The House opened May 16, 1940. Two days later, at a meeting of the CCF national executive with the caucus in a committee room off the Parliamentary Reading Room, Woodsworth had a severe stroke.

"I remember so well the scene," Grace recalled. "My father was the chairman of the meeting with David Lewis on one side of him and Coldwell on the other . . . and he reached for a glass of water and his hand just fell and he said 'I think I've had a stroke.' And all the time Mother never budged. She believed in letting him alone; she wanted to budge, but she didn't. Then one of the members of Parliament who was a doctor, he was a Liberal member, we called him."

Completely paralyzed on the right side, Woodsworth spent two months recuperating in hospital and nursing home before leaving with Lucy for the Cavan farm and then for the family home in Winnipeg. Grace wrote sadly, "Father had come home to a home peopled only by memories, the memories of those who had been here and were gone. Now he had been struck down. There was no one left to keep the old home alive."

Grace fought a family battle in fine style at the July meeting of the Canadian Youth Congress (CYC) in Montreal. The conflict erupted between Grace, in her role as CCYM national president, and her cousin Ken Woodsworth, national secretary of the CYC, over the abrupt reversal of the CYC position on the war. By the end of the three-day meeting seven major national organizations had withdrawn from the CYC and many others, including the CCYM, dissociated themselves from the report of the congress.

Grace believed her cousin Ken was doing the work of the Communist Party of Canada (CPC), if he was not actually a member. The policy the CPC had pursued since 1935 of building a united front against fascism with other "progressive" groups had been reversed by the August 1939 German–Soviet non-aggression pact. When the 1940 CYC meeting did a similar flip-flop, Grace vigorously objected. Trade union groups, church groups and the Young Liberals withdrew from the Youth Congress in protest.

Her report to the CCYM outlined the points of conflict. "Since its inception in 1936," Grace wrote, the CYC had "put its weight solidly behind the efforts of the democratic nations to halt the spread of aggression." In 1939 the Congress had favoured conscription in the event of direct military attack on Canada, or if Canada participated in a group of nations "in defence against aggressors." The CYC had then issued a statement that until the Nazi system was destroyed there could be no peace. The CCYM had actively supported the CYC in that position.

"From the outset of this year's congress," Grace went on, "it became evident that a fundamental change had taken place in policy . . . . Delegates heard with amazement the secretary's report. All mention of the war was completely excluded except in so far was it related to civil liberties and economic conditions within Canada." The planned discussion group on conscription and war aims had been dropped.

Grace and David Lewis, two of the nine CCYM delegates, attempted unsuccessfully to debate Ken Woodsworth's report; the chair ruled it was not debatable. Attempting to advance CCYM positions in the democracy and civil liberties group, Grace proposed the nationalization of industry and a one hundred percent excess profits tax. But the group would hear nothing except "wholesale condemnation of the Government," Grace wrote.

In a final attempt to secure clear-cut endorsement of support for the war as taken by earlier youth congresses, Grace supported an amendment to the report of the democracy and civil liberties group which said, "Youth in particular is anxious and willing to discharge its duty to the full in support of the war against Nazism and fascism, recognizing that a victory for the totalitarian forces would mean the complete destruction of all liberty and democracy." When this amendment was attacked and overwhelmingly defeated, Grace wrote, "We realized that Congress leaders had allowed certain elements in the Congress to bring about changes in Congress policy since the meeting last summer in Winnipeg." Those elements, Grace believed, were the communists.

Grace wasted no time in letting the general CCF membership know of her concerns. In an article for *Canadian Forum* in August, "Crisis in the Youth Congress," she attacked the congress for conducting its meeting undemocratically, for cutting out all direct discussion of the war and for not truly representing Canadian youth. On this last point, Grace meant that the 1940 congress was packed with delegates from Toronto and Montreal listed as "miscellaneous." Coupled with a decrease in delegates from legitimate groups, she believed the result was a congress stacked with communist sympathizers. She pointed out a parallel crisis in the American Youth Congress, accusing it too of being "controlled by and in the interests of an organization whose policy, both domestic and foreign, is dependent upon the turn of Soviet foreign policy."

Ken Woodsworth responded immediately in the pages of the *Canadian Tribune* newspaper, published in Toronto by the Communist Party of Canada. He pointed to a statement approved by the 1940 CYC, "We believe the forces of totalitarianism must be defeated," but admitted a change in the CYC program which "reflected the profound changes which have occurred in events . . . which took place through free and democratic discussion during a whole year, a natural expression of the changing thoughts of the young people." Canadian youths held a variety of convictions about the war, Ken observed, pointing out the very evident divisions within the CCF. "Her [Grace's] criticism of the congress on this score is nonsense," Ken wrote, "and dragging in the usual 'whipping-boy' of communism hardly increases one's respect for her argument."

He acknowledged that attendance was lower than in previous years and attributed this to "widespread and open intimidation, both official and private." A 1941 memorandum on the Youth Congress lists Royal Canadian Mounted Police (RCMP) activities with regard to the CYC, including a raid on the Montreal office in April 1940, interrogation of the national chairman in May followed by his resignation, and a threat to close the Saskatchewan CYC meeting in June 1940 if any subversive opinions were expressed. After the Montreal CYC meeting in July, some French Canadian members of the CYC national committee were arrested but released without charges.

Grace found herself in the uncomfortable position of championing a stand taken previously by the united front, to which she had long been opposed, and standing up for vigorous pursuit of the war—a complete turnaround from her previous pacifism.

But she was not alone in her suspicions of communist domination of the CYC. A general "Dear Sir" letter circulated in 1941 by the CYC national committee and signed by Kenneth Woodsworth, secretary, was sent to J.S. Woodsworth. In it Ken described the CYC as a thoroughly democratic organization that had wide and representative support and had never acted illegally. Objecting to "a series of intimidating acts during the past year," he wrote: "Now the Minister of Justice intimates quite directly that it is a communist organization; and therefore, we assume, may be declared illegal." Ken appealed for help "in securing a fair judgment on the basis of facts" and did not forget family links. A personal "hope you are well" note to his uncle James appears in the margin of the letter.

J.S. Woodsworth was seriously ill and could do little. But the point became moot June 22, 1941 when Germany attacked Russia, voiding the German–Soviet non-aggression pact and mandating yet another total turn-around in the attitude of the CPC.

Within the family the very public breach between Woodsworths was submerged. Grace recalled, "Father was dead against communism or any communist ideas or thinking. But I remember one day when Mother said that Ken was coming to lunch or something, and I said, 'Well, I'll be going out.' And Mother said, 'Now look, I know how you feel about Ken.' She didn't even say 'You're right' or anything. 'But remember, your Father has family ties that mean a great deal to him, so you just put your pride in your pocket and come.' And I came. But again, there was this wall. I was a very strait-laced person when it came to—you see I'd had to fight for the life of the party against communist control. And I could sniff it out a mile away. I knew what it was and I knew how to recognize it . . . . There wouldn't be any talk [about political differences]. My father knew perfectly well the situation too. It would be purely family affairs. Well, purely family affairs never interested me as such."

In Ottawa the House adjourned August 7, 1940 after declaring Nazi, fascist, communist and Jehovah's Witness groups illegal under the Defence of Canada Regulations. The MPs had passed a law giving the government the right to conscript men for training and service in Canada but not overseas. Grace and Angus climbed into their first car, a black Austin, bound for Vancouver.

On August 17, the day Prime Minister Mackenzie King and US President Franklin Roosevelt were creating a Permanent Joint Board of Defence in Ogdensburg, New York, Angus and Grace had a car accident. On a narrow gravel road in Plains, Montana, the car brakes failed. "The car turned over several times and stopped in loose rock right side up," Angus wrote. "We were shaken and bruised but not badly hurt. I was mad, but also glad that I was driving myself, otherwise I would be cross with Grace and perhaps blame her for the accident. Grace was magnificent. She did not complain or find fault." The car was restored at the "enormous cost of $510" but, as good as new, it served for years.

When they reached the coast, for the first time in twenty-seven years Angus found himself without a place of his own in Vancouver. His mother had died and his sister Christine, in poor health, had rented out the MacInnis family home on Prince Edward Street. Grace and Angus rented "a rather poor apartment," but would not stay long. At the end of September Woodsworth had a relapse which impaired his speech, and Grace travelled to Winnipeg in October to persuade her parents to give up their house for a smaller place. They decided to move to Vancouver where several of the children were settled and winters were milder. Grace described those last melancholy days at 60 Maryland Street. "For several weeks we spent our evenings reading old letters and looking at faded souvenirs while Father lost himself in the years and among the friends of long ago. Some of this mass of material he sent to other members of the family; much of it he burned, accompanying Mother or me to the furnace and watching the last flare as it died down to ashes." By vigorous persuasion Grace managed to save a few precious notebooks for the archives.

At the end of October the sixth CCF national convention took place in Winnipeg. Woodsworth was in the city, but too ill to attend. He tried again to resign, but his resignation was not accepted; instead the beloved leader was eased into the newly created position of honorary president. Coldwell was again elected national chairman; Angus was unopposed for national vice-chairman. Grace had the satisfaction of receiving an enthusiastic vote of thanks for her work as secretary of the parliamentary caucus. Postwar social planning emerged as a prime CCF issue at this convention.

Christmas 1940 brought a big Woodsworth family dinner in BC at the Langley Prairie home of Dr. Arthur Rose and his wife Edith, James's youngest sister, with whom James and Lucy had moved in after leaving Winnipeg. James sat up with the family most of the day, but the celebration was overshadowed by his poor health. Angus wrote frankly, "Mr. Woodsworth . . . is burnt out. I doubt very much if he was ever very happy at home or if the family was happy when he was at home. My own feeling when visiting there, both before and since Grace and I were married, was that he was morose and tense to a very marked degree. He seemed afraid that he might waste a minute. There was no joking, no relaxing, no fun. The family must keep quiet when he was working . . . and when he went to sleep, day or night, everyone had to keep still.

"He was seldom in good humour for conversation unless he could do most of the talking or he had 'persons of quality' to talk to. At this time his strong views on the war and his illness makes it rather difficult to talk freely when he is present." Angus was patient and forbearing while sharing an Ottawa apartment with his father-in-law and Grace during parliamentary sessions in the late 1930s, but he was relieved when Woodsworth moved out in spring 1940, leaving the younger couple to their private life.

Grace walked a tightrope between the two men she most cared for, her father and her husband. Each defined one pole of opinion within the party they all loved and served. She was devoted to her pacifist father, the courageous fighter for human rights and social justice who had moulded her ideals and helped her to realize them, the man whom she had followed through an open door to her life's work. She was deeply in love with her upright, compassionate, capable husband who hated war but championed the cause of democratic freedom. Angus represented the most militant of the CCF inner circle, and he was willing to shape the new socialist values required to preserve that freedom.

CHAPTER 7

Wartime MLA

G race had been asked to run for office in every province while she was working in Ottawa, but she had always refused until the demands of wartime altered her outlook. During the pinched Depression years it was thought to be greedy and unkind for a husband and wife both to work when one of their jobs could be supporting an otherwise jobless family. But war pulled all able workers into the job market; women and men alike pitched in to win.

So, when Grace was approached to contest the nomination for Vancouver–Burrard in the BC provincial election of 1941, she agreed to try her luck. "In these times," she said, "it is the duty of everyone to be in the place where most needed. My party thought my experience would be useful on the floor of the [BC] House, and so I ran."

Grace campaigned on a platform of "a Socialist government for an all out war effort." She pleaded until she was hoarse for the economic well-being of Canadians at home, who were producing the greatest contribution to Canada's war effort: essential war materials, commodities, food and clothing. "No country is stronger than the morale of its people," Grace declared convincingly, "Poverty, misery, neglect and cynicism are the greatest saboteurs in wartime." In fact Grace and Grant talked so vigorously that during this campaign they earned the nickname "Windy Burrard."

Under the leadership of Harold Winch, all the CCF candidates promised: conscription of wealth and public ownership of industries before conscription of manpower; democratic control of the war effort with representatives of farmer, labour and consumer groups on war boards; a planning board to direct housing, roads, reforestation, government-held industries and postwar plans; a graduated income tax rather than taxes on food and other necessities; community control of public utilities; universal health insurance; increased old age pensions; a provincial marketing board for agriculture; and an extension of labour's right to organize.

"THE OLD ORDER IS DYING," proclaimed the blue-and-white CCF campaign brochures, which promised a "NEW ORDER: NEW IDEAS— VICTORY ABROAD and SECURITY AT HOME."

Grace and her running mate, former MP Grant MacNeil, triumphed on October 21, 1941. Grace's eyes sparkled under her red turban as returns from riding after riding showed CCF candidates elected. "We started working eight years ago for this victory tonight," she jubilantly told her Vancouver radio audience from a microphone in the editorial offices of *The Province* newspaper. At an election-night rally, she said, "Personally, I feel a great sense of responsibility at the thought of my own election."

It was a proud night for the CCF. Fourteen party members won seats in the provincial assembly, doubling their representation and making the CCF the official opposition. The Liberals with twenty seats and Conservatives with thirteen were forced into a coalition government headed by Premier John Hart when it became apparent that neither of the old parties could command a majority. Former Premier Duff Pattullo had held his seat by the skin of his teeth against the CCF contender, and the consensus was that he could not head the next government.

J.S. Woodsworth had lived to see his eldest daughter win elected office, but "he was quite disappointed that it wasn't the House of Commons." It seemed that no matter how devotedly she worked or how much she achieved, she could never quite live up to the patriarch's standards. Still, Woodsworth was cheered somewhat by Grace's photograph on the front page of the *Vancouver Sun* the day after the election. Although he could no longer take part in Parliament, technically Woodsworth still held his seat as MP for Winnipeg North; with Angus also in the House of Commons, Grace's election victory made her the first person in Canada to hold elected office simultaneously with a parent and a spouse. Her election also meant Grace would earn her own living for the first time since 1931 when she had left teaching.

One prominent Liberal who went down to defeat in that election was BC Attorney General Gordon Wismer, KC. He lost to the CCF in Vancouver Centre, even though he tried to scare voters by linking the CCF with its old enemy, the Communist Party of Canada. When Germany had attacked the Soviet Union on June 22, 1941, breaking the German–Soviet non-aggression treaty and turning the Soviets into war allies of Britain and Canada, the CPC had once again beaten the drum for a united front, and the CCF had again rejected it. Wismer tried to tag the CCF as communist, producing as ammunition a directive sent from one section of the CPC to another which spelled out tactics for drawing the CCF into a united front.

Immediately Grace and Grant denied any association with the CPC. "We believe in all aid to Soviet Russia and none to the communist party in Canada," Grace told a rally two days after Wismer's attack. "The only labour

The three CCF women MLAs in the BC Legislature, October 29, 1941. From left: Laura Jamieson, Dorothy Gretchen Steeves, Grace (wearing a red turban).

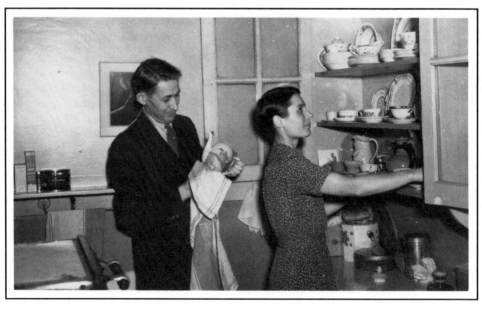

Equality reigns in the MacInnis kitchen. Angus dries a cherished coffee pot while Grace arranges the china cabinet, Vancouver, 1941.

party is the CCF. It is a Canadian product based on what is good for Canada, not what is good for Soviet Russia." The CCF provincial executive did send a speaker to a September meeting called by the Anti-Fascist Mobilization League to Aid the Soviet Union, a move Angus objected to. "The purpose of the 'League' is not to aid the Soviet Union but to rehabilitate the C.P.," he wrote. "The prestige of the CCF is being used to raise funds for the Communist Party which will be used to destroy the CCF."

But Wismer's tactic of linking the CCF with the CPC backfired. Ironically, he was bested at the polls by Wallis Lefeaux, a longtime BC socialist intellectual whom CCF MLA Gretchen Steeves termed "the best informed Marxist in the country."

Steeves was re-elected for the third time in North Vancouver, but her speech of November 1939 questioning the Canadian government's war aims was not forgotten by voters, and she was attacked as unpatriotic. Grace had disapproved of the speech, but she defended Steeves during a rally at her old alma mater, Kitsilano High School. Grace voiced the pride of the CCF in Mrs. Steeves whose only son, Hugh, was serving as a pilot officer in the RCAF during the election. He was later killed in battle. Grant MacNeil's son was also serving as a pilot officer with the Royal Air Force. Opposition charges of disloyalty did not stick in the face of facts like these.

CCF newspaper ads asked "Who Are The PATRIOTS?" The old line parties, they declared, "are prepared to endanger even our War Effort for the Sake of PROFITS. The CCF Will Eliminate War PROFITS so as to ensure Victory and Protect the People." From being the party of pacifism in 1938 the CCF had now been drawn into a contest of wartime patriotism with the old line parties.

But Grace had made up her mind, however painfully: Hitler must be defeated, and if that meant conscription, she reluctantly accepted it. She insisted, though, on the accompanying conscription of wealth, and never let people forget the supreme importance of planning for a secure postwar world. As she told a campaign audience at the old Peter Pan Ballroom, "This is a people's war, the people pay in blood and treasure; the people must plan the kind of peace to follow."

All CCF candidates used recent elections of socialist and labour governments in other parts of the Commonwealth to good effect. Grace repeatedly told her audiences: "The British kicked out Chamberlain's outfit and put in Bevin and Morrison under Churchill. New Zealand returned its 1935 Labour government in 1938. Australia turned in its old Conservative administration on a new Labour government two weeks ago. These countries are now all advancing social legislation as an essential part of their war effort. Mr. Pattullo will delay social advances. Only the CCF will push them through."

MacInnis's support for the civil rights of Japanese Canadians surfaced only once in the newspaper coverage of the campaign. The Liberal candidate in

Vancouver East, Ted Burnett, told an audience that before he left on military service he wanted to make sure the country was protected from "our real enemies, Hitler, Mussolini and 'Tokio MacInnis'." Burnett had protested proposals to extend the vote to citizens of Japanese ancestry, and Angus had branded him a Hitler. The push to move the Japanese out of BC had not yet begun.

Five women, a greater number than ever before, would be seated when the BC Legislature convened in December. Three of them were CCF members: Grace, Gretchen Steeves, and former juvenile court judge Laura Jamieson, who was re-elected to a second term. Homemaker Tilly Rolston won in Point Grey, the first Conservative woman to sit in the BC Legislature, and Victoria voters chose Liberal newspaperwoman Nancy Hodges. All except Rolston had independent careers, yet newspaper headlines echoed the prevailing belief that a woman's place is in the home: "BC Women Take Flying Leap From Kitchen to Rostrum." The *Vancouver News Herald* "Meet the Candidate" profile on Grace was headlined "Eloquent on Platform Grace MacInnis Is Still a Homemaker." In a pre-election article the *Vancouver Sun* made a point of portraying the women candidates in their traditional role, campaigning "over backyard fences, in clubrooms, over luncheon tables . . . . They are willing to forego well earned leisure to do a little 'mothering' for their less fortunate neighbours."

Most Canadian women had gained the vote a mere twenty-five years before; Quebec women only in 1940. Women in politics were still so unusual that newspaper editors seemed to feel it necessary to reassure readers that the homes of successful women politicians would not go neglected.

The only BC party leader who seemed to appreciate the role of women was the handsome, mustachioed "Clark Gable of socialism," Harold Winch, re-elected in Vancouver East. "The CCF nominated more women candidates than any other," he told a reporter. "Our recognition of the contribution of women in administrating the affairs of the province has been completely vindicated by the electors."

One of those defeated at the hands of the CCF was the party's former leader, Grace's friend from the early 1930s, Dr. Lyle Telford. The flamboyant doctor had run as an Independent–Labour candidate in Vancouver East where he was defeated by Harold Winch and Arthur Turner, CCF provincial president. The loss put an end to Dr. Telford's political career, and it was all the more ignominious after the heights to which he had risen.

When Parliament opened in November, J.S. Woodsworth was again in his seat. Broken in health, partially blind, his right arm and leg semi-paralyzed, he refused to accept that he might never again take his seat in the House. Charles, then a Vancouver *Province* reporter, described his father's last great effort. "In his tired mind a plan had formed. We thought he was too ill to get back into active work, did we? Well, somehow, some way, he would outwit us all, return to Ottawa and take his rightful and necessary place with his colleagues in the House . . . .

"Anticipation aided Father to survive that trip to Ontario. Sheer resolution prevented a breakdown on the way. But the effort cost him dearly. When, to his wide-eyed wonder, he and Mother ended up in Ottawa and he hopefully suggested he might look in on the House for a moment, his physical condition was tragically poor. As he hobbled weakly, but proudly, into the Chamber, members gave him an ovation of the kind accorded only the brave. It was his final triumph in this scene of his greatest struggles and moral conquests. A few hours later a second stroke laid him so low that even he was forced to concede his active life was over." Soon James and Lucy were back on a train, heading one last time for Vancouver.

The issue of a successor to James in Winnipeg North had arisen on that last trip to Ottawa, during a stopover James and Lucy made in Winnipeg. Grace said, "They tell a story about my father which is very revealing about his character. A group of them was discussing who his successor would be and he was in the group. They were trying to press him . . . and he said he really didn't have any idea, the convention would decide and there were a number of candidates. As the group was leaving through the door, he called after them, 'Remember, it's got to be Stanley Knowles.' I always liked that story."

During the opening days of the new session of Parliament, Angus was pressed into service as acting CCF House leader due to Woodsworth's illness and Coldwell's absence. In that capacity he urged the King government to open diplomatic relations with the Soviet Union. "Russia is now our ally," Angus argued. "If we are ultimately able to defeat Hitler and all he stands for—and God grant that we may—Russia will have an important part in making the peace and determining the new order that will follow."

In mid-November Grace celebrated her election at a CCF victory dinner in the deluxe Commodore Ballroom on Granville Street with its famous sprung dance floor. The white card program featured photographs of all fourteen CCF MLAs. They dined on crab cocktail and roast chicken and enjoyed entertainment which included accordion songs, Hawaiian novelty numbers, tap dancers, acrobats, and the Hand Hill Lariats. As Grace described the evening, "We were all a pretty spirited crowd, as rank a set of individualists as you ever saw. We were making these speeches at the banquet. We'd come fresh from the hustings, and it was inevitable that each of us would tell our best campaign story. And it became a matter of one-upmanship and the stories got a little more and more racy as they got up to some of the more outstanding members. We all had a rollicking good time, and then a few days later the provincial executive here in Vancouver received a letter from the Victoria executive saying the Vancouver executive should discipline the Members of the House because they had put on a disgraceful exhibition . . . . I loved that story." This lighthearted occasion was one of the last Grace was to enjoy for a long time.

On Thursday December 4, 1941, as the twentieth British Columbia legislative session convened, Grace first took her seat as a legislator. She occupied the second chair in from the aisle in the second row, diagonally behind Harold Winch. This first assembly took just an hour and a half to hear former Premier Duff Pattullo tender his resignation, and to choose Liberal Norman Whittaker as Speaker.

On the far reaches of the Coalition back bench sat another first-term legislator with a bright political future, William Andrew Cecil Bennett from Kelowna. Grace described him later: "He was a little bit of a smart alecky person . . . . He didn't figure much then. He was like myself; we were just both neophytes and freshies." Bennett would be elected Premier of British Columbia a dozen years later, and would be succeeded by his son.

The media dubbed Grace and Angus Vancouver's number one political family, "a couple of swell people with a sure-fire recipe for happiness." One photo showed Angus drying the china while Grace arranged it on the kitchen shelves. This happy image of equality became a MacInnis Christmas card. Angus captivated guests with the story behind each treasured piece in his extensive collection, displayed with Grace's blue baby cup and her great-grandmother's mahogany tea box.

But their comradely life was about to enter a long distance phase. They had lived and worked closely together for ten years, but now Angus would go alone to Ottawa for the session, and on January 23 the couple would celebrate their tenth anniversary apart. "Grace's election spoils one part of our life together," admitted Angus sorrowfully. Their duty to the cause must be done, but work was really only fun when they were together.

On December 7, three days after Grace took her seat in the Legislature, the Japanese bombed Pearl Harbor in a sneak early-morning attack, wiping out most of the American Pacific Fleet stationed at Honolulu. During the next four days Japan attacked Hong Kong, Manila, Singapore and various points in Malaya and Thailand. Canada declared war on Japan within twenty-four hours, before other Commonwealth nations, and even before the United States. Canadians realized with a profound chill that their own country was in mortal danger, and those living on BC's Pacific coast were the most fearful of all Canadians.

"It is hard to believe now the atmosphere of real panic that developed here after Pearl Harbor," Grace recalled. "There was a fear that we were going to be invaded from Japan or attacked from Japan, and that all these people who were here of Japanese origin would then be available for combat troops for the Japanese, and that there were spies in all the little coves and inlets. Now that was the general perception, not that of some of us in the CCF. The whole difference was that some of us firmly held to the fact that these are not Japanese, these are Canadians. Other people called them 'Japs,' and to them, they were aliens. But some CCFers were very much alarmed because of the political consequences of our stand, and they really wanted to backwater and keep quiet on the thing."

The day after Pearl Harbor, the Royal Canadian Navy began to impound the twelve hundred vessels in the Japanese Canadian fishing fleet. All Japanese in Canada were compelled to register with the government, thirty-eight Japanese aliens were taken into RCMP custody, Japanese language schools and newspapers were closed, and the twenty-one thousand Japanese Canadians in British Columbia were plunged into extreme anxiety.

The outbreak of war in the Pacific made Woodsworth incomparably sad. Grace later wrote, "My father lay in bed in our little apartment in Vancouver, the windows blacked out against the danger of Japanese invasion, listening to the drone of planes overhead, thinking about the horror of this new world conflict. Doubts came upon him of the value of his work, of the value of human existence itself in the face of such barbarity, but always he regained his faith that somehow right would triumph, that some day humanity would outgrow the brute within it."

For the last time the family celebrated the Christmas holiday with Father in Grace and Angus's suite at the Montrose Apartments. James, Lucy, Charles, Bruce, Angus's sister Christine and his niece Violet gathered around the dinner table. At that moment determined Russians were driving German tanks from the gates of Moscow; the Germans were falling back in the same bitter cold that defeated Napoleon in 1812. Across the Pacific in Hong Kong, Canadian and British forces capitulated under Japanese attack. The Christmas 1941 fall of Hong Kong crystallized Canadian attitudes against Japanese Canadians, particularly on the West Coast, and prompted scattered incidents of violence. It also led Premier John Hart, many other BC politicians and a large segment of the public to furiously demand internment for Japanese Canadians.

When the BC Legislature reconvened early in January, the legislative buildings were ready for an air raid. Only one door to the classical stone buildings was open, most windows were blacked out, and glass panels in office doors were covered with cardboard and wood. The light bulbs in the long corridors were now amber, and some complained the darkness made it difficult to negotiate stairs. In the stairwells signs directed people to basement air raid shelters far below the earth's surface. The division bell would be used to warn of attack.

Grace was appointed to the Committee on Municipal Matters, as were the other CCF women, and to the Social Welfare Committee along with all the other women in the House. Other social welfare committee members were former Premier Duff Pattullo and Ernest Winch, father of CCF House leader Harold, who had refused to name Grace a Socialist Party of Canada delegate for the first national CCF convention at Regina.

For the six-week provincial legislative session, Grace took a room in the historic Churchill Hotel on Government Street, built on the site of Victoria's original fort. A five-minute walk along the Inner Harbour seawall by the grand Empress Hotel brought her to the Legislative Building.

The second member from Burrard gave her maiden speech January 15, 1942 in the debate in reply to the throne speech presented by a Liberal–Conservative coalition government. The CCF had declined to join the coalition, preferring to play a role in vigorous opposition to the entire capitalist system. Some observers believed the political situation in British Columbia foreshadowed what would happen across Canada. As the CCF gained in strength, they believed, it would force the Liberals and Conservatives into coalition and thereby become the only opposition with a real alternative program.

In this first speech Grace advanced the urgency of planning to serve community rather than private interests. "We in this group are not fighting to maintain a system of free enterprise in this country, nor are the voters who sent us here," she declared in her fine, firm voice. "We have no intention of allowing Huntley Drummond [President, Bank of Montreal] or anyone else to have us fight this war if it is to shove us back into a system of private enterprise with its unemployment, degradation and insecurity."

Despite the wartime environment of fear and intolerance, Grace idealistically affirmed that racial hatreds should not be stirred up as a substitute for giving the Canadian people a real goal for democracy. "Our way in the CCF is to take the mock out of democracy," she told the MLAs. "Our group in the Legislature has no intention of lending ourselves to this system of race hatreds, or any other Nazi-inspired hatreds. If the people of Canada too did not feel that way we might just as well call off this war now. The people of Canada, we feel, are fighting this war so that democracy might be born."

The war effort in Canada would not be sincere, she said, until equality of sacrifice occurred. She called for a ceiling on incomes and a minimum standard of living. Rationing had to come, and a minimum diet sufficient to maintain nutrition and health would have to be established. Social justice determined civilian morale, Grace insisted, in war and in peace. No pressure by minority groups should be allowed to stand in the way, she finished with a flourish.

Always working for ways to interest the public in the political process and attract publicity for CCF ideas, Grace was the first to advance the idea of radio broadcasts from the Legislature. When she made the suggestion in that speech, "tradition-steeped members of the legislature skipped a breath." At that time there was no hansard, no written record of debates, so Grace believed radio broadcasts were essential to keep the public informed. Live broadcast coverage of the legislature would not become a reality for nearly forty years; meanwhile her maiden speech was considered significant as a news event, and was covered by the three Vancouver and two Victoria daily newspapers.

The *Vancouver Sun* made it the subject of editorial comment the following Saturday. The writer acknowledged her concern for social justice, but reminded readers that Canada and her allies were engaged in a deadly war for survival, "not only as democratic nations—but as nations at all." The writer advised Grace to put aside for the time the "minor issues of free enterprise and planned economy." But the *Province* staff correspondent saw Grace as highly radical: "in her advocacy of the new order as viewed by the CCF she is a militant of the militants." The writer gave her credit as a clever and experienced speaker with a "splendid command of language and attractive personality."

Provincial Secretary George Pearson, a Liberal from Nanaimo and the Gulf Islands, was not in the House for Grace's maiden speech. He was on his way back from Ottawa, quite satisfied with himself for leading a delegation of BC politicians to press the King government to intern the province's twenty-two thousand residents of Japanese ancestry. The BC politicians ran into opposition from the Canadian General Staff, the RCMP, and Hugh Keenleyside of External Affairs, who feared further discrimination against Japanese Canadians might cause Japanese retaliations against Canadian prisoners of war. Pearson and his delegation told the government they feared destructive rioting by enraged whites unless the Japanese were controlled. But while there was evident suspicion and uneasiness on the BC coast, the Office of the Prime Minister received only forty-five letters and resolutions on the subject of Japanese Canadians; twenty-eight demanded incarceration and six were in support of their loyalty. Still, the King cabinet in Ottawa gave Pearson and the BC politicians part of what they wanted. Order in Council 365 was issued, ordering the removal of all male enemy aliens of military age from the coastal defence zone before April 1, and granting the right to detain any resident of Canada without trial on the grounds of national security.

Personally, Grace was convinced that the Japanese in British Columbia posed little or no threat to other residents, but she believed that widespread fear made their removal from the coast an unfortunate necessity. The newspapers seethed with articles advising people where best to take shelter if Vancouver were bombed, and with interviews of Caucasian citizens who feared the Japanese as "fifth-column" traitors, and called for the immediate evacuation of women along with men. The BC Legislature rang with warnings of "this yellow peril," and predictions that if the Japanese were not checked, BC could be under "Oriental dominance" within twenty years after the war. Grace had to accept the relocation of Japanese Canadians. "To have continued agitation for equality at that time would have been worse than useless, just like going into a north wind, a blizzard," she acknowledged later. "But what we concentrated on at that stage was trying to get, and the party as a whole was wholehearted on this, . . . the rights of citizens in every way we knew. I know I tried in the Legislature and outside it."

The problem for Grace and all provincial legislators during the war was that their field of influence had drastically diminished. With the War Measures Act, the Dominion government regulated many functions normally administered by the provinces: transport by air, road and rail; supplies of petroleum products, electricity, construction materials, liquor and foodstuffs; and rents, wages and prices. The scope of provincial power shrank.

Grace's first attempt at lawmaking was aimed at obtaining an increase for old age pensioners to keep up with the cost of living bonus just granted wage-earners. She first proposed a legislative committee to investigate the problems of old age pensioners, but withdrew the motion. Two weeks later the government voted BC's old people a bonus of five dollars per month, but Grace charged it was not enough. She urged a return to "the original humane intention in administration of the Pension Act." She was shot down by the coalition government, but not without a fight.

Provincial Secretary Pearson, Grace's opponent regarding Japanese Canadians, was also in charge of the Pension Act. Since the regulations had been set up by inter-provincial conference, he claimed, they could not be changed unilaterally. On advice from the federal Finance Minister, Grace argued for a lenient interpretation. In the end BC pensioners got only the five-dollar bonus, but Vancouver newspapers ran Grace's complaint that it was only "a quarter or half a loaf" when pensioners were entitled to "a full loaf."

When Grace's first legislative session ended in February, a Post-War Rehabilitation Committee was in place. As a junior MLA, Grace was not on the committee. Harold Winch, Grant MacNeil and Gretchen Steeves represented the CCF, but Grace would also soon contribute to federal postwar planning.

In Ottawa, Parliament reconvened January 22, 1942. The speech from the throne gave notice of a government plebiscite in three months on conscription, to remove the current restriction that manpower could be drafted only for home defence. The CCF supported the plebiscite, but Coldwell wanted it broadened to include "complete and effective conscription of war industries, accumulated wealth and financial institutions."

When Singapore fell to the Japanese February 16, apprehension in BC escalated. The Japanese would now be free to attack the West Coast, and many felt poorly protected by Ottawa. The Canadian General Staff discounted the possibility of invasion, viewing enemy strategic aims as "limited to raids which may include carrier-borne air attack, sporadic naval bombardment, small landing parties for the destruction of selected objectives and submarine activity." But even the potential of such "limited" Japanese activity raised fears in BC to fever pitch.

On February 19 US President Roosevelt issued an Executive Order giving the War Department the power it needed to remove the 110,000 men, women and children of Japanese ancestry in the Pacific Coast states. On February 24 the King cabinet passed an almost identical order giving the Minister of Justice authority to remove and detain "any and all persons" from any designated "protected area" in Canada. By order of the Minister of Justice a dusk-to-dawn curfew was imposed on Japanese Canadians, and they were made to surrender all motor vehicles, cameras, radios, firearms and ammunition.

The clash between her civil libertarian and pacifist upbringing and the demands of wartime continually kept Grace on the defensive. In mid-February a biographical speech about her father at a Vancouver United Church turned into a public grilling. Members of the congregation peppered Grace with challenges about CCF support of the war effort in view of her father's absolute pacifism. "This is not a black-and-white world where we can say 'this is so,' or 'that is right,'" Grace replied. "It is a grey world. We can follow the teachings of those who have gone before, but we change our ideas and beliefs as we see them, if we are to be true to our leaders. We have to do our own thinking in 1942 . . . . J.S. Woodsworth washes his hands of this present social conflict as absolutely and completely as he did in 1914, but that does not mean that those who follow his principles do not change their ideas."

The British Columbia CCF assembled for its annual convention Friday, March 20, 1942 at Burrard Hall in Vancouver. The night before the convention opened, J.S. Woodsworth, so frail he could no longer walk around the block, had been taken from Grace and Angus's home to a bed at Vancouver General Hospital on the advice of his son Ralph, now a medical doctor.

Lucy had been at his side day and night for months. At the end only her steadfast cheerfulness and potent painkillers were able to quiet her beloved James. Charles wrote of his father's last days, "He turned sleepless and tormented in the confines of his bed, unable to move without intense effort or draw breath freely."

Friday night, as the great pacifist founder of their party lay dying a few blocks away, the CCF convention considered whether to recommend to party members a vote of "yes" or "no" on Mackenzie King's upcoming conscription plebiscite. Grace's eloquent speech to the delegates that night swung them behind the party executive's motion for a "yes" vote. She charged that the plebiscite represented political trickery on the part of the Prime Minister, but she warned that a "no" vote would be playing into the hands of a group in Quebec which was not only fascist in tendency, but was working in active co-operation with the Axis.

The motion for a "yes" vote warned that a negative would "encourage the fascist-minded groups to be found in all parts of Canada." But it insisted that members accompany their affirmative vote with "a campaign demanding that Federal authorities use their powers to affect a complete mobilization of wealth and industry in addition to manpower." Two days later the CCF national council issued a statement calling for a "yes" vote in the plebiscite, accompanied by a six-point plan for the conscription of wealth.

The Japanese were leaving BC, but the federal government's silence on coastal defence plans had created much public anxiety. That night the provincial convention passed a motion exhorting the government to begin "training and arming all able-bodied men; providing all necessary equipment for civilian protection" and creating an international production council to co-ordinate war and industry in Canada and the US.

The CCF was not alone in pressing the government to do more for coastal defence. The *Vancouver Sun* ran a series of articles pointing out the inadequacy of military preparations on the coast and quoting military sources, articles for which the King government threatened to sue the newspaper. Public fear was further fuelled by front page accounts Saturday morning of Japanese bombs falling on the west coast of Australia, where the Tokyo fleet was reported to be twenty-four hours from Perth harbour. Fighting raged across Burma and New Guinea, and that day US General Douglas MacArthur formally assumed command of the United Nations forces in the southwest Pacific Ocean.

Saturday night, March 21, 1942, the first day of spring, James Shaver Woodsworth died peacefully in hospital with his son Ralph at his side. He was sixty-eight. His constant companion, Lucy, was not there at the moment of his death. Family friend and CCF comrade Mildred Osterhout Fahrni had come for a visit and suggested that Lucy take a break from her constant bedside vigil to see the spring blossoms in a nearby park. When the two women returned, they found James had passed away.

Grace hurried over from the convention with her brother Bruce, a teacher and delegate from Gibson's Landing. Charles and Lucy completed the family gathering. Grace sent a simple wire to Angus in Ottawa conveying the news and a self-reliant, "Found it was too late for you to catch tonight's train so will not expect you. Love, Grace." Angus wired her right back, but his message was about the public reaction to the death of her father, without a word of condolence. Grace and Angus kept the wires humming over the next few days as they arranged for a private family funeral to be followed by public memorial services in major cities across Canada, each featuring a prominent CCF speaker.

When the news of J.S. Woodsworth's death reached them Saturday night, delegates at the CCF convention stood for an emotional two-minute silence in his memory. Leader Harold Winch proclaimed, "Mr. Woodsworth burned with a passion for human justice. He did not live to see its fruition. But through his inspiration and work, a torch has been lighted that shows to a world in darkness the path to a fuller life." A treasured word of condolence came from Prime Minister King who wired Angus, "Mr. Woodsworth has left a name greatly respected in our country and which will be increasingly honoured with the passing of the years."

The short informal funeral was held on Tuesday morning after the cremation. In the hushed chapel the organist played James's favourite hymn, "Dear Lord and Father of Mankind." James's two sisters Mary and Edith were present, and all of his children except Howard and Belva, who were both in eastern Canada. As James had asked, fellow pacifist Mildred Osterhout Fahrni spoke simply of his deep faith in God and his vision of a world of caring and sharing.

The family then boarded Charles's thirty-foot cabin cruiser *Fourth Estate,* freshly cleaned and repaired for the ceremonial journey. The little boat headed across the sunlit whitecaps of Burrard Inlet to a spot outside the Lions Gate near the Stanley Park shore. Charles saw it as a day "which in many ways symbolized the turbulent, yet transparently honest and cleansing character of the man whose memory we were honouring." Grace wrote, "In the immensity of sky and sea the launch rode at anchor while Mother carried out his last wish. Slowly she cast his ashes on the waves that they might mingle with the elements that touch all shores and know no boundaries. Then we saw that she held in her hand a few leaves of her shamrock plant, a growing slip from the love-token he had given her before they were married. She looked at the living green for a moment and then very slowly let it drift into the waters."

As his ashes touched the ocean, Mildred spoke: "Following James S. Woodsworth's request that his body be freed from any national boundaries, we cast these elemental remains to wind and wave, thereby making one last gesture of his commitment to the spirit of internationalism." She ended with a promise from Kahlil Gibran's *The Prophet*: "Yea, I shall return with the tide, and though death may hide me, and the greater silence enfold me, yet again will I seek your understanding . . . . And not in vain will I seek."

More than thirteen years before his death, Grace had expressed her most sublime thoughts on her father's life and purpose, in a message for Father's Book from her Christmas in Paris. The vision she had then was often in her mind during that week between his death and the public memorial services. In "To One Of Them" she wrote: "Each individual in his own lifetime must repeat the history of the race. There are some people—a very few—who are able to do more than that. They are the ones who busy themselves only with what is most advanced at each step in human progress. Instead of following the little detours in the road they guide themselves by some landmark high above them.

"Most people struggle painfully up the steep slopes of experience, held back at every step by the thickets of tradition, or bruised by the rocks of disillusion or bewildered by the forests of confused detail. These people spend their lives climbing countless slopes, and like the race, they are forced to come down into the dark valleys of doubt between the mountain tops.

"The other people, the very few, keep their eyes fixed on the summits of experience. They follow the steep trails which lead directly to the peaks. From each new summit they can see a little more of the line of shining peaks which stretches toward the unknown horizon. They arrive long before the rest at the limits of human discovery. But they do not remain there. They feel that, hidden in the mist before them is another peak which no one has yet discovered. They push on alone into this pathless solitude, and no one knows what becomes of them. But the next travellers follow the trail which they have blazed, and penetrate farther into the trackless forests where they too are swallowed up by the darkness. And so, when the great mass of humanity arrives, the trail is ready."

Grace attended the overflowing memorial service in Vancouver, one of twelve held across Canada. On national radio William Irvine evoked the fountainhead of J.S. Woodsworth's motivation for social change. "It was his supersensitiveness to the touch of another's pain which made his soul a flaming passion of protest against injustice and drove his frail body into prodigious dynamic action," testified his colleague of twenty years. Newspapers across the country joined the Woodsworth family in their grief. "He created a spiritual movement," said one editorial, and journalist Bruce Hutchison referred to Woodsworth as "a saint in our politics."

Encouraged by both parents to think for herself, Grace had not rejected her father's lofty ideals and methods. Instead she had internalized them, and their radical nature had satisfied the rebellious side of her nature. She took pride in her place as the companion of this great socialist warrior, battling at his side to free humanity from the fetters of entrenched power and privilege, greed and exploitation. Now, at this moment of his passing, when all Canada paused to recognize his achievements, Grace felt herself ennobled as the inheritor of the enormous task still to be accomplished. It would be her life's work to carry forward her father's dream. She felt the weight, but she was young and strong, and she could count on many willing helpers.

The BC Legislature was not sitting, so Grace returned to Angus in Ottawa where Parliament was still in session. In April the Canadian people voted Yes on the conscription plebiscite, a vote in accord with the policy of the CCF national council.

In June a Liberal member on the floor of the House accused the CCF of aiming at a system of "state socialism." Although Coldwell immediately denied advocating "state socialism," the *Ottawa Journal* printed an editorial, using the accusation to denounce the CCF for wanting to bring "everybody down to the same financial level . . . even the defiers of law and order and social decency." The editorial claimed control of a socialized economy by the "community as a whole" could only operate through a government or leader, "say a government like the German, or a leader like HITLER or MUSSOLINI [capitals in original]."

The old charge that the CCF was a collection of "social fascists," as they had been labelled by the Communist Party in 1934, had now resurfaced in a more conservative quarter. The CCF's brief holiday from editorial barbs while in mourning was over. A new period of editorial ferocity designed to counter the party's growing popularity was beginning.

Grace responded to the editorial with a letter to the editor of the *Ottawa Journal* printed three days later. Some believed the community as a whole could "continue to operate through a Roosevelt or a Bevin or a Walter Nash," she wrote, "because we have faith in the methods of democratic Government and prefer to extend them as in the United States, Britain and New Zealand, rather than to dangle Hitler in front of people as a means of frightening them away from building social security through community ownership and control."

As a skilled debater, Grace took her strongest point from the paper's own pages. The obituary for her father printed by the *Journal* in March had editorialized, "if the fathers stoned the prophets, the sons adopted the policies for which the prophets had fallen. Each struggle leavened the mass by a process of permeation until ideas deemed highly heretical became the commonplace of orthodoxy." Grace riposted, "Why cannot the *Ottawa Journal* leave the job of stoning the prophets to others? Their sons are already supporting the new policies." In fact, the *Journal*'s editorial had touched on "permeation," the very social process by which the British Fabian Society believed masses of people were converted to socialism. The CCF, modelled on Fabian ideas, had permeated the mainstream of Canadian thinking with the emerging social security system. On Dominion Day 1941 the Unemployment Insurance Act came into effect, due at least in part to creation by the CCF of a public attitude that laid responsibility for Canada's unemployed at the feet of the federal government.

In early July 1942 Grace toured Quebec and New Brunswick, speaking to provincial CCF conventions and service clubs about the conscription of wealth and industry as well as manpower in "an all out war effort." She accused the government of trying to divide the country by raising race and religious differences for its own political advantage, and promised the CCF would "prove it can unify Canada." She urged the "United Nations" to "lay the basis for future collective security among the nations." The term United Nations was first used January 1, 1942 in reference to the twenty-six nations at war with the Axis powers who signed the Washington Pact not to conclude any separate armistice. This pact became the nucleus of the present-day United Nations. It was clear that the League of Nations had failed to achieve its goal of collective security. Grace and her CCF colleagues believed the goal was worthy, but the League had been too weak a vehicle.

The CCF celebrated its tenth anniversary in Toronto at the end of July. After solemn tributes to its founder, J.S. Woodsworth, the new leader, M.J. Coldwell, presented delegates with a five-point program of mobilization for total war. It included public ownership or government control of industry; industrial planning councils with representation from labour and management; an extension of the rationing system; a 100 percent tax on all profits in excess of 4 percent; a fixed ceiling on income; and a floor below which no person's income could fall. It featured an especially strong appeal to remedy the neglected position of agriculture with revision of the price ceiling policy to "place farmers on a parity with other workers."

But nowhere did the CCF's tenth anniversary policy statement use the words socialism, socialized or socialization. The word socialist appeared once, referring to the Regina Manifesto: "As a statement of democratic and socialist policy, not a word of it need be changed." Instead phrases like "social planning on a democratic basis" and "a common social objective" and "public ownership" expressed CCF aims.

Grace was elected to the national council as a member from British Columbia. Angus was elected vice-chairman after declining the nomination as national chairman in favour of Frank Scott; he detected a strong feeling in the party that Scott should be in the top spot.

With the convention behind her, Grace took on the job of campaigning for the election of Stanley Knowles in her father's old riding of Winnipeg North Centre. The by-election was to be held November 30, 1942. Lucy Woodsworth issued an open letter to the Women Electors of North Centre asking them to vote for "young, keen, intelligent" Knowles as "the man my husband hoped to see chosen as he believed Stanley well prepared to carry on his work." Grace and Angus spoke in Winnipeg from November 18 as part of the group of CCF "stars" brought in to counter the Liberal "stars"; the Conservatives did not contest the race. Knowles won the seat with seventy-one percent of the vote.

The winter of 1942–43 was a cold and hungry one for many British Columbians, particularly the old, the poor and the Japanese Canadians shivering in hastily constructed resettlement camp shacks in the snowy valleys of the province's interior. When the BC Legislature reopened February 1, a sombre speech from the throne took the first steps toward publicly owned hydroelectric power development and promised an ambitious postwar public works program, but did nothing to address the acute shortage of food and fuel or the Japanese Canadian issue. The provincial all-party Post-War

Rehabilitation Council tabled a massive interim report outlining vocational and land settlement schemes for returning soldiers, plans for construction of a steel mill in the province, the opening of northern BC by road and rail, maximum power generation and rural electrification. Still it proposed no plans for dealing with the Japanese or the food and fuel shortages.

The two CCF members from Vancouver–Burrard set out to rectify these omissions. As senior member from the riding, Grant MacNeil spoke first. He was recognized as a voice of authority on the Japanese question because of his position as executive secretary of the advisory board to the British Columbia Security Commission, the three-man group charged with the job of relocating the Japanese. As a wounded veteran of World War One and former head of the Great War Veterans Association, MacNeil's patriotism was unquestionable.

MacNeil told the House that the evacuation had been conducted as a security necessity and not through hysteria and prejudice. He addressed the question of education for the twenty-five hundred Japanese Canadian children; the Security Commission had taken responsibility, but a conflict over which level of government should pay had stalled plans for schools. MacNeil advocated government sales of Japanese assets with the proceeds going to a trust fund for their welfare. Turning to the contentious issue of relocating more than twenty thousand uprooted Japanese Canadians once the war ended, MacNeil said the thousands removed to other provinces expected to return to BC. Many would be impoverished, and they would return in the middle of postwar rehabilitation of the general population. To the Liberal and Conservative calls for their "repatriation" (many of them were Canadian born) to Japan, MacNeil objected there could be no repatriation to "an economically chaotic, defeated Japan" until many years after the armistice.

Grace was also eager to speak about issues affecting Japanese Canadians, but she was cautioned by provincial party president Arnold Webster not to mention the topic in her upcoming speech. So, when she took the floor the following week, she did not approach the issue. Instead she focussed on shortages of food and fuel during Vancouver's recent cold spell—and she was dramatically aided by a sudden drop in the temperature inside the legislative chamber that set everyone shivering most realistically.

Talking about the basics of food and nutrition, Grace cited a recent survey that showed forty percent of Vancouver families not eating proper meals, and only three percent consuming an "excellent" diet. The greatest needs in the city were for green vegetables, milk and fruit. This, she indignantly said, in a province noted for its fruits, vegetables and dairy products. Grace went on to say that lack of sufficient income was the major cause of malnutrition in the "hungry thirties" and was still the cause for people on pensions and those with low incomes and large families to support. To achieve minimum standards she advocated family allowances and collective bargaining with strong labour unions. These themes, first sounded on the chilly floor of the BC Legislature, were to become part of Grace's signature as a lawmaker as she tried to pry the necessities of life for low-income Canadians out of a series of governments.

Her ability in debate during this session impressed more than one newspaper reporter. The *Vancouver Daily Province* called her "a most capable young woman" who has "a way of getting down to solid, hard facts and suggesting remedies. She also has a knack of wrapping those facts up in language that gets her purpose over to the government and beyond the administrative benches to the public at large." The *Vancouver Sun* called her "very able," and the *Victoria Daily Times* observed: "Mrs. MacInnis is a small, wiry woman with jet black, shiny hair. She looks only a slip of a girl, but she can hold her own in debate with the toughest men . . . . The coalition benches just gave up trying to argue with her."

Grace's speaking ability and her hair both made a hit with former Premier Duff Pattullo. Two notes that he passed to her across the floor of the House were enjoyable enough that Grace kept them in her files. The first said, "Mrs. MacInnes [sic] You speak as well as you look which is high compliment." The second, more personal, said: "Mrs. McInnis [sic] Have you given consideration as to how hair should be parted? Most of those whose hair is parted in this House are parted on the left side. I am wondering whether the right side is not much more attractive. Experimentation would be very interesting." Then CCF House leader Winch passed Grace a joking note. "Grace, I have instructed the whip to inquire into the notes and flirtatious looks passing between the Premier and 2nd member for Burrard. Harold." Of course, it was all in good fun; no one took these expressions of personal interest seriously.

Despite the distance of the continent between them, Grace and Angus were working together. Two days after her speech on fuel shortages in the BC House, Angus took up the issue in the House of Commons. Fuel supply difficulties in British Columbia demonstrated the "manpower muddle," he told the House, and fuel production should be declared an essential industry. At the first sign of shortage, rationing should be imposed.

In November 1942 Britain's plan for postwar social reconstruction written by Sir William Beveridge was published. It set out plans for a comprehensive and universal social insurance plan, with a children's allowance. This prompted Prime Minister King to commission distinguished McGill University social economist Dr. Leonard Marsh to put together a comprehensive plan for Canada. In March 1943 the Marsh Report was presented to the House of Commons committee on reconstruction and rehabilitation. It touched off a nationwide debate about social insurance. The newspapers were full of it; the BC Legislature was full of it. "Social insurance was the burning topic before the Legislature," reported the *Vancouver Daily Province* March 11, 1943. Grace was "locked in earnest debate" with her old adversary George Pearson, now Labour Minister, for over two hours.

Pearson's motion asking the federal government to establish as soon as possible a comprehensive plan of social insurance got support from both sides of the BC House. Commenting on it on the floor, Grace agreed that handling social insurance on a countrywide basis was the only logical way, but she insisted on a co-operative socialized approach in a mixed economy—small businesses, government-owned businesses, co-operatives, public utilities and banking—everyone was welcome except profit-making monopolies.

The war had demonstrated that Canada could achieve full employment, and CCF policy statements during the war always included full employment as the economic basis for national social insurance. "Until the BC government is prepared to stop thinking in the old fashioned terms of free enterprise we shall not get far," Grace told the House. "To say that social security can be brought in without taking measures for the control or ownership of the means of production is to deceive the people."

The Coalition's move to hire a nutrition expert for the Provincial Secretary's Department won Grace's approval. Good nutrition was the best cure for spiralling health care costs, in her opinion, and she had learned her father's lesson well—a person with an empty stomach could not appreciate the higher things of life.

Pleading for financial help for unmarried mothers ineligible for mothers' pensions, Grace told the House of such a mother with no financial resources, who could not work because the child was too young to leave. No government-funded day care was available, but the number of children born out of wedlock had been on the rise in BC since the start of the war.

Throughout the session Grace urged that Vancouver's unsanitary and overcrowded tenement housing be replaced, but the issue was sidelined by the need to house war workers. Grace pressed the government to look ahead to peacetime, and build for returning soldiers, sailors and airmen.

With her illustrious family connections and national experience, Grace added some flair to whatever issue she addressed. She had a youthful, modern presence, especially compared with Conservative Coalitioner Tilly Jean Rolston of Vancouver–Point Grey or with Liberal Coalitioner, the British-born society page editor Nancy Hodges of Victoria. Matronly CCFer Laura Jamieson was a contemporary of Grace's mother. Gretchen Steeves, brilliant and showy in debate, was seen by CCF whip Colin Cameron as a peacock, while he likened Grace to a guinea hen, scratching away industriously. Grace said she thought the comparison "very accurate," but she enjoyed the centre stage spotlight quite as much as Steeves. She was not flamboyant, but she made proposals that seemed radical—proposals which on examination were sensible and struck straight down the middle of the CCF party line.

The party was in a triumphant mood when the Legislature opened in

January 1944. In a mid-summer by-election Revelstoke voters had chosen CCF candidate Vincent Segur, a locomotive engineer; the CCF now had a record total of sixteen MLAs. On the day Segur was to be introduced to the Speaker Grace happened to be wearing a red scarf, which, on impulse, she cut dramatically into sixteen pieces. The CCF men pinned these tiny red flags on their lapels, the women on their hats or suits, and they sat smiling in the Legislature as Opposition Leader Harold Winch led Segur up the centre aisle to the Speaker's chair. Segur's election was part of an unprecedented wave of CCF popularity across Canada as the public forgot its fear of centralized planning and endorsed whatever was effective in the drive for victory.

For Grace the red flag idea was a show of solidarity rather than a declaration of revolution. She may have seemed radical to Liberals and Conservatives, but within her own party she defined the moderate middle of the road. In 1943, for example, she found Harold Winch's comments too inflammatory in a 1943 speech he made, threatening that under a CCF government "the police and military would be used to force those opposed to obey the law . . . . Those who defied the government's will would be treated as criminals . . . . If capitalism says no, then we know the answer—so did Russia." It was a tough call for many Canadians. People could conclude from the words of the Regina Manifesto that Canada's socialist party was no threat to their individual freedoms, and from the repeated statements of Woodsworth and other CCF leaders that a richer, fuller life for individuals was the party's goal. But many Canadians found it hard to square assurances of individual freedom with CCF programs of centralized government planning, confiscation of industry and redistribution of income from the rich to the poor.

In her own riding of Vancouver–Burrard, Grace was starting what proved to be a long battle to prevent a takeover by communists. The tactics she and riding-mate Grant MacNeil used now would serve them well when the same conflict intensified in the 1950s. Grace compared these radical left-wingers with a cuckoo which lays its eggs in the nest of another bird. "We had the Marxian socialists from Vancouver Centre who wanted to start a branch in the Burrard area," she said. "So they came to us, the CCF. They'd come to our meetings and talk to our membership. They would scrap over points of order and prolong this. When the audience was getting restive, they would start in on business that was convenient to them. They wanted to send purified water to Timbuctoo, or address some outrage on the other side of the world, practically passing the hat at that stage. They would use this to keep us from building the CCF agenda."

Grace and a few original CCFers decided that two of them would attend every meeting to keep things under control. "One of us would get up and we'd start asking questions. 'Now who is behind this contribution appeal? How do you know this money will be used for relieving so and so that's in the dungeon?' People who had been swayed by their first appeals would think, 'This sounds very reasonable, we ought to know more about it.' But the other crowd would wait. The innocents, the ones we wanted to recruit, would quietly slip out under this perfectly boring, ghastly, deadly dull meeting and then the trouble would start." When the interlopers had a quorum they would pass a resolution to control a seat or two on the CCF executive. Grace fought them for months. "We were just as honey-toned and gentle and persuasive, but persistent like no end." Finally the Vancouver Centre group appealed to the provincial council for a separate charter.

"The provincial executive was by no means clear in its mind at the time," said Grace. "It was pretty badly poisoned with communists too, but we got them to hoist the idea of a charter for six months." In the interim, Grace worked to expose her opponents for the communists they were, and they dropped the idea of a separate charter. "I never used to inveigh against communists at all publicly. If anybody asked me about them I would explain why I thought they were nefarious, but we would fight for their liberty the same as anybody else—but not inside us!"

CHAPTER 8

A House Divided

The CCF hit a record high in the Gallup poll of September 1943—if an election had been held that day, the CCF would have polled twenty-nine percent, the two older parties twenty-eight percent each. The Canadian Congress of Labour overwhelmingly endorsed the CCF as "the political arm of Labour in Canada," and recommended all CCL unions affiliate with the party. Grace and the rest of the party's inner circle were elated. They concentrated on converting their lead in the polls into election victories.

But undermining CCF attempts to increase its popular support, the old struggle over whether or not to join a united front with other left-wing parties had erupted again within the British Columbia CCF. The party nationally was only as strong as its weakest link, and even as the CCF climbed in the polls its enemies were quick to call Canada's attention to the tug-of-war in BC. At the CCF provincial convention in April 1943, vice-president Hilary Brown of Hornby Island caused a minor storm when her report termed the CCF attitude toward the Soviet Union "equivocal."

Eager to show the CCF supported the Soviet Union as Canada's war ally, Grace contradicted Brown, pointing out that Angus had been first in the House to press for renewed Canadian diplomatic relations with the Soviet Union. Coldwell had acted early in the 1943 parliamentary session, Grace said, by demanding to know when the government would lift its ban on the Communist Party in Canada. Angus and the caucus, as well as Grace, supported Coldwell on this free speech position, although a legalized CPC, in its new guise as the Labour Progressive Party (LPP), was to make constant trouble for the CCF.

At this 1943 convention Bert Herridge, first-term MLA from Rossland–Trail in eastern BC, took the pro-communist stance that would divide him from Grace and Angus in the coming years. He said, "I would suggest that in future we make plain that we are behind the Soviet Union, that we support the Soviet Union, and that we are friends with the Soviet Union."

It was always an uneasy position for Grace. She distrusted communists and rejected a united front, but believed they had a right to freedom of speech and assembly. When the CPC was illegal her attitude was: "All aid to Soviet Russia, none to the Communist Party of Canada." She was clear on her own attitude, but members of the public who could not split such fine hairs lumped the CCF in with the communists anyway. Others, of leftist sympathies, saw the CCF rejection of a united front as an obstinate refusal to unite with natural allies.

When the 1943 provincial convention was over, Grace worked on educational materials for the CCF summer camp, campaigned in the Revelstoke by-election in June, then joined Angus in Ottawa. She spoke in Ottawa, Toronto and Pembroke, Ontario. In Montreal she shared the platform with CCF stars Frank Scott, David Lewis and Clarie Gillis to press the case for a social democratic new world order.

The party grew quickly through 1943 and by 1944 there were a total of one hundred and nine members sitting in seven provincial legislatures. It won thirty-four of ninety seats in the Ontario legislature in August 1943, and was the official opposition in Ontario and BC. In 1942 total membership had been less than thirty thousand. At the end of 1944 this had tripled to nearly a hundred thousand. There were over two thousand local CCF organizations, clubs, constituency associations and study groups. Party news was published in one French-language and six English-language papers. The *Canadian Forum*, a fortnightly journal of research and comment featuring CCF views, boasted a total circulation of over ninety thousand.

Grace had a different outlook on many aspects of life from most British Columbians, but nowhere did she differ from them more than on the Japanese Canadians. In June 1942, while Grace was with Angus in Ottawa, a Japanese submarine had reportedly shelled the Canadian naval and communications installation at Estevan Point on Vancouver Island. The shelling caused no damage but stimulated local fear of invasion to a new high point. Fear spoke: the Japanese Canadians must leave the coast.

By September most of the province's more than twenty-two thousand Japanese Canadians had been moved through the dismal processing centre in the livestock buildings at the Pacific National Exhibition in Vancouver and sent to internment camps in BC's Kootenay Mountains or to jobs in other provinces. Permitted to take only a hundred and fifty pounds each—bedding, clothing, a little food—they forfeited homes, automobiles, boats and land. The near-total lack of provision for the education of their children was one of the worst parts of the war for many Japanese Canadians in the Kootenay camps.

During the 1943 session Grace began her effort to secure better education for the internees by asking the BC Minister of Education for figures on costs and student enrollment in the province's correspondence courses. That summer she journeyed through the Kootenays by bus, visiting the internment camps and speaking at CCF meetings to drum up support for schools for the Japanese Canadians. On her way through the Kootenays Grace touched base with CCF colleague Helena Gutteridge, who was handling welfare work at Lemon Creek, and with Mildred Osterhout Fahrni, teaching in the New Denver evacuation camp.

One day Grace got an unexpected lift when she met the wife of the Japanese newspaper editor she and Angus had entertained at home in prewar days. "I had not intended to stop over at Slocan City," Grace wrote twenty-five years later, "but for some reason my contact did not arrive. As I waited disconsolately, I saw a woman running towards me, her arms held out in greeting. It was Mrs. Umezuki, and never did anyone receive a warmer welcome as she invited me to stay with her. Just then my driver arrived and I had to go. But the warmth of that welcome has stayed with me all through the years."

Recognizing the need to clarify the CCF position on the contentious Japanese Canadian issue, Grace and Angus collaborated in writing a pamphlet, *Oriental Canadians—Outcasts or Citizens?*, in fall 1943. They tried to balance protection for the human and civil rights of the Japanese Canadians with the nearly universal public opinion that they were not welcome in BC. At that time, British Columbia alone did not permit Orientals to vote. Angus had long been on record as opposed to permitting people to settle in a province where they would not have full citizenship rights. In the pamphlet he and Grace first urged BC to grant the franchise to all and restore their rightful property to the Japanese Canadians. If not, they held, "the Dominion Government should now plan to protect the Coast area against any sudden return of an impoverished Japanese community; seeking re-establishment as a racial group, at a time and under conditions provocative of disturbances."

This was also the position of the provincial CCF as resolved at the April 1943 convention. The resolution stated in part, "That Japanese be now assisted to obtain productive and permanent employment outside the protected area, and in other provinces at prevailing rates of pay to protect labour standards, and under conditions enabling them to re-settle with their families. This will substantially relieve the present manpower shortage and mitigate against any future concentration on the Coast in BC." Publicly the party appeared to have a unified position, but within the BC CCF there was still a deep split between the civil libertarians and the fearful.

The Japanese Canadian question was not the only issue dividing the BC party. When the 1944 CCF provincial convention opened, the schism within the party over a united front was sharper than ever, and Angus's temper shorter. Old Rio Hall rocked on its foundation of stumps during a closed-door meeting of the national and foreign affairs section where Angus branded as "stooges and stool pigeons of the Communist Party" the left-wing CCFers who wished to refrain from attacking other left-wing parties.

Later a resolution from MLA Bert Herridge's riding of Trail urging the principle of consultation and co-operation with other "left-wing groups," came to the floor, provoking another enraged outburst from Angus. "The stool pigeons of the Communist Party are here," he shouted, "and the best thing they can do is get out! I am sick and tired of hearing about the communists." Hilary Brown demanded that he name names, but was ruled out of order. One delegate attempted a motion censuring Angus for making "malicious and slanderous" statements. It was lost for lack of a quorum, and the convention broke up acrimoniously.

The insurgent feeling in the CCF for co-operation with communist leader Tim Buck's new Labour Progressive Party (LPP) was strong in 1944, understandable when Soviets were fighting the Nazis alongside Canadian soldiers. A recorded vote on co-operation at the 1944 BC CCF convention was lost sixty-eight to a substantial minority of forty-two.

Grace tried to restrain Angus's fiercer outbursts, knowing that he alienated many people within the party. Hilary Brown, who favoured a united front, was on the national council with Grace and Angus. She remembered Angus's attack at one council meeting. "I made some observation, and Angus just plowed into me. He just went at it bull-headed, you know? And I heard a very quiet little voice saying, 'You've done it again.' And it was Grace speaking to Angus."

Angus did not stay around Vancouver to face his adversaries. He left at the end of April 1944 for a three-month all-party parliamentary tour of Australia and New Zealand in company with Members of the British Parliament.

In late spring 1944 Grace took part in the Saskatchewan provincial campaign that elected Tommy Douglas and the CCF to form the first socialist government in North America. The party brought in all of its star speakers, Grace among them, to persuade Saskatchewan voters to cast out the incumbent Liberal government of William Patterson. When the votes were counted June 3 the CCF had won forty-seven of the fifty-two seats in the Saskatchewan Legislature.

Grace believed it was the personal charisma and leadership ability of Tommy Douglas that carried the day. A slight man with glasses, curly hair, a brilliant grin, and a vast store of jokes and pointed stories, Douglas knew how to hold an audience. Grace said of her friend and colleague, "He is a great story teller. The audience is afraid not to listen. Afraid they'll miss something . . . . In 1944 the media couldn't create a leader as they can now," she reflected. "He had to do it himself."

While Angus was in Australia and Grace, along with most of the CCF federal caucus, was electioneering in Saskatchewan, the Soldiers Vote Bill wound through Parliament unopposed by the CCF. The measure would give the vote to Canadian soldiers serving overseas with the exception of "any person whose racial origin [was] that of a country at war with Canada." Because German and Italian Canadians would lose their voting privileges the bill was amended to leave disenfranchised only those Japanese Canadians who had previously been without the vote as BC residents. Prime Minister King said he was afraid granting the franchise to Japanese Canadians might result in riots on election day.

When Grace found out about CCF inaction on this issue, she wrote an indignant letter to David Lewis. "Here we have a bill whose purpose is to disenfranchise Japanese Canadians in all sections of the Dominion. The CCF has been tenaciously fighting to wipe out discrimination in BC and to fit the Japanese Canadians into the other provinces as ordinary Canadians in the full sense of the word. We have been winning through, too . . . . Yet when Bill 135 comes up in the House of Commons there isn't a single world of protest from the CCF members . . . . This legislation is of the same kind that Father spent the 1920s protesting against again and again." Lewis apologized profusely and invited Grace to draft a resolution for the upcoming CCF national convention condemning the clause disenfranchising Japanese Canadians.

Enfranchisement, conditions in the internment camps, sale of confiscated assets, repatriation to Japan, resettlement across Canada, all these issues were but parts of the larger question vexing Canada: what to do about the Japanese Canadians? By the summer of 1944 all three major parties agreed the Japanese Canadians must not be resettled in coastal BC at the end of the war, but they differed on how far to carry the discrimination. At the extreme of anti-Japanese opinion, the Liberal Minister of Pensions and National Health, Ian Mackenzie of Vancouver Centre, told his re-nomination meeting he would answer the campaign of "our socialist friends" with the slogan 'No Japanese from the Rockies to the seas.'"

Speaking in Kamloops, BC, near many Japanese Canadian internment camps, Progressive Conservative leader John Bracken said Japanese Canadians should be barred from a zone five hundred miles inland from the BC coast. Howard Green (PC–Vancouver South) said it was in the Japanese Canadians' own interest "to see that they are kept away from the Coast." Even CCF leader Harold Winch said that summer, "Japanese assets in BC should be liquidated, and they should never be allowed to congregate in any one Province or section of a Province again, but rather they should be spread out across the Dominion."

Grace stated her position to a CCF audience in September: "We propose to settle the twenty-three thousand Japanese Canadians across Canada in all the nine provinces. Race discrimination must be wiped out and the vision of this larger Canadianism is going to grow in this country." That was in fact the policy of the King government. That September Arthur MacNamara, national director of National Selective Service, revealed in Vancouver that the BC Security Commission would be assigned to handle the re-establishment of Japanese Canadians after the war. "When the twenty-three thousand BC Japanese have been evenly distributed across Canada, there will be no restrictions on their movement into industry." But the MacInnis pamphlet stating nearly identical views on resettlement, though not on the franchise, ran into trouble almost at once. The CCF national executive had decided to postpone putting out *Oriental Canadians—Outcasts or Citizens?* as a national publication in 1943, even over Angus's urging that the issue was "of the utmost importance." Evidently it did not have the urgency across the country that it did in BC. By May of 1944 Grace was still pressing the national office, without success, to publish the pamphlet.

The Japanese Canadian issue caused a split within the CCF in British Columbia that became painfully apparent during the 1944 provincial convention. Grace and Angus's pamphlet had been circulated only within the party, and the convention was considering the whole issue: the motion before them called for a provincial plebiscite on voting rights for Japanese Canadians. The two hundred delegates listened in silence to Vancouver Island MLA Sam Guthrie's dire warnings of defeat at the polls if the CCF persisted in urging equal rights and the vote for Canadians of Japanese origin. Grace took the moral high ground. "I would rather see myself and the party I represent go down to defeat than lower the flag on this issue of equality for all races," she told Guthrie and the delegates. The resolution was defeated. The BC CCF executive called Guthrie on the carpet and extracted a promise that his opposition to the CCF policy of support for Japanese Canadian rights would "be kept for private conversation or CCF gatherings—not for public meetings."

Early in 1946, after Tommy Douglas had appointed a Japanese Canadian man, Grace wrote to congratulate him, saying that Harold Winch was "always terrified of this issue and did his best to prevent any reference to it being made in the Legislature. At times, by devices such as that only one member should speak . . . he got the caucus pretty well tied down. It was the same way in election campaigns, but we went right ahead."

By autumn 1944, Angus expected a federal election at any time, and he wanted to ensure that the CCF policy on the Japanese Canadian question was crystal clear. He did not wait for the national office to get around to publishing *Oriental Canadians—Outcasts or Citizens?* It was published from the office of the *Federationist*, a BC newspaper that supported the CCF. Angus outlined the positions advanced in the pamphlet wherever he could: in the House of Commons, in an article commissioned by *Maclean's* magazine, even from the pulpit of one of Vancouver's largest churches.

Grace saw "the Oriental issue" as just one facet of a much larger racial question. "In Quebec they hate the Torontonians and the Jews; in Toronto they hate the French-Canadians and the Jews; on the prairies it's the Mennonites; out here it's the Orientals, East Indians and Doukhobors. The CCF will simply have to deal with race hatred as a single issue, showing that it is fomented for a purpose by those who hate the CCF and what it stands for."

Building cross-cultural bridges between Quebec and English-speaking Canada was a growing CCF priority in 1944. Party strategists realized that without substantial support in Quebec the CCF would never govern Canada, so courting Quebec was emphasized as a crucial element of national policy. At the national council meeting at the end of 1943, Quebec organizer Jacques Casgrain, KC had hopefully reported "keen interest in the CCF in Quebec and phenomenal growth in the organization."

The national Convention of 1944 was held in Montreal, and three members from Quebec were elected to the national council: national chairman Frank Scott; Omer Chartrand, Quebec provincial secretary; and co-vice-chairman François LaRoche of Montreal who shared the position with Angus. An emergency resolution was passed to provide for two national vice-chairmen instead of one, one French-speaking and the other English-speaking.

It was the first national convention Grace had missed since Regina, as she was unwell and had a pressing volume of work, but she campaigned in the summer 1944 Quebec election fight. Maurice Duplessis and the Union Nationale were returned to power after four years of Liberal government, but one CCF candidate was elected, the first ever in Quebec. The CCF carried on its campaign literally without any organization, often without any membership in the constituency, and always without funds. But Grace was optimistic. As one of the few French-speakers in CCF ranks, she had travelled to Quebec each summer during her term as MLA to build support for the party. She sincerely believed that the CCF could bring cultural unity to Canada. On the West Coast she tried to convince her own constituents that their interests were in harmony with those of Quebec residents, but this was an uphill struggle.

When the Legislature opened in 1945, Grace tried again to obtain government-funded schools for the Japanese Canadian camps. She was turned down. Then she tried to have the provincial government fund correspondence courses for them, but the BC government passed the buck to the Dominion government. In other provinces the Dominion government was paying sixty-five dollars per pupil for the education of Japanese Canadian students, but BC Education Minister H.G.T. Perry admitted he had never asked for this funding. Eventually correspondence courses were made available at nine times the price other British Columbians paid for the same course, an injustice Grace vigorously protested.

In the fierce debate on whether to "repatriate" Japanese Canadians at the end of the war, many CCFers in British Columbia were signing a petition to send them to Japan. Ninety percent of voters in the fishing town of Steveston, where Japanese Canadians had been numerous before the war, voted to "repatriate." Grace pointed out that these people were Canadians, not Japanese. "You can't repatriate Canadians," she insisted. "Where would you send them?"

It was purely a British Columbia question, but in March of 1945 people of colour across Canada watched closely as BC Provincial Secretary George Pearson introduced an amendment to the provincial Elections Act giving all veterans who were British citizens the right to vote whether their skins were yellow, black, brown or white. At one the next morning, by a show of hands after a ninety-minute debate, the right of franchise for Hindus was killed by just four votes. Grace voted for the franchise along with the other fifteen members of the CCF caucus and Coalitionists Nancy Hodges, Dr. J.J. Gillis of Yale, and Education Minister H.G.T. Perry.

By the end of April 1945, when the Allied world was rejoicing over the fall of Berlin and victory in Europe, Grace appeared out of step with the prevailing public mood, thrown off-course by her unpopular stand on the Japanese Canadian question and her preoccupation with the damage that the lack of Quebec CCF support was doing to the party nationally. She was becoming impatient with the resistance of Quebec to socialism. Her public comments about Quebec plunged her into hot water with the CCF national office and in *la belle province*. The re-election of Maurice Duplessis's Union Nationale government had created a chilly climate for reform, let alone for the creation of a socialist Canada. Duplessis was a believer in provincial autonomy, totally opposed to the centralized federal government economic planning which Grace advocated. His government had in 1937 passed an extension to the Padlock Law that sanctioned locking a building not only for prostitution and gambling, but also if communist propaganda was found there. It was a law Grace and the CCF abhorred as limiting to freedom of speech.

Grace told a CCF open forum in Vancouver April 30, 1945 that the combination of church, industrialists and politicians was keeping French-Canadians "ignorant, uneducated and helpless . . . . This blunt truth must be kept in mind if Canadians are to approach the problem with a solution in view. The people of Quebec are told what to think by their leaders, and the industrialists further exploit the Quebec workers who lack modern education and strong unions."

Grace had said precisely the same thing without incident in August and in October of 1944. But this time the French-language press picked up her comments and used them to condemn the CCF. In the Quebec legislature Duplessis called her remarks "unfair and inadequate." Grace did not back off, and immediately replied that Premier Duplessis "with his extreme isolationism is one of those most guilty of keeping the people of his province cut off from their fellow citizens in the rest of the Dominion." Immediately the CCF national office was besieged with requests for a statement repudiating what Grace had said. Lewis wrote her, "Your statement is doing us a good deal of harm, according to the complaints of our people in these areas," but he did not issue a repudiation.

Still Grace believed that "French-Canadians want exactly the same thing that everyone else in Canada wants—adequate food, shelter, education and health," she said. "Other parties tell them the reason they can't have them is because English-speaking Canadians prevent them from getting them. The truth is that capitalists—both French and English-speaking—are the ones responsible for that isolationism . . . . Real economic interests are the same everywhere," she told a CCF audience at Rio Hall.

As a French speaker and a socialist, Grace believed she understood the aspirations of Quebec residents and the proper way to satisfy them. "If you want to bring the French-Canadians in with the rest of us," she said, "you must protect and save their economic rights. We must see that Quebec workers have the same wages as others in Canada." She would meet every obstacle—language, religion, customs—by saying to French-Canadians: Let us work together to build a system where the people through their elected government control the means of production.

In January 1943, Grace was one of ten women appointed to the federal government's Subcommittee on Post-War Problems of Women. As part of the James Committee, the Advisory Committee on Reconstruction headed by McGill University principal F. Cyril James, the subcommittee was to examine the economic and social implications for women of the transition from war to peace.

Chair of the subcommittee was Dr. Margaret Stovel McWilliams, journalist, Winnipeg councillor, president of the Manitoba Historical Society, organizer of women's groups, and the wife of the current Lieutenant-Governor of Manitoba, Roland F. McWilliams. The other Vancouver woman chosen was Evelyn Lett, prominent in the University Clubs of Canada and wife of Brigadier Sherwood Lett, a decorated war hero. The other subcommittee members were: Margaret Mackinzie of Fredericton, Thais L. Fremont of Quebec City, Margaret Wherry of Montreal, Dr. A. Vibert Douglas of Kingston, Helen Smith Agnew and Marion Findlay of Toronto, and Susan Gunn of Lloydminster.

The subcommittee met four times during 1943 and tabled its final report in November. The thrust of the report was revolutionary: after the war, women should have the right to choose whether or not to work outside the home. Women were divided into four groups: married women working at home; married women working outside the home; single women earning their own living; and farm women. The subcommittee report emphasized the right of each woman to choose her occupation. "To women in each group the right to choose what occupation she will follow must be conceded as a right to which every citizen is entitled. She must also have the right to equality of remuneration, working conditions, and opportunity for advancement . . . . It is the right to choose which is demanded."

Grace and the other members of the subcommittee recognized in their report that many women war workers were earning their own money for the first time, and had "gained an entirely new realization of their skills and capacities." The widely held opinion that married women should not work outside the home suited Depression-era economic conditions when jobs were few and desperately needed by heads of families. But in a postwar Canada where full employment was to be the "objective of all economic policy," the subcommittee put forth as a basic assumption the expectation of Canadian women "to be full members of a free community."

One in four working women in 1942 was married. To bolster their right to work, the subcommittee recognized that married women workers in the lower economic ranks had always been conceded this right. "It is only when we come into the ranks of the better-paid women that the weight of public opinion creates difficulties for her, as for example, in the teaching profession where in our judgment the married teacher would really be of great value."

The subcommittee calculated that of the 1.2 million Canadian women working in 1943, after the war 180,000 women would have to be taken care of by government action of some kind. Training and retraining for occupations in demand after the war was urgently recommended, "upon precisely the same basis" as the training provided for men war workers.

The subcommittee's recommendations for women working in the home were also revolutionary. Household workers would be covered by the Labour Code, Minimum Wage Act, Unemployment Insurance, and Workmen's Compensation. In other words, women would receive wages for housework. The status of household workers would be raised with a government-funded training course and recognition of graduates as skilled workers.

The need for children's allowances and national health insurance was stressed, and in general the subcommittee supported the recommendations of the Marsh Report tabled in the House of Commons in March 1943 for a comprehensive social security scheme in Canada. The recommendation on housing shows clearly that Grace never abandoned J.S. Woodsworth's ideas: "Well-planned dwellings have a beneficial effect on the health, morale, and development of the family and so of the community." The subcommittee strongly urged that women have "an immediate and responsible share in the planning and carrying through of all housing programs."

For the first time, the need for government-sponsored day care in peacetime was asserted. A few joint federally and provincially funded day nurseries had been set up as a war emergency service, and the subcommittee recommended they be continued, as half-day care only, leaving mothers free to work part-time or participate in volunteer activities. "Every woman should for her own sake and that of her family have time for outside interests," the report stated, thereby defining a new standard for Canadian women. In the 1944 BC legislative session, Grace attempted unsuccessfully to get the provincial government to enact the provisions of this report.

Women had served with distinction in wartime production work, but many still believed women did not belong in the workplace. A poll taken in Vancouver in March 1945 for the radio program "Public Opinion" showed 83.8 percent of those polled believed "a woman's place is in the home." Still, Grace spoke often to women's groups in 1944 and 1945 about the issues raised by the subcommittee, and her controversial remarks made the news. And, although she had served on the Subcommittee on Post-War Problems of Women, she had no hesitation in criticizing the full report of the James Committee of which her group was a part. In the Legislature, she declared it startlingly similar to that presented by the Canadian Manufacturers Association. She charged that it recommended a return of industry to big business, the immediate reduction of corporation taxes, elimination of the excess profits tax and the withdrawal of all war control measures except those covering labour. These were all measures opposed by the CCF, and all measures which Grace believed would make it tougher for women to make a living for themselves in the postwar world. She did agree with the James Committee's conclusion that while full employment after the war was the goal, there would be an economic slump, requiring the federal government to provide social welfare benefits such as unemployment insurance and health insurance.

But regardless of the pros and cons of the James plan for reconstruction, it was constitutionally impossible to implement. Despite nine months of meetings, the 1945 Federal–Provincial Conference on Reconstruction failed to agree on a new balance of Dominion and provincial powers. The James Committee proposals were shelved and forgotten.

In fall 1943 Grace and Angus bought their first house, a two-storey wooden building at 355 West 14th Avenue near City Hall in Vancouver's Mount Pleasant area. They were well satisfied with their new home overlooking False Creek, but their pleasure was overshadowed by the miserable housing in which some of their constituents had to live. Grace told her fellow MLAs the homes were "dismal, dingy and damp . . . overcrowded rabbit warrens where people are herded together like animals and old people and children shiver through winter days."

During the last two sessions of the twentieth BC Parliament in 1944 and 1945, Grace made housing her number-one issue. Premier John Hart's throne speech of February 1944 made no mention of housing; when Grace's turn came in the throne speech debate, she scored the government for its neglect of housing in favour of a million-dollar office building for downtown Vancouver. "In our opinion," she told the House, "a large scale low rental housing program under the auspices of this government ought to be considered public works project number one, the minute men and material become available."

A month after her initial speech on housing, the CCF's "girl orator" sparked one of the hottest debates of the session when she introduced a resolution urging the Dominion government to consider a large-scale low-rental housing program. Angry at being upstaged, Liberal Coalitionist Nancy Hodges advanced her own housing plan as a detailed amendment. Tempers flared as each side tried to score points on this previously neglected issue. When the vote was taken Grace's resolution passed with the Hodges amendment tagged on.

When the Legislature reconvened in February of 1945, Grace continued her crusade for replacement of Vancouver slum housing, although again there was no mention of housing in the throne speech. *Vancouver News Herald* reporter J.K. Nesbitt wrote, "Mrs. MacInnis is a persistent little woman, bright as a dollar. She's still on the sunny side of forty and may be expected to have a long, long public career before her. She stays with the same old subjects, year after year, hoping to wear down the government as rain drops might wear down stone.

"She lectured the government about housing, seeming to say the government worries more about people in Point Grey houses than people in East End houses. When she gets mad she bounces about swinging her arms, as if she'd like to punch some people on the nose—figuratively speaking that is, she is much too much a lady to literally punch anyone on the nose."

With words, Grace took the members on a tour of Vancouver slum areas. She told of flats without bathtubs, toilets or sinks, of small children sitting on dirt floors, of hundreds of people in Vancouver living on less than 499 dollars a year. The 499 dollars figure created a storm on the Coalitionist benches, as several members could not believe it was possible. These slum housing conditions were breeding grounds for disease, delinquency, crime and insanity, Grace declared. She urged that a Dominion housing authority be established to work with provinces, regions and municipalities. When she thought she was making progress, she geared up again on the issue March 6, 1945. But that day the spectacular explosion of a freighter at Pier BC rocked Vancouver's downtown business section, killing nine people. Grace's housing speech, carefully timed for maximum publicity to coincide with the Vancouver visit of Dominion Director of Housing F.W. Nichols, never made the papers.

Grace did take up other matters besides housing, particularly the extension of the Vancouver municipal franchise to all adult citizens over twenty-one, not just householders and property owners.

Meanwhile the Coalition government was finally accepting some CCF demands. In 1945 Premier Hart brought in a bill providing for public development and administration of hydro-electric power, daring the CCF to attack it. They did not. That same day, Provincial Secretary George Pearson moved his social assistance bill through second reading. Grace called it "a first attempt by BC to provide a social security network through which no person could fall."

The CCF program was becoming blurred as the Coalition co-opted some of its most important issues and attacked the rest. Grace even found herself on the same side as Attorney General Royal Maitland and Nancy Hodges in the matter of bringing Canada's divorce laws up to date. In a debate just before the 1945 session wound up, Grace urged that adultery, insanity, long periods of desertion and habitual criminality now be made additional grounds for divorce. "Once love and respect are lost," Grace told the House, "it is immoral for a man and a woman to live together—it is an immoral atmosphere in which to bring up children." She said it might be a good idea to make marriage more difficult in the first place.

The spring of 1945 was a joyous one as the Allies recovered one German-held territory after another. The eleven days from April 28 through May 8 was the victorious culmination of the entire Allied war effort in Europe. Yet joy in victory was mixed with mourning for the vast destruction war had wrought. The great cities of Europe lay ruined, fifty-five million were dead, thirty-five million wounded, ten million more were displaced persons and refugees. An estimated $1.5 billion US had gone up in smoke. The most deadly device in history, the atomic bomb, had just been exploded secretly for the first time in the New Mexico desert.

Naturally Grace was delighted by the news of victory for the world as a whole, but she also had personal reasons to celebrate. Her brothers were all in the armed forces: Howard as a soldier, Bruce as an intelligence officer in Europe, Ralph as a doctor and Charles on the British Ministry of Information staff in the Far East.

That year a charter and structure for the UN emerged from a gathering of fifty nations in San Francisco, but so did the fundamental cleavage between communism and democracy. Canada was negotiating to maintain her status as an independent dominion, rather than as part of the British Empire, a priority of Prime Minister King during all his terms in office. King represented Canada in San Francisco; the CCF was represented by leader M.J. Coldwell.

With victory in Europe assured, Prime Minister King dissolved Parliament and called an election, and the CCF was confronted by the appearance of an improbable alliance of the communists and the Liberals, the Liberal–Progressive Party. In January 1944 Tim Buck had said, "Masses of Canadian people are turning away from the Liberal and Tory parties, but reactionary interests are preparing for an unscrupulous struggle to keep the old parties in power." But in June 1944, five days before the Saskatchewan election, the CPC took out a large ad in the Regina *Leader-Post* declaring, "TIM BUCK proposes a Liberal-Labour Coalition in the coming Federal Elections." In August Buck published an article, "Why I Support Mackenzie King."

The BC CCF studied and re-studied the problem. In 1944 a committee of five was selected to "study the whole question of the relation of the CCF to the Communist Party, the Communist–Labour Total War Committee, and other progressive groups, and to consult with these bodies to discover whether or not a basis of future cooperation on matters of mutual interest and concern may be effected." That committee included Grant MacNeil, Arnold Webster, Nathan Nemetz, later Chief Justice of the BC Court of Appeals, and Bert Herridge. Herridge, MLA for West Kootenay, was expelled from the CCF in May 1945. When his name was put forward as a federal candidate while he was still an MLA, the application was rejected by the BC CCF executive, as two simultaneous elective positions were not allowed. Herridge ran anyway as an Independent–CCF, or People's CCF candidate, and won, but this incident turned Angus and Grace against him. To Grace, Herridge was a hypocrite, a big landlord who dabbled in communism. Angus, among others, believed Herridge was really working for the LPP, boring into the CCF from within, and he never acknowledged Herridge's presence in the House of Commons, even to say good morning, although they were both part of the CCF caucus from 1945 until Angus retired in 1957.

In retaliation for his anti-communist views, the LPP mounted a fierce campaign against Angus in his own riding of Vancouver East. While Angus was in Australia, Harold Pritchett was nominated to run against him. David Lewis in Ottawa and Grace in Vancouver recognized the danger. "In my opinion," Grace wrote him, "certain ridings are in a bad way because they are allowing a few of those well-known CP supporters to remain right in the organization. They say they have no proof and can't turn them out. Our people aren't half tough enough to survive."

For their part Liberals did not return the LPP embrace, but, paradoxically, they painted red those very CCF candidates who had just rejected the LPP. "Who are these CCFers who demand that we toss away a thousand years of parliamentary freedom together with our common laws and replace them with the vaporings of a German named Karl Marx?" Gerry McGeer, Liberal MP for Vancouver–Burrard, thundered erroneously during the federal campaign.

In the federal election June 11, 1945 the CCF elected only 28 members. It was a gain of 20 seats for the party, but not a very strong showing when compared with the CCF's twenty-nine percent in the Gallup poll of September 1943. The Liberals stayed in government with 125 seats; the Tories won 67 ridings; 13 went to Social Credit and 12 to independents. Angus retained his seat in Vancouver East, but ironically he did so partly due to campaign literature quoting written expressions of gratitude from LPP leaders Nigel Morgan and Tom McEwan for his efforts in Parliament to have the ban on the Communist Party lifted.

Grace served as campaign manager for Vancouver–Burrard CCF candidate Arnold Webster, a former president of the BC CCF. Despite her best efforts, Webster lost by 1,872 votes to the Conservative candidate, Lt.-Col. Cecil Merritt, a war hero. It was a classic case of the success of Labour–Progressive tactics, although the Tories and not the Liberals harvested the seat. Webster and Merritt had contested the riding against LPP candidate Minerva Cooper, a well-known communist who polled 2,130 votes. If she had not split the labour vote, and if her votes had gone to Webster, he would have won Vancouver–Burrard. Coldwell blamed the communists for the CCF's poor showing. "Tissues of falsehoods and distortions" were spread across the country, he told reporters, "confusion deliberately created . . . in the interests of the Liberal party by communists under the guise of Labour–Progressives." Still others had painted the CCF as fascists; one Liberal candidate identified the CCF directly with German Naziism.

A week before the federal election, on June 4, the CCF had dropped all but eight of their seats in a disastrous Ontario election that returned the Conservatives to power under George Drew. CCF supporters in Ontario were shattered. A week later, CCF supporters across the country were totally discouraged.

At the end of July, the British Labour Party led by Clement Attlee defeated Winston Churchill's Conservatives. Attlee, Stalin and Truman decided in a meeting at Potsdam, Germany that Germany would be disarmed and demilitarized, Nazi institutions would be dissolved, and German leaders would be tried as war criminals. Meanwhile, across the Pacific, the United States was preparing to bring World War Two to a decisive end.

On August 6, the world's first atomic bomb used in combat fell on Hiroshima, killing one hundred thousand Japanese people. Another hundred thousand died later from burns and radiation sickness. Three days later a similar bomb dropped on Nagasaki, killing seventy-five thousand outright and fatally burning seventy-five thousand more. August 10, Japan sued for peace. August 14 was declared V-J Day for Victory in Japan.

Grace lost no time in using these events to illustrate the need for racial equality at home. Commenting on the refusal of a Vancouver hotel to accommodate the black cast members of the musical *Carmen Jones,* Grace wrote in a letter to the *Vancouver Sun*, "V-E Day was supposed to celebrate our victory over Hitler and his Nazi creed. It would seem however, that his ideas of 'Nordic Superiority' have won the day .... If it isn't Negroes, it's Japanese. If it isn't Japanese, it's Chinese. If it isn't East Indians, it's Jews. In short, it's anyone but you and me. And tomorrow it may be you! It's high time we stopped playing with this atomic bomb of race prejudice."

Now Grace would have to defend her views to her constituents. On August 31, 1945 Premier John Hart dissolved the Legislature and called a provincial election for October 25.

As the long, bloody war ended and reconstruction began, socialism sank like a stone across Canada, and Grace sank with it. Voters in Nova Scotia and Manitoba provincial elections held during the BC election campaign rejected CCF candidates overwhelmingly. Manitoba returned a Liberal–Conservative Coalition; Nova Scotia voted Liberal. In the previous few months Ontario had gone Conservative; New Brunswick, Liberal; and Alberta, Social Credit. Saskatchewan was the only CCF province in the country. These hard electoral facts were used by opponents of the CCF in British Columbia to convince voters that socialism could only succeed if it were nationwide, and across the nation Canadians were not supporting the CCF.

Grace and Grant MacNeil contested Vancouver–Burrard against Coalitionists Vancouver parks commissioner Don Brown, a Conservative, and Dr. George Weir, a professor and a Liberal who had served as Minister of Education and Provincial Secretary in the Pattullo government of the late 1930s. The LPP and Social Credit each ran two candidates. Much of the campaign controversy in BC revolved around co-operation with parties of the right or the left. What party insiders like Grace saw as maintaining CCF integrity, many outsiders saw as a refusal to live by their own principle of co-operation.

In her opening campaign speech Grace blasted the Hart government for hoarding surplus revenue of more than sixteen million dollars instead of investing it "to create new industry and jobs for the post-war years." But in the mouths of Coalitionists those surplus funds became the assets that would make possible their forty-three-point program. This program included many of the CCF social insurance measures: better health and hospital services, municipal ownership of transit services, and funding for low-rental housing and slum clearance.

CCF candidates were painted as doomsayers and calamity-howlers for predicting a postwar depression, as inexperienced idealists who would freeze all wages and jobs, and as heavy-handed dictators who called the tune and ejected from the party anyone who refused to dance.

The CCF issued a blue book outlining its campaign platform and featuring its Regina Manifesto declaration, "We aim to replace the present capitalist system." That alone was enough to scare off many voters who just wanted a return to normalcy as they had known it before the war. The blue book promised to socialize transportation, brewing and distilling industries, refining and distribution of oil and gas, and to start a public logging and milling enterprise and a government steel industry. As the *Vancouver Sun* pointed out repeatedly, the CCF program would "go farther than the Labour government proposes to go in Britain." That too frightened many voters.

Remembering that French-Canadians had bitterly opposed conscription, voters did not respond to Grace's calls for understanding of French Canada and unity with Quebec. Grace had been optimistic on this score. She told a campaign meeting in Rio Hall that "uniform living standards, minimum wage rates, high health standards and advanced standards of education" would entice Quebec to stay within a happy, solidly united Canada. But BC voters did not seem to care.

Most devastating to Grace personally was the public reaction to her insistence on equal and just treatment for the Japanese in Canada. Some saw her as a traitor. "The CCF," one Coalition candidate declared, "took sides with the Japanese and have consistently done so ever since." It did not help Grace's cause when people recalled May 22, 1945, the day Japanese incendiary balloon bombs were found in BC loaded with explosives designed to ignite massive fires in the heavily forested interior mountains. Another Coalitionist warned, "If the CCF comes back, you will have the Japanese on your hands . . . these same men who used our soldiers for bayonet practice. They would have the vote in this province and they would not vote individually but en bloc. Yes, the CCF would bring the Japs back to British Columbia."

No matter that the policy in Grace's pamphlet *Oriental Canadians—Outcasts or Citizens?*, the CCF's official policy, was the same as that of the federal Liberal government: to spread the Canadian Japanese amongst all nine provinces; voters were still fearful. During the campaign newspapers printed a barrage of stories detailing Japanese war atrocities. "Japs Used Live Prisoners as Rifle Practice Targets," "Japs Tortured Victoria Repat" and "Children Eaten When Japs Held Hong Kong" were typical examples.

On election day the *Vancouver News Herald* ran a story highlighting Coalition Attorney General Gordon Wismer's anti-Japanese remarks the night before. "I am not being unchristian by suggesting that the people who committed frightful atrocities against helpless prisoners be shipped back to Japan," he said. If the CCF gets in, those [interned] Japanese will come back here . . . they will get the vote. How many Japs will the CCF bring over here to bolster their hold on the province?"

A record turnout was predicted for election day, but on October 25 BC experienced its worst storm in years. Heavy rains and flooding made it hard for voters to get to the polls, and the turnout was lighter than expected.

When the votes were tallied, Grace had lost her seat by more than three thousand votes. The Coalition swept to victory with thirty-five seats, and only nine went to the CCF. All three CCF women were defeated; Grant MacNeil as well as Grace lost in Vancouver–Burrard. Wallis Lefeaux lost Vancouver Centre. Harold Winch, who retained his seat in Vancouver East, blamed the losses on the CCF's limited campaign budget. Grace was reduced to finding comfort in "a definite increase in the popular vote" for the CCF, while Grant MacNeil called it "a great moral victory."

Grace did score one minor point. For years she had been pressing the City of Vancouver to allow full suffrage in civic elections. Grace campaigned on the idea that voters qualified to choose MPs to deal with peace and war and a federal budget of billions should be able to vote for aldermen to handle a few million dollars for Vancouver. Just before election day 1945 a city council committee decided in favour of broadening the franchise to allow full suffrage, but full council approval was still years away.

Grace travelled to Ottawa to be with Angus, her champion and bulwark of strength in defeat. A week before Christmas a bill giving MPs an annual salary increase of two thousand dollars came up for third reading. Angus objected to the increase, which he termed, "colossal impudence . . . until we can raise the living standard for the low-paid citizens twenty percent or so." Prime Minister King sternly rebuked him, but Social Credit leader Solon Low hit below the belt. "I was trying to imagine what his [MacInnis's] logic would be if suddenly he were to find himself the father of six or more children," Low said. "I would suggest, Mr. Speaker, that it might make a better man of him if he was married to a wife rather than to a brilliant member of the BC Legislature."

Angus jumped to his feet, furious. "I think that members of this House could have the decency to leave wives of their members out of the debate," he rasped. Low's sexist comment was doubly an insult because Grace had just failed to keep her legislative seat, and triply insulting because her full-time work for the CCF had always been unpaid.

No longer on the CCF national council, Grace attended the 1946 national convention in Regina as delegate from the Burrard CCF association, of which she was now president. But Grace won a greater achievement at this convention. She succeeded in carrying the first full CCF resolution on the status of women. During the 1944 convention two resolutions regarding women had been introduced—one on general equality for women, and the other requesting equality of opportunity and wages for women—but both had been judged to be covered by the Regina Manifesto. The new resolution was based firmly on Grace's work with the James Committee on women's postwar reconstruction issues. The national CCF council was instructed "to formulate a policy which will enable women to participate on a basis of equality in the economic and cultural life of Canada," equal opportunities for training, access to all occupations, equal pay for equal work and "discontinuance of the present practice of dismissing married women or refusing them jobs."

The resolution specified modern housing for both farm and city; family allowances or a salary for homemakers or both; trained household workers to be paid the minimum wage; availability of publicly owned or co-operative restaurants, laundries, nursery schools and community centres; and shopping centres conveniently located. Finally, the council was to press for the establishment of a Women's Bureau under the Dominion Department of Labour. This CCF convention also advocated a guaranteed annual income, a way of ensuring at least minimal economic independence for women.

Grace had lost her seat in the Legislature, but she had retained her dignity and her essential vision of herself. She saw herself standing firmly on principle—as her father had done, as Angus did—as long as the cause was right, regardless of whether or not it was popular. She saw herself carrying on her father's role as an instigator and educator for socialism. She would still try to realize the ideal: a Canada governed by a democratically elected socialist administration, serving not the interests of individual profiteers, but the basic human needs of the greatest number of Canadians.

CHAPTER 9

Citizen of the World

Scarlet maples spread a flaming carpet across the Catskill Mountains amid the rich smell of burning leaves in October of 1946, when two hundred women from around the world gathered in an old carriage house in South Kortright, New York. The carriages pushed to the sides of the huge hall and antique quilts on the walls provided a rural homey touch, but the subjects of discussion were serious and far-reaching: nothing less than creation of international understanding that would make world peace a reality.

Grace was one of the six Canadian delegates at the ten-dayInternational Assembly of Women, convened by the National Women's Organizations of the United States and timed to coincide with the first New York meeting of the United Nations General Assembly. Chairman Alice T. McLean, head of the American Women's Voluntary Services during the war, invited the gathering to her twenty-five-hundred-acre farm deep in Rip van Winkle country. At the opening session McLean told the delegates, many from former enemy countries, "We don't mean to have it a pressure group. We hoped it would become a road of understanding, to a broad common denominator."

Grace arrived in New York City October 10 to meet women representing fifty-five nations: members of parliaments, club leaders, educators, professional and business women, and one princess. The other Canadian delegates were Mrs. Rex Eaton, Associate Director of the Department of Labour, and, during the war, Director of the Women's Division of Selective Service; Miss D. Shearwood-Stubbington, of Montreal who worked with the United Nations Refugee Relief Agency; Mrs. Tannis Murray of Toronto, producer and director of the CBC radio program "Citizens Forum"; Mme. Thérèse (Mrs. George) Garneau, a champion of women's rights from Montreal; and Alice Keenleyside, who served with the Canadian American Women's Committee and the Pan Pacific Children's Association. Alice was sister to Grace's friend, the Canadian diplomat Hugh Keenleyside.

On the first day delegates were greeted by the assembly's sponsor, Eleanor Roosevelt, then a member of the US delegation to the United Nations and a member of the UN Human Rights Commission. "This meeting will be effective," she said hopefully, "because it is bringing together women from all parts of the world with a willingness to discuss their differences."

Differences there were in abundance. One delegate was a Filipina who had been captured by the Japanese and tortured; another was Haru Matsui, head of the Japanese desk of the US Office of War Information. Gabrielle Strecker, a physician from conquered Germany, was there. Lady Reading of Great Britain played a prominent part in discussions. Mary Caradga, head of the Greek Red Cross, brought an olive branch from the Acropolis to symbolize peace. Ruzena Pelantova, vice-mayor of Prague who was jailed for years by the Nazis, was there, as was Kyllikki Pohjala, a member of the Finnish Parliament since 1931.

The United Nations was about to celebrate its first anniversary, and UN Secretary General Trygve Lie had recognized the International Assembly of Women. He expressed admiration for the conference's aims at a dinner honouring Mrs. Roosevelt at the Waldorf Astoria Hotel.

Grace took an active part in the assembly. The women debated a two-part question: the world of the present, and the world they wished to create. Grace was tapped to head a discussion group on the current economic situation, where participants stressed that the needs of people everywhere are the same: food, education, housing, health services and the right to be responsible citizens. But, looking back, Grace said the women from various countries were on such different economic levels that reaching a consensus on ways and means was next to impossible. "I remember particularly one American woman discussing the pros and cons of unemployment insurance. These people had no idea what a) unemployment was or b) what insurance was. It was miles over their heads. We didn't realize in the western world that the only thing that could mean anything was an attitude of friendship, because all the things on the agenda were mostly beyond their control." When a small group from the Assembly visited nearby Hartford, Connecticut for a panel discussion on "The Contribution of Women Toward One World," Grace was selected as a panel member.

While resting from their consultations the delegates enjoyed the choicest farm food. They slept in nearby hotels and inns. Grace stayed at the same hostelry as one German representative who carried an enormous load of guilt for the behaviour of her countrymen. "She came in just like a timorous little mouse," Grace said. "The Americans are nothing if not generous in their personal ways; they set to work to make her feel comfortable. I remember she had nothing but the clothes that she had on her. She went out of her room to the bathroom and when she returned they had left some curlers in a little saucer on her dressing table. Well, it touched her heart, you see. A lot of us made a point of visiting her and making her feel at home."

Although no formal proposals were supposed to issue from the assembly, several groups of women coalesced during the ten-day meeting. One group started a voluntary international information exchange aimed toward the women of the world. Another group of thirty women from underground movements in occupied countries held a news conference to urge the United Nations toward a quick solution of world problems. A group of women from Latin America held a news conference urging that their countries be made to live up to the United Nations Charter and cease discrimination against women. Many women pressed for sanctions against Spain, then still under Franco's rule.

"One thing I did," Grace remembered, "was to stop the strong communist influence there. There were some French delegates that were communist and they had a strong Communist Party at the time. They did what communists do, tried to gain control of the thing. What I did was to expose them. You talk to people quietly about it and point out examples. But they were trying to get control, and I just knew it would bust things up if nothing else."

The Sunday before the United Nations met for the first time in the US, Mrs. Roosevelt drove the few miles to South Kortright from her home at Hyde Park, New York to address the assembly of women. She expressed faith that the UN could break down the barriers of prejudice between countries, but only if it received the support of the peoples of the world. She urged the women to back the UN in their home countries. "Such meetings as these are a tremendous help in wiping out unthinking prejudices that exist in the world because we've never faced them," she told the delegates.

That day Grace learned a lesson in diplomacy from Mrs. Roosevelt by which she guided her actions ever after. "She said that when you are dealing with other peoples it isn't important that you should agree—in most cases you disagree very vigorously. But what is important is that you find the thinnest edges of agreement and you build on them. And it works."

When the International Assembly of Women held its final session at the Waldorf Astoria Hotel in New York City on October 24, the first United Nations Day, Grace was one of the speakers to address the final plenary meeting. She presented democratic socialism as the only sensible solution to the extremes of individualistic capitalism on the right and communist dictatorship on the left. She spoke practically of socialist methods of postwar reconstruction—helping all people to obtain adequate food, shelter, education and health care—by means of equal democratic participation for all.

Grace was inspired by her experiences in New York. She felt that in this group of women from around the world she had found a new and wider peer group. "It was both heart-warming and heart-wringing to listen to the women from victor and vanquished countries alike," she wrote. "White and black, industrialized and emerging, comfortable and war-scarred—as the days passed these differences became submerged in a common resolve to return home with a practical vision of the first steps to be taken to enable each country to fit into the jigsaw of a world pattern, wonderfully varied and rich in our shared humanity." The vision was still with her twenty-eight years later when she wrote those words.

A new home awaited Grace on her return from New York. The MacInnis establishment was moved to 442 West 15th Avenue, close to Vancouver General Hospital and three blocks from City Hall, in the same tree-lined neighbourhood as the house on 14th Avenue. In mid-November they were ready for their first guests, Angus's niece Violet and her new husband Jack Cameron. Angus's mother had died and his sister Christine lived with the MacInnises during this period. Her presence motivated the move from Grace and Angus's first house after only two years. "I found out that it just didn't work," Grace explained. "There were two ways of living. She had the idea of getting up bright and early and doing everything. She was a superb house-keeper. What I did, you see, was my writing and thinking and that sort of thing in the good hours of the day, and then I'd do my housework and ironing in the evening when I could listen to the radio. So it just didn't work. She was always doing all the work, and my pride wouldn't let me do it . . . . When she would see an unmade bed at the wrong time of day, the bed would have to be made.

"So we then decided, and very wisely, to buy a house with two suites, one upstairs and one down. And this worked magic. We had the lower suite. She had her own place insulated upstairs, and she could run it and polish the brass off everything. She loved the place."

In her role as caretaker for her siblings, Grace helped her youngest brother Howard in his search for a home. He and his wife Joan, an English war bride, wanted to settle near Toronto, but could not afford suitable housing. Grace organized a scheme under which the five Woodsworth siblings contributed to a loan which enabled Howard to buy a house in the Toronto suburb of Scarborough. The low-interest loan was paid back meticulously and in full.

As New Year's Day 1947 dawned the position of women around the world was beginning to improve. Canadian women took another step on the long road toward legal equality when the new Canadian Citizenship Act recognized the equal status of women. Formerly, women applying for citizenship were classed as persons "under a disability" in the same category as minors and insane persons. French women had gained the vote in 1945 and Italian women in 1946. In American-occupied Japan women gained the franchise, and thirty-four women were elected to the Japanese Diet in 1946.

Now that the war was over the jobs of most of Canada's 255,000 women war workers disappeared. Many single women wanted to stay in the labour force, but the majority turned to marriage and homemaking. Birthrates began to soar as reunited couples and newly married husbands and wives started their families. The baby boom had begun. Prices rose when wartime controls were removed, but so did wages. Inflation ballooned. Newly built suburbs began to fuel consumer demand for major appliances, the novel television sets and new cars.

When Grace and Angus's fifteenth wedding anniversary came up January 23, 1947, they were apart as they had been so often for the past five years. Yet they were still very much in love: from his Ottawa office Angus sent the traditional anniversary roses to Grace in Vancouver with a romantic card.

Grace quickly began to reconstruct her own political life after losing her legislative seat. In January 1946 she was named president of the Burrard CCF Association, demonstrating that her power base in the party locally was strong. She wrote educational material for the CCF such as the fifteen-page pamphlet *It's Up To You: How you can be an active citizen through the CCF*, published by the national office in 1946. She served as the national adviser to the CCYM. She and Angus were both on the national council. She attended the Commonwealth Conference of Labour Parties in Toronto in September and worked with the national office as a strategist and writer. But all this activity was not enough; Grace still wanted an elected position. Her only choice was a municipal election.

In early 1947, as publicity chair of the BC CCF civic affairs council, Grace was blasting the current Vancouver City Council for planning to build a new police station rather than replace the city's slum housing. "They'll probably need the police station if they continue to do nothing about Vancouver's housing conditions, which are breeding delinquency and crime faster than His Worship can talk about them," Grace said. In November 1947, when Vancouver civic elections were called for the upcoming year, Grace was ready with her nomination papers for one of the four seats on Vancouver City Council. In the space marked "occupation" she wrote "housewife."

Some of Grace's CCF friends were also in the running: Laura Jamieson for alderman, Gretchen Steeves for parks board and Mildred Osterhout Fahrni for school board, a position she had filled for two years in the 1930s. The issues were funding for a new civic centre with an art gallery, museum and library; the removal of the poll tax; delinquency; education; a universal adult franchise in civic elections; and, most important, housing.

Grace's most important campaign speech was her radio broadcast December 4, 1947 on CKWX. She blamed the civic Non-Partisan Association (NPA), in control of city hall since 1939, for being "Liberals and Tories masquerading as Non-Partisans, who are responsible for the housing chaos, the lack of civic planning and the betrayal of the public interest to BC Electric . . . because they are the tools of vested interests operating for their own gain and not for the public welfare."

Since 1943 Grace had pressed a plan for low-cost housing in Vancouver. In this campaign the NPA adopted the issue; they claimed to have housed four thousand people. "I don't know what they mean by that," Grace told her audience indignantly, "unless they are alluding to the basements, the cabins and little stores into which families have been driven by the city's neglect. The City Council has not built one single house."

When the votes were counted on election night, December 10, 1947, Grace failed by just 256 votes to win one of the four seats on City Council. She came fifth in a field of thirteen. At one point in the evening she surged into third place, but in the end lost to fellow CCFer Laura Jamieson and to NPA men Alex Fisher, R.K. Gervin and Halford Wilson, a long-time adversary on the Japanese Canadian question.

Although Grace had lost her seat in the Legislature partly because of her insistence on equality for those of Japanese origin, she soon had the satisfaction of watching the provincial and federal governments take steps to restore their civil rights. After the bombing of Hiroshima and Nagasaki and the end of the war, Canadian public opinion began to favour a relaxation of restrictions against Japanese Canadians. By December 1946 the camps were practically empty. Four thousand Japanese had gone to Japan; more than thirteen thousand resettled east of BC. Only 6,776 Japanese Canadians remained in the west coast province.

In December 1946 the British Privy Council upheld Canada's right to deport undesirable Japanese, including naturalized British subjects of the Japanese race. Just over a month after this decision the Supreme Court of Canada was made the final court of appeal, ending recourse to the British Privy Council. But the federal government was no longer interested in using its power to deport. Prime Minister King feared an embarrassing debate in the House and a possible split in his Cabinet. One month after the Privy Council decision, King revoked the deportation Orders in Council. But he permitted orders to stand restricting the movements of Japanese Canadians, and prohibited them from fishing on the West Coast. Still, sympathy for them was mounting. In addition to MacInnis, Coldwell and the CCFers, the King government was facing Conservative John Diefenbaker, who had already begun his crusade for a Canadian bill of rights.

Meanwhile, in Ottawa on January 25, the CCF officially opened its new national headquarters in a classic three-storey brick residence at 301 Metcalf Street not far from Parliament Hill. To all the CCF MPs and staff Woodsworth House was, as national secretary David Lewis wrote, "a defiant symbol of survival and permanence. The Liberals could filch our policies, the Tories besmirch our name, the communists disrupt our activities, and editorialists and columnists misrepresent our ideas, but none could halt the work of democratic socialism, not even in temporary defeat." Lucy represented the Woodsworths at the opening ceremony. Grace was in Vancouver pressuring the BC government to extend the franchise it was about to grant Canadian-born Chinese and East Indians to include Japanese and native Indians. "Only when we recognize common humanity will there be no cause for butchery and strife," she told a Sunday evening church forum.

A March 1947 editorial in the *Vancouver Sun* criticized the Toronto Co-operative Committee for trying to have revoked the Orders in Council restricting Japanese fishing and re-entry to the coastal area of BC, and Grace took a swipe at it. "Does the *Sun* know that persons of Japanese origin are forbidden to travel over fifty miles from home, anywhere in Canada, without an RCMP permit . . . forbidden to go from one province to another . . . forbidden to change their place of residence . . . . Or to be absent from home for over thirty days without an RCMP permit? It sounds like Hitler. It *is* like Hitler." By this time Grace was advocating unrestricted return of Japanese Canadians to coastal BC in addition to full rights of citizenship for them. Within weeks she was in Ottawa with Angus, upholding the same standard of racial equality. In April the CCF MPs had failed in their attempt to have the freedom of movement Orders In Council rescinded. Although the vote was one hundred and five to thirty-one, and many members did not even show up for the vote, the press began to swing behind civil rights for Japanese Canadians.

The MacInnis view was starting to prevail. In July, the King government appointed a judge of the BC Supreme Court to investigate Japanese claims for the loss of personal property amounting to an estimated ten million dollars, although the inquiry did not cover the 950 Japanese fishing boats seized and sold. As reporters pointed out, "All of the Japanese in Canada today have been cleared by the government of any suspicion of disloyalty." Yet in March 1948 the King government decided to continue for another year the Orders In Council restricting freedom of movement for Japanese Canadians. In April 1948 the BC government again decided not to grant Japanese Canadians the provincial vote. But their attitude appeared outdated when, just two months later, the federal government just two months later changed the Dominion Elections Act to allow Japanese Canadians the vote in federal elections. Angus, a member of the House of Commons elections committee, told the committee he would ask the House for a deletion of the discriminatory section, rather than an amendment to the act giving Japanese Canadians the vote in 1949. Members of the government did not wait for MacInnis to upstage them; a government-sponsored motion deleting the offensive section was passed by the House without a single dissenting voice.

In April 1946 a joint American–British committee investigating the problems of European Jewry and Palestine brought down its report. Grace studied the report thoroughly, heavily underlining the salient points in her blue paperback copy as she framed a resolution on the issue for the upcoming CCF national convention. She agreed with the report's conclusion that "the whole world shares responsibility for them and for the resettlement of all 'Displaced Persons' . . . irrespective of creed or nationality."

She recognized that in Palestine existed the Jewish National Home, created by the Balfour Declaration of 1917. In 1939 one-third of the population and twelve percent of the land in Palestine were Jewish. The Anglo-American Committee recommended Palestine's borders be opened to one hundred thousand Jewish immigrants, although it recognized that Palestine was "an armed camp" controlled by large illegal armed forces.

Most heavily underlined and starred in Grace's copy of the report is the recommendation that Arab and Jew live together in peace, which sets forth three principles of conduct to achieve this. "I. That Jew shall not dominate Arab and Arab shall not dominate Jew in Palestine. II. That Palestine shall be neither a Jewish state nor an Arab state. III. That the form of government ultimately to be established, shall, under International Guarantees, fully protect and preserve the interests in the Holy Land of Christendom and of the Moslem and Jewish faiths." Grace's long-term view of the Jewish–Palestinian conflict was founded on these principles. As late as October 1973, she reiterated her belief that the area "should be neither an Arab nor a Jewish state."

The resolution placed before the 1946 CCF convention in August bore the stamp of her approval. It resolved that the CCF wholeheartedly support the report of the Anglo-American Commission of Inquiry on Palestine, and urged the Canadian government to accept "a fair share of displaced persons from Europe as citizens of this country." Of the nearly ten million Jews living in Europe in 1939, the Anglo-American Committee report estimated just 391,000 remained alive in 1946. In all, the war left an estimated twenty-five to thirty million Europeans (sixty percent of them Germans) outside the borders of their homelands. What proportion of these needy people, if any, should Canada admit? Grace confronted this enormous problem in an April 1947 article for the *Canadian Forum*, entitled "Immigration? On What Basis?" The refugee issue, she declared, must be considered "from the standpoint of our responsibility as world citizens, regardless of what effect the admission of displaced persons will have on the life of Canada." She urged the government "without further delay" to open Canada's doors to a "fair share" of the world's refugees."

Many Canadians, concerned that an influx of displaced people from Europe would increase competition for jobs and housing and change the racial balance of the country, wanted "selective immigration." If Canada was to be the country of her dream, Grace believed it would need more immigrants to build that dream. But, she warned, Canada would only get desirable immigrants by treating them well once they arrived. She never forgot the misery of the immigrants she had seen growing up in Winnipeg, and campaigning across the prairies during the Depression. "Never again must we dump them on the prairie or in the bush and leave them to fend for themselves," she wrote. "Never again must we allow them to settle in racial or religious blocks. Never again must we keep them as second-class citizens, deprived of rights which we native-born Canadians regard as inseparable from democracy . . . freedom is one thing we can have only when we are prepared to see that others get it too."

When the annual Vancouver civic election campaign opened in November of 1948 Grace's name was again on the ballot for alderman. The leading plank in the CCF platform was "Votes for everybody." In response to years of CCF prodding, City Council had decided on a plebiscite to test public opinion on a full franchise for all adults.

All CCF candidates urged a Yes vote on the plebiscite. They were opposed by powerful voices, including that of the *Vancouver Sun*, which pointed out in an editorial that ratepayers had had the power to elect their own public boards since the city was born. "The CCF would take it from them," the *Sun* warned. For the general public, the CCF platform emphasized the still desperate need for housing, mobile classrooms and travelling classes to relieve the overcrowded schools. But underneath there was a struggle for the labour vote, especially between Grace and NPA candidate Birt Showler, president of the Trades and Labour Council. The local branch of the rival Canadian Congress of Labour took out newspaper ads declaring, "Labour supports Tom Alsbury for Mayor and all CCF candidates for civic office. The CCF is the political arm of Labour." Angus, acting as campaign manager for the CCF mayoral candidate, teacher Tom Alsbury, felt Grace had a good chance to win against Showler. But again, when the ballots were tallied, Grace came fifth in the race for the four council seats. Birt Showler was elected.

Nonetheless, Grace's strength and optimism were valued in party councils, and many looked to her for leadership despite her recent electoral defeats. One observer wrote in November 1948, after attending the CCF national convention at Winnipeg: "Without detracting from the great personal capabilities of M.J. Coldwell, it is widely suspected that Grace, daughter of the late Hon. J.S. Woodsworth, the party founder, and now the wife of Angus MacInnis, CCF MP, is the real leader of that group. Certainly her voice is listened to with great respect and would be even more so if the party won its way into the East Block at Ottawa."

Grace did have her eye on the East Block where federal governments had their offices. Her next election bid was for a seat in the House of Commons in the federal election of 1949. At the end of March she won the nomination in Vancouver South, an area that included many provincial and municipal

CCF voters. Recent redistribution took in a portion of Angus's old riding, Vancouver East. The election was called for June 27, 1949. For the first time Grace and Angus were fighting for seats in the same election. Their ridings were side by side and their hopes were high. It was to be the first federal election (apart from the 1917 election) not contested by Mackenzie King since 1908 when he was first elected to the House of Commons.

Two issues dominated the Canadian scene on a national level: Canada's entry into NATO, and Newfoundland's entry into Confederation. Prime Minister Louis St. Laurent, chosen Liberal leader after King resigned, wanted to see both of these issues brought to a successful conclusion before he set the date for an election to confirm his position. In the second of two close referenda, Newfoundland voted by a narrow margin to join Canada. The issue was relatively simple to resolve and Grace was not involved. But NATO was a different kettle of fish.

As the Cold War deepened it became clear that the United Nations, despite high ideals, could not guarantee world peace and security. NATO was born out of fear of Soviet aggression. In Canada officials felt there was reason to fear. In September 1945 Igor Gouzenko, a cypher clerk in the Soviet Embassy in Ottawa, defected. He took with him documents that proved conclusively that a Soviet spy ring in Canada and the US sought to obtain secrets of the atomic bomb. Coincidentally on the same day, September 5, Canada's first nuclear reactor, ZEEP (Zero Energy Experimental Pile), started up at Chalk River, Ontario. And Soviet military might loomed over Europe. As Canada's Secretary of State for External Affairs, Lester Pearson's job was to assess the Soviet threat. "It appeared that Moscow's advance would not stop as she brought under her control hundreds of thousands of square miles of territory in East and Central Europe and more than ninety millions of people," Pearson wrote in his memoirs.

Late in 1947 Angus attended a session of the UN General Assembly in New York as parliamentary advisor to the Canadian delegation. He returned home convinced that Soviet Russia was the chief obstacle to co-operation and achievement at the UN. "The Soviet is preventing action by use of the veto, and if deprived from using the veto, she will boycott," he told the *Vancouver Sun*, his distaste for communism strengthened by his observations.

In July 1948 Soviet occupation forces in Germany set up a blockade to cut off rail and highway traffic between West Germany and the city of Berlin, and the next day US and British aircraft began flying food and supplies to the two million people in West Berlin. The airlift continued until September 1949, months after Soviet officials lifted the blockade.

Canada was, with the United States and Britain, party to the earliest negotiations to organize a regional group of North Atlantic nations for collective security. The majority of Canadians approved of this new alliance, signed April 4, 1949, but some pacifists opposed it as a step toward conflict.

Soviet sympathizers opposed it as well. Grace identified a third group in opposition who were "much harder to define and very much more difficult to deal with. These people are, basically, isolationists who justify their position in the name of socialism."

Some of the loudest of NATO's opponents were members of the British Columbia CCF. Grace had a lonely fight in support of NATO in her own Burrard executive meeting soon after the CCF national council came out in support of the pact. "We shall have to work hard," she wrote David Lewis, "to the end that the provincial convention shall not come out with a blaze of publicity attacking or at least dissociating itself from the national council stand."

One of the most troublesome dissidents was a newly elected CCF Member of Parliament. Rodney Young was a name Grace preferred in later years not to mention; when questioned about his activities, she "didn't want to waste any time on him." But from 1948 until 1954 Young caused Grace many trials and tribulations.

Rod Young had been a member of the CCF in British Columbia since the early days. At the second national convention in Winnipeg in 1934, the twenty-four-year-old Young made a bid for the leadership of the newly formed CCYM but lost to the youthful Tommy Douglas. In 1937 Young, still a member of the Young Socialist League, was suspended by the BC CCF executive for "stirring up trouble," according to Gretchen Steeves, then an MLA. "Young belonged to a leftist faction opposed to the United Front," she wrote. "A motion to lift his suspension was defeated after some delegates had denounced him as a disruptive element."

When the nine-month suspension was over, Young again became active in the CCF. He served in the Canadian Army, received an honourable discharge in 1946 and began studying for a law degree at the University of British Columbia. When the riding of Vancouver Centre was left vacant in 1948 by Liberal Ian Mackenzie's elevation to the Senate, Young contested the seat in a by-election and won by more than two thousand votes. But his appearance at the same May Day rally as members of the communist-dominated LPP, prompted an angry telegram from Coldwell threatening to cancel a meeting rather than speak on the same platform as Young.

On June 21, 1948, acting as CCF House leader in Coldwell's absence, Angus led Young to the Speaker's chair for the traditional introduction. From that moment Young caused trouble for federal CCF caucus. "It was not long before CCF members learned to be very careful what they said in caucus," Grace wrote in a letter to BC party executive member Frank McKenzie, "because what they said was so frequently repeated outside. There had been no leak prior to the election of Rod Young." The most controversial topic of discussion in caucus was the party's position on NATO, and the press got hold of the details of caucus discussions. Young's guilt in the matter was proved to Grace's satisfaction by a letter Young wrote to Manitoba MLA Barry Richards, who had been suspended and was later expelled by the CCF in that province for proven collaboration with the LPP. "There has undoubtedly been some discussion in the corridors of this building," Young wrote to Richards on March 24, 1949, "which has led the Press to assumptions which should have remained the secret of the Caucus, but in view of the publicity, I do not think I would be breaking any confidences now to tell you that I am in principle opposed to a military pact as an instrument for maintaining peace . . . . My own opinion is that there must be formed an expression or third force among the nations whose Governments are composed in part or whole by members of Social Democratic Parties and that these Governments co-operating in the United Nations and refusing to be influenced either by the Russian Government or the American Government, might form a power sufficiently great to prevent either of the aggressors from plunging civilization into an atomic war."

The rejection of NATO by the BC CCF made front page headlines in Vancouver, where Grace was at the time a declared candidate for federal office. No matter that the CCF federal caucus supported the pact, no matter that Grace had attempted to rise on the floor of the BC CCF convention to explain CCF thinking about NATO after a resolution to support it was defeated; she was ruled out of order. Young was a CCF candidate for Vancouver Centre, and Grace was on the same slate, contesting the riding next door. She was linked with the rejection of NATO in the public mind.

Even Angus had to clarify his position and that of the national CCF. He wired the city editor of the *Vancouver Sun*, "Policy made by national convention, national council and Parliamentary Caucus and all three bodies approved Atlantic Pact in principle. I feel that Canada should join pact as signed. Failure of United Nations to organize world peace has made regional Pact necessary. Pact is for economic co-operation as well as military co-operation . . . . I am satisfied I am representing the majority of my constituents by supporting Pact. Personal conviction and party decision guided my action."

After the BC convention Young returned to Ottawa, and on April 29 addressed the House in support of NATO, a complete reversal of his stance at the BC convention. He assured the House of "the complete and absolute solidarity of the CCF in the position of our leader." He said, "In supporting this Pact it is our sincere belief that it may be a step toward peace and not a step toward war." No one spoke against the NATO pact; a recorded vote showed 185 for; zero against. Young voted in favour of NATO.

The LPP, as a communist front, was outspoken in its denunciation of the NATO pact. It was the only party mobilizing Canadians to block signing of the pact. The *Pacific Tribune*, the communist newspaper in Vancouver, blasted Grace early in 1949 for impeding their efforts: "Such official CCF stalwarts as Grace MacInnis are exerting every effort to solidify that party on common ground with George Drew and St. Laurent behind Wall Street's blueprint for aggression."

The federal election campaign went into high gear in June. Grace was contesting Vancouver South against Liberal Arthur Laing, then a division manager with a farm supply company and president of the BC Liberal Association. He had the backing of BC Premier Byron Johnson and of James Sinclair, then parliamentary assistant to the minister of finance. Laing's campaign literature stressed current prosperity and a national health plan.

Grace's Progressive Conservative opponent was Jack Cornett, a former mayor of Vancouver and a former BC MLA. His platform focussed on freedom of the individual without government interference, fair wages and government housing for low-income tenants. He also advocated health insurance and contributory old age pensions at sixty-five without a means test.

Cornett made the most of the split in the provincial CCF over NATO. "Some of the policies of the CCF would so weaken our country that, in time, it could fall an easy victim to communists," Cornett's campaign literature proclaimed. "The opposition of the CCF in BC to the North Atlantic Pact is a good example of this. I believe that socialism is the first step in the direction of communism."

The entire CCF slate was adversely affected by attacks on Rod Young's candidacy in Vancouver Centre. His Liberal opponent, Ralph Campney, challenged Young's position on the NATO pact. "What has Mr. Young to say about charges in the provincial election campaign that the CCF is being infiltrated with communists?"

In the middle of the federal campaign, a BC provincial election was set for June 15, 1949. Grace was held responsible for one embarrassing moment that left the CCF vulnerable to "Red Scare" tactics. As chair of the CCF rally climaxing the provincial campaign, Grace opened with the fervent singing of "The Red Flag," the theme song of the British Labour Party. The crowd of twenty-four hundred raised the roof as Grace cried, "A great wave is rising toward the King Canutes of capitalism who are trying to hold back the tide of the peoples' movement." Rod Young did not attend, but that did not stop Campney from raising a press furore over the singing of "The Red Flag," which many people mistakenly linked with communism.

Grace's own campaign literature for the federal vote two weeks away featured bread and butter issues. "Vote CCF and Stop the Boom from becoming a Bust," her leaflet enjoined voters. Emblazoned above a photo of Grace looking serious and competent was the national CCF slogan, "The CCF Can Do The Job!" She referred repeatedly to the success of Clement Attlee's socialist government in Britain. She campaigned for reduction of food prices to consumers by means of federal subsidies to farmers. Bread is eight cents a loaf in Britain but fourteen cents a loaf in Canada, she pointed out, suggesting cheaper prices in Britain were due to price controls and subsidies implemented by a socialist government.

She slammed Canada's government for lifting wartime price controls. "The Liberal government struck a body blow at home markets when they lifted ceilings on food and other consumer commodities," she declared. "Every dollar in subsidies during the war saved the Canadian buyer twelve dollars. Removal of controls swept away these savings. Now farmers and manufacturers are finding their products rotting in warehouses because Canadian families cannot afford to buy everyday needs. The CCF is the only party which tried to prevent decontrol. The CCF believes that steady prices within the range of low-income families are the cornerstone of security for the nation."

A national health insurance plan was a plank in all three platforms, but Grace described Laing's health care promises as "pure election bait," a 1945 campaign promise the Liberals had broken. Grace's campaign leaflet emphasized national health care. "Have your doctor and hospital bills paid by a National Health Insurance Plan," it invited. "In Britain everybody has it, in Canada everybody wants it." In addition Grace's leaflet promised old age pensions of fifty dollars a month to all at age sixty-five with no means test and higher unemployment benefits.

Late in the campaign, Grace struck at Laing's limited influence even if he were to win. He and Cornett had been vying with one another in promising a bridge from Vancouver South to Richmond where the airport was located. "The most pathetic figure in parliament is a back-bencher on the government side who has ideas of his own," Grace declared. "No one is more powerless. He will either toe the line of government policy or he'll be told . . . that he'd better make his criticism from the opposition side of the House." The next day Laing indignantly hit back, calling Grace's warning "tall talk."

The most controversial topic in the campaign was housing. Liberal Laing invited PC opponent Cornett to debate the issue. Cornett turned him down, but Grace shouldered her way into the debate by challenging Laing. When the debate was held three days before the vote, Victoria Hall was packed and five hundred people were turned away. On the platform stood an empty chair decorated with a prominent sign, "For ex-Mayor Cornett."

Grace called housing "our number one headache" and blamed the Liberal government for the "appalling shortage of housing . . . . We are failing to keep pace with the increase in numbers of families, and haven't even touched the backlog of over a million homes unbuilt or needing major repairs." Laing defended Liberal policies and explained that the housing problem was worldwide, caused in Canada by "lack of building before and during the war, an increase in population and a tremendous rise in civic assessments." Grace countered that fifty percent of Canada's workers earned less than twelve hundred dollars a year, "making about forty-five percent unable to borrow from the National Housing Act . . . . People live like animals in the shadow of the Parliament Buildings in Ottawa, and in Toronto families of five live in single rooms for eighteen dollars per week in rent." Responsibility for housing should be shared by civic, provincial and federal governments, Grace concluded.

She had run an intelligent, principled campaign; she had generated interest at high-powered rallies and garnered a great deal of media attention. But when the votes were counted June 27, Grace lost to Arthur Laing by 2,685 votes. She had the consolation of coming second, ahead of Cornett.

Angus retained his seat for a fifth consecutive term, but most other CCF candidates in BC lost. Provincial party president Gretchen Steeves was narrowly defeated in Burnaby–Richmond. Bert Herridge kept his Kootenay West seat, and Owen Jones was elected in Yale. The CCF took just twelve seats across the country. It was a Liberal sweep—193 seats out of 262, the greatest proportion of seats ever won by a political party in Canadian history. Prosperity and the trusted figure of Louis St. Laurent carried election day on June 27, 1949. The CCF and many Canadian economists had guessed wrong. The postwar economic needle pointed to growth for the Canadian economy, not depression.

Again Grace was stoic in defeat. While Angus blamed it on fear of a Canada under Conservative leader George Drew, Grace told the *Vancouver Sun*, "I see two reasons for our defeat. One was fear of Drew. The other was a reluctance on the part of the people to change horses in what they consider a troubled midstream. I fear the public has sought security in the evasion of facts. The time will come when they will realize that the facts must be faced."

But Grace herself had to face one fact: in the past five years she had lost provincial, municipal and federal elections. She was just not electable, at least for the present.

CHAPTER 10

Intimate Enemies

In the brilliant sunrise of July 26, 1950, the Hotel Vancouver hulked grey and sad over Georgia Street. Within, CCF delegates from across Canada assembled for their eleventh national convention, the first to be held in Vancouver. Grace had worked for months to ensure smooth functioning of the event and plenty of positive attention from her hometown media.

But the CCF convention was to be upstaged. Former Prime Minister Mackenzie King had died four days before, alone at Kingsmere amidst his collection of *faux* ruins of world-famous buildings. Compounding the national sense of loss, on the day the CCF convention opened, Liberal Minister of Labour Humphrey Mitchell died suddenly in Ottawa. First elected as a Labour MP from Hamilton in 1931, he had been part of the earliest CCF parliamentary caucuses. Grace, Angus and many others at the Vancouver convention knew Mitchell, and mourned him even though he had turned Liberal.

Still, the convention must continue. Frank Scott, tall and intense at the podium, addressed a CCF convention for the last time as national chairman. He tried to reassure delegates that the party to which they had dedicated so much was still valuable in a world that persisted in confusing socialism with totalitarianism and communism.

Embroiled in a Cold War detonated by the fierce race for nuclear and ideological supremacy, the world paid little attention to Scott's wisdom. One month earlier armed forces from industrialized communist North Korea had invaded agricultural South Korea, where the US military had established a government under Syngman Rhee after the war. The governments of both North and South Korea now claimed jurisdiction over the entire peninsula. The US was organizing a collective security force under UN auspices and had called on Canada to contribute. The country was divided on the proper extent of its involvement. Agreement to send a volunteer brigade was reached only after several heated cabinet meetings.

The CCF was sharply divided too. The national executive and council supported the UN action in Korea based on the precept that World War Two had proved in blood: aggression must never be appeased, it must be attacked early to prevent its growth. At a large convention-eve rally in Vancouver, M.J. Coldwell declared the council's position on Korea to be CCF policy, a move that earned him the righteous anger of the party's pacifist left wing. They opposed the national council's position, and were determined to be heard. To them, Coldwell was acting arbitrarily by declaring the CCF position on the eve of a national convention without waiting for the delegates to vote. They felt especially betrayed since the CCF promised prospective members a direct role in the policy decisions of the party in contrast to Liberal, Conservative and communist methods of policy-making by the party elite.

Grace had used this promise as the main point of her 1946 pamphlet, *It's Up To You!* "In all other political parties the policies are made by leaders who hand down their decisions to the rank and file," she wrote. "In the CCF, it's the rank and file who make the policies." She described the path of a resolution from local club or constituency organization to unit meeting, to yearly provincial convention, to biannual national convention. "Your vote is just as important as the vote of any other member in making the policies and in choosing the leadership of the movement," Grace wrote. "The CCF is challenging the old idea that the people are unfit to rule, that only a small clique has enough brains and determination to do the job. The CCF maintains that the people themselves are capable of governing themselves—if they only will."

Grace was still committed to these ideals of democracy, but now she found herself enmeshed in a sticky web. The left wing had a point: Coldwell's Korean War speech flatly contradicted the promise of *It's Up To You!* and other similar CCF statements. Grace had been manoeuvring to block this group's activities. Two weeks before the convention she had confided her strategies to David Lewis, as was her longtime custom, although he was now in private law practice after fourteen years as CCF national secretary.

"The Steeves–Young axis has been working hard and will have, I believe, more than fifty percent of the BC delegates on their side," Grace wrote, referring to former MLA Gretchen Steeves and former MP Rod Young. Grace blamed this left-wing group for the spread of apathy and dissension in BC. Also, they did not object to working in a united front with the communist LPP. Grace knew Young was the delegate from Vancouver Centre. Referring to the Vancouver East delegate as "a man with a fellow-travelling record and a loud voice," Grace pointed to her biggest fear. In these "red scare" days, pro-communist "fellow-travellers" were considered subversive.

Grace thought "the other crowd" was anxious to drive a wedge between CCFers from British Columbia and those from the rest of Canada. "We have already discovered an attempt to foist the 'Red Flag' on the big public meeting. We have squelched it, of course and are keeping convention arrangements very closely under control. But here's what I am afraid of. They know that Mr. Coldwell has been rubbed raw by BC antics. So have you and some others. They will try to create a public scene where one of the national figures—preferably Mr. Coldwell—may be tempted, in a moment of sudden feeling—publicly to renounce BC's habit of messing up the CCF for the rest of Canada. Such a gesture would be absolutely *fatal* for our hopes of making the split come where it should—in the BC. delegation."

Grace wanted Lewis to advise national officers, particularly Coldwell, to BC CCFers who wanted to work with the rest of Canada to defeat the "other gang." As it turned out, Lewis and others broke Angus's heart and sparked the public scene she feared.

The national council met in Vancouver a few days before the convention to establish the order of business and choose a nomination slate of national officers to endorse. Grace and Angus hosted two pre-convention gatherings in their back yard attended by, among others, national council members Frank Scott, M.J. Coldwell, Thérèse Casgrain and Stanley Knowles. Yet they received no warning of the coming blow.

Scott had announced his decision to step down as national chairman. Angus had been vice-chairman during Scott's eight years at the top; he was deputy leader in the House; he had been continuously re-elected for twenty years. It was natural for him to hope he might succeed Scott as chairman. But during June, at the invitation of Labour Minister Mitchell, Angus had gone to Geneva to advise the Canadian delegation at the thirteenth annual conference of the International Labour Organization (ILO). Grace spent May and early June in Ontario with her mother and returned to convention arrangements in Vancouver. Neither was aware of forces within the party moving against Angus.

The national council nominated Percy Wright, the MP from Melfort, Saskatchewan, as national chairman. Saskatchewan was the only province with a CCF government, they reasoned; it had a strong party organization; Wright had been in Parliament since 1940; since Scott was an easterner, a westerner was next in line. Lewis recalled, "The conversations on the subject were, of course, informal and private. Several other council members, including Scott and myself, were canvassed and agreed. None of us, all friends of MacInnis, had enough sensitivity to appreciate the affront to his pride and self-respect which our decision entailed." Meanwhile Grace and Angus, both council members, were left in the dark.

Grace felt totally betrayed. "David worked to get Percy Wright in there. He didn't say a word to either Angus or me. It was a very, very bad blow. Angus stood [for election as national chairman] because he said he would stand, and he was defeated by Percy Wright. It was a very crushing blow for me. I could have borne it better if they had come to me and laid it out cold.

I would have objected, but at least I would have known about it. But they didn't do that. It never made any difference in our relations with Percy, but it did with David."

Later Lewis felt badly about his part in shouldering Angus aside. For years he never mentioned it to Grace or Angus, but after Grace had retired and Lewis had been defeated, he wrote a letter of apology. "All I want you to know is that from the day it occurred I regretted doing something that obviously hurt Angus. This regret has been strengthened lately by my research in the files of the CCF. This has confirmed my belief that Angus's contribution to the building of our party, in its early years, has not received the recognition it deserves. His logical mind, practical sense and moral courage were the strongest influence in the direction of a realistic approach to difficult problems in policy as well as in organization . . . . I should have known that the interests of the party would be well served by Angus as chairman."

Lewis's lack of sensitivity is surprising: he had been in almost daily contact with Grace and Angus socially and on CCF business since 1935. Yet as early as the mid-1930s Grace had reservations about Lewis. "David tried to undermine my father as a leader way, way back," she said. "He felt he wasn't militant enough. I think he felt that we should have had a more vibrant and noisy kind of a leader, I mean a vigilante sort of a fighter.

"And you see, he didn't understand the temperament of Canadians like Angus and me, and on the other hand, we didn't understand the people born in those European, tough anti-Semitic backgrounds. Angus and I were both born and raised on this continent. We had a fairly straight kind of moral code given to us by our parents, and it was probably easy sailing to know where we stood on things. David was born of a family that was in a Jewish ghetto in Poland, where they had to be quick-witted to get along, much more flexible than either Angus or I. We were pretty rigid. I think a whole lot of it was temperament. Then I think David had a sort of a quality, almost a secretiveness that we didn't have.

"When he wanted to put Percy Wright as national chairman instead of Angus, instead of letting Angus know about it and talking it over with Angus and me, it was all done under the guise of love and friendship, but the first we knew about it was when he had already put Percy Wright on the executive slate. Angus was overturned without so much as a word."

It was the most bitter disappointment of Angus's political life, and the beginning of his decline. His health deteriorated and his political influence waned. For the first time since the CCF's founding in 1932, he was not on the national council. To add insult to injury, other retiring members of the national executive were honoured during the 1950 national convention, but because he was displaced so abruptly, Angus was not.

As the convention proceeded, Grace was elected to the council as representative from BC, and Lewis was elected national vice-chairman. But Grace's troubles during that pivotal convention were not at an end. There was one discussion she wanted to continue until everyone was talked out; Angus wanted to shut off debate after forty minutes. A vote was called, and Angus's side won. Grace hurried on to other business without roasting Angus for voting against her, but the split was apparent to Jim Nesbitt, covering the convention for the *Vancouver News Herald*. The event was an echo of a public argument between the MacInnises at the 1948 national convention, which had also made the newspapers. Angus said a proposed ten-point socialization program should be the first-term program of a national CCF government; Grace told him he was "off the beam" and ought to know better. The article is illustrated with a news photo showing Grace reproachfully pointing a finger at her husband while he faces her sternly, arms akimbo.

Grace's parents would have been appalled—they never publicly disagreed. But these incidents illustrate Grace's growing independence of thought, and also her ability to take part in the democratic process of discussion, dissent, voting, and support of the majority position even when she was in the minority.

And still another blow was about to descend. At the entrance to the convention hall was a display table of socialist literature for sale, staffed by BC provincial literature secretary Eve Smith. The presence of one pamphlet provoked a ferocious controversy. *Is the Labour Party the Way to Socialism?* by the Socialist Party of Great Britain criticized the policies of the governing British Labour Party and its leader Clement Attlee. No one is sure how the pamphlet got there, but on the third day of the convention T. Eggerton, a CCF member-visitor to the convention from Trail, BC, objected to the presence of "Trotskyist literature" on the display table, and he objected in what Smith considered an offensive manner. David Lewis instructed Smith to remove it. She refused. He repeated his request in stronger language. Smith again refused. According to Smith's later recollection, Harold Winch then jumped to the platform, grabbed the microphone and, holding the offending pamphlet aloft, demanded, "Do you want this sold on the table?"

A wild debate on the issue of free speech ensued, with delegates ignoring rules of order and making venomous personal comments. Eve Smith's brother-in-law John Smith recalled, "The convention was so out of hand, I know I spoke. I had no right to speak but since they were all disobeying the rules I had my speech . . . . David Lewis and M.J. Coldwell with a kind of goon squad behind them were using pretty rough tactics. They were simply taking the microphone whenever they wanted." The free-for-all was climaxed by a close vote which held that the pamphlet should not be on sale. Finally, according to Eve Smith, an exasperated Donald MacDonald overturned the literature table, dumping all the books and pamphlets onto the floor, and pushing her out of the way. MacDonald says he simply put the offending materials in a carton and got out of Eve Smith's way.

In August 1950 Eve Smith wrote a letter to the editor of the *Vancouver Sun* claiming the national leadership of the CCF wanted the pamphlet removed because its socialist message was in conflict with the leadership's newly perceived need to revise the Regina Manifesto. "It should be understood quite clearly that the trouble at the convention was over no Stalinist or Trotskyist publications, but over socialist ones," Smith wrote. Grace and the BC party executive were indignant over this airing of the party's dirty linen, but the increasingly prosperous and well-fed Canadian public was not interested in distinctions among socialist, Trotskyist and Stalinist literature, and it was quickly losing interest altogether in the squabbling CCF.

The "literature incident," as it came to be called, was the inflammatory public scene Grace had feared, and the issues behind it did split the party. The CCF establishment, which Grace called the "moderates," believed that the party would never appeal to a wide cross-section of Canadians unless it updated its socialism and toned down some of the more radical statements in the Regina Manifesto.

The left wing viewed the incident as a free speech issue, another intolerable instance of authoritarian control by the national CCF inner circle. This left-wing group, which included Rod Young, Gretchen Steeves, Colin Cameron, Ernie Winch and Eve Smith, did not believe Canada should be a member of NATO but should maintain a foreign policy independent of the United States. This group wanted to see the Regina Manifesto retained. Yet they joined in a unanimous vote against the "peace petition" circulated at the convention by the Canadian Peace Congress, which the convention believed to be a communist front organization.

The CCF was more than usually eager to distance itself from communist and Marxist left-wing associations. Canada and the US in summer 1950 were rigidly intolerant of all left-of-centre views. In September 1949 the Russians had announced that they too had the atomic bomb. US President Truman announced his country's intention to develop a hydrogen bomb. NATO was another response to this new Soviet threat. Any pacifist, anyone not supportive of private enterprise capitalism, was tagged a "commie pinko" or a "red." Liberal views were "dangerous"; fear of espionage by traitors and spies was commonplace.

Many Americans were convinced of an internal communist conspiracy to undermine the US government. In 1947 the US Attorney General had published a list of organizations considered to hold communist, fascist, totalitarian or subversive views. US Senator Joseph McCarthy was not yet a household name but was already hunting for "reds" in the State Department and accusing Secretary of State Dean Acheson and President Truman of being "soft" on communism. Alger Hiss, president of the Carnegie Endowment for International Peace, was convicted of perjury in January 1950 regarding his links to the Communist Party. (He was not cleared until January 1993.) People from many walks of life were subpoenaed to appear before congressional committees and pressured to name friends and acquaintances as communists.

These events received wide publicity in Canada, and Canadian opinion took on a similar tone. Canada's own red scare began in September 1945 with the Igor Gouzenko incident, and the government passed a secret Order In Council allowing the RCMP to detain anyone suspected of passing information to a foreign power. The Royal Commission on Espionage held closed-door hearings; persons before it had no right to bail or counsel.

Canadian trade unions too were purging their ranks of communists. In 1949 both the TLC and the CCL called on all affiliated organizations to remove communists from union office. In this distrustful political climate, Marxism was as suspect as communism in the eyes of most Canadians.

Grace thought of herself as a defender of free speech and had often supported the right of minority dissent, yet in the "literature incident" she stood with the CCF establishment to protect the national party from communist infiltration and factional splits. She allowed this conviction to supersede her anger over Lewis's cavalier treatment of Angus. Grace's guiding ethic was to get all CCF members working co-operatively together. Her stance earned her the undying antagonism of the left-wingers, even those who knew her well. John Smith recalled much later, "I liked Grace MacInnis personally. I spent many weekends in her house, and she was an attractive, pleasant kind of woman. But Grace would support free speech if free speech was going to further Grace's political ambitions—otherwise not. And Grace MacInnis could be one of the most politically minded people that ever was in the CCF, and it was striking because it was in such contrast to her own father and her mother too. Grace MacInnis was the arch politician inside the CCF."

For political reasons Grace suppressed her annoyance with Coldwell for his inflammatory Korean War speech and her anger with Lewis for his treatment of Angus. She continued to work with them purely for the good of the party. And she sincerely believed the Regina Manifesto appeared outdated and was partly responsible for the CCF's slide from its twenty-nine-percent approval rating in 1943 to just thirteen percent in 1950. She voted for the convention resolution instructing the national council to "prepare a statement of the application of democratic socialist principles to Canada and the world today." In March 1951 the national council named Grace to the committee that would draft this new statement of principles.

Fallout from the angry split at this convention began less than twenty-four hours after it closed. Hundreds of disillusioned CCFers met in the auditorium of the Medical Dental Building to form what came to be called the Socialist Fellowship. Its purpose was preservation of the Regina Manifesto, and opposition to German rearmament and Canadian participation in NATO. Its members saw the attempt to restate CCF principles for the modern world as "an attempt *led* by David Lewis and Grace MacInnis, to discard the Regina Manifesto." [emphasis added] Rod Young, Gretchen Steeves, Colin Cameron, and Eve Smith were prominent at this gathering.

Although Ernie Winch declared at the convention, "Marxism is the basis of the Regina Manifesto. As long as it stands as an expression of the principles of the CCF, we are safe," he did not rock the CCF boat. As long as his son Harold had a chance to be BC premier, the old socialist would be cautious. But the British Columbia CCF was in no shape to face the electorate. Over the next few months the party turned inward, consuming its energy in an orgy of meetings, letters, trials, and accusations on both sides that others were betraying socialist principles. Once again the philosophy of Karl Marx was the focus of contention.

Grace took notes at an August 6 meeting of the Stanley Park Open Forum as Rod Young reviewed the convention from the left-wing perspective. "It is easy for people to fall into the trap which I think Professor Scott fell into," Young said, "that Marxists advocate violence and bloody revolution. No Marxist today believes in that," he scoffed. Young acknowledged he was viewed as "too extreme, too radical—even communist—too idealistic" but denied that he or any other delegate on the convention floor was a communist "in the sense that they were members of or supporters of the LPP."

A verbal duel broke out at the forum between Tom Alsbury, who held that CCF members publicly attacking CCF policy should be disciplined, and Colin Cameron, who upheld freedom of speech. Cameron charged Alsbury with conducting an organized campaign of character assassination against him. At a CCF trial board hearing in September Alsbury was acquitted, but hard feelings on both sides persisted.

The worst, from Grace's viewpoint, was yet to come. On August 25 seventy people met to organize the left wing of the CCF under the name Socialist Caucus (later changed to Socialist Fellowship). With veteran CCFer Marxist lawyer Wallis Lefeaux in the chair, Rod Young moved that the group "disaffiliate from the CCF" because "it was impossible to put forward Marxian ideas within the movement." After much debate the majority voted to stay in the party, "trying to accomplish something, by carrying on definite socialist activity."

The meeting approved the actions of Eve Smith in the literature incident and censured Lewis and MacDonald. It passed a resolution upholding the Regina Manifesto and another endorsing Section 10: "We stand resolutely against all participation in imperialist wars." To forestall retaliation by the provincial council they sent a committee to the next council meeting with a statement of renewed socialist principles and a threat of "concerted action" if disciplinary measures were taken.

In October this caucus began to call itself the Socialist Fellowship. It agreed to co-ordinate activities of the left wing across Canada, and decided that membership in the fellowship be restricted to CCF members. It set up an independent financial structure, collecting dues of twenty-five cents per month. It outlined a Marxist study program and urged complete socialization of the Canadian economy, including land. In November the fellowship reported organization of groups within the CCF in Nanaimo, Victoria, Kamloops, Trail and Hedley. Significantly, it urged fellowship members to give precedence to fellowship activities over all other CCF activities. In January the fellowship proposed a separate annual convention prior to the CCF annual convention. To Grace it appeared as if the fellowship was establishing a new political party within the CCF.

Although in the past Grace had been friendly with Gretchen Steeves and Colin Cameron, their friendship paled. Ironically, while Grace and Angus were still smarting over David Lewis's manoeuvre to install his chosen man as national chairman, Grace herself was strategizing frantically to prevent her opponents from capturing the CCF from within. Each side self-righteously saw itself as correct and the other side as hopelessly wrong. So, during the early 1950s, the split within the CCF widened into a chasm.

In British Columbia the battle over Marxism was fought in the pages of the *CCF News*. Soon after the 1950 convention, Grace wrote a letter to the editor to prepare CCF members for the changes which a restatement of CCF principles would bring. In an answering letter Steeves asserted that the basic principles of the Regina Manifesto on which J.S. Woodsworth based his integrity were "derived from Marxist economic theories." Steeves declared the primacy of Marxism, argued that the Regina Manifesto should remain the guiding creed of the CCF and criticized Grace for lack of adherence to her father's principles.

Grace replied, "All his political life J.S. Woodsworth warned against the uncritical acceptance of Marxism exactly as he warned against the uncritical acceptance of any other dogma." She was confident that her father would have supported revision of the Regina Manifesto. He had said, "We do not believe in unchanging social dogma. Society is not static. Knowledge grows, and each age must work out a new and higher synthesis. Such growing knowledge is dependent upon experience and action."

Grace needed all the faith she could muster in that fall of 1950 as her troubles rose to mountainous proportions. At the end of October, when she was striving mightily to keep the CCF on an even keel, Angus was admitted to Royal Columbian Hospital in New Westminster for a major operation. To protect his privacy, Grace would not divulge the nature of Angus's illness, but some family members believed the successful surgery removed intestinal cancer. Grace spoke of recurring "cankers" Angus suffered in his mouth and esophagus, which tormented him in his later years. He did smoke the occasional cigarette, even after this operation, but Grace denied he was a heavy smoker.

Because of Angus's illness, Grace missed the winter meetings of the national executive and thus avoided confronting David Lewis until the pain of his betrayal diminished. She stayed in touch with the new national secretary, Lorne Ingle, whom she found more congenial. To a colleague, Grace described Ingle as "a broad, smoothly running, sunny river," in comparison with Lewis who was like "a dark stream running swiftly underneath."

Grace was always more comfortable when taking action to overcome her problems: in May 1950 she had started a biography of her father. She would write the story of J.S. Woodsworth so vividly that no one could misunderstand the roots of his philosophy, undermine his leadership, underestimate his accomplishments or ignore her faithfulness to his legacy. As she researched her father's life, Grace felt strengthened in her struggle to keep the CCF free of radical left-wing influences such as the Socialist Fellowship.

Toward the end of January 1951, Angus had recovered enough to tolerate informal family gatherings at the Vancouver homestead. On January 27, Grace attended a meeting of the BC provincial council as an observer. The executive was divided between "moderates" such as Grant MacNeil, Tom Alsbury, Laura Jamieson, Alex Macdonald, Harold Winch and Frank McKenzie, and "left-wingers" like Rod Young, Gretchen Steeves and Dave Stupich.

Stupich, elected in 1988 as NDP MP in the BC riding of Nanaimo–Cowichan, was in many ways typical of Socialist Fellowship supporters. He had joined the CCF in 1947 while a student at the University of British Columbia. Stupich had met fellow student Rod Young at UBC and canvassed for him in the 1948 Vancouver Centre by-election that vaulted Young into Parliament. Stupich joined the Socialist Fellowship and was elected to the provincial executive in time for the January 1951 council meeting. There provincial secretary Jessie Mendels gave an official report on the Socialist Fellowship, detailing its activities and defining as its central mistake "not . . . its determination to carry on 'socialist activity' but arrogating to itself the right as a group to decide what constitutes socialist activity and to pursue their objective, not through individual action in established bodies of the CCF but as a distinct entity."

That spring, with Grace and Angus in Ottawa, BC president Grant MacNeil led the provincial executive offensive. He publicly alleged that the Trotskyist Workers' Revolutionary Party had agents in the fellowship "in the guise of CCF members." It is still uncertain whether the fellowship actually had Trotskyist members. One rank-and-file member wrote, "There were no Trotskyists in the Socialist Fellowship. The idiotic claim, that whenever members of the CCF disagree with Grant McNeil [sic], Alex Macdonald, Tom Alsbury and Frank McKenzie, must be Trotskyists, is hardly worth refuting." But another member of the left-wing Stanley Park Club said that although Rod Young was a Marxian Socialist, not a Trotskyist, "usually the allies of the left in the CCF were Trotskyists who were really communists. They were the other side of the coin from Stalin."

Nevertheless, CCF moderates did not want fellowship members in the party. Under MacNeil's guidance the provincial executive declared that the fellowship was a political party operating within the CCF. Since the national CCF constitution did not allow CCF members to belong to another party, Socialist Fellowship members and supporters were liable to expulsion. This move won the unanimous approval of the CCF national council at its March 17 meeting which Grace attended. The council noted the situation in BC "with deep concern" but left its resolution to the BC executive.

In response to the provincial executive's ultimatum, the Socialist Fellowship itself fractured. One group was most concerned with capturing the CCF provincial executive with a left-wing slate, while the others wanted to build majority fellowship support within the rank and file that would pressure party leaders to carry out their will. By the opening of the BC provincial convention in May 1951 the fellowship had formally dissolved.

When MacNeil was re-elected provincial president, Grace congratulated him. "Had it not been for your courage in grasping that particular nettle of the Fellowship and obtaining the help you needed at the time of the national council meeting, BC might now be in the column of the lost as far as the CCF is concerned." Even from Ottawa Grace was instrumental in the defeat of the fellowship, encouraging CCFers she considered loyal and gathering support from national council members. Now she turned her attention to keeping Steeves out of any position of responsibility for the *CCF News*.

"The group here at Ottawa," she wrote MacNeil, "feels very regretful that Gretchen is back on the executive. But it is all the more essential that she not be put in a position where the group she represents can use *CCF News* as a means of building themselves up again and fostering the fog of confusion which led to trouble before." Too, Grace wanted to stop other "little dissident groups" in Alberta, Saskatchewan and Manitoba from using fellowship tactics to take over their provincial newspapers.

Steeves's position seemed to alternate between support for the fellowship and support for the CCF establishment. She would promise to support the national council, then renege on her promise. In March 1951 MacNeil and Alsbury had a long talk with Steeves and, at Easter break, Angus too lectured Steeves. In a letter to Harold Winch Angus now seriously questioned Steeves's loyalty to the party. "The reason the CCF is not making progress is that these people are continually destroying the public's faith in the CCF by their continual attack on leadership."

The situation was becoming critical. British Columbia's Coalition government, in power since 1941, came unglued in spring 1951. An election in the near future was inevitable. "The failure of the Coalition has presented us with the kind of opportunity that we have been waiting for years," Angus wrote to Winch. "However, now that it is here, the movement is so weak from internal conflict that we are not able to take advantage of this opportunity."

Soon after Grace and Angus's twentieth wedding anniversary January 23, 1952, Angus fell ill again. Late in February, soon after he got home from three weeks in hospital, Angus wrote CCF leader M.J. Coldwell to explain why he would not be at the opening of Parliament: "I was extremely ill with what the doctors cannot more clearly define than stomach flu, septic throat and a very greatly swollen tongue . . . I am so thin that I have to stand up twice to make a shadow." During this dark and painful time Grace found relief from her worries and inspiration in writing her father's biography. She drew closer to her mother as together they summoned up the past and once again brought it to life. Lucy's faith in her daughter did much to heal Grace's troubled heart. Angus, too, supported her biography project, encouraging Grace when her confidence weakened.

By March 1952 they were back in Ottawa, two weeks late for the session, with Angus still sick. He had decided to relinquish chairmanship of the CCF caucus, but his name was not struck from his regular committees: Labour, External Affairs, National Health, and Finance.

During 1951 and 1952 Grace took a central role in national CCF organizing. Back on the national executive in 1951, she intensified her collaboration with Thérèse Casgrain of Montreal. Since 1948, this outstanding worker for women's rights had been CCF national French-speaking vice-president; in 1951 she was elected CCF leader in Quebec, the first woman in Canada to head a provincial political party.

Thérèse Casgrain had much in common with Grace. Both were eldest children of powerful fathers who became MPs. Born Thérèse Forget in 1886 into one of Quebec's oldest families, Thérèse said her father Rodolphe Forget took the side of the underdog, the working class, just as Grace's father did. Both men cultivated humanitarian values and independent thought in their daughters. Grace and Thérèse were both wives of long-serving MPs. Thérèse married Liberal lawyer Pierre Casgrain the year before he was elected in her father's riding of Charlevoix. During his twenty-four years in the House Casgrain served as Speaker from 1936 to 1940 and as Secretary of State in King's wartime government.

In 1921, Thérèse helped to found the Comité provincial pour le suffrage féminin (The Provincial Suffrage Committee) seeking the provincial vote for Quebec women. In 1927 the suffrage committee was reorganized as the La ligue des droits de la femme (League of Women's Rights) with Thérèse as president. After nineteen years of annual appeals to the Quebec legislature by this group, in 1940 Quebec women were enfranchised. In 1941 Thérèse had been inspired by a visit to the dying J.S. Woodsworth in Vancouver. In 1946 she joined the CCF. Thérèse Casgrain was key to creating a CCF bridgehead in Quebec, and Grace consulted with her frequently from the early 1940s.

At the national executive meeting in May 1952, Grace formed a three-member group with Percy Wright and Lorne Ingle to prepare policy resolutions for the upcoming national convention in Toronto. They worked on a world plan to end poverty, race conflict in South Africa, agricultural marketing, social security, the government's high-interest-rate policy and housing. This meeting also scheduled a conference on trade union–CCF relations before the national convention. The executive felt the time was ripe for such a conference "in view of the growing importance of trade union political action and of the development of healthy relations between the CCF and labour." Henry Weisbach, executive secretary of the Political Action Committee (PAC) of the Canadian Congress of Labour (CCL), was invited to the next national executive meeting to straighten out "misunderstandings." These revolved around CCL dissatisfaction with CCF policies and CCF fears of trade union domination. Both sides felt closer liaison was the solution. Weisbach joined the CCF national council where he served throughout the 1950s.

As she drafted a new statement of principles for the CCF, Grace kept track of ideas from provincial sections across the country. A first draft of the new statement was submitted to provincial and national council members in June 1951. This draft was considered by the national council in October 1951, and changes suggested. Grace and Lorne Ingle re-edited the draft and circulated it for comment during the winter of 1951–52, hoping to present it at the 1952 national convention. But the March 1952 national council meeting found that many CCFers believed the re-edited draft was inade-quate. A new drafting committee was appointed, but the statement would not be ready for the 1952 convention.

In British Columbia, a crucial provincial election was called for June 12, 1952. With the BC CCF so divided and Angus so ill, Grace was in no position to contest a seat.

MLA W.A.C. Bennett, a Kelowna hardware merchant elected as a Conservative in 1941, was now creating the Social Credit party of BC. In March 1951 Bennett declared lack of confidence in the Coalition govern-ment's hospital insurance funding scheme and crossed the floor to sit as an independent. In December he joined the Social Credit Party, which governed neighbouring Alberta under Premier Ernest Manning, but had never won a seat in BC It was generally considered to be a "funny money, Bible punching party." But the Conservatives and the Liberals had lost the confidence of their usual supporters, the CCF had the socialist vote, and Bennett believed Social Credit could appeal to the discontented.

For the first time in 1952 the controversial transferable ballot was used, a method CCF leader Harold Winch told Grace was "one unknown in the democratic world." Voters marked their ballots with first, second and third choices. A candidate with more than fifty percent of first choices was elected. If no one received a majority, the candidate with the least number of votes was eliminated, and the second choices on his ballot were added to the other candidates' first choice votes, and so on. He liked the transferable ballot because it gave minor parties a better chance of election and worked to the disadvantage of the CCF. The disadvantage was that counting the votes took more than a month. Bennett toured the province tirelessly in support of his neophyte candidates.

The day after the polling four Socreds were elected, including Bennett. Social Credit was leading in ten ridings, but the CCF was leading in twenty-one. Three weeks later the Socreds and the CCF were tied with fourteen seats apiece. Six weeks after the election, leaders Winch and Bennett, with eighteen seats apiece, were still anxiously awaiting the final recount in just one constituency, Vancouver–Burrard. The CCF men in suspense were Grant MacNeil and Alex Macdonald, both moderate social democrats. The complex new system was most controversial in their riding, particularly the breadth of discretion allowed the returning officer. Vancouver–Burrard was a double-member riding; voters cast two transferable ballots, "A" and "B." At first the returning officer in Vancouver–Burrard produced ballots with the two incumbents, Brown and Gould, on the same ballot, together with Grant MacNeil. Macdonald appeared on the other ballot. The effect would have been certain defeat of at least one incumbent. A few days later the returning officer placed Brown and Gould on separate ballots. Macdonald condemned the change as a violation of the Election Act, designed to hurt CCF chances.

Ballot B in Vancouver–Burrard went to a fourth count, which Social Credit man Bert Price won by 246 votes over Grant MacNeil. The BC Supreme Court granted the CCF request for a recount, but a lower court judge refused to carry it out. Ballot A went to a fifth count which declared Socred Eric Martin the victor over Alex Macdonald by 644 votes. When the tallies were complete the CCF had eighteen members, Tom Uphill had won his perennial seat as an independent, and the Socreds had nineteen seats. The Liberals had six seats and the Conservatives four.

Lieutenant Governor Clarence Wallace was undecided about who should form the government—Bennett's Social Credit novices, or Winch's CCF Official Opposition which had polled twenty-seven thousand more votes than the Socreds. Wallace had counted Uphill on the side of the CCF until Bennett, in a secret meeting with the Lieutenant Governor, showed him

Uphill's written promise to vote with Social Credit. While BC stood without a government for six weeks of vote counting, Bennett had shrewdly formed a cabinet, prepared the papers and made himself available to be sworn in the night of his secret meeting with Wallace. Winch was finessed, and the first Social Credit government of British Columbia was sworn in August 1, 1952.

Just 891 additional votes for the CCF candidates in Vancouver–Burrard would have put the CCF on the government benches. Grace believed those extra votes would have been secured if the Vancouver–Burrard CCF had not been impaired by the bitter fellowship struggle.

Grace also felt she could have been the deciding factor if she had been able to contest Vancouver–Burrard where she had won in 1941. Grace had worked for nearly twenty years to form a CCF government in BC but, as Angus had predicted, at the moment of truth the socialist movement was so weak from internal dissension it could not seize the opportunity. The chance was lost to political neophytes who had contested only two previous BC elections and lost them both miserably. Grace strengthened her resolve to battle the Socialist Fellowship to the death.

CHAPTER 11

Policy Maker
Behind the Scenes

G race struggled to keep the party on the straight and narrow path of democratic socialism during the materialistic 1950s, and she found that writing her father's biography renewed her own inspiration, keeping her focussed on the socialist spirit of sharing and co-operation he had embodied. As she delved deeply into J.S. Woodsworth's life to clarify its meaning for others, she refreshed her own central self-concept as the pioneer's front-rank standard bearer.

The "red scare" during these Cold War years isolated Canada's democratic socialists from many potential supporters. Grace worked continuously to correct public confusion between communism and socialism, her task made more difficult by the machinations of the CCF's left-wing in BC.

Despite disturbing defeats and divisions within the party, Grace soldiered on through 1952. At the twelfth CCF national convention at the King Edward Hotel, sweltering in Toronto's early August heat, Grace was again elected to the national council with Hazen Argue, William Dodge, Carl Hamilton, Lorne Ingle, William Irvine, Stanley Knowles, Morden Lazarus, Donald C. MacDonald and CCL man Henry Weisbach. Lorne Ingle moved a message of greeting be sent to Angus in Vancouver who skipped a national convention for the first time since the CCF was founded. Grace was installed as chair of the two-member publicity committee with national organizer MacDonald to handle media relations. It was a position that did nothing to endear her to free-speech, pacifist, left-wing delegates such as Gretchen Steeves, who was also in Toronto, on the resolutions committee.

Grace drafted the national council resolutions on foreign policyCo-operative Commonwealth Federation (CCF), foreign policy with Percy Wright and Ingle, demonstrating her remarkable ability to work harmoniously for the overall good of the party with Wright, the man who was national chairman instead of her beloved Angus. They wrote the far-sighted War on Poverty resolution passed by this convention. A CCF government would "plan the development of world resources to the highest possible degree, provide technical assistance to underdeveloped areas on a wider scale, take international action to achieve maximum production of food and provide its equitable distribution, and establish international development corporations free from control by private capitalism or by any one country." The also convention resolved to lower the Canadian voting age from twenty-one to eighteen and extend the franchise to North American Indians and Doukhobors, now barred by race and religion respectively. A universal social security package without a means test was approved.

After the convention Grace went home to Vancouver, and by the end of September Angus's health was greatly improved. He had gained weight; his energy and stamina were restored. They returned to Ottawa, and just before Christmas 1952 Angus was gratified to receive a two-minute ovation from all sides of the Commons when he rose to speak for the first time in more than a year.

Another BC provincial election took place in June 1953 and a federal election in August. While Grace was not a candidate in either race, she was closely involved in both contests as a strategist behind the scenes. Despite her efforts, Bennett's Socreds increased their plurality in the BC Legislature to a majority of twenty-eight seats and the CCF lost ground, winning only fourteen seats.

Grace was upset by the news that Rod Young was again positioning himself to capture the federal seat in Vancouver Centre. When the provincial executive was asked approve Young's nomination, Grant MacNeil questioned Young's loyalty to the party and appealed to Grace as a member of the national executive to get that body to protest the nomination. "It's beginning to look as though the Fellowship is once more ganging up on the convention," MacNeil warned Grace. "Nominations for the incoming executive are obviously showing a block support for Steeves, Cameron, May Campbell and Stupich." The BC moderates preferred that Vancouver Centre nominate Alex Macdonald, a young lawyer "with a fine reputation for defending Trade Unions and individual workers in their struggle for justice."

Grace immediately took the issue of Young's nomination to the national executive, but it decided that only the provincial executive could disqualify Young. "All of us feel," wrote Grace, "it is of the highest importance that it should be done definitely at this coming week-end meeting . . . The very fact of his being a candidate would be bad publicity for the CCF . . . . Should Rod be elected there would be difficulties in caucus. His disloyalty there in times past would scarcely allow the members to admit him again."

That weekend an emergency meeting of the BC CCF executive in Victoria decided to withhold approval of Young's nomination; Steeves, Cameron and McKenzie dissented. Vancouver Centre nominated him regardless. Grace provided the executive with an exhaustive history of Young's disloyalty and

Grace skips with ropes of kelp, accompanied by two unidentified friends from CCF Summer School. Gabriola Island, BC, summer 1951.

Grace corrects the proofs of her award-winning biography of her father, J.S. Woodsworth: A Man to Remember. Vancouver, October 1953.

treachery. But she could not prevent Young's nomination in Vancouver Centre from being approved by the BC provincial convention in April.

In early April Grace and Angus were urgently consulted on who would fill the provincial leadership left vacant by Harold Winch. The legislative caucus selected Arnold Webster, principal of Magee High School on Vancouver's wealthy west side, and a member of the CCF executive since 1935. Webster penned an anguished letter to Angus and Grace asking for frank advice. Webster was not an MLA, he had just won a federal nomination; he did not feel familiar with provincial issues; he had recently lost his beloved wife and political comrade Gladys; and moreover, he considered MacNeil and Alsbury more in line to contest the leadership for the moderate faction. Would Grace and Angus advise him to seek the provincial leadership?

Grace and Angus preferred Tom Alsbury for the position. They wrote Webster in a kindly tone that he must make up his own mind, but that they would welcome him in the caucus at Ottawa. In letters to Webster, MacNeil and Alsbury they indicated Alsbury was their first choice, Webster their second choice and MacNeil their third choice, only because MacNeil himself was so reluctant. As it turned out, Webster relinquished his federal nomination and won a seat in the provincial legislature in June. Grace gave a number of campaign speeches for CCF candidates around the province, but despite her efforts the party dropped four seats. Bennett's Socreds formed another government and Webster became leader of the opposition.

But the conflict over Rod Young drove a wedge between Webster and the MacInnises, close as they were before the election campaign. The trouble was over M.J. Coldwell's refusal to appear on the same platform as Young. Webster insisted that once a candidate had been nominated, no leader had the right to refuse to support him. "We supported M.J.'s position," Grace said. "The result was that Arnold was furious with us and for a short time would barely speak to us." Fortunately the rift was temporary.

In the federal contest, Young was renominated early in July to run against incumbent Ralph Campney. He lost again by more than thirty-three hundred votes, to Grace and Angus's great relief. Across the country the CCF gained ten seats for a total of twenty-three. Angus was easily re-elected in the newly redistricted riding of Vancouver–Kingsway which took in much of his old territory. It was to be his last election campaign. Harold Winch vaulted into the House of Commons representing Vancouver East, Angus's old riding. The CCF federal caucus was delighted to gain such an experienced man. St. Laurent's Liberals held the majority with 170 seats; the Tories took fifty-one and Social Credit fifteen.

In November 1953 Grace's biography of her father was published. *J.S. Woodsworth: A Man To Remember* immediately attracted favourable reviews. Wilfred Eggleston, a well-known national journalist who had covered Parliament in Woodsworth's time, wrote: "It is unlikely that anyone will ever write of him as a human being with greater insight than his daughter has done . . . . An outstanding portrait." Veteran *Vancouver Province* parliamentary reporter Torchy Anderson called it "an important contribution to Canadian history." Jean Howarth's review in the *Province* magazine section devoted more attention to Grace the writer. "When you meet Grace MacInnis, you know at once that you have met Somebody. I remember the first time I saw her. She had risen in a meeting to correct a statement made by a former speaker. She is a pretty, graceful little woman, and she spoke with such gentle womanliness that the former speaker hardly realized that he was being corrected, except that she also spoke with such flawless logic that he was completely demolished."

In the biography Grace attempted to be objective, but recognized that she fell short of that mark. "I couldn't escape from the fact that he WAS my father, as well as J.S. Woodsworth. In the end I wrote about him as I had felt about him. When I was a little girl, he was my father. When he became a political figure, he was—to me and in my book—J.S. Woodsworth, leader and fellow worker in the movement. But when he was old and sick and drawn back at last from the battle, he was my father again." In the closing pages of Woodsworth's life story she wrote: "His was a person-to-person influence, the warm contact of heart with heart, the leaping flame of ideas from mind to mind." Grace could have been writing about herself. She breathed new life into his ideas and actions.

The biography sold briskly and earned Grace an award from the Canadian Authors' Association. The following year it won a national award for popular biography from the University of British Columbia. But, much as Grace appreciated the public recognition, she enjoyed her eighty-year-old mother's response even more. In her Commonplace Book for 1953 Lucy wrote, "Grace's splendid book has had much public praise and is selling well. I think she did an excellent job. I was much touched by her dedicating it to me and presenting me with her first copy of the book."

On January 23, 1954, Grace received a big bunch of golden roses from Angus in celebration of their wedding anniversary. On the card, this man who turned a hard carapace to the rest of the world wrote, "It is hard to find words to express how happy you made me during the past year. It was the best of the twenty-two. You grow more lovely each year."

When Parliament opened in February, Angus made the pages of *Time* magazine for opposing an increase in his pay. MPs were then paid four thousand dollars a year plus two thousand dollars for expenses. The increases went through, but as a result of Angus's protest the maximum pension for MPs was capped at three thousand dollars instead of the contemplated six thousand dollars annually.

Agnes Macphail, the first woman Member of Parliament and Grace's valued colleague, died that February in Toronto, just before her appointment to the Senate was to have been announced. Grace grieved the loss of her friend, but concern for Angus's health prevented her from attending the funeral.

As spring approached Grace reaped the benefits of her literary as well as her diplomatic skills. She and Angus attended a formal dinner hosted by the first Yugoslavian Ambassador to Canada after World War Two, Dr. Rojko Djermanovic. At the head table next to the guest of honour, External Affairs Minister Lester Pearson, Grace glowed from flattering comments about her biography. "Pearson expressed pleasure in having read my book," she noted in her diary. "Dr. Djermanovic turned from his neighbours to say with enthusiasm, 'I have not read one comment against your book, Mrs. MacInnis.' To which honesty compelled me to admit, 'There was one, Mr. Djermanovic.' He asked where it was and I told him in a little Canadian communist paper. To which he rejoined scornfully, 'It is nothing! They do not count!'" It was an unusual statement from the ambassador of a communist country. By now Grace and the ambassador were good friends. But the MacInnises had exercised skillful diplomacy before reaching such a comfortable state with the ambassador.

Dr. Djermanovic had visited Grace and Angus in Vancouver the previous July, at the height of the federal election campaign. At first he was wary of going to their home, Grace recalled years later, but Coldwell had suggested the meeting. An aide anxiously warned Grace to receive the ambassador alone and not to offer him any food or drink. Soon Dr. Djermanovic and his aide arrived, attired in black coats and homburg hats despite the summer heat. After some careful small talk broke the ice, Grace did get the cautious men to accept a cup of coffee, and Angus offered to take them around Vancouver in his little Austin. The ambassador expressed the wish to see an Indian reserve and some "real" Indians.

"Angus knew Capilano Joe quite well," Grace recalled. "So we went over to the North Vancouver waterfront. Here was Joe in his shirtsleeves, with big brawny arms beachcombing with his granddaughter. The ambassador's eyes popped open." He thought here was real peasantry, kept in drudgery by capitalist Canadians. "Joe showed him two of his boys carving a totem pole, and the ambassador asked, 'What do you do with that?' Joe said, 'We sell it to the Americans, and we ask them a good price for it.' The ambassador began to look a little doubtful. Then Joe said, 'Here's my ceremonial costume. When I'm dressed in that I'm worth $8,000.' The ambassador was looking puzzled by this time. We went back to the beach and sat on a log. Joe said to Angus, 'It was nice of you to send me the speech that [General Douglas] McArthur made when he got back to the United States.' By this time the ambassador gave up completely. He had seen the 'down-trodden natives' and had heard Joe say, 'This property is really valuable. We have no intention of selling it at all.' He came back a very chastened ambassador from that excursion."

With genuine friendliness and belief in the equality of all people, regardless of cultural differences, Grace and Angus made it possible for insight to take the place of ignorance, and understanding to replace fear. Grace was becoming an effective amateur diplomat. And her contact with Canada's diplomatic community kept her from being imprisoned in the limited world of BC politics.

Angus felt well enough in April 1954 to suggest a trip to Washington, DC during Easter week. Lester B. Pearson alerted the Canadian Embassy in Washington to their arrival, and Angus's old friend from the Canadian Congress of Labour, Pat Conroy, labour attaché with the Embassy, invited Grace and Angus to stay at his home.

Pat Conroy was active on the international labour scene as an executive member of the International Confederation of Free Trade Unions. He and Angus saw eye-to-eye on the matter of rooting communists out of the unions. The day they arrived, Conroy took his guests to meet John L. Lewis, head of the United Mineworkers of America. Grace wrote of the burly, cigar-smoking union leader: "Pat was quite right in saying that John L. was a staunch defender of the capitalist 'free enterprise' system. At no point did his thinking appear to get beyond its framework. I had the impression that we were watching one of the last of the old-style trade unionists—the men who saw only the workers and the bosses and who had to fight ruthlessly against ruthless opponents. They were colourful and dynamic, but one felt that John L. Lewis had been overtaken by newer lines of thinking in response to changed conditions."

The next day, Thursday, April 22, was the opening day of Senate hearings into Senator Joseph McCarthy's accusations against the US Army of protecting and sheltering communists. Grace and Angus had an opportunity through a friend of Conroy's to attend the hearings, but Conroy turned it down on their behalf, and they watched McCarthy's downfall on TV.

Grace and Angus went with Conroy to meet George Meany, head of the American Federation of Labour (AFL). Grace noted perceptively, "The man and his surroundings were quite a contrast to John L. Lewis and his setting. George Meany's office is relatively unpretentious." The conversation centred on unemployment. "Meany felt the government should have a shelf of public works in constant readiness for use as unemployment pockets developed," Grace wrote. "In the same way he wanted to see a large scale program of public housing, as private builders had demonstrated that they could not solve the housing problem for low income groups . . . . We found Meany interesting. Here was a man brought up and living within the framework of free enterprise thinking who, nevertheless, was applying the practical test of workability to the system."

Less than a year later the AFL and CIO merged and elected George Meany president. Grace's contact with these two powerful American labour leaders, Lewis and Meany, and Pat Conroy with his international affiliations, extended and deepened her understanding of the world of organized labour in ways that would prove valuable in her future work with Canada's labour leaders in forming the New Democratic Party.

While the parliamentary session stretched on into June 1954, Grace remained in Ottawa with Angus, and so missed the climax of Rod Young's attempt to capture the British Columbia CCF. But both Grace and Angus had strategized with Young's opponents by air mail. Vancouver Centre was the hotbed of trouble, especially the Stanley Park Club where Young had established his power base. Jim McKenzie joined the Stanley Park Club in 1952; there he first heard Grace speak. The Stanley Park Club took a Marxian view of the world, but invited a wide variety of speakers from Liberals to Trotskyists to speak at its Sunday meetings. Their ideas would be torn apart in discussion later, McKenzie recalled.

"We spoke of revolution, discarding bourgeois values and religious cant," McKenzie explained. "Subservience was frowned upon and fierce competition existed in the party. The contest of wills had its parcel of dirty tricks, shameful tactics that pandered to the paranoia of both left and right. We used to have tic-tac signals from the back of the hall, we had spokespeople, we had well designed caucuses."

Young started 1954 with a show of strength. At a University of British Columbia meeting sponsored by the campus CCF Club, he told the students, "There is no difference between theoretical communism and socialism . . . the problem is not to show that the CCF is different from the communists, but that it is different from liberalism." Although Young addressed just seventy-five students, his remarks sent a shudder through the CCF. The BC Federation of Trade and Industry ran ads quoting the speech, and the Liberals lost no time passing it around the Liberal caucus and using it in the House.

Young's goal was to take over the 1954 BC CCF convention and win the presidency of the provincial party. "Rod has been actively building a machine in Vancouver Centre with aid and comfort from other quarters," Grant MacNeil wrote Grace. "Stanley Park Club has been recruiting members from all corners of the province in support of Rod. He has surrounded himself with a group of young members who regard him as the leader of a great crusade to save the movement for scientific socialism." MacNeil, busy with crucial IWA negotiations, arrived late at the convention. "I got there toward the end of the second day, to find that Rod and the Stanley Park Club had virtual control of the convention debates, and that he was slated for the Presidency."

But Young overplayed his hand. His faction introduced a resolution condemning "the drive against communists, the witch-hunting and red-baiting" as "merely a screen for the attack of Big Business on all working class organizations" and called on members to reject it. Tom Alsbury, Trades and Labour Council president, had written to Grace and Angus a week before the convention that he was "sick and tired of finding myself in the labour movement being attacked and opposed by CCF card holders who follow a pro-communist line." On the convention floor he vigorously denounced Young and the "reds." "I don't agree communists are fine class-conscious workers," declared Alsbury. "Their first loyalty is to the Soviet Union."

Young then seized the microphone to announce, "I'm proud to have people tell me I'm a communist . . . I can personally introduce you to fifty former communists in the CCF." His dramatic statements sent a shock wave across the convention floor that appeared on the front pages of Vancouver newspapers the following morning.

That morning, a Saturday, Grant MacNeil scolded Young at the convention for "wholly irresponsible remarks which set the CCF movement back by ten years." Less than an hour later Young lost the fight for the BC presidency to Vancouver lawyer Frank McKenzie seventy-eight to forty-three. Young and McKenzie were both lawyers in the office of the dean of BC socialist lawyers, Wallis Lefeaux. Their rivalry struck to the heart of the group.

Young's supporters were still able to defeat MacNeil's emergency resolution to force Young to resign from the CCF. MacNeil immediately put through a motion dissociating the convention and the CCF from Young's remarks regarding communism, but the damage was done. Ironically, the motion to dissociate carried while Young was in the chair as deputy chairman.

MacNeil warned Grace and Angus that Young might be at the national convention six weeks away in Edmonton. He had persuaded the Vancouver Centre Constituency Association to withhold contributions to the provincial and national sections for his travel expenses to attend the convention. The idea that Young might be seated as a delegate at the national convention struck horror into hearts at the CCF's highest levels. Leader M.J. Coldwell privately told Lorne Ingle he would resign if Young got into the convention, and Ingle reported this to Grace in a letter from Toronto, where he was conferring with Ontario CCF leaders on the Rod Young question. Coldwell had threatened to resign before over Young's behaviour, Ingle acknowledged, but assured Grace that this time he was dead serious.

Ingle judged that the anti-Young faction was not strong nationally; even a well-documented case against Young might not persuade national delegates to expel him. Then, he wrote to Grace, "we'd be placed in the position of having to slap down a whole provincial section." Ingle worried that BC might defy such a national decision. He strongly suggested that Grace gather enough strength in BC to get the provincial executive to handle the matter. Grace agreed.

By this time Grace was thoroughly disgusted with the behaviour of

Gretchen Steeves, who was playing both ends against the middle. She insisted to moderate CCFers that she had forsaken Young and his crew, while continuing to work with them. Grace was relieved when Steeves left for Europe at the end of June—it removed her influence—but thought Steeves's European background was responsible for her attitude of superiority. "Mrs. Steeves took pride in being one of the leaders. She was a continentalist. She was born in Holland, she lived there, became a lawyer, met her husband and married there. I often thought to myself, 'Now you wouldn't talk that way if you'd been born in Canada, particularly of parents and grandparents who lived in Canada. You don't understand Canadians'."

Grace and Angus were determined not to be pushed around by the Young–Steeves–Cameron group. In Vancouver during the last week of June, they hosted a strategy meeting of their own supporters which included most of the executive. Everyone present believed Young should be "thrown out of the movement," Grace informed Lorne Ingle. "Every member of the provincial executive except Dave Stupich is of the same opinion. Unfortunately the provincial council . . . has a pro-Rod Young majority."

In the event, ousting Young was easy. During its July 10 meeting, at which Grace was not present, the BC provincial executive received six written complaints about Young's behaviour from CCF clubs and constituency associations. A resolution was passed that Young made his "proud to be called a communist" statement knowing that "he would misrepresent the CCF and bring it into undeserved disrepute, contrary to his duty as a member, and contrary to the constitution of the CCF." The resolution ordered Young to stand trial on this charge, and suspended his membership in the CCF pending the trial set for July 24. Young refused to submit to a trial and resigned from the CCF the day after the provincial executive suspended him. "It is my opinion," he told the *Vancouver Province*, "that no honest person will expect me to appear before a trial committee hand-picked by an executive which has already condemned me."

Coldwell's rage was defused, but he became wary enough to warn Saskatchewan CCF Premier Tommy Douglas that he must handle a similar group in his own province promptly and firmly. The national convention took place in Edmonton undisturbed by the Rod Young controversy. Once again Grace was elected to the national council; she was given the job of international liaison with the Socialist International and socialist parties around the world. Angus did not attend, pleading ill health, but in fact he was still sore over his rejection at the 1950 convention in Vancouver.

The Young faction made several more unsuccessful drives toward power in BC. It tried to take over the provincial council meeting in September, hoping to discredit the executive and force its resignation. Angus was so eager to forestall this tactic that he asked every MP and MLA to attend the meeting. He even sent a letter to Bert Herridge, the CCF MP whom he had refused to acknowledge for years. At the meeting the executive was sustained by a vote of twenty-eight to thirteen. Emboldened by this success, it passed a strong, new Program For Action to reverse the drastic slide in memberships and refill the empty treasury. Grace was delighted.

In fall 1954 Young's group anonymously began to publish mimeographed notices to loyal members from "Box 16" in Vancouver. It denounced the new Program For Action and affirmed the right of any CCF member or group to present dissident views and attempt to win converts within the party. A Box 16 mimeo in March 1955 circulated to Ottawa as well as BC tried to gather support to oust the moderate executive at the upcoming provincial convention.

In letters to CCF provincial secretary Harold Thayer, Grace strategized to keep the left-wingers from taking over the 1955 BC convention. She was even more motivated than in years past because British Labour Party leader, former British Prime Minister Clement Attlee, was to speak.

Grace's plan to urge all the "useful" BC MPs to attend the convention was adopted. On the convention floor she argued successfully for a motion approving an executive decision to bar Young from speaking at any CCF meeting. It was a long debate and the vote was close, eighty-nine to sixty-six, so Grace's strategy and arguments likely did sway the undecided to the executive's side. Attlee gave an inspiring speech, undisturbed by left-wing machinations, and that night Grace entertained Attlee at home with a party of sixteen that included people from all CCF factions.

Grace wished she herself were free to take a position on the BC executive. She wrote Thayer just before the convention, "We've got to have people who will simply refuse to be 'nice,' or 'reasonable,' or to have 'peace in the movement at any price.' I wish to goodness I were in a position to try a year's battling instead of advising others to continue getting their heads bloodied!"

Grace and Angus travelled to Ottawa early in January 1955 for the opening of Parliament and to take part in a fierce debate in the CCF national council and caucus on German rearmament. CCF official policy for years had firmly opposed rearmament, but conditions had recently changed.

The Soviet Union was anxious to prevent West Germany from being accepted into a military alliance of European nations known as the Western European Union. The Soviets were manoeuvring instead for withdrawal of all occupation troops and reunification of the two German sections which would create a new nation they hoped to control. But in October the western nations signed the Paris Treaties allowing for admission of a rearmed Germany to the WEU and to NATO. Germany pledged to furnish three hundred thousand troops to NATO, but was not allowed to make atomic or chemical weapons, guided missiles, long-range bombers or heavy warships. On these terms the US, France and Britain ended their occupation and recognized the full sovereignty of the German Federal Republic.

The western powers believed that Germany would rearm with or without their permission, and they wanted German strength on their side. It was ten years since the end of World War Two. Now, instead of Hitler and the Axis against the world, the enemy was Stalin's Soviet Union. Canada, not a member of the WEU, was asked as a NATO member to ratify the Paris Treaty covering admission to NATO of a rearmed West Germany. Parliament was to debate the ratification on January 25.

The CCF national council met in Ottawa to thrash out its position the week before this debate. As usual with political hot potatoes, Grace and Angus had discussed the issue privately before the council meeting. They expressed their position to Coldwell in a letter that Angus dictated while Grace typed. While recognizing the arguments on both sides, Angus opposed reunification with free elections which he considered "far more dangerous to the world than Germany rearmed and associated with the Western Powers . . . . If the fear of the opponents of rearmament is based, as they claim, on the resurgence of Nazism, the danger of a Nazi resurgence is much greater with a Germany 'on the loose' than with a Germany armed and associated with the Western Powers. As I see it, Germany will, sooner or later, arm anyway, and it's much better to have her on our side with some control than making her own way in the world against every nation."

In the council meeting Grace was one of only eight to argue for the admission of a rearmed Germany into NATO; sixteen opposed it. She voted with Coldwell and Frank Scott, and was the only BC council member to take this position. Her speech in favour of ratification of the Paris Treaty so pleased Angus that he passed her an unprecedented note of approval.

"He wasn't one for giving praise," Grace reflected later. "You knew when he liked what you'd done or when he didn't. The question under discussion that day was whether Germany should be allowed to rearm, and I spoke on the thing. Later on he passed me a note saying he was very proud of my speech. He said, 'The next member for Vancouver–Kingsway.' That was the first and only indication that he considered me of a stature with the other MPs." Grace carried that precious prophetic little note in her "inside wallet" until the day she died.

Agitation in the CCF caucus was acute right after that divided council meeting. The CCF parliamentary caucus had to decide what to do about the ratification of the protocol admitting Germany into NATO. Angus's own speech in the House took note of his "peculiar position" in opposition to the CCF members sitting behind him, aligned instead with the Liberals.

Angus blasted the communists and those who wished to negotiate with them for reunification of Germany before allowing her to rearm. Gone were the days when he identified with Marxian socialism and spoke admiringly in the House of Stalin's activities. This time he declared, "In the last fifteen years ever since the beginning of World War Two, the CCF has refused to

associate with them in any way, at any time in any place on any issue . . . .
The experience of the trade union movement has been the same . . . . It is no
different in international affairs."

Here then was Angus's recompense for the many slings and arrows he had
taken from the CCF left wing. He could proudly stand in the House and
declare his total independence from the treacherous communists. Of course,
the radical left wing accused him of being in bed with the Liberals, but when
Angus was convinced he was right, no critic could change his mind. Canada
ratified the NATO Protocol and a rearmed West Germany was admitted to
NATO.

In April 1955 Angus was again troubled with high fever, weight loss, and
infections in his mouth and esophagus. Grace nursed him in Vancouver, and
tried to make cooking an artistic adventure to entice him back to health, but
his condition remained poor during most of the spring.

That spring brought a fresh crop of troubles for the CCF federal caucus.
Renewed charges of communist sympathies were highlighted by the defection of three-term CCF Moose Jaw MP Ross Thatcher to the Liberals. In his
resignation speech, Thatcher accused the majority of the CCF as following
the communist line on the issue of German rearmament. Angus pinpointed
the problem in a letter to MP Stanley Knowles: "I fear that some of us in the
CCF have not yet made up our minds as to which is the real enemy—world
communism or world capitalism. Wherever communism exists as a ruling
force, no socialists are allowed to live . . . and advocate socialism. For that
reason alone, in the struggle between communism and democracy, it should
never be in doubt where the CCF stands."

To heal the deep division in the CCF group, Angus suggested to Coldwell
that the leaders of the different schools of thought should "get together for
a few weeks in a quiet place and discuss the world we're living in today . . .
where we are going and how we are going to get there." By return mail,
Coldwell agreed that a soul-searching session was in order.

Grace was sidelined at this time, her energy consumed in trying to improve
Angus's state of health, but his illness remained stubbornly resistant. The
CCF caucus had to replace him on the House Industrial Relations and
External Affairs committees, but Angus was eager to get back to Ottawa.
Grace wrote Stanley Knowles: "Angus is very miserable and very frustrated
these days and it is hard to have to watch him and be unable to help. As soon
as there is any letup in the acute discomfort he begins to think of the group
at Ottawa . . . His whole life is in the work of the movement." By mid-May
Angus had given up the idea of returning to Ottawa in the current session.
Grace travelled east to pack their things for shipment to the coast. She too
was missing executive meetings and feeling frustrated to be out of the
mainstream of events.

But the summer and fall of 1955 did hold some joy for Grace and Angus. They celebrated Grace's fiftieth birthday on July 25 by moving into a new home at 2880 West 39th Avenue, in the quiet Vancouver residential neighbourhood of Kerrisdale. They delighted in the spacious house with its generous garden, and named their new establishment *Tigh Cairdeil,* Gaelic for House of Happiness.

Three days later, July 28 marked the twenty-fifth anniversary of Angus's election to the House of Commons, where he was now the longest-serving MP. The newspapers took note by asking Angus the reason for his twenty-five-year survival record. He gave top honours to Grace. "A good wife and lots of luck," he told the *Vancouver Sun.*

Lucy came to live with Grace and Angus in their new house that fall. Grace enjoyed spending time with her mother, but it meant an even greater burden at home. She was forced to miss another CCF national council meeting rather than leave eighty-two-year-old Lucy with the household responsibilities while Angus was ill. His health improved a little that fall, but Angus had no reserve strength. He prowled the house at night, seeking relief from insomnia.

The CCF threw a twenty-fifth anniversary dinner for Angus October 28 in Vancouver which featured addresses by national leader M.J. Coldwell and provincial president Frank McKenzie, with provincial leader Arnold Webster in the chair. A photograph the next day in the *Vancouver Sun* showed a three-way handshake: MacInnis–Coldwell–Webster. In Angus's other hand he held a burning cigarette.

The national council wanted to present Angus with a token of appreciation at the dinner. Grace advised Lorne Ingle of an appropriate gift in a letter revealing of Angus's character. "He does not care anything for ornamental plaques or dustcatching objects in silver," she explained. "However, a year ago he bought himself a record player . . . . If anyone could take time out and buy a collection of records and they could be presented in a suitably-inscribed container, I know he would play them and enjoy them indefinitely . . . . He loves singers Paul Robeson and Enrico Caruso . . . . Among his favourites are any and all of Robbie Burns, and almost any of the old, pre-jazz ones. Melody, rhythm, understandable words—these are the things he likes." On the night of the testimonial dinner Coldwell presented Angus with the gift—recordings of some of his favourite music in a leather-covered case inscribed in gold.

The CCF inner circle was feeling a growing urgency to modernize the public perception of the party. Angus's idea of a two-week retreat to harmonize the diverse factions became a three-day meeting of the national council January 13–15 which Grace and Angus attended. From the outset it was agreed that a restatement of fundamental policies was needed to reverse the party's decline. Douglas pointed to "a world reaction against the things in which we believe," and suggested bringing other organizations into "a new alignment" with the CCF. The aim was still to weld a farmer–labour–socialist party, but there was general agreement that the Depression-era assumptions of the Regina Manifesto were no longer valid.

Grace emphasized meeting the needs of individuals in Canada, while strengthening links with socialists and trade unionists internationally. "The CCF is different," she said, "because we believe in human beings." She urged the party to "push harder for greater economic justice." And in a complete reversal of her stance at the 1933 Regina convention, she said, "there is no merit per se in social ownership."

The council decided to draft a statement of principles in time for the 1956 national convention. Grace's contribution to the list of recommendations read: "Our industrial society has taken from the individual his sense of worth and significance. A cooperative society will restore to him this sense of belonging. We must emphasize that the new society can be built only in the measure that each person participates according to his ability in affairs of his community local, national, international."

The party was already groping toward what would be its metamorphosis into the NDP in 1961. Douglas's comments at this council meeting were the most prophetic. He said, "If the tide begins to turn the farm, co-operative and labour organizations might come in with the CCF, or merge in some alignment of which the CCF would be the dynamic core—a new type of federation or the same type of federation enlarged for a genuine farmer–labour–socialist movement in Canada. I think that ought to be our aim."

Organized labour took a step toward securing more political power when the Trades and Labour Congress merged with the Canadian Congress of Labour to form the Canadian Labour Congress in April 1956. David Lewis and many CCF trade unionists had been working for a long time toward a closer relationship with labour. Although the merger convention did not formally endorse CLC–CCF co-operation, the door was left wide open. In July 1955 Lewis and Claude Jodoin, then TLC president, had arrived at an informal agreement that "although the merger convention itself should avoid any direct partisan commitment for the new Congress, a further step would have to be taken in 1958, either through the CCF or through some broader political alignment."

Some CCFers and trade unionists were already talking of the creation of a new party. But Grace and Angus resisted this line of thinking. When Lorne Ingle visited them in Vancouver during the 1956 Christmas season, Grace let him know that as the daughter of the CCF's founder she was upset by references to a new party. He wrote back apologizing for using the "new party" terminology, but not backing down from the concept.

Summer 1956 brought the fourteenth national CCF convention in Winnipeg which adopted a new statement of principles, the Winnipeg Declaration. It was a reformist document which affirmed: "Private profit and corporate power must be subordinated to social planning designed to achieve equality of opportunity and the highest possible living standards for all Canadians." The aim of the CCF was now "the establishment in Canada by democratic means of a co-operative commonwealth in which the supplying of human needs and enrichment of human life shall be the primary purpose of our society." It spoke of the folly of wasted resources and declared capitalism basically immoral. It endorsed the United Nations and called for "a world society based on the rule of law."

The controversial last sentence of the Regina Manifesto, "No CCF Government will rest content until it has rededicated capitalism," was replaced by: "The CCF will not rest content until every person in this land and in all other lands is able to enjoy equality and freedom, a sense of human dignity, and an opportunity to live a rich and meaningful life as a citizen of a free and peaceful world."

While she had supported the need to modernize the CCF statement of principles, Grace did not approve of the Winnipeg Declaration. "It was neither fish, nor fowl, nor good red herring, in my view," she commented. She was happier with a resolution presented in Winnipeg calling for government-funded monthly salaries for mothers of children under sixteen, if they were not otherwise employed. "In every other field of public service or business . . . it is a recognized principle that the labourer is worthy of his hire. Only in the field of home-making do we expect to have a vital service rendered without paying for it," she said. The resolution was not passed, but referred to the national council for research. Grace had advocated salaries for full-time homemakers as early as the 1943 Report of the Subcommittee on Post-War Reconstruction for Women. Now at least the idea was under consideration.

When Grace left Vancouver for the Winnipeg convention she had been determined not to allow her name to stand for the national council again. But as Angus put it, "The political virus dies hard, and I had the idea that if pressure and circumstances coincided, she would be very likely to succumb." She was once again elected to council.

Poor health and lingering resentment at being denied the national chairmanship kept Angus from the Winnipeg convention. But in Winnipeg his long years of service to the CCF were honoured with the presentation of a painting which Grace received on his behalf. Stanley Knowles's speech of appreciation and Grace's acceptance speech were taped and made into a record for Angus to play on his new phonograph.

On May 28 Angus gave his last important speech in the Commons in the infamous Pipeline Debate. He was protesting the St. Laurent government's unprecedented move to threaten closure before the debate even began. The government wanted to counter anticipated objections so that funding for a cross-Canada gas pipeline could be finalized for an American company, Trans-Canada Pipelines, before a deadline of June 7. In his twenty-five years in the House, Angus told the members, "I have never yet seen a Speaker who would make a ruling on an anticipated situation . . . . It is intolerable," he declared, "that free men should come here and be told what they may or may not discuss on the word of the Prime Minister or anyone else." Heckling of previous speakers had been fierce; even the courteous Coldwell had stormed the Speaker's Chair at one point, shouting and shaking his fist, but Angus's speech was received respectfully in what one reporter termed "breathless silence." Fifteen years later as an MP Grace would draw on Angus's contribution to this debate in her own fight against closure imposed by Prime Minister Pierre Trudeau.

During the 1956 session Angus announced that he would not contest the next election, so ending thirty-four years in politics, starting with his 1922 election to the Vancouver School Board. Throughout 1956 honours were heaped upon Angus's head while poor health dogged his heels. In February, forty-eight of Ottawa's most powerful men had gathered to pay him tribute at a testimonial dinner. At the end of October, Angus received an honorary Doctor of Laws degree from the University of British Columbia, a distinction which touched him deeply. This self-educated man now held a degree from one of the most respected universities in Canada.

BC Premier W.A.C. Bennett called a snap provincial election for September 19, 1956, on the issue of a controversial government tax rebate plan that would return twenty-eight dollars to property owners. Barely three weeks before election day, Grace was nominated to contest the three-member Vancouver–Point Grey riding with CCF running mates Norman Hill, an electronics technician, and Bill Pierce, a carpenter. Grace ran against two formidable opponents, incumbent Attorney General Robert Bonner and Liberal Leader Arthur Laing, who had defeated her in Vancouver South during the 1949 federal election but who was not in the House of Commons in 1956. The CCF campaign slogan was "Let's Clean House," and its symbol was a broom. There was plenty of scandal to sweep out.

Management of BC's natural resources was the campaign issue Grace chose to focus on. The province was in an uproar over the management of its forests by Forestry Minister Robert Sommers, who had recently been forced to resign under opposition allegations of fraud. Bonner was under attack for keeping an RCMP report on the Sommers case out of sight until the election results were in. In Grace's first television appearance, which happened to fall on her fifty-first birthday, she shared the stage with the recently elected CCF provincial leader Bob Strachan in a discussion of BC's natural resource policy. "It seems to me," she told viewers, "that expecting profit-hungry private logging corporations to conserve the woods is a little like putting a weasel in a hen-coop and expecting it to raise chickens!"

Closer to election day Grace told a meeting of the Stanley Park CCF Forum the Social Credit government was "giving away resources lavishly to big corporations on either side of the border. If the CCF can't get in there this time," she warned, "it may very well soon be too late to save the resources."

But Grace's efforts were not rewarded with success. She and Laing both were defeated by Bonner and Socred candidate Mrs. Buda Brown. The disgraced Sommers was re-elected by a large margin. When the votes were counted by the usual method, not the transferable ballot, Social Credit scored a landslide victory. Only ten CCF candidates were elected, down four from the last election. Grace was discouraged. It was her fifth election defeat in eleven years, and it would be her last contest for another nine years.

CHAPTER 12

A New Era

Clouds of pale pink cherry blossoms glowed in the late April sun along the Vancouver streets. At 2880 West 39th Avenue, the two inhabitants of Tigh Cairdeil gathered their forces for yet another attempt to make socialism appealing to the Canadian public. But in 1957, the CCF's twenty-fifth year of existence, gearing up for another political season seemed to take more effort than ever before.

A federal election had been called for June 10, and the BC provincial CCF convention was coming up at the end of April. But despite these opportunities to re-invigorate the CCF, the very foundations of the party Grace had helped to build with such love and care seemed to be crumbling. CCF national leader M.J. Coldwell was battling poor health: he had fallen in January and suffered a bruised chest complicated by a bad cough that developed into bronchial trouble. Then, during a caucus meeting in February, Coldwell suffered what may have been a heart attack for which he was hospitalized. Angus's own physical problems had forced him to bow out of the House of Commons. He had missed the first 1957 session of Parliament, and the CCF caucus knew of his decision to resign. Coldwell and Ingle persuaded Angus not to announce his resignation publicly until the election was called, to avoid weakening the CCF. Stanley Knowles packed his files and personal papers and sent them to Vancouver.

With Angus out of the picture, Coldwell felt the lack of Woodsworth–MacInnis support. He wrote to Angus expressing hope that Grace would be nominated to replace her husband in Vancouver–Kingsway. There was a move to offer her the nomination; she declined. With relief Lucy commented in her Commonplace Book, "Grace wisely decided not to accept nomination for his seat. Impossible. She chose to care for him [Angus]. She couldn't take on two full-time jobs."

CCF national secretary Lorne Ingle had announced that he would be leaving his position to join the law firm of Joliffe & Lewis in Toronto. There he would be closely involved with David Lewis in guiding the expanding trade union–CCF alliance. The remaining CCF leadership was convinced that the party was immovably stalled. It was becoming evident that the CCF had to change or die. But Grace at first strongly resented the usurpation of her beloved father's party by any other political entity.

Grace was finding CCF work "slow and difficult" at a time when Canadians were prosperous and complacent. "The public is too much absorbed in working long hours to buy new major appliances on credit," she complained to Ingle, "or in watching TV for endless periods, or in anything of a comfortable and comforting nature, to care about the leg work and brain work involved in a movement like ours. Result: the faithful and aging little band—among which all of us can be separately counted—tries to shoulder a somewhat thankless load."

Still, when the BC provincial CCF convention took place the last weekend in April, Grace was elected first vice-president, serving under president Alex Macdonald and alongside moderate colleagues Grant MacNeil, Arthur Turner and Harold Thayer. Although left-winger Dave Stupich was on the 1957 provincial executive, the Socialist Fellowship seems to have faded into the background.

Grace felt the old era passing with the death of Ernie Winch in January. When the BC convention honoured the memory of its longest-serving MLA with a moment of silence, all the events of her long relationship with the elder Winch passed through Grace's mind. Though they had often disagreed, she felt keenly that a vital element of the BC socialist movement was gone.

The Canadian people went to the polls June 10, and the new era took on a Tory blue colour. Voters turned the shocked Liberals out of office, electing John Diefenbaker and the first Conservative government since R.B. Bennett's defeat in 1935. BC CCF president Alex Macdonald was elected by a wide margin in Vancouver–Kingsway. Nationally the CCF elected twenty-five MPs, up two from the previous parliament. It was a slight improvement, but no vindication of CCF-style socialism.

As 1957 drew to a close, Grace was caught up in arrangements for the party's twenty-fifth anniversary celebration the first week of December. Despite Angus's precarious state of health, Grace planned for banquets across the country and with Morden Lazarus edited a hundred-page souvenir album featuring articles by CCF luminaries. During the anniversary week, Grace delivered the keynote address to the Victoria banquet. She promised that the CCF would continue as a "major political force" and spoke of "pioneering fresh territory," hinting at the closer co-operation with organized labour already taking shape.

Grace's power base was now British Columbia rather than Ottawa. No longer at the centre of national policy making, she was still on the national council. As first vice-president of the BC CCF, Grace presided at provincial executive and council meetings through late 1957 and the first half of 1958

A new CCF broom would sweep out the Social Credit government during the 1956 BC election campaign. But lean CCF coffers could support only the single ad in Grace's left hand, while the ads in her right hand were placed by the Socreds every week. September 1956.

Grace and Angus at home on the joyous occasion of their twenty-fifth anniversary. On a card accompanying the traditional bunch of anniversary roses, Angus wrote: "Our 25th but the happiest yet. The years have all been lovely." Vancouver, January 23, 1957.

in place of president Alex Macdonald, who was now in the House of Commons.

Prime Minister Diefenbaker had called another election for March 31, 1958, in an attempt to strengthen his slim seven-seat lead over the Liberals. In Victoria on February 1, with new CCF national secretary Carl Hamilton in attendance, Grace presided over a joint BC executive-caucus meeting to map policy for the federal election. With a strong track record as president of the CCYM, the CCF youth movement, thirty-year-old Hamilton was part of the Ontario group working on the promising new alliance with labour.

Hamilton and the national executive saw the two key issues for the 1958 campaign as the agricultural crisis and unemployment. So, although labour law was a provincial responsibility, the CCF promoted a National Labour Code to provide an "adequate national minimum wage, a forty-hour week . . . two weeks annual vacation with pay and eight statutory holidays each year, union security and check-off, and prohibition of injunctions which infringe on basic labour rights." Other features of the national program were: 200,000 low-cost homes annually; better highways, hospitals and schools; a publicly owned national investment and development bank; increased corporate taxes; a national fuel and energy authority; public ownership of the trans-Canada pipeline; national marketing boards and removal of monopoly control of agricultural industries; and an old age pension of seventy-five dollars a month at age sixty-five with no means test. It was a good, solid social reform package with something to appeal to labour, farm and small business voters. Yet it failed miserably.

When the votes were counted on March 31, the Conservative government swept in with 208 seats; the Liberals took only 49. The CCF won a mere 8 ridings, a third of the 25 they had held. M.J. Coldwell and Stanley Knowles lost their seats; Vancouver–Kingsway fell to a Tory. The CCF leadership was shaken to its foundations. It was obvious that the party could not continue in its present form.

Grace wasted no time crying over the results. She turned at once to the BC provincial convention slated for the last week in May. To forestall disruptive activities by the party's left wing, she pressed for a national CCF position on the international questions she knew were of concern to them. Two days after the election she wrote to Carl Hamilton, "This year they are very likely to redouble their efforts to influence national CCF policy through the BC convention—not only on the floor but through the press across Canada."

To head them off, Grace wanted Hamilton to ask the next national executive meeting to define CCF positions on the value of NATO; a detailed "ban the bomb" policy; arms versus aid to underdeveloped countries; German reunification; and the hot issue of American bases in Canada. Grace would support any national policy they worked out for the sake of unity, putting aside her personal views for the moment. She knew that the public would never vote for a party of co-operation in which the members could not co-operate amongst themselves.

The pacifist CCF left wing had an enormous effect on foreign policy, more than ever in 1958 when global nuclear war seemed imminent. The provincial executive presented a nuclear test ban resolution to the April 1958 convention that also called for a stop to the manufacture and distribution of nuclear weapons, and destruction of the world's nuclear stockpiles under the inspection of the United Nations. In Winnipeg in August 1959, Grace represented BC at a national council meeting which passed a resolution that Canada refuse to allow any nuclear weapons within its borders.

A year earlier, the Diefenbaker government had agreed to allow the US Eisenhower government to construct two bases, one in North Bay, Ontario, and the other in La Macaza, Quebec. In these locations US Bomarc surface-to-air missiles would be installed in addition to the string of Bomarc bases planned for the US. The Canadian government had understood that the Bomarc missiles could be armed with either conventional or atomic warheads. In February 1959 Diefenbaker informed the House that the government was in consultation with the US on "questions connected with the acquisition of nuclear warheads for Bomarc . . . and the storage of warheads in Canada." It would prove to be an explosive issue for the Diefenbaker government.

After the March 1958 federal election, Grace finally accepted the inevitable. The BC executive, with Grace as first vice-president, passed a special resolution for the provincial convention welcoming the decision of the newly merged Canadian Labour Congress (CLC) to "participate in a broadly based people's political movement which embraces the CCF, the labour movement, farm organizations and other liberally-minded persons interested in basic social reform and reconstruction through out parliamentary system of government."

The last weekend in May the CCF provincial convention elected Grace president of the BC–Yukon section. As president Grace would play a key role in what she termed the "unprecedented but remarkably close and efficient linkage of the CCF and BC Federation of Labour organizations," which brought significant gains for the CCF in the BC election of 1960. Usually, once Grace decided to do something, she was exceptionally effective. But in spring 1958 there was still indecision about who would lead in the dance between the CCF and the CLC. Grace wrote Carl Hamilton to ask: "Are the national CCF officials planning to let the CLC take the lead in forming a labour party with the CCF, the farmers' organizations, the cooperatives and possibly other groups tacked on? This question, in some form, is in quite a few minds. It was sharpened by Mr. Coldwell's widely publicized statement that he wouldn't mind if the name CCF were changed; that he had never liked it anyway. For a good many people such a change would imply the dropping of the essence of socialist thinking and the inevitable watering-down of policy."

Grace travelled to Montreal for the 1958 CCF national convention, where she stayed at the home of Frank and Marion Scott, consulting with Scott about the metamorphosis the party was undergoing. On her fifty-third birthday the CCF convention once more elected Grace to the national council, a position she would hold in addition to the presidency of the BC section. In this dual capacity, she had a pivotal role in the soul-searching and policy reformulation which continued until August 1961 when the CCF joined with the Canadian Labour Congress to create the New Democratic Party.

What Angus and many others had endeavoured all their political lives to accomplish was finally coming to pass: organized labour was beginning to work as a partner with the CCF. Knowles, now no longer an MP, was named CLC executive vice-president. CLC and CCF executives set up a joint political committee to implement the CLC's new party resolution. Knowles chaired this committee; CCF national secretary Carl Hamilton was vice-chairman and secretary.

But within the CLC, most former Trades and Labour Congress leaders and members remained reluctant to engage in any sort of political activity, believing that trade unions should not get "mixed up" in politics. A parallel feeling existed within the CCF about trade unions. Grace saw the union–socialist relationship in Canada as the reverse of that in Great Britain. "In Britain," she explained, "it was the union movement that gave rise to the political movement and the political party [the British Labour Party]. In Canada it was the other way around, the party gave rise to changes in the unions."

During her two years as provincial CCF president, Grace reversed the party's failing financial fortunes with successful appeals to the membership and a policy of holding expenditures down to rock-bottom. More ridings than ever before sent in one hundred percent of their "quota" of funds. In January 1959 the party hit a high in memberships and in financial support. Grace also presided over the construction of a new hundred-thousand-dollar provincial headquarters on East Broadway in Vancouver. She and Angus had loaned the building fund a thousand dollars in December 1956, and enough additional support had been collected by January 1959 to put the roof in place. The building was nearly complete by the opening of the 1959 provincial convention in early April. The convention heartily approved of her efforts, and re-elected Grace president by acclamation.

But the troublesome left-right split surfaced again at the convention, this time over provincial forest policies. Leader Robert Strachan was reluctant to

Grace in 1958. {Vancouver Province}

introduce socialism into the BC forest industry. But the "old guard" socialists such as Colin Cameron, former and future MP for Nanaimo and currently a member of the provincial executive, wanted a CCF government to enter the logging business. While Strachan's faction won by a large margin, the party's platform called for public ownership of BC's private power companies, natural gas firms and the BC Telephone Company, as well as compulsory government auto insurance.

Delegates went home in hopes that organized labour would support the CCF in the next election, particularly in view of the Bennett government's new bill: it restricted picketing, and it stripped unions of protection against civil lawsuits filed by employers seeking damages from striking unions. As a prominent member of the provincial CCF–BC Federation of Labour liaison committee, Grace was satisfied with the convention's endorsement of its report recommending joint financing, joint political education programs and close consultation in the selection of candidates.

Grace worked smoothly on the liaison committee with all CCF factions as well as the labour men. But at a very deep emotional level she still resisted allowing the name Co-operative Commonwealth Federation to become history. She was sad that the old ideals, the evangelistic fervour of Regina in 1933, had not brought the CCF to power. Nevertheless, as a realist she could see the necessity for the new alliance, and as BC party president she went on the road to campaign for it. "Ontario and the East had lost heart," Grace reasoned. "They thought they would never get anyplace, and they wanted to make a new party. They felt that they would be able to get the unions in a big way then. Well, my attitude always was, at that time and has been subsequently, all right if they want to have it, it wasn't going to hurt us to change our name. We would continue as the same party, but if it helped them we would do that, if it would make a strong party."

Grace travelled through BC as part of a four-member new party preparation team. It met acceptance in most areas, but was outright refused entry into the mountainous riding of Kootenay West, long controlled as a personal fiefdom by the MacInnises' political enemy, MP Bert Herridge. "He didn't want any orders coming to him from Ottawa or Victoria or Vancouver," Grace recalled. "So, they wouldn't let us in. He was head and forefront of opposition to that."

During her two years as provincial president from 1958 to 1960, Grace many times put aside personal feelings to focus on bringing the new party into being. It was not an easy birth. "We had rows, quite a few rows and a lot to overcome," Grace recalled. "We knew that David Lewis was very anxious to pull in the unions on the basis that there was a brand new party for them to join, that they weren't joining any old party. I understand why he did—they were a big potential source of funding.

"A lot of us were worried about David Lewis's anxiety to entice the trade unions to the point where we thought he was in danger of dominating us with trade unions. Well, we didn't need to worry. As president in BC I discovered it was the hardest thing in the world to get trade union representation on our club councils or our executive or anything. They would simply say, 'Now, we're busy people. You go ahead and run the party how you see fit. We'll help at election time.' And so we were no longer afraid of being dominated."

By the time Grace relinquished the provincial presidency to Owen Jones at the 1960 BC convention, she had overcome earlier misgivings to become a vigorous advocate of a labour–socialist partnership. She told the delegates that the CCF movement had been helped enormously by the BC Federation of Labour, "whose constant vigilance over the living standards and liberties of the whole community has given the lie to its detractors."

Grace might have run again for the presidency of the BC party, but her body was showing painful signs of stress. That year she fought her first battle with the rheumatoid arthritis that would become her constant tormenter. "I think it really had something to do with triggering off my first big attack of arthritis, the general heaviness of the presidency when we were preparing for the advent of the NDP," Grace told a reporter.

The perennial struggle against communist infiltration, especially her fight to keep Orville Braaten of North Vancouver off the provincial executive, plagued Grace in the second year of her presidency. "Even the general populace knew he was communist," she recalled. Grace asked the national inner circle to prevent Braaten from representing the CCF at the 1960 CLC convention. "I even worked on trade union people in the east," she said. "And then, two of our executive members went back and got the convention to admit him. Frustrating! With all that kind of kerfuffle, the public felt that we were lying when we said that we didn't have anything to do with the communists."

At the landmark CLC convention where a thunderous ovation met passage of the new party resolution, Grace's fears were realized. "We watched Bratten [sic] perform during the convention," Carl Hamilton reported by mail. "As far as I was able to see, he took the straight 'Commie' line on practically every issue." Grace lost that battle, but she felt vindicated by Hamilton's view.

Grace and Angus overcame their respective health problems sufficiently to travel by train to Regina for the final CCF national convention August 9–11, 1960. Grace acted as the delegate from Vancouver East, served on the resolutions committee and was once more elected to national council. For Angus it was the first CCF convention he had attended since 1950. He was seated on the platform, and had the heart-warming experience of greeting many longtime friends and reliving old memories.

The exact form the new party would take was still crystallizing. The 1960 convention went on record as favouring the name Social Democratic Party for the new political entity, and elected as national leader Hazen Argue, who had been CCF federal caucus leader since 1958. In other business, the convention declared the CCF pro-United Nations and anti-nuclear. A resolution urged Canada to withdraw from NORAD, the North American Air Defense Agreement, on the grounds that "the keystone of NORAD in Canada is to be the BOMARC anti-aircraft missile, which can be made relatively effective only by the use of atomic warheads." By the same vote Canada was advised to leave NATO, which had become "a purely military organization."

After the convention Grace and Angus returned home, but Grace travelled east again that sweltering August 1960 for a three-day seminar convened in Winnipeg by the national joint committee of the CLC and the CCF. While the more than three hundred seminar participants took no votes, they reached a consensus on a broader political party with a program and philosophy almost indistinguishable from that of the CCF would be founded at a convention in 1961. Canadian Labour Congress president Claude Jodoin assured the seminar that the CLC had no desire to dominate the new political party. The CLC would not affiliate to the new party, but would support it and urge its affiliated unions to join. To Grace's relief the new party, unlike the British Labour Party, would have no bloc voting—that is, one person casting a large number of votes on behalf of his or her union—which would have given unions a dominant position in the new partnership.

Grace, now completely resigned to the political transformation underway, took part in many phases of this crucial seminar: constitutional drafting, promotional planning, and especially community planning to end construction of rows of identical shoddy suburban houses. Grace wanted to see shopping centres, schools, churches, parks and places of work more fully integrated with housing to form whole communities.

Seminar participants shared their concern over American investment in Canada and growing American control of the Canadian economy. They noted with alarm that inflation was nibbling away at social security benefits, and urged that these benefits be indexed to the cost of living. There was universal agreement on the need for a national health insurance plan to provide full medical, hospital, nursing, dental and optical care.

Now that the democratic left appeared to be creating a truly powerful alliance, the drum roll of press criticism grew louder. The media reported that "every imaginative split conceivable" had occurred at this seminar. But, as BC CCF secretary Harold Thayer told radio audiences in October, the charges were distorted. The delegates had agreed, he reported triumphantly, to support a "program of public ownership in all its forms, national, provincial, municipal and co-operative." Another commentator wrote, with greater accuracy, "It was quite clear that it was the aura, the image, the reputation of the CCF that was being abandoned, rather than basic principles and programs."

Lucy had been living with her sons and daughters in turn, but she spent the most time during the late 1950s and early 1960s with Grace's sister Belva and her husband Ralph Staples, a prominent leader of Canada's co-operative movement, on their farm near Ottawa. Belva preferred a quiet family life to being out in the public eye. When she married her first cousin Ralph Staples, a younger son of Lucy's brother Richard Sandfield Staples, it was the second such marriage in the Staples family. Lucy's mother Hannah had married her first cousin, Richard Staples, two generations before.

When Belva married Ralph he was a farmer, interested in producer and consumer co-operatives. In 1949 he became president of the Co-operative Union of Canada. Belva and Ralph had two sons and a developmentally disabled daughter. Maureen Staples had trouble learning to speak and was unable to learn to read and write. After some training at home, she had been placed in a special residential school. Belva had become depressed, likely because of her inability to help her daughter, and this problem may have been complicated for her in 1959 when her mother became part of her household. Ralph wrote Grace and Angus in summer 1959, describing Belva's state of mind and asking if they could find a place for Lucy on the West Coast, either in their home or with brother Bruce or Ralph. "Belva is currently comparatively well—as evidenced by the fact she felt able to lead the boys on two days of intensive Washington touristing while I attended a meeting," Ralph informed Grace. "She still has moments of panic, but these too will soon pass. The real problem does, of course, remain. How to prevent or minimize these distressing periods of depression. She spends a period reluctantly each week with Dr. H.—two years plus now—but this brings no miracle. Belva seems unable to bring herself wholeheartedly to reach out for help. When unwell she just wants, 'to be let alone to get a grip on herself,' an attitude which makes treatment difficult."

Lucy Woodsworth moved to the West Coast during summer 1959, first living with Ralph and Vivian, and then in September moving into Tigh Cairdeil with Grace and Angus. Grace dearly loved her mother, but Lucy's presence did add to her workload. Grace wrote in her diary, "I imagine we had not thought of the extra strain—her deafness, her constant talking when Angus was worn from a sleepless night, her need to have time spent with her on shopping, getting her hair curled, visiting friends, etc. I know that in addition to the other things I was doing, it was too much. I suffered increasingly from guilty irritation and trying to be strong-minded." In addition to her work as BC party president and national council member, Grace had responsibility for the large house and garden. She kept the spacious lawns cut and canned a plentiful supply of fruit from their own trees.

Grace enjoyed all her varied activities, but her health buckled under the stress. In February 1960 she developed pneumonia after a case of flu. Her arthritis, which had given its first warning the previous winter, was now in her hands and knees continually. The doctor advised rest, advice which Grace had trouble following.

It seemed to her that an end to responsibility would never come. As soon as she returned from the CCF–CLC seminar in Winnipeg, she plunged into the last two weeks of campaigning for a BC provincial election September 12. "I was sick," Grace wrote in her diary, "but I made up my mind I was going to do what I could." She did office and committee work, gave campaign speeches around the province and introduced Tommy Douglas at a luncheon welcoming him to the BC campaign trail. Finally, at the climax of the campaign, Grace undertook the most exhausting task: chairing an enthusiastic rally in New Westminster with five thousand people in attendance. When the votes were tallied her efforts had paid off to some degree. Social Credit, with thirty-nine percent of the vote, still formed the government under the leadership of W.A.C. Bennett, but the CCF had increased its representation from ten to sixteen seats, polling nearly thirty-three percent of the vote.

"When all was over," Grace told her diary, "I was at breaking point. Mother had decided they needed her at Belva's, and she left toward the end of September. I did her packing. Then I went to see the doctor and devoted myself to a winter of illness, with everything cut off. Angus has been wonderful." In her diary Grace planned her future: "FIRST comes Angus. I must have time always to be with him, to think more about the little things that give him pleasure and that give me pleasure in doing them. We have earned some time to ourselves now. I must think of myself as HOME-BASED, and not as we did for so many years as being first at the service of the movement."

When she went into seclusion, Grace was so racked with arthritis she had trouble turning over in bed. But she was determined to be well enough to care for Angus at home. With her doctor, she worked out a schedule of forty minutes' exercise first thing in the morning followed by a hot bath. By spring 1961, after eight months of rest, daily exercises and twice-weekly treatment at the G.F. Strong Rehabilitation Centre in Vancouver, Grace felt she was on the road to convalescence. Her doctor prescribed the drug prednizone and simultaneous injections of gold salts, but Grace recognized that despite any treatment no one really recovers from arthritis. She could only hope to keep it suppressed with luck and by good management.

Sadly, Grace gave up the plan she had cherished through that long, painful winter: to travel to Ottawa for the founding convention of the new party. "All I could do, being more or less confined to barracks, was listen to reports. We didn't have much in the way of a TV set, and Angus didn't like too much noise around. He wasn't able to take any interest by that time. His energy was down to zero. I was sick too. One of the hardest things, if you've never had a devitalizing health experience, you don't realize what happens to you when your energy suddenly gets chopped off. You don't have what it takes."

As it happened, the start of the new party left a bitter taste in Grace's mouth. She was sickened, in the turbulent time between March 1958 and November 1962, by what she viewed as treacherous actions by two of the party's small band of eight MPs: Bert Herridge and Hazen Argue. Coldwell stepped down as leader in 1960, and the new national leader and federal caucus leader, Hazen Argue, aspired to the national leadership of the new party. But the CCF establishment—particularly David Lewis, Stanley Knowles and Grace—did not want him; they backed Saskatchewan Premier Tommy Douglas. Argue began an all-out campaign against Douglas that placed him at the top of Grace's list for the meanest tricks ever played in politics.

During five suffocating days at the beginning of August 1961, more than two thousand delegates from CCF, labour, and a few farm and professional groups met in Ottawa to create the New Democratic Party (NDP). Grace stayed at home but vigorously rooted for Douglas. For the rest of her life she remembered that leadership struggle. "One of the dirtiest things that was done was the steady campaign that Hazen Argue waged to defeat Tommy Douglas. He pretended to be his friend right up until Tommy emerged as the person [who was elected NDP leader]." Douglas was still premier of Saskatchewan and as yet had no seat in Parliament, and Argue remained federal caucus leader for another seven months. Then, to the utter shock of Grace and the rest of the NDP inner circle, without warning on February 25, 1962, Argue abruptly turned Liberal.

In June, during the first federal election after the birth of the NDP, Douglas failed to win the federal seat he contested in Regina. Erhardt Regier, re-elected since 1953 in the BC riding of Burnaby–Coquitlam, voluntarily resigned and invited Douglas to run for his seat. The voters of Burnaby–Coquitlam turned out in force for Douglas, who won the October 1962 by-election by a large majority.

In the inter-regnum between Argue's defection in February and November 1962, when Douglas took his seat in Parliament and became caucus leader, Bert Herridge was caucus leader but never national leader of the party. Grace still distrusted him as a maverick who often supported left-wingers and had barred her new party organizing team from Kootenay West. It galled Grace to see evidence that Herridge was accorded the same leadership status her father had once held so honourably, especially whenever she saw Herridge's photograph hanging next to that of her father in the Parliament Building; all the other photos were of genuine party leaders. She confided later: "I used to wish that there was some way of getting rid of that picture. I thought of all the ways—of tearing it away, getting it broken—but there was a special friend who had connived with him about this picture. To have stirred him up and to make trouble in the caucus, I just figured it isn't worth it. You just swallow your pride and figure it will be gone some day."

Grace had to swallow her pride and work with Herridge in the federal caucus until 1968 when he was replaced in Kootenay West by NDPer Ran Harding with whom she collaborated easily, particularly on environmental issues. In suppressing her distaste for Herridge, Grace acted to preserve party unity and maximize the effectiveness of the caucus.

Although she was not in Ottawa for the birth of the NDP, Grace did participate in the three-day founding convention of the BC section of the NDP in Vancouver in late October 1961. Her name topped the list of the BC Committee for the NDP, albeit as an honorary member. The other members were party stalwarts with whom she had worked for years: Frank McKenzie, Owen Jones, Bob Strachan, Alex Macdonald, and Jessie Mendels. Gretchen Steeves and Grant MacNeil shared administration committee duties with a new man on the scene who would soon take a very active part, Thomas Berger.

On Hallowe'en night 1961, Grace and Angus moved from their beloved Tigh Cairdeil to a more manageable four-room house at 2114 West 48th Avenue, still in pleasant Kerrisdale. Soon after the move, while wandering at night under the influence of a sleeping pill, Angus tripped and fell, breaking a shoulder and a hip bone. He was in hospital for several weeks and hated being there. Grace dedicated herself to keeping him comfortable at home.

They kept up the traditions of their love. Each year on January 23 Angus had presented Grace with a bouquet of golden roses to commemorate the bouquet she had carried on their wedding day. "The last two years he wasn't able to get out and get them at all," Grace said. "He got me to go and get the roses, but we always had them."

On federal election day 1962 the NDP came a disappointing fourth place with nineteen seats, though they were up from eight in the previous House. It was encouraging that Knowles regained his seat in Woodsworth's old riding, Winnipeg North Centre. Diefenbaker led his Tories back to power with 116 seats, despite lack of public confidence in his handling of the Bomarc missiles. The Liberals took 100, Social Credit 30. The minority parties had the balance of power, an unstable situation that would be changed by another federal election within the year.

The MacInnises led a quiet life for the next two years, enlivened only by a visit from Frank Scott in September 1962, and a trip Grace made to see Lucy and Belva in Ontario in May 1963.

On January 1, 1963, the centennial of the Emancipation Proclamation, Grace and Angus listened with hope as the Reverend Martin Luther King, Jr. addressed the great march on Washington: "I have a dream that one day . . . sons of former slaves and the sons of former slaveowners will be able to sit down together at the table of brotherhood." It was a dream Grace and Angus shared.

They watched the hopes of the fledgling New Democratic Party falter in the federal election of April 8, 1963, the second financially draining election within a year. It was triggered by a fight over nuclear weapons. On February 4, 1963, Diefenbaker's defence minister, George Harkness resigned over the government's refusal to accept US nuclear warheads for the Bomarc missiles based in Canada. The following day the government was defeated in a non-confidence motion on the issue.

Liberal leader Lester Pearson, winner of the Nobel Peace Prize for defusing the explosive Suez Canal crisis of 1956, had given many Canadians the impression that he was against the basing of nuclear weapons in Canada. But the Cuban missile crisis of October 1962 changed many North American minds, and possibly Pearson's, about the necessity of a nuclear defense for Canada. Soon afterwards, Pearson was advocating the acceptance of nuclear warheads by Canada. In a January 12 speech in Scarborough, Ontario, he said, "[The Canadian government] should end at once its evasion of responsibility, by discharging the commitments it has already accepted for Canada. It can only do this by accepting nuclear warheads, for those defensive tactical weapons which cannot effectively be used without them but which we have agreed to use."

Grace, the CCF and later the NDP had long opposed the placement of nuclear weapons on Canadian soil, but the Canadian public generally agreed with Pearson. The Liberals won 129 seats in the April 8, 1963 election, wresting power from Diefenbaker's 95 Tories. The NDP made a disappointing showing: the party dropped two seats, winning only 17 and remaining in fourth place, behind Social Credit. On domestic issues the Liberals co-opted the NDP platform to promise full employment, a national pension plan, a national health care plan and better markets for farmers. Barely a month after he won the election, Prime Minister Pearson signed an agreement with US President John F. Kennedy to equip Canadian forces with US-supplied nuclear weapons.

During the spring and summer, the Front de libération du Québec (FLQ) planted a series of bombs to blow up mailboxes in the wealthy English community of Westmount, Montreal, to dramatize the FLQ demand for the separation of Quebec from Canada. In an effort to resolve the conflicts between French and English Canada, Prime Minister Pearson formed the Royal Commission on Bilingualism and Biculturalism in July.

A social explosion on another front was triggered in 1963 when Betty Friedan's book *The Feminine Mystique* raised the long-smouldering issue of the suppression of women and second-class status of the female half of the population. Female Canadian reporters began to question why so few women had been elected to Parliament and to provincial legislatures. One *Vancouver Sun* reporter sought out Grace.

Earlier feminists had achieved suffrage and struggled to improve conditions for women workers during two world wars, but after the wars most women had retreated to become homemakers and consumers. At this point Grace had little hope that women would ever again be a source of political strength. "I don't think feminism cuts any ice now," she said wearily. "When it existed, women were inspired to enter politics so that they might lend their support to idealist programs involving such things as health, welfare or educational opportunities. Other idealistic women supported them. Now it is an age of materialism—an age of roads and bridges. And materialism has contaminated women voters so that they elect the candidate who makes the most generous promises of material, not spiritual benefits."

Angus's long and painful illness ended on March 2, 1964. As he had wished, he died peacefully at home. Grace felt a mixture of deep grief and relief that her precious husband need suffer no more. Her aunt and good friend Mary Woodsworth, who was staying at the MacInnises' home at the time, provided Grace with solid emotional support. Ninety-year-old Lucy wrote to comfort her daughter: "Strength will come to you though we cannot explain it, and there is a reservoir found in the fact that you and your strong, brave companion have tried to be and do the best you knew. You have indeed, 'made earnest with life' and you who remain will grow in strength."

The funeral took place on March 5. Flowers from Lucy, Charles, Howard, and Belva and Ralph arrived as messages of love from the east. Arnold Webster gave the main funeral address, and Grace took comfort from his view of Angus's accomplishments. Angus was cremated, and in a private ceremony Grace scattered his ashes on the trail around tranquil Beaver Lake in Stanley Park, where he had loved to stroll.

Despite Grace's view of Angus as "the power behind the throne, not a headline hunter," many editorial tributes were published in his memory. The *Vancouver Sun* called him "A tireless fighter for the common man." Arthur Laing, then Northern Affairs Minister in the Liberal government, said, "The coin that can buy Angus MacInnis will never be minted." The *London Times* recognized him as "one of the architects of the Co-operative Commonwealth Federation in Canada." Coldwell was too ill to attend the funeral but his letter of condolence cheered Grace with a personal tribute: "To me he was a tower of strength as he sat beside me in the House of Commons . . . He was the comrade in whom I confided and from whom I sought advice when I was worried or perplexed. Always he helped me as none other could."

All during the grief-filled days of Angus's death and funeral, Grace kept a stern hold upon herself and remained equal to all the demands of the time. In accord with her father's high expectations of her, Grace had always required of herself a flawless performance, regardless of personal cost. She spent Easter with her brother Bruce and his family in Westbank, BC, then took a short holiday with some friends in Oregon. After several weeks she made plans to visit Lucy and Belva in Ontario, but before she could get there, Lucy broke her hip in a fall down a flight of stairs. She remained in hospital for the rest of her life.

The vale of sorrow seemed to stretch on forever. At the end of June Grace's dear friend and colleague Laura Jamieson died in Vancouver at age eighty-two. Grace spoke at her funeral and a few days later broadcast a tribute on CBC Radio praising her for living to give in the face of a materialist world. "Where the prevailing idea is to get . . . she plunged into the work of securing equality for women—full voting rights with men, and later, full economic and social rights."

That same month, after trying for years to protect Belva's privacy, Lucy confided to Grace: "For all these days now she lies helpless in bed until afternoon she comes down and makes the dinner, and Ralph doesn't know how her day has gone." In summer 1964 Ralph Staples decided to sell their family house and three acres of ornate terraced gardens in Manotick, near Ottawa, and relocate his family to an apartment in the capital, where he could be closer to his job as president of the Co-operative Union of Canada. He and Belva asked Grace to come and help with the move, and she arrived at their country place in time to take charge of the packing. Her presence was a great relief to Belva, who felt overwhelmed by the task. "I was surprised to find I was able to do that moving and sorting," Grace recalled. "It was good restoration for me because the scene was quite different and it pulled me out of things, and I was able to help get the move achieved." By allowing the urgent needs of others to absorb her energy, Grace began her own healing process.

When Angus died, her old way of life died with him. She grieved very deeply the loss of her dearest companion. For several years after his death, kind friends who understood the depth of their love sent Grace roses on their wedding anniversary as Angus had always done. And yet as the immediate oppression of her grief began to lift, Grace found there was a certain new freedom to life. While she was an intelligent and capable woman dealing with the world of politics and everyday life, one of Grace's primary motivations had always been to please the most important man in her life. When she was a child, an adolescent and a young woman, this man was her father. Once she married, Angus became the man to please; she had chosen him precisely because he was like her father in many ways. At times Grace was then agonizingly caught between the two strongest men in her life.

Now she could lay to rest some demands of the past. Some things could never be: Her father's wish for a first-born son could never be fulfilled; as a woman Grace could never be the party's leader within the cultural context of her time. Yet, while attempting to fulfill her father's impossible expectations, Grace had already reached higher and accomplished more than most other women.

If the relationship of father to daughter was rooted in inequality, Grace and her husband had worked together as equals, companions and friends in a rare way. In the last years she had sacrificed her career opportunities to care for him. All her patience was required, because Angus in pain could be every bit as irascible and demanding as her father. Grace had always felt overshadowed by the giant stature of these two, her father and her husband. Now, at fifty-nine, she was poised to emerge from their shadows.

PART III

HARVEST

CHAPTER 13

Ambition Fulfilled

G race returned home to Vancouver in time to watch the first snowfall
soften the North Shore mountain peaks. Truly alone for the first time
since Angus died, she did not give way to self-pity. Instead, she replanted
herself on the political field. The seed from which her new life sprouted was
an informal study group she started for the federal ridings of Vancouver East
and Vancouver–Kingsway.

That winter twenty-five to thirty people met weekly over tea and cookies
to consider current questions: Quebec's uneasy place in confederation; the
newly proposed Canadian maple leaf flag; the rise of automation; the recently
signed Canada–US free trade Auto Pact; the impact of American capital and
culture on Canada's identity; roadblocks to a national medicare plan; demands for equality by a new generation of feminists; the escalating conflict
in Vietnam; the possibility that Canada would join France in recognizing
communist China; the role of the United Nations in averting nuclear war.

By the time her backyard dogwood tree was in bloom, Grace was
blossoming on the political scene. Locally she helped NDPer Bob Williams
in his successful campaign for a seat on Vancouver's City Council. At the
NDP provincial convention in May 1965 she rejoined the party executive as
first vice-president.

In the international arena, Grace advocated a strong role for Canada in
the United Nations. On the radio program "Town Meeting in Canada," far
ahead of her time, Grace insisted: "The UN must have a peace-keeping force
and the power to use it, no matter who the belligerents may be." At a June
meeting she and the BC NDP executive issued a press release opposing
Canadian participation in Vietnam. "Involvement of Canadian troops is
completely at variance with the aims and objects of the UN to which Canada
and Canadians are pledged," it stated. Grace led the BC delegation to the
third federal NDP convention in Toronto in mid-July, where the BC
resolution on Vietnam was adopted.

In August Grace joined childhood friend Kathleen Inglis Godwin at her home in Nanaimo. They swam and beachcombed on Gabriola Island, site of many happy CCF summer schools. Grace spent time with family members and made plans for an autumn banquet and dance to celebrate Tommy Douglas's thirtieth year in politics.

Yet beneath her cheerful exterior Grace was uneasy and impatient. Rumours of a fall federal election were everywhere, and she was anxious for the contest to begin. "So much of life consists of waiting, and it's not always easy to hustle while you wait," she confided to her diary. "Most of us old hands claim we're not a bit impressed . . . but, one by one, we join the ranks of the glory shouters . . . . I'm tired of waiting!" Grace sensed that her life's path was about to take an unprecedented turn.

Right after Labour Day Prime Minister Pearson dissolved Parliament and called an election for November 8 in an attempt to refresh his scandal-plagued minority government. Grace was again offered the nomination in Vancouver–Kingsway, and this time she accepted. The seat had been held since 1962 by her old friend Arnold Webster, who was now retiring.

Women candidates have often been sacrifice candidates, but that was not so for Grace in this district of working people in the southeastern quarter of Vancouver. These families had voted CCF or NDP since 1930 when Angus took over part of the area from the Conservatives by winning Vancouver South. The growing population was split into two new ridings over the years, but they kept voting for Angus. After he retired, the riding remained CCF and NDP except after the disastrous 1958 election. By standing for election in Vancouver–Kingsway Grace was demanding the ultimate performance from herself. If she lost Angus's riding she would be disgraced in her own eyes. Her whole life had prepared her for this contest, she had a fighting chance and she was determined to run for all she was worth.

Deciding what to put down as her occupation on the nomination form took some thought. The only paid work Grace had ever done was her two and a half years of early teaching, her term as an MLA, and the biography of her father which had generated royalties. Was she merely a political volunteer? Some suggested she put "widow," others proposed "homemaker" or "retired." But these labels were not for Grace. "Being a widow is a sorrow," she explained. "Angus told me housewife was an exaggeration; retired, I'm not." An award-winning writer she certainly was. She filled in "writer" on the nomination form.

In Vancouver–Kingsway Grace was opposed by Liberal Jack Austin, later Senator Austin. Then he was half her age, an energetic thirty-three-year-old lawyer making his first election bid. As personal assistant to Northern Affairs Minister Arthur Laing, he had been the Canadian government's international

Grace shares a victory dance with her old friend and colleague Harold Winch on the night of her election as the first woman Member of Parliament from British Columbia. November 8, 1965.

Grace inhales the fragrance of water lilies in a constituent's pond, on a tour of Vancouver–Kingsway with Toronto Star columnist Lotta Dempsey, proving with one image that her arthritis was in remission, and that being an MP had not made her pompous. August 1967.

law adviser on the Columbia River treaty negotiations. The Conservative candidate was Garfield Milner; the Social Credit candidate, Arthur Holmes. From the start the real race was between MacInnis and Austin.

Grace's discussion group formed the nucleus of her campaign team of more than two hundred people. The riding contained 17,000 single family homes, but few apartment blocks. Under the direction of campaign manager Jim Dickson, Grace's workers twice visited each home. Arnold's wife Daisy Webster supervised thirty women in the Rio Hall committee room freshly redecorated with "Elect Grace MacInnis" signs in the striking new NDP colours of orange and black. Grace's whole campaign had a well-organized, neighbourly feeling rather than an aura of slick professionalism. Early in October a stand-up coffee party at Rio Hall featured beautiful girls serving sandwiches. Grace's old friends BC NDP leader Bob Strachan, MLAs Alex Macdonald and Arthur Turner, MP Harold Winch and incumbent MP Arnold Webster turned out to man the coffee pots. An overflow crowd listened to Grace lash out at her perennial enemies, the large corporations.

She drew support from a wide variety of quarters. The elderly M.J. Coldwell spoke on her behalf. Alderman Bob Williams wrote a blurb for her campaign leaflet: "a lady with guts . . . willing to stand up for important principles, regardless of consequences." Trade unionists and Japanese Canadians campaigned for her.

Grace's main platform planks were job security; retraining to deal with job loss due to automation; government funded education from child care centres, then called nursery schools, through university; immediate full medicare; protection of consumers from high prices; an increase in the Old Age Pension to $100 per month at age sixty-five; and an independent Canadian foreign policy focussed on peace.

The hottest point in the campaign flared over consumer protection, a long-standing concern for Grace. During the Depression she had cut her political teeth on consumer issues of low wages, price controls, and availability of food, shelter and clothing. As an MLA during World War Two she had crusaded against rising costs of food and fuel. The crux of the current crisis was deceptive packaging and advertising, a made-to-order platform from which Grace could attack the large corporations. For the campaign the national NDP had produced a newspaper ad and a television commercial to support its packaging bill, introduced in 1964 by Winnipeg MP David Orlikow. The newspaper ad showed a woman pouring something from a box labelled "Biff Bam" beneath the words, "Who protects you against misleading advertising and labelling? The New Democrats." Although the NDP had purchased space, the Southam-owned *Hamilton Spectator* refused to print this ad. Similarly, a sixty-second TV commercial asked viewers to demand a law against misleading advertising of an unidentified detergent, a law that a New

Democratic government would bring in. The NDP bought air time and the Board of Broadcast Governors approved the ad, but the CTV network, a Tory-leaning private corporation, refused to air it.

Grace was indignant over what she called "a gross violation of the right of free speech." NDP leader Tommy Douglas called it "censorship and suppression" as did federal president Eamon Park, but Grace was most frequently quoted, probably because consumer issues were viewed primarily as women's issues. But Grace framed the question of misleading advertising and deceptive packaging, as well as the suppression of ads, in the wider context of the need to control the power of large corporations.

Election day, November 8, 1965, was victory day for Grace. She took Vancouver–Kingsway with a margin of 5,736 votes, earning her place in history as the first woman of any party elected to Parliament from British Columbia. For ninety-four years, since the province sent its first Members to the House of Commons in 1871, it had been represented solely by men. Indeed, Grace was only the eighteenth female ever elected to the Canadian Parliament. Across the country the NDP won twenty-one seats in three provinces, Ontario, Manitoba and BC. The party now ranked third in the House and had tallied 17.9 percent of the popular vote, its best showing yet. Pearson's Liberals won only a minority government, its third in a row; the NDP and Social Credit held the balance of power.

For Grace victory was sweet after so many election defeats, but her response was measured. "I'm mindful of the honour," she told reporters. "Kingsway is a very precious jewel in the NDP crown. I would hate to have lost it." She was undoubtedly thinking of her beloved husband and of the little slip of paper still tucked away in her wallet on which Angus had written to her more than a decade ago, "The next Member for Vancouver–Kingsway."

Grace vehemently rejected the opinions of those who put her election vistory down to a widow's sympathy vote. She pointed to the four elections since Angus's last win in 1953, and to her own term in the BC Legislature and party activities on both provincial and national levels. "I know myself it was no consolation prize at all," she told a reporter defensively. "I had done enough on my own. I am always very pleased about that because so often, you know, they say, 'She succeeded because her husband died.'"

On election night all quibbling was laid to rest for a brief glorious moment. At the Golden Horseshoe Cabaret, Grace, wearing a corsage of pink rosebuds, happily shared a victory dance with her old comrade Harold Winch, re-elected for his sixth term in Vancouver East.

Early in January, Grace rented her Kerrisdale cottage to a young couple, packed the old leather suitcase Angus had bought years ago in Australia, and boarded Air Canada's Silver Dart flight to Ottawa. She rented an apartment in the Bronson Street building where Belva and Ralph lived, a twenty-minute walk from the Parliament buildings and just a block away from Saint-Vincent's Hospital where Lucy was about to celebrate her ninety-second birthday. Her mother had supported Grace with frequent letters of encouragement during the campaign, and was thrilled at the successful outcome. "How lucky you were to have had private coaching from the head man himself," Lucy wrote when she heard of Grace's election. "All the secrets he has used are now yours forever."

Because Stanley Knowles understood what it would mean to her, he arranged for Grace to have the same sixth floor office she had worked in with her father and with Angus. Originally numbered 616, it was by then 639C. When she stood in that room again for the first time in more than ten years, her heart was flooded with loving remembrances—her little desk in the corner under the cartoons of J.S. Woodsworth, her first meeting with Angus in that very room, all the socialist history that had been made there. She unpacked her papers, placed her carefully nurtured shamrock plant on her desk, and hung the famous Karsh photograph of the first CCF caucus, in which she was honorary secretary. Then Grace took a deep breath and vowed that she would, in the best Woodsworth–MacInnis tradition, champion the rights of ordinary Canadians in the stony face of power and privilege.

When Parliament opened on January 18, 1966, Grace was welcomed warmly by Prime Minister Pearson and by Opposition Leader Diefenbaker as heir to a proud legacy of integrity. As she surveyed the green-carpeted chamber from her seat at the back of the NDP corner, Grace saw some familiar faces. On the government front bench were Minister of Transport Jack Pickersgill, her old friend from the University of Manitoba, and Minister of Indian Affairs and Northern Development Arthur Laing, who had defeated her in Vancouver South in 1949. The "Three Wise Men" of Quebec were among the Liberals: Pierre Trudeau, Jean Marchand and Gerard Pelletier, all three former CCF sympathizers. Trudeau had already been singled out with the job of parliamentary secretary to Prime Minister Pearson.

Three other women sat in this parliament: Secretary of State Judy LaMarsh from Niagara Falls; Margaret Rideout, a Liberal from Westmorland, New Brunswick, parliamentary secretary to the minister of national health and welfare; and Jean Wadds, a Tory from Grenville–Dundas, Ontario. Aside from Ellen Fairclough, Canada's first woman cabinet minister, and the outspoken LaMarsh, most women MPs since Agnes Macphail had turned in performances that were competent but undistinguished. If the 261 male MPs in the House expected the same from Grace, they were about to be surprised.

Her maiden speech January 24 made headlines from coast to coast, and gave notice that her legislative agenda would be centred on the home and family. She began simply, thanking Pearson and Diefenbaker for their tributes to her husband and father. She then marked out the foundation for all her work in Parliament. In resonant tones, she quoted a giant of democracy she had long admired, who said, "'The proper job of government is to help a community of people do for themselves collectively what they need to have done and what they are not able to do for themselves as individuals.' In case anyone should think that is a radical definition of the job of government," Grace said, "let me hasten to assure them it is one given by Abraham Lincoln about a hundred years ago."

She rapped the throne speech as "woefully inadequate" in dealing with the twenty-three percent of Canadians living in poverty on less than $3000 per year. "They are the old workers and the pensioners, the unemployed and the underemployed, the school dropouts and the undereducated, the widows and fatherless families, the disabled and the sick, the retarded and the mentally ill, the small farmers and the commercial workers, the native Indians and the new immigrants . . . . They live on the margin of misery." To that point it was a compassionate speech, nothing unique. But the fuse was lit, and the bomb was about to explode.

Grace declared mothers had a right to work outside the home, and called for adequate "nursery schools" and part-time hours of work. Then Grace proposed a measure so "far out" that many members could not believe their ears, "suitable and adequate wages" for "women who desired to make a full-time, good career of motherhood." Grace concluded her maiden speech in French by drawing an image of her ideal Canada—one diverse family under a single roof. "It would not house only wealthy and influential families but all families down to the smallest farmer and the most humble workers. They would all be accepted as essential to the welfare of the country . . . . In the various parts of our huge country, we could keep on living in our own room while being free and happy to go in any part of the house, as masters in our own home," she finished with a flourish.

Editorial pages across Canada ridiculed Grace's proposal of salaries for homemakers. The *Globe and Mail* smirked, "Government payment would turn mothers into civil servants. We have nothing against civil servants. Some of our best friends are civil servants, but would you want your father to have married one?" The *Ottawa Journal* ran a front page story headlined, "Widow MP's Plea: 'Pay Housewives'" and a photo of a common scene, mother vacuuming while two squalling kids scatter toys in her wake. The Montreal *Gazette* ran a straight story, but the *Toronto Star* took a sarcastic tone, suggesting that everyone, MPs included, should at least pay lip service to the idea by kissing their mothers on the cheek. Grace received only a few letters giving serious consideration to what such a measure would mean in terms of taxes and a woman's share of her husband's estate.

Now that Grace had served notice in the House that she was not just going to follow tradition tamely, she focussed on women's issues and on consumer questions. Each of these themes was but a different facet of the core of Grace's work—her championship of healthy families as the foundation of a strong Canada.

One of Grace's primary interests throughout her parliamentary career would be the advancement of women, but she utterly rejected the feminist label. "I am not a feminist," she declared early and often in English and in French. To her, issues of women's wages, family planning, day care and equal treatment before the law regardless of gender were not women's issues, they were human issues. Before she had been elected to Parliament, Grace had not specialized in the social and legal problems of women as a group, but now that she was in the House, she felt obliged to take up these issues, because few other MPs were addressing them.

Grace was assigned to the Health and Welfare Committee, where she and Margaret Rideout were the only women. Shortly after Grace was seated the committee began its inquiry into reform of the law governing birth control information and contraceptive devices. These were criminal activities at the time, punishable by two years in prison, although prosecutions were rare. Diaphragms and condoms were available only from physicians who were willing to break the law. Birth control pills were first licensed for use in Canada by prescription in 1960; they were soon in great demand. Grace was quick to advocate removing birth control from the Criminal Code. She wanted all restrictions lifted on the advertising of birth control devices, so that everyone could have full and free access to information about the choices available. More timid committee members worried that such advertising in popular magazines would lead to promiscuity, particularly amongst unmarried teens.

"I have an open mind on the business of people being unmarried and using contraceptives," Grace said. "I have an open mind as to how early sex ought to be indulged in, but it should not be indulged in without safeguards, without foolproof contraceptives until the couple is not only married but well-adjusted to each other and until they both want to have a child, and have the means of looking after that child. And if they don't want a child they shouldn't have to have children."

In December the Health and Welfare Committee tabled a report recommending that birth control be removed from the Criminal Code of Canada and placed under the jurisdiction of the Food and Drug Directorate, with restrictions on the advertising of birth control devices for commercial purposes. Grace believed family planning was best left to each woman and her doctor, but when these measures were approved by Parliament in 1969 as part of the Trudeau government's Omnibus Bill, the distribution of birth control information and devices was finally decriminalized.

During her first year in Parliament Grace often pressed other issues of importance to women. She demanded a female deputy commissioner be included in the penitentiary system to handle problems at Kingston Prison for Women. She urged tax changes for working wives that would permit an increase in the amount they were allowed to make before wiping out the married exemption of their husbands. In May 1966, four years before the Royal Commission on the Status of Women made its official recommendation for a nationwide day care system, she used every opportunity to press for such a program of day care centres, and for full training of staff.

Back in her riding at the beginning of October, Grace found the city council debating a measure to ban topless dancers from Canada's first topless bar, the Cat's Whiskers, which had opened in Vancouver in August. "Moonlighting mothers should cause the city fathers more concern than a few bare-breasted beauties in night spots," Grace told a meeting of the Vancouver Council of Women. She turned the incident into another call for nursery schools, equal pay for equal work and stabilization in the cost of living, and urged women's organizations to battle for "a full and equal partnership with men."

Since 1963 Pearson's only woman Cabinet Minister, Secretary of State Judy LaMarsh, had urged the Prime Minister to set up a royal commission on the status of women. Pearson had balked until the chair of the Committee for the Equality of Women in Canada, Laura Sabia, threatened to lead two million women in a march up Parliament Hill. Demonstrating the truth of Grace's adage, "if there is no pressure, there will be no action," the Prime Minister capitulated.

When Grace arrived back in Ottawa in early January 1966, she found a letter on her desk from Grace Hartman, vice-president of the Canadian Union of Public Employees, requesting her input for a follow-up meeting of Sabia's committee. Grace replied, "Frankly, a lot of women, including NDP women, have not been too keen on this Committee, largely for the reason that they feel it is composed almost exclusively of business and professional women who have a middle class outlook on life . . . the things in the Committee's brief do not concern working class women in any real way . . . . If there is to be either a Royal Commission, or any other form of enquiry, it should deal with the status of women on all levels and in all capacities."

By February 1 Grace knew that an inquiry would be announced any day, and in a letter to Hartman, she predicted the appointment of award-winning bilingual broadcaster Anne Francis (the pseudonym of Florence Bird) as chair. Grace began at once to urge reluctant NDP women to get involved in the commission process. "You and other people with an NDP viewpoint will need to be vigilant about the personnel of the Commission and its terms of reference," she wrote Hartman. On February 3 Pearson indeed announced that Anne Francis would chair a Royal Commission on the Status of Women.

The current status of women in Canada was aptly illustrated by the *Globe and Mail* article announcing the commission. Anne Francis was the pen name used by Florence Bird, wife of John Bird, parliamentary columnist for the *Financial Post*. On February 4, *Globe* reporter Michael Gillan wrote, "The commission to be headed by Ottawa free-lance journalist Mr. John Bird, will study . . ." Not only was the new chair of the Royal Commission on the Status of Women referred to by her husband's name, she was denied even the designation Mrs. In official lists of commissioners, and in the final Report, the chair was referred to not by her own first name, but as Mrs. John Bird.

In addition to Florence Bird, the originally appointed members of the Royal Commission on the Status of Women were: Elsie Gregory MacGill, the first Canadian woman aeronautical engineer; Lola (Mrs. Ottomar) Lange, a rancher's wife and farm union woman; Jeanne Lapointe, professor of French literature at Laval University and member of Quebec's Parent Commission on education; Doris (Mrs. Robert) Ogilvie, a lawyer and Juvenile Court judge; Jacques Henripin, head of the Department of Demography at the University of Montreal; and Donald Gordon, Jr., a broadcaster and political science professor.

A few months after the commissioners were appointed Gordon resigned. Chairperson Bird said Grace was influential in having another man, rather than a woman, appointed in his place. "I was told that Grace MacInnis had gone to see [Prime Minister] Pearson and persuaded him that it was important to have more than one man on the commission and that, if the report were to be acceptable, he should appoint a well known, respected, experienced man right away." Bird rejected two cabinet suggestions, then "accepted with enthusiasm" John P. Humphrey, McGill professor of law and political science, from 1946 to 1966 director of the Division of Human Rights for the UN Secretariat.

Bird recalled that Grace was not alone in her concern that the commissioners did not represent a broad enough spectrum of Canadian society. "The Canadian Labour Congress was so indignant that the president announced that the Congress was going to boycott the commission and refuse to present a brief at the public hearings," Bird recalled. She invited CLC executives in for a private meeting and persuaded them not to lose this opportunity to speak publicly for organized labour. "As time went on," Bird said, "I realized that the academics on the commission were thinking more about the problems of educated, higher income women than about the majority of women in our society. I was so anxious to remind the commissioners of the needs of disadvantaged women that I got hold of the photographs of poor people, taken for a conference on poverty, and hung them on the walls of my new office . . . . I explained I had put the photos there to remind us that we were required to find ways of giving equal opportunities to women in all aspects of Canadian society."

Regardless of her private misgivings about the RCSW, in public Grace was always supportive. She impelled the NDP to write a brief for the Commission. First she mentioned the matter to Tommy Douglas, then at his request she put it in writing. "The brief should be undertaken by the Party as a whole rather than by the Women's Committee," she instructed Douglas. "The committee should be a broad one, involving men and women from political, trade union, home-making, farm, industrial, professional and communications sectors, held together by our socialist outlook . . . the overall planning must come from as broad a spectrum of human beings as the Party can find."

The first bill to legalize abortion in Canada was Bill C-122, authored by Grace MacInnis. On May 30, 1967, when the bill was called for first reading, Grace rose to explain that she proposed to legalize abortion only under certain circumstances. "This bill seeks to end a situation where a law which cannot be enforced is brought into disrepute, and where illegal and bungling methods endanger the lives and health of growing numbers of women," she declared. Her bill provided for a legal abortion to be granted at a woman's request on the advice of two registered medical practitioners, under any of three conditions: "that the continuance of the pregnancy would involve serious risk to the life or grave injury to the health, either physical or mental, of the pregnant woman; that there is a substantial risk of a defective child being born; or, that the pregnancy is a result of rape or incest."

Grace's abortion law reform bill was not entirely unheralded. In 1963 NDP MP Barry Mather had asked if the government was considering a royal commission on the laws affecting abortion. The government's answer was no. In February 1966 Mather again raised the question of a royal commission. This time Prime Minister Pearson replied that the government was considering it. On February 27, 1967, in response to a question from Stanley Knowles, the Prime Minister acknowledged that his government intended to introduce legislation regarding birth control and abortion "this year." Six weeks later Tommy Douglas again asked for clarification of the Criminal Code. Pearson brushed him off, saying he had already told the House the government was considering such legislation.

Two other abortion reform bills were also introduced on May 30, 1967, but Grace's was first to reach the floor of the House. One, sponsored by Liberal Ian Wahn, attempted only to clarify the existing law. The other, by Grace's nemesis Bert Herridge, was based on the British law passed in April, and included a "social clause" that considered the mother's standard of living as a possible ground for abortion. Justice Minister Pierre Trudeau indicated that any action to make abortion legal would be part of a package, and all three bills were sent to the Health and Welfare Committee for study.

With the introduction of her bill, Grace began to include the abortion issue in speeches, but listeners were divided on the reform proposal. At the BC NDP convention in early June, the delegates passed a resolution supporting legalization of birth control, voluntary sterilization, and sex education in schools, but made no mention of abortion. In a rare approving editorial the *Vancouver Sun* backed Grace's views on abortion, birth control and divorce law reform.

Her research into population issues led Grace to what she saw as inescapable conclusions. The poor always have more children, she noted, while the well-to-do and educated have fewer and fewer. By controlling disease, she wrote, we have thrown out natural selection; humankind has now taken over the direction of its own evolution. She read widely: Malthus's 1798 essay, Darwin, socialist birth control pioneer Margaret Sanger, Rachel Carson's more recent books, Marston Bates, Paul Ehrlich, the Vatican's Papal Study Commission, and Catholic dissenters. She studied Japan's Law of Eugenic Protection (1948) which established nationwide contraception and abortion clinics, and she kept close watch on the progress of abortion law reform in other countries.

The world population was doubling every thirty-five years; she estimated that it would hit six billion by the year 2000. Could enough land be saved for food? Would the non-renewable resources of the world support so many? Could six billion people live together without war? Would the price of such numbers be totalitarian organization? "The question has always been, who dies?" Grace observed. "The new question must be, who is born?" She was well aware of the moral and political implications of this question. Eugenics posits the selective breeding of a quality population—the definition of "quality" is the crux of all the questions this concept raises. Between the world wars, before Hitler used the theory to justify mass murder, eugenics gained some popularity amongst more ingenuous socialists.

Grace was convinced that birth control and abortion were in the public interest. To her a "quality" population was one in which every child was a wanted child—healthy, nourished and loved—who would develop into a contributing, productive individual. If a family's situation precluded that outcome of a pregnancy, Grace favoured whatever could be done to ease their burden—abortion, birth control or child care—the ABCs of Grace MacInnis. "I thought to myself, this is a logical thing," she explained. "There are so many people. If for the past number of years we hadn't made information about birth control illegal, there would be no reason in the world why there should be all these people wanting abortions now. Once I got that through my head I didn't care whether it was popular or not popular, I just went ahead with it."

On October 3, 1967, discussion of Grace's abortion law reform bill C-122 opened the Health and Welfare Committee hearings on abortion. The hearings and the splashy publicity surrounding them placed the divisive issue in the public arena for the first round of a debate that, twenty-five years later, is still going on. Grace, Wahn and Herridge all presented their bills on opening day, but only Grace would remain involved with the abortion legislation. The other two MPs returned to other concerns; Grace attended every committee hearing and questioned many witnesses.

Her own presentation started off smoothly. She outlined the bill's main features, then argued, "Our choice today is not between having abortion in Canada and not having abortion in Canada. Our choice is whether we will have abortions performed legally under proper conditions or whether we will continue the practice of back-street bungling and butchery . . . to which we have been closing our eyes." She quoted some fearful statistics on criminal abortions and resulting injury and illness. "I believe Canada is ready for a change in our abortions laws," she asserted, quoting a 1965 Gallup poll in which seventy-one percent of Canadians said just that.

Any public discussion of abortion at all was truly shocking to many Canadians in late 1967, particularly in mixed company. But Grace was by then inured to the risks of discussing "forbidden" topics in public; she had been doing it for years. Still she was quite unprepared for the committee's reaction to what she presented as "the positive side" of her bill. "I think it is time that we began to work toward quality population in this country," she declared. "To have children born into a country as the result of rape or incest is not going to be too helpful when one considers the environment that they are likely to encounter. Also, I want to say that if conditions like those of thalidomide babies or congenital diseases are known ahead of time, I do not think it is a good thing for Canada to allow those beings to come into the world . . . . I think it is time we gave parents a chance. I think that women ought to have far more control over what happens to them when monstrosities are to be born. I have known women who have had to put up with lifetimes of that sort of thing, and it would have been far far better, both for them and for those poor little deformed creatures, to have never been brought into the world."

The outcry began immediately at the idea of a quality population. Liberal MP Robert Stanbury said he was offended by population selection, which to him smacked of the Nazi idea of creating a master race. Conservative Lewis Brand of Saskatoon objected to "the thought of setting up a super race in Canada." Grace began to explain. "Some people honestly believe that every child that is conceived ought to be brought to life no matter what the result may be. Other people do not; they feel it is a tragedy and, even more than that, if it can be prevented it is a crime for people, or for themselves, to bring something into the world that will have no chance at life or living as we understand it . . . . Because we are a democratic country I think it is very important that we provide a freedom of choice."

Stanbury said, "There seems to be a step in the direction of a sort of big brother approach to people's problems." Grace countered, "It is just the reverse." Stanbury then raised the problem of restricting abortion to cases of rape or incest: the need for doctors to determine when rape or incest had taken place. "It implies coming to conclusions which would, in effect, convict third parties without a trial, unless you are going to wait for a trial, in which case it might be too late for a therapeutic abortion," argued Stanbury. Flustered, Grace admitted she was not too sure of exactly how it would work either.

A more hostile opponent, York–Humber Liberal Ralph Cowan, a director of Toronto's Northwestern General Hospital, asked if Grace had seen the portrait of Queen Victoria in the Senate lobby, showing one arm shorter than the other. "Do you think she should have been born?" he probed. Startled, Grace said, "What was all right in 1861 is not all right in 1967." Angrily Cowan demanded to know how anyone could tell before birth if a child is defective. Grace handed that off to chairman Harry Harley, MD, who pointed to German measles and the tranquilizer thalidomide as probable causes of birth defects. Cowan contended, "Why not let the child be born and then if it is defective, kill it? Why would you not favour that?"

Recognizing the ferocity of the opposition arrayed against her, Grace invoked Eleanor Roosevelt's "edges of agreement" strategy. She insisted accommodation was possible. After all, she reminded the MPs, the committee had begun its deliberations on birth control speaking "very many different languages," but after much discussion and many witnesses "found out that there was ground on which we did agree, and we were able to come to an almost unanimous report."

Over time, Grace would work toward agreement, but she would never give up on her ultimate goal. Even at this point, although this first of her abortion bills did not reflect it, she believed that the entire matter should be removed from the Criminal Code. The three restrictions in her first bill were there because she judged that the Canadian public was not ready to go further. Now she put the government on notice that regardless of the fate of C-122, she would not give up. "I have learned all my life," she told the Health and Welfare Committee, "if I want a loaf of bread to take half a loaf if I cannot get a whole loaf, and if I cannot get that, to take a few crumbs, knowing that each attempt will strengthen me to get a little more of the bread later on."

It was a vivid example of the Fabian streak in her socialist upbringing, but this gradualist attitude was partly responsible for the way Grace was misunderstood by the new generation of radical and socialist feminists emerging in the late 1960s. As Grace addressed citizens' groups and gave interviews during fall 1967, she never made a secret of her desire to decriminalize abortion entirely. "My bill is pitched to what the Canadian people are ready for," she often said. "We've got to get into the twentieth century about this, but we've also got to move slowly and then build on it later."

In the months that followed that first hearing the committee took evidence from the Canadian Bar Association, Canadian Medical Association, the Women's Liberation Group, Catholics and other right-to-life people. It all came down to one basic question, "When is a human life a human life?" The sessions were stormy, and Grace's convictions were the lightning flashes that sparked emotional conflagrations. "I remember the Member from Halifax then," she said, "Mike Forestall, a good, solid Catholic, coming up to me after one of the committee sessions on abortion and just shaking his fist under my nose, he was so angry. If I had been a man he would have knocked me down."

Grace first met Dr. Henry Morgentaler that October when he presented evidence to the committee. As a medical doctor and past president of the Humanist Fellowship of Montreal, Morgentaler viewed the foetus not as "an individual being" but as a "potential human being." He expressed his desire to keep the government out of it and "leave it to the judgment of the woman." Liberal MP Joseph O'Keefe, a Newfoundland supermarket owner, became infuriated. "Who gave you the right to try to influence people to allow the killing of unborn babies?" he yelled. The chair demanded order. Morgentaler cited the opinions of other scientists that "children who are brought into the world and who remain in institutions . . . who do not have a mother figure or a home in which they are taken care of usually grow up suffering from tremendous psychological damage. Many criminals and antisocial characters, people who eventually become neurotic or psychotic, became so because of tremendous psychological deprivations in the first three years of life." Grace had made the same point in speeches back as far as the 1930s, as had her parents before her.

Grace's argument for abortion rights was two-pronged. On the one hand she believed with Dr. Morgentaler that the environment in which children are raised determines their future success in life. At the same time she believed in developing a "quality population" by making birth control information and contraceptives freely available to people of all income levels, so that family limitation would not take place solely in middle and upper class homes. But she did not expect birth control alone to bring about a "quality population." She knew low-income women who could not afford good food would produce low birth weight babies, with possible physical birth defects or mental retardation. To prevent these tragedies, Grace focussed her work on ensuring a basic adequate diet for every Canadian, through public education backed up by a guaranteed annual income and a network of social services. Because she endorsed the old adage "An ounce of prevention is worth a pound of cure," Grace placed birth control before abortion and placed adequate nutrition, housing and education before crime and punishment.

Just before Christmas the Health and Welfare Committee tabled its interim report recommending the Criminal Code be amended to allow abortion, "where a pregnancy will seriously endanger the life or the health of the mother." In all, ninety-three witnesses from legal, medical, church and citizen pressure groups gave evidence; and thirty-five briefs as well as numerous letters, petitions, telegrams and letters were received. Before the committee's final report was tabled March 13, 1968, Justice Minister Pierre Trudeau introduced a wide-ranging bill to reform many sections of the Criminal Code, among them the section on abortion. His wording was slightly more vague than that of the committee. Chairman Harry Harley urged his committee's more direct wording, and recommended continued study of abortion. There the matter rested, for the time being.

Involved as she was in national affairs, Grace still found time to keep abreast of BC politics and to offer advice where she thought it was needed. Generally she believed in leaving the province to handle its own affairs, but she felt obliged to intervene in late 1966, when news reports revealed that young labour lawyer and former NDP MP Thomas Berger was being considered as a replacement for BC leader Bob Strachan.

After ten years with Strachan at the helm, the NDP was still far from governing the province. In a September election, they had won sixteen seats, but W.A.C. Bennett's Socreds remained in power. The question of a change in leadership naturally arose. In October, after reading a *Globe and Mail* article presenting Berger as the best bet to succeed be Strachan, Grace immediately phoned the provincial NDP office to express concern that the news media was playing a role in the selection of a party leader. Berger undoubtedly heard from BC president, Norm Levi, for he wrote Grace at once, explaining that he had given only a profile interview to the *Globe* reporter, and had stressed that the leadership decision would be made at the annual convention.

By return mail Grace admonished Berger and advised him to refrain from discussing the leadership issue with the media. "The sole result is to weaken the party in the eyes of the public and to tear it to pieces organizationally . . . . In my view," she wrote, "leaders must prove their capacity to lead, or continue leading. I have no faith in the method of drafting leaders before they have had an opportunity to prove themselves." At the June 1967 BC party convention, Berger challenged Strachan for the leadership and was defeated. Not until the 1969 convention would Berger become the BC NDP leader, winning over Dave Barrett by a mere thirty-six votes.

Commenting much later, Berger said he viewed Grace's intervention as evidence of her conservative attitude in party matters. "She represented the continuity, the origins of the movement, its greatest figures. She was one of them herself. Who could blame her for wanting to lay down the law to us? A whippersnapper like me."

On cost of living questions Grace devoted most of her first year in the Commons to supporting the goals of the NDP caucus. She warned against inflation and the rising cost of living, and advocated a sharply increased universal old age pension at age sixty-five without a means test or a ceiling on additional income. To recover superfluous pensions from wealthy older people, she advised taxing them back rather then destroying the principle of universality. And she lost no opportunity to remind the House that it was J.S. Woodsworth who had manoeuvred a minority Liberal government into enacting the first Old Age Pension legislation in 1927.

In an effort to give consumers more clout, Grace introduced a private member's bill in 1966 to replace the Registrar General with a Department of Consumer Affairs that would operate under a Consumer's Bill of Rights with four provisions: the right to safety and quality; the right to truthful information; the right to a dollar of stable purchasing power; and the right to be heard. Consumers' rights were a hot issue in 1966. As the cost of living continued to spiral upward, a new consumers' movement was born of frustration and privation. In tune with these times of citizen activism, consumers were willing to demonstrate and boycott. To further public debate, Grace had her Consumer's Bill of Rights speech printed up as a pamphlet for mailing. The *Vancouver Province* condemned the Bill of Rights in a scathing editorial that called Grace "an old-time socialist, a sworn enemy of capitalism convinced that Business is out to grind the faces of the poor, hoodwink the consumer and wreck the nation." Grace probably took that comment as a compliment.

NDP leader Tommy Douglas was the first to call for a prices review board to control soaring inflation, and Grace supported this idea in many speeches that first term. She demanded a board that would regulate profits as well as wages and prices. Her words were given added strength by a nationwide boycott of supermarkets started in early October by housewives refusing to pay skyrocketing prices for basic foods.

In answer to a growing number of consumer protests and boycotts, Prime Minister Pearson appointed a Joint Senate–Commons Committee on Consumer Credit in March 1966 to take a serious look at the reasons for rising costs. In debate Grace often reminded the House that many Canadians were unable to afford basic foods listed in the Canada Food Rules like meat, milk, fresh fruits and vegetables. In the face of bland smiles and brushoffs from government members, Grace grew still more persistent. In early November she was named to the Joint Committee on Consumer Credit, replacing another NDP member. She had worked and waited all her life to be in a position to challenge the men she believed were at the root of Canada's economic and social ills, and she lost no time in sharpening her questions.

Grace confronted the president of the Kellogg Company of Canada, which advertised its cereals through television characters and toy giveaways, asking if "in merchandising practices children are used as a club over the parent's head by firms to buy things they cannot afford in the family budget." She asked the president of Green Giant of Canada if it were not true that the consumer had to pay the cost of the company's advertising and of gimmicks. "Would it not be cheaper for the consumer if you cut out all of that, and sell her your goods without the express trains, the dolls and all the other stuff?" she demanded. Grace maintained that the increased costs of advertising promotions which lowered the prices of goods by a few cents were passed directly to the consumer; instead she argued for a constant pricing policy without fluctuations. The executives did not concede that their advertising practices drove up costs, but they squirmed under Grace's tough questioning, and she made many of her points in the eyes of the other legislators on the committee.

At one November committee hearing, Grace suggested to the astonished president of Colgate–Palmolive that he should be required to go before a government prices review board to justify the firm's pricing. "Before any trade union can get an increase in wages today it has to go through an elaborate process of collective bargaining and a great deal of red tape to justify it. On the other hand, in the matter of prices there is no such machinery whatever." In December she interrogated the president of the Institute of Canadian Advertising. "Twenty percent of the people in Canada get four and a half per cent of the income. Yet these people have to spend over forty percent of their budget on food . . . . Does advertising, by helping these big firms to get into the position of monopoly or near monopoly, ultimately reduce competition at the expense of the consumers who suffer?" This question came just two days after the *Financial Post* revealed the hitherto unknown extent of the far-flung Weston empire.

The fact of the matter was that Grace disliked excessive advertising, especially on television. She told the CBC television show *Marketplace*: "My number one beef is consumer advertising. Consumers are never let alone to buy what they want. They go in to buy soap flakes or a detergent. They are confronted with something New! New! or Blue! Blue! a package that mixes some blue crystals in with the white for no apparent reason except that of novelty. Informative advertising is one thing. Pressure advertising where the consumer is enticed, cajoled, frightened and browbeaten into buying something she neither needs nor genuinely wants, is quite another."

In its interim report to the House at Christmas the Joint Committee on Consumer Credit recommended that a Department of Consumer Affairs should be established with a full-time minister to look after the needs of consumers—Grace was in enthusiastic accord—but the report did not support Grace's call for a price review board with teeth.

A new spirit of co-operation surfaced in North American during the late 1960s and early 1970s, and many co-op grocery stores were established.

Grace pressed for national legislation on co-operatives that would afford them the same types of financial advantages available to other businesses. While housewives and farmers demonstrated on Parliament Hill and boycotted supermarkets, Grace worked closely with her brother-in-law Ralph Staples to promote co-operatives as a practical way of reducing food costs. As president of the Co-operative Union of Canada, Ralph had started a co-op store, the Supplies Depot of Ottawa Ltd., as a study project in 1962. It offered basic items at about two-thirds of the typical retail price. By 1967 the study project was an expanding enterprise with more than four hundred families as members. From her high-profile position, Grace publicized the advantages of co-operative buying throughout spring 1967 with trade unionists, housewives and other groups. At the same time she was living in an apartment adjoining Belva and Ralph's and took a protective, nourishing role in her sister's life, spending time with Belva and drawing her out of her depression.

That spring, when the Joint Committee on Consumer Credit was writing its final report, Grace presented her own recommendations. First and foremost, she wrote, "the Department of Consumer Affairs should have a full-time minister and be consumer oriented, not linked with corporate affairs or any other sectional interest." She also called for a prices review board, unit pricing, generic sections in grocery stores, and federal legislation as a framework for co-operatives.

The throne speech on May 8, 1967, opening the next session of Parliament, ended her hopes. The government paid lip service to the need to take consumer interests "fully into account," but then proposed "a department of corporate and consumer affairs." Within this department would be a branch "to assist the consumer and protect the small investor." To Grace this sounded ominous—a ministry with a full-time minister, but serving the needs of corporations first, consumers and small investors second. Three days later she introduced her own Consumer Protection Bill, C-48. If it were passed, a Department of Consumer Affairs would deal with corporate affairs too, but corporate affairs were listed as the fifth area of jurisdiction, after patents and trademarks.

Grace did not expect to have her private member's bill approved, but introducing it gave her an opportunity to take the government to task for its plan. "The government has given notice . . . that it is going to thumb its nose at our major recommendation, that it is going to thumb its nose at the committee," Grace said hotly. Both of the committee's reports, she said, had made it perfectly clear that what Canada needed was a department "the sole purpose of which is to protect consumers," Grace told the House. "This point was made by every organization which spoke on the subject as we travelled across Canada. Not one single organization asked for a department of corporate and consumer affairs."

When the supply estimates for the department came up for debate in

June, Grace attacked the policies of the new minister, John Turner. "To mix the consumers and the corporations in one department is simply the same as trying to have the lion and the lamb live peacefully together," she told the House. Turner responded only to say the government was studying a law for co-operatives and, as he had told the House earlier, in his view prices did not come within the jurisdiction of his government.

Grace pestered the Pearson government all year on this issue, and she succeeded in one respect. On December 21, 1967, the ministry was renamed Department of Consumer and Corporate Affairs, but it was a change in name only. Grace's battle to obtain a better deal for low-income consumers was far from won.

Objections to the US war in Vietnam escalated during 1966 with a demonstration on Parliament Hill in March, an international day of protest, an encyclical from Pope Paul VI, demonstrations at American universities and an unsuccessful challenge to the legality of US military intervention by US Senate Foreign Relations Committee chair J.W. Fulbright. During the summer recess that year, Grace attended a Canadian–American anti-Vietnam war rally at the Peace Arch on the border at Blaine, Washington. The August 6 Hiroshima Day rally was sponsored by peace organizations and churches from both countries. Grace made a powerful plea for sanity in international relations. She called for greater United Nations involvement in peace efforts, and warned that peace would never be achieved if countries meet with an olive branch in one hand and a bomb in the other. She had supported Canada's involvement in World War Two and in the formation of NATO as necessities of their eras, but Grace now placed more emphasis on developing the United Nations as the world's peacekeeper. In spite of all protests, by the end of 1966 there were 400,000 US troops in Vietnam. US dead numbered 6,358; enemy dead, 77,115.

When Expo '67 opened in Montreal at the end of April to celebrate Canada's centennial year, Grace soon took time to visit the exposition. She found pleasure and hope for rapprochement between Canada's anglophones and francophones in what she saw as a successful blend of English practicality and a distinctly French flair for art and drama in the fair's colourful displays.

In mid-May Grace addressed the Quebec NDP convention at the new Bonaventure Hotel in Montreal. She delivered the same hard-hitting speech she had given in other parts of Canada for nearly two years, calling for a Canada-wide network of government-funded child care centres to allow women both a career and a family. Grace did not soften her approach in Quebec, although it seemed radical in a province where the law still gave the husband of a married woman control of her property, including her earnings, and women rarely ran for public office.

In his keynote address to these five hundred NDP delegates, Tommy Douglas declared himself in favour of special constitutional status for Quebec. "Unless Quebec is accorded special status Confederation will keep Canada in constant turmoil," he said prophetically.

That weekend Grace attended a testimonial dinner for her friend Thérèse Casgrain, in honour of her more than forty-five years of service in advancing the rights of women in Quebec. Through Casgrain, among others, Grace kept abreast of the strong currents of nationalist feeling sweeping Quebec. Since 1958 when Pierre Trudeau's landmark articles in *Vrai* challenged the prevailing dogma that political authority comes from God, and declared that political authority derives from the consent of the governed, the Catholic–Duplessis church–state power arrangement was on the defensive. By 1966 when the Union Nationale party under Daniel Johnson took power, the "quiet revolution" was displaced by stronger separatist feelings.

This spirit was encouraged by a centennial visit from Charles de Gaulle, who displayed the Canada–Quebec split for the entire world to see. Premier Johnson had persuaded de Gaulle to start his Canadian centennial visit not in the federal capital of Ottawa, but in Quebec. In Montreal on July 24, 1967, the French leader proclaimed, "Vive le Québec libre!" to the delight of half a million cheering Québecois nationalists.

Since 1945 Grace had been warning of trouble if Quebec's legitimate aspirations for respect and recognition by Canada were not met. Now Canada could no longer ignore these aspirations.

Queen Elizabeth was the star of Canada's centennial birthday show in Ottawa on July 1. While most Canadians were enjoying parades and hundred-gun salutes, Grace was more concerned with the fortunes of her party. Delegates to the NDP federal convention were gathering in Toronto, bringing with them the seeds of dissent that would divide the national party as the BC CCF had split in the 1950s.

Tommy Douglas's opening speech to the convention called for a stronger Canadian economy with less American control, and an international declaration calling on the US to end the bombing of North Vietnam. He stopped short of supporting special status for Quebec, but the convention did approve a resolution on special status, swayed by a strong appeal from broadcaster and historian Laurier LaPierre. An early sign of discontent was a set of resolutions adopted by New Democratic Youth calling for massive nationalization of industry, withdrawal of Canada from NATO and NORAD agreements, and support for the communist side in Vietnam. In a challenge to the NDP establishment, NDY members claimed the party was becoming irrelevant, and would never attract young people unless the NDY seized leadership of the larger radical youth community.

In this internal dispute between the radical left wing and the old guard,

Grace sided as always with the party establishment. Her own resolution on the creation of a Department of Consumer Affairs—worded precisely as were her speeches in the House—passed easily. The department would support co-ops, a tax on advertising, TV shows to educate consumers, production of low-cost generic drugs, and low-cost credit for debt consolidation. The delegates also voted for a national automobile insurance plan; a cabinet-level Department of Science and Technology to stem the brain-drain to the United States; a comprehensive air, water and soil pollution control program; an end to the production and testing of chemical and biological weapons by the Canadian Defence Research Board; abolition of the Canadian seal hunt; the treatment of drug addiction as an illness rather than as a crime; and the abolition of capital and corporal punishment. In later sessions of Parliament Grace spoke in support of most of these goals.

While the convention was wrapping up in Toronto Grace was in Ottawa advocating in a major speech to the House the "guaranteed minimum annual income plan" she had urged since the early 1940s. "The idea that those who are on welfare are the only ones who feed from the public trough is surely a little bit of an understatement," she declared. "The only problem is that people like ourselves and other public servants are so close to the trough, in the front row, that the welfare cases are elbowed so far away they cannot get enough feed from the public trough."

In the idyllic summer of 1967, Vancouver's 4th Avenue was a mirror image of San Francisco's Haight–Ashbury. Young Canadians, dreaming of freedom on the open road, hitchhiked west to the coast. They frequented the beaches and parks, attended concerts with psychedelic light shows, and danced all night to the Jefferson Airplane up from California or local bands Fireweed and Mock Duck. Young at heart herself, despite her sixty-two years, Grace did not fear the youthful revolution. Her attitude toward marijuana, for instance, was pragmatic and tolerant. "These things will always be with us until we make reality good enough that people don't want to escape from it," she told one curious reporter. "I can understand young people feeling it's unfair to penalize them for smoking pot, when liquor, which is probably more damaging, is legal." She saw hippies in a positive light. "I feel hippies are the advance guard of a new society. But flower power and love-ins are only recognition that change is needed," she told another reporter.

Before she returned to Ottawa for the fall session of parliament, Grace was chosen by acclamation to fight the next election in Vancouver–Kingsway. Modestly she told her nominating meeting it was not her legislative skill but her persistence that was most effective. "I'm not under any illusions that I'm a brilliant fighter, but I am good at bugging people," she said with a grin.

Just before the Christmas 1967 recess, Prime Minister Pearson announced his retirement from the Liberal leadership, setting the stage for a leadership race just as the international situation was heating up. At the end of January 1968 the North Vietnamese and Vietcong staged the Tet offensive against thirty South Vietnam cities including Saigon. The heavy attack caught the Americans and South Vietnamese off guard and touched off another round of anti-war protests in the US and Canada. Grace and the NDP were outraged by what they saw as morally and legally unjustifiable American intervention in another nation's civil war. On March 3 the NDP federal council passed a resolution urging that Canada "terminate the Defence Production sharing agreements which have been used for channelling military aid to one side in the conflict." The council called for an embargo on the export of military supplies that might be used in Vietnam, and urged that medical supplies and other Canadian aid be sent to all Vietnamese people, North and South alike.

Grace brought up the issue of medical and relief assistance for Vietnam in the House, directing her question the next day to Prime Minister Pearson. In response Pearson sent her a news release from the External Aid Office dated March 1, announcing $200,000 in aid, in addition to the $3,000,000 already allocated for 1967–68. In Grace's view it was not satisfactory; all the milk, rice, clothing, medicine and medical personnel were going to South Vietnam.

Her fervent crusade against the war did not abate over time; it grew. She celebrated Easter Sunday 1969 by delivering a passionate speech from the steps of the Vancouver courthouse to fifteen hundred cheering demonstrators. Canadians who want US troops out of Vietnam should first pressure Ottawa to sever Canada's military and defence industry ties with the US, Grace proclaimed. "Let's get our own hands clean before we go after bloodier hands. In Canada our hands are bloody because our complicity in this war is tremendous. It is a monstrous crime," she insisted, "a crime that has the double evil of wiping out the people in Vietnam and sparking the next world war which will be the last world war." She was once again in accord with her pacifist upbringing, at peace within herself now that she no longer had to defend war.

As spring 1968 thawed Ottawa streets and flower beds brightened on the Hill, Grace hammered away at her basic concerns, the related issues of women's rights and consumer protection. A bill was before the House that would widen the grounds for divorce—at the time virtually only adultery— to include sodomy, bestiality, rape, homosexuality, bigamy, physical and mental cruelty, and permanent breakdown of marriages. Grace urged Justice Minister Trudeau to replace this long list with just one ground for divorce, marriage breakdown. She believed, as had Angus, that it was immoral to force a couple to remain together when mutual love and respect were gone.

In November 1967 and again in January 1968 Grace proposed in the House that the government pay salaries to women who work full-time at home. She made the case for maternity leave for women in the federal civil service, and rose in the House eight times in March alone to assail the faltering minority Liberal government about the rising cost of food. The report of Judge Mary Batten on the cost of living in the prairie provinces was tabled. It called for a federal inquiry into grocery retailing, particularly the dominance of Canada Safeway and the Weston group. Grace demanded that his inquiry be held immediately.

Grace had met with very little overt sexism in the House of Commons during her first two years, but now she ran into a setback. The International Parliamentary Union was holding a seminar in Dakar, Senegal, in mid-April 1968. "It was a French speaking place, and David Lewis and I were the only two who could manoeuvre in French. David was too busy, so I was on the delegation," Grace recalled. "The leader of the delegation, a Liberal, met me in the hall and he said, 'I'm very sorry you won't be able to go with us on this trip.' It was some story about someone being left over from the last time and having to go.

"Well, I was very mad inside myself because I knew exactly why. They didn't want to be burdened with a tag-along, and they'd never had a woman on their delegation before. So I didn't bother with him at all. I just went to Stanley Knowles and David Lewis and Tommy Douglas and let them go to the Speaker. And I went, and it was a very pleasant time we all had."

At the conference sessions in Senegal Grace discovered people from developing countries were not especially interested in food assistance, but cared more about obtaining education, scientific know-how and help to build their own industries. Grace's own area of concern at the seminar were the conservation of natural resources and the pollution of fresh water. Her experiences at the Dakar seminar set the stage for Grace's future work on the condition of Canada's water.

On April 20, while Grace was in Senegal, Pierre Elliott Trudeau became Prime Minister. Three days later he dissolved the House and called an election for June 25. The curtain was rising on a new era in Canadian politics.

CHAPTER 14

One Woman, 263 Men

On June 25, 1968, Grace woke with the sunrise in her Vancouver apartment. She completed the twenty-minute daily exercise routine that kept her arthritis at bay and breakfasted on her customary half grapefruit and two cups of coffee. She lingered a few moments longer than usual over the second cup, reading the paper and luxuriating in the first less-than-frantic day in months. She allowed her thoughts to dwell on Angus, appreciating all the election battles he had won.

It was election day once again. By midnight Grace would be the only woman in Canada to win a seat in the House of Commons, although thirty-seven women were running.

Trudeau swirled across the country like a tornado, gathering 155 seats into Liberal hands and forming a Liberal majority government for the first time since St. Laurent. The Tories took 72 seats under their new leader Robert Stanfield, former premier of Nova Scotia. The NDP was third with 22, but leader Tommy Douglas narrowly lost his seat to Liberal Ray Perrault in the new riding of Burnaby–Seymour. Créditistes took 14 seats; one went independent.

During her fifteen hours a day on the hustings, Grace emphasized bread-and-butter issues, positioning herself on the side of ordinary people, in contrast to Trudeau, who had declared during the Liberal leadership convention in April, "In the field of social welfare programs it is my belief that we have enough of this free stuff . . . . We have to put a damper on this revolution of rising expectations . . . . We must not be afraid of this bogeyman, the means test."

Grace's opponents this time were Liberal motel operator Ed Bodnarchuk, Conservative sheet metal salesman Claude Britton and Social Crediter Lorena Green. Her campaign slogan was "The MP who works WITH you." Dodging sprinklers and dogs, Grace climbed endless flights of steps. She talked with people about lower living costs, a prices review board, budget-priced housing and the NDP pledge to build 250,000 housing units a year until all needs were met. She talked about day care and free university education to all who qualified academically, and how these measures would multiply job opportunities. She spoke of fair taxation, decent pensions and allowances, getting Canada out of NATO, and making peace not war.

As a bilingual candidate Grace toured the Montreal ridings, too, speaking on consumers' issues and salaries for mothers who worked full-time in the home. On behalf of Charles Taylor and Robert Cliché she campaigned in hopes that the NDP would win its first Quebec seat. It didn't.

Cliff Scotton, NDP federal secretary, was national campaign director in the 1968 election. He noted that while some people saw Grace as "pushy," this alleged aspect of her personality never bothered him. "She was held in quite great esteem, first because of her intellectual and judgmental capacities, and being the daughter of J.S. Woodsworth didn't hurt at all. The interesting thing is for people who knew the family even a little bit, that Grace was the oldest son that should have been."

When the votes were counted, Grace proved she had the kind of staying power as an MP that would have gratified her father. Her victory as the only woman MP was covered in most of Canada's major daily newspapers, with comparisons to Agnes Macphail. At a time when women's liberation and a new wave of feminism seemed to be surging in Canada, why had Canadians elected but one female to Parliament? And why was Grace Woodsworth MacInnis that woman? Her election was partly due to her high-profile first term, despite her radical stand on abortion. While seventy-one percent of Canadians favoured abortion reform, Grace's stand for repeal was not endorsed by nearly so many. But her re-election in 1968 proved to Grace forever that the voters would not necessarily reject or accept a candidate on this issue alone.

Some put Grace's electoral success down to her family pedigree. Judy LaMarsh was one of them: her 1968 book *Memoirs of a Bird in a Gilded Cage* added to the confusion with the erroneous statement that "Mrs. Grace MacInnis, the daughter of J.S. Woodsworth, began her career running for and winning, her husband's seat in British Columbia's provincial legislature." Of course Angus never sat in the BC Legislature. While acknowledging her debt to her father and to Angus, Grace knew she had earned every step of her advance herself. In addition she recognized how childlessness had favoured her political career. She knew that without affordable, convenient day care, many women with young children could not enter politics.

Grace would tell women who sought advice about a political career: "The initial stages are to get busy locally. You don't think of election to begin with. The first thing a person has to think about is fixing one or two of the worst abuses in the community. You gain experience and expertise. You gain knowledge about how to work with people, that's the vital thing. Then, when you've had a few years of this you can cheerfully run for one of the city bodies, maybe not for alderman right away; parks board is a fairly soft touch. This is the period of apprenticeship. I don't think anybody can skip that. After you've been at this for a few years then comes along a possibility of Victoria [the BC provincial legislature].

"You could do politics at home with children if you've got a co-operative husband and a chance of paying a babysitter or nursery school. Then, when the children are independent, Ottawa is possible. But Ottawa is not possible, in my view, for young women with children who don't live near Ottawa."

Grace was a role model for many women interested in public life. One of those she inspired during this election campaign was Margaret Mitchell, a pioneer community development worker in the neighbourhood of the Little Mountain Housing Project. "We met with tenants from public housing," said Mitchell, "and called a big meeting with representatives from all the different systems, the welfare department, the housing officials, and confronted them about the problems that were facing low income mothers. On the one hand they were being told they couldn't look for work unless they had day care, and day care wasn't available unless they had work. Anyway, there were many complications, but Grace inspired me at that time and certainly inspired those mothers. The program went on and was called MOMS, the name she suggested, More Opportunities for Mothers."

Grace led by example, Mitchell said. "She was always so practical. In working with bureaucracy she would be very courteous, but very firm as well. She had the respect of everyone, but she was tough, there was no question about that. The community people knew that she was their friend and would work with and for them." Inspired by Grace, Mitchell went on to become a committed and respected NDP Member of Parliament.

The last of the summer flowers and vegetables brightened Byward Market as Ottawa filled once more with politicians, bureaucrats and office workers fresh from restful weeks at their lakefront cottages. A new feeling pervaded the House of Commons when Grace took her seat September 12 for the opening of the first session of parliament under Prime Minister Pierre Trudeau.

Hope and optimism ran high. During the election campaign Trudeau had acquired a reputation as a charismatic, swinging millionaire bachelor with a sense of humour. He gave parties for young people; rock music pulsed from his campaign convertible; crowds followed him like groupies. The media dubbed the phenomenon "Trudeaumania." Convinced that Quebec's rightful place was within Canadian federation—that it would be weaker, not stronger, as a separate nation-state—the new Prime Minister was determined not to allow anger and ignorance to divide the country. Instead he aimed to create a truly bilingual Canada, so that French Canadians would have greater opportunities and would no longer feel like strangers in their own country.

His throne speech promised the inauguration of a "just society and a prosperous economy in a peaceful world." He vowed to do a great deal: streamline parliamentary procedures, deal with continuing poverty, protect consumers, strengthen bilingualism, improve domestic investment and resource development, handle the increasing problem of pollution, modernize the Criminal Code, encourage scientific technology, and establish a satellite communications corporation.

Grace had grave doubts about this man who promised so much. She viewed him not as the great shining hope, but as a former CCF supporter who had turned Liberal for political advantage. She saw a politician who was "very able, very arrogant, very rational . . . . Mackenzie King with a flair."

With NDP leader Tommy Douglas temporarily out of Parliament, Stanley Knowles, the longest-serving NDP member, took over as caucus leader. Colin Cameron, longtime BC Socialist Fellowshipper, had been re-elected for a sixth term in Nanaimo–Cowichan–The Islands but died before taking his seat. Douglas returned to the Commons after winning this safe NDP seat. Meanwhile, in caucus, Knowles was in charge. He and Grace had a firm bond of comradeship and trust, and Knowles admired her very much. "She was inspiring to people," he reflected later. "When she made public speeches she was very impressive. She really worked hard for pensions, put pressure on the government. Her effectiveness was very significant."

Grace was assigned again to the Health and Welfare Committee, now renamed the Standing Committee on Health, Welfare and Social Affairs. Within caucus she worked on committees dealing with resources and agriculture, urban and social affairs, and consumer and corporate affairs.

Two future NDP leaders were in this caucus. David Lewis, in his third term, was now a seasoned parliamentarian. Newly elected York University political science professor Ed Broadbent was just getting his feet wet. He recalled one caucus discussion during which he disagreed with Stanley Knowles: "Grace came strongly to his [Knowles's] defence. How dare I attack her beloved Stanley! She had enormous loyalty to those who helped build the social democratic movement with her."

Grace remained personally as well as professionally close to Knowles. Marjorie Nichols, a press gallery journalist, recalled how the sight of Grace and Stanley putting their heads together over apples and cheese for lunch was a fixture of the fifth floor House of Commons cafeteria.

The sight of an apple always reminded Harold Winch of Grace too. Back for his sixth term, Winch was NDP critic for finance and the solicitor general's ministry. "The members didn't take her seriously at first," Winch said, "but it didn't take long. I can't think of any progressive legislation, provincial or federal, in this country, that wasn't initiated and turned down repeatedly, but eventually accepted, and the initial move—the speech, the motion, the amendment—came from people like Grace."

At twenty-two, NDPer Lorne Nystrom from Yorkton–Melville, Saskatchewan, was the youngest person ever elected to the House of Commons. "Grace had tremendous respect," he said, "partly in a patronizing sense because of who her father was, J.S. Woodsworth. But she certainly had a lot of respect in her own right, and that was quickly realized by members of all political parties."

Freshman NDP member Mark Rose, a University of British Columbia professor of music education from Fraser Valley West, admired Grace but felt intimidated by her at first. "She was an outstanding figure because she was really one of the saints. Saint Tommy, Saint Grace and Saint David. And I was just new and just off the street." Rose recalled how Grace welcomed his participation in caucus and made him feel at home. "She was generous. I remember in contrast to some, who shall remain nameless, [her treatment of] a newcomer asking questions about her field or area. Her answer was the more the merrier. And she was certainly not jealous, whereas some of the others would nail down an area, they were the expert, and they resented it if somebody else happened to venture into their particular field."

With the volume of correspondence her work was generating, Grace really needed a super-secretary when she met Betty Irwin. "She was older and I didn't know what she'd be like so I invited her to have lunch with me downtown," said Grace. "We liked the look of each other. So I said, 'Well, suppose we take a period of three months and see how we get on.'" They got on beautifully, and Betty Irwin became one of the pillars Grace could lean on. "She was a wonderful person," Grace said. "She did everything. She tried to fence me off from some of the nuisances, but I wouldn't let her fence me off. But she would help a lot. Visitors would arrive, and she knew right away which kind I would want to serve a cup of tea to, and she'd go down and get it without any questions in the cafeteria. Or, when I'd get there in the morning, she'd say, 'Oh, Mrs. MacInnis, you've got lint on your coat or your glasses are all fogged up.' She'd clean me up. I got to depending on her because I paid no attention to those things myself." Betty Irwin and Grace remained a team until Grace retired in 1974.

It might have been all work and no play for the NDP members, except for the presence of Mark Rose in the caucus. An amateur trumpet player and music educator, Rose wrote uproariously funny musical skits for the NDP caucus Christmas parties that provided a welcome break from parliamentary pressures. The skit that still had people laughing years later was the Christmas 1969 spoof of Snow White and the Seven Dwarfs in which Grace starred as Snow White. Stanley Knowles played Prince Charming and the seven shortest men in the caucus—including David Lewis, Andrew Brewin and Tommy Douglas— were the dwarfs.

Rose chuckled recalling rehearsals with Grace. "Her opening line was, 'Mirror, mirror on the wall, how come I look like bugger all?' And she had never used that phrase, and she'd say, 'Bugger all? I've never used that, Mark. What does it mean?' I said, 'It means nothing. How come I look poorly?' And I'd say, 'Bugger all.' And she'd say, 'Bugger all?' 'No,' I'd say, 'you haven't got the right inflection, try it again, Grace.' And she'd be shouting at me, 'No, it's not right! Bugger all!' And I remember having such a great kick out of this." The night of the show Grace did say it, though the words never comfortably rolled off her tongue. Then, said Rose, "she ate something and went to sleep and Prince Charming came in. It was Stanley. He looked like a sack of deer horns most of the time; he is very angular. He kissed her and woke her up. And her line was, 'Where have you been all my life?'" This moment had everyone laughing until their sides ached. All agreed, Grace was a good sport.

Grace's first major speech of the session late in September was naturally critical of the new government. The streamlining of parliament would not run smoothly, she forecast, if "the opposition will be silenced or restricted in bringing to the attention of the government the conditions in this country and the needs of our people." She chastised the government for refusing to increase family allowances and old age pensions "while the cost of living has risen tremendously." She pleaded for better housing and for a guaranteed annual income for the one in five Canadians living in poverty. This was all standard Grace MacInnis material, but it seemed weak in this new context. Many social security measures were already in place; the country was not in a recession; she had to stretch for a "modern" definition of poverty to prod the government into releasing more tax money for social benefits.

From this first speech Grace made it clear that the advancement of women and consumer issues were again to be the primary themes of her legislative work. Her most powerful statements that day were in support of equal opportunities for women and action on Royal Commission on the Status of Women recommendations when tabled. "The biggest single waste of human resources in this country now is the waste of womanpower," she declared emphatically, but her words were met with yawns from the government benches filled with male MPs.

Charles Lynch, a journalist, often observed Grace from the press gallery. He respected her as a person of principle, but said that many of her fellow MPs did not. "She suffered," he said. "Being a woman was a great handicap all through her life in terms of impact. The acceptance of a woman as an equal, while it may have existed inside the party, it did not exist inside the House."

Grace kept trying to educate the men in her life, in particular the NDP men. For instance, Wally Ross, BC provincial secretary and editor of the

NDP newspaper the *Democrat*, received a courteous but firm letter from Grace asking for a change in the heading of the parliamentary column, "Our Men in Ottawa." Grace wrote, "I look to our Party for a more up-to-date title than one which embodies the old fashioned idea that 'man' embraces woman! It is a minor irritation, but one I have to put up with far too often down here. I am no feminist, but I surely object to being herded under the same headline with 'Our Men in Ottawa,' in spite of the fact that I love them all very dearly."

During the first week of October, Florence Bird and the Royal Commission on the Status of Women were in Ottawa for their final week of public hearings. Women from the Caughnawaga Indian reserve near Montreal had asked Grace and Thérèse Casgrain to appear with them before the Commission to present their case for a new Indian Act which would remove discrimination against Indian women. The Indian Act at that time provided that an Indian man who married a non-Indian retained his Indian status and conferred it on his wife and children, although an Indian woman who married a non-Indian lost her status and all attendant financial benefits.

On October 2, 1968, a delegation of thirty women from Caughnawaga, accompanied by Grace and Thérèse, appeared before the RCSW. No hearing drew a larger crowd of listeners nor evoked a more sympathetic response. Chairperson Bird recalled, "They were bitter, and like the majority of Indian women who appeared before us, they were dramatic and compelling in the way they made us feel that bitterness." "They did us the honour of having us appear with them before the Commission," Grace told a Vancouver radio audience a few days later, "but they didn't need us. The justice of their cause gave them power to put their case forcefully and simply. In their own way they were helping all women in their battle for equality in the many fields of human experience today."

"That night in Ottawa," Bird said, "the delegation of Indian women told us that they would be beaten up by their men for daring to appear before us. We heard later that is exactly what happened." The Royal Commission's report, released in 1970, recommended that the Indian Act be amended to allow an Indian woman, upon marriage to a non-Indian, to retain her Indian status and transmit this status to her children.

Grace opened her legislative strategy for 1969 by introducing Bill C-161 to create a Human Rights Code for Canada. It would ensure complete equality of treatment as a person "regardless of race, creed, colour, sex, nationality, ancestry or place of origin, whether in employment, in residential or business accommodation or in access to other facilities or services customarily available to the public." Grace envisioned a Canadian Human Rights Commission established to administer the Code. It would have two divisions, one to consider "complaints and studies on the basis of sex, the second on the basis of the other listed headings."

Her Human Rights Code was based on the United Nations Universal Declaration of Human Rights and the Ontario Human Rights Code. Even idealistic Tommy Douglas, who as Saskatchewan premier led the first Canadian government at any level to enact a Bill of Rights, did not include protection against discrimination on the basis of gender. In line with Section 12 of the Regina Manifesto, Douglas did outlaw discrimination on the grounds of race, colour or religious creed. That was in 1946, fourteen years ahead of Prime Minister John Diefenbaker's federal Bill of Rights in 1960. This law did prohibit discrimination on the basis of sex and national origin as well as on grounds of race, colour or religion. By 1956 the CCF had come to recognize the need for special protection of the rights of women; the Winnipeg Declaration called for a Bill of Rights guaranteeing the "enjoyment of all rights without distinction of race, sex, religion of language."

Grace saw such protection for women as fundamental, a necessary first stage in establishing the legal framework for the right of women to control their bodies. But the Code she prepared with such hopeful and meticulous care was lost in the storm raised by the Trudeau government's Omnibus Bill.

Grace was scheduled to introduce her Human Rights Code on January 27, two days into debate on first reading of the Omnibus Bill. Aimed at renovating the Criminal Code on a wide range of measures including divorce and birth control, homosexuality, firearms and lotteries, the bill had no section more divisive than the one covering abortion. Trudeau's abortion section allowed "a qualified medical practitioner in an accredited or approved hospital to procure a miscarriage if the hospital's therapeutic abortion committee, by a majority of its members, has certified in writing that the continuation of the pregnancy would endanger the life or health of the woman." Trudeau buried it in an avalanche of other amendments to the Criminal Code in an attempt to make a Yes vote possible for the many Liberal Catholic MPs, including his own Justice Minister, John Turner, who personally objected to freedom of choice on religious grounds.

Grace's first abortion reform bill, C-122, introduced in the previous session, had also embodied some legal limitations. Now, speaking on first reading of the government's Omnibus Bill, Grace argued for the complete removal of abortion from the Criminal Code. "Public crime and private sin are entirely different matters," Grace declared, directing her comment in particular to the Catholic MPs. "On this question I commend the insight of the Prime Minister because he was quite right in saying the law has no business in the bedrooms of the nation." Trudeau had made the comment in reference to removing homosexuality from the Criminal Code, but it was widely quoted to shield all sex-related activity from government regulation.

"There is now one law for the rich woman," Grace told the Commons, "who can get an abortion by a doctor at home or abroad, and another for the poor woman who must bear an unwanted child or find a backroom butcher."

The law did not go far enough, she contended. "If doctors are to be large-spirited and humane they will still have to conduct illegal abortions even under these amendments." She suggested free-standing abortion clinics, with "a trained staff including doctors, as is the case in respect of birth control clinics, so that a woman could come there and have her abortion dealt with in the very early stages of pregnancy without waiting for the stage at which it becomes dangerous, difficult and disgusting even to the physician who has to deal with it."

The Omnibus Bill went to the House Standing Committee on Justice and Legal Affairs for clause by clause study, to re-emerge for second reading and debate in May.

Grace believed that David Lewis was a stumbling block on the way to repeal of Canada's abortion laws because she knew he did not approve of abortion. In addition to his moral qualms, Lewis may have thought it was a poor issue for the party. Yet during this debate on the Omnibus Bill he spoke in favour of her amendment to remove it from the Criminal Code. In Grace's view this was purely a gesture of caucus solidarity. "I don't think David Lewis had any use for abortion," she reflected. "I used to watch for times when he'd be out of town on meetings when I'd have a chance to get up and air it. I didn't pull any punches on the thing at all, and I'm rather glad because I think it all helped."

Whenever Grace presented a position in the House, especially on a highly controversial subject as abortion, she wished to ensure that she had the latest, most accurate information available. When Dr. Henry Morgentaler wrote in March 1969 asking her to his Montreal clinic to witness an illegal abortion using the new vacuum suction method he was pioneering, she accepted his invitation.

The House of Commons exploded in an uproar when Grace stood to speak of this experience. She knew that she had the equivalent of diplomatic immunity to discuss the illegal act she had seen, because Members cannot be taxed with what they say in the House. She took advantage of this privilege to let her colleagues see the realities of abortion in Canada.

It was a lovely May afternoon. Shafts of sunlight streamed through the high arched windows into the green-carpeted chamber, the peaceful light throwing the conflict on the floor into bold relief. For the past two weeks the Créditistes, francophone and mostly Catholic Social Crediters, had been filibustering the abortion clause of the Omnibus Bill. They wanted the law to stay as it was—abortion should remain a crime punishable by life in prison for the abortionist and up to two years in jail for the woman terminating her pregnancy.

Grace rose with a tingle of anticipation, knowing she would create a whirlwind. She quoted a Gallup poll taken less than a month before: seventy-three percent of those polled were in favour of legal abortions "to preserve a mother's physical or mental health." With firm conviction she stated, "I believe that the state has no right to compel a woman to continue a pregnancy which she feels unable to cope with, whether for reasons of physical, mental, or emotional health or of economic circumstances. I believe the state has no right to compel an unwanted child to be born . . . . I say with all the force at my command that today the world needs an increasing population in exactly the same way that we need the nuclear bomb."

Grace was alarmed and indignant that some MPs saw women seeking abortions as frivolous, concerned mostly with dress sizes and incapable of exercising responsible judgment in such a life-and-death decision. "They have treated women purely as baby machines, without minds, feelings or rights of their own," Grace accused them. "They have suggested that it is the duty of women to have any number of children without complaint. They have suggested that therapeutic abortion boards should include a psychiatrist for the purpose of telling women that maternity under any circumstances is good for them.

"The knife is not the only way," she argued. "We have been told over and over again by some witnesses before the committee that an abortion is a dreadful thing, that it involves the loss of vast quantities of blood, haemorrhaging, mutilation, and all kinds of other complications. This is a great exaggeration. For example, the new suction or vacuum method is in wide use in countries behind the iron curtain as well as in other countries, notably Japan and Israel." The MPs began to make comments. "I myself have witnessed such an abortion which was performed on a two-month foetus," Grace began. A storm of heckling rose around her. "It required only a local anaesthetic," she continued, "took fifteen minutes to perform, and was carried out by a regular qualified doctor in Canada. It caused practically no bleeding." The din increased as MPs, shocked and outraged, tried to drown her out. The Speaker demanded order; eventually he got the permission of the House for Grace to go on.

"This operation relieved a woman in her late thirties who had several children," Grace explained. "She had health problems which her doctor had told her were serious. Her income was very modest and her husband had refused to consider any sterilization of himself even though he was in sympathy with what she was doing and in full knowledge of it. I may say that I witnessed this operation with her permission. This woman had conscientiously but unsuccessfully tried birth control methods, with the acquiescence and co-operation of her husband. The operation brought about relief from a situation with which neither she nor her husband felt able to cope. Within fifteen minutes of the operation being performed the woman got up from the table, had a cup of coffee and on the arm of her young daughter went home and has been perfectly well ever since. This is the truth about abortion and I wish it were better known."

Grace concluded with another plea to the government to "remove the subject of abortion completely from the Criminal Code" and leave it to women and their doctors.

She was far ahead of her time. The Omnibus Bill passed unamended and came into effect August 26, 1969. Grace voted for it as half a loaf, the most she was likely to get for the time being. But even after the Omnibus Bill was law, she did not give up. "She was just a tiger on that issue," Marjorie Nichols recalled. "She was up day after day after day after day, kicking the government over the lack of access and providing statistics. And she was alone, I'm telling you, I mean all, all alone on that. She didn't have a lot of her colleagues in the NDP standing up and applauding her."

When the bill on birth control came up for second reading in the House, a week after her revelation about witnessing the illegal abortion, Grace was specific in calling for birth control advertising. "We have become accustomed to advertising for patent medicines of all kinds, beauty aids, toilet paper, deodorants, feminine douches . . . . I see no reason why contraceptives should not be advertised in the same way."

On some issues Grace agreed with the Trudeau government. Her heartiest support went to the effort to place the French language on an equal basis with English. She minimized western discontent and said the resolution to make both English and French the official languages of Canada, was "long overdue." Whether English or French, we are all Canadians, she affirmed. In French she said: "I am tired of hearing people of French origin call us English. I am not English, I am the end result of a mixture of three or four other races . . . . I am a Canadian and you, you are Canadians regardless of our origin . . . . Let us forget our differences and let us work all together in order to build and develop a beautiful country, a friendly Canada."

But it was not to be so easy. The province was in turmoil. In Quebec City on October 12, 1968, two days before Grace's speech to the House, two separatist organizations—Mouvement souveraineté–association and the Ralliement national—united to form the Parti québécois, with television journalist René Lévesque as president. Quebec students demanding a French-language university in Montreal had closed the provincial colleges for most of October. Quebec Liquor Board employees had been on strike since June. To combat separatism and unrest, Trudeau implemented his program of accelerating opportunities for qualified French Canadians in the civil service. "Trudeau began by placing quite a large number of French Canadians in high positions, like heading up Crown corporations or other higher placed administrative jobs," Grace said approvingly. "It wasn't too noticeable at the time; it became increasingly so.

"In doing so Trudeau did a number of things. He showed the very high value that he put on the idea of French Canadians being in the position of equality as far as government service went. Also, where there had been in ridings throughout Quebec a great hostility toward things emanating from Ottawa, this had the magical effect of transforming those ridings into Liberal government or pro-Canadian. And it gave a great deal of morale boosting to French Canadians trying to gain equality and bilingualism in the civil service. Now I think those things have to be set down very definitely to Mr. Trudeau's credit."

As the last leaves blew off its trees Ottawa bundled up for the winter of 1968–69, and Grace set about her perennial task of getting a better deal for low-income consumers. Her objective was to limit the powers of large corporations with monopolies on food distribution. The Batten Report, product of the Prairie Provinces Cost Study Commission, gave Grace the ammunition she needed in its recommendation for a combines investigation of Canada Safeway and of the Weston corporation which operated Loblaws, O.K. and Economy markets, Mini Marts and Shop Easy stores.

In committee she quoted the Batten Report. Ron Basford, the new Minister of Consumer and Corporate Affairs, replied that the Batten recommendations and evidence were not grounds enough for a prosecution. Grace kept at it. At the next sitting of the Health, Welfare and Social Affairs Committee she questioned the minister again about a prosecution under the Combines Investigation Act. Basford said he had to wait for the results of a study underway by the Economic Council of Canada.

Still she had a few tactics in reserve. Grace had been receiving letters from George Strong of Calgary, who complained that the Woodland Dairy fudgsicles sold in his neighbourhood were half an ounce short. One day Grace posed a question in the House about this discrepancy. The members rolled with laughter. Speaker Lamoureux ruled the question out of order. It was not a matter "of urgent public concern."

A few nights later Grace grabbed attention by breaking the rule that Members could not bring commercial products, exhibits or food onto the floor of the Commons. Waving a fudgsicle, she recounted the whole story. The Calgary man had become suspicious, weighed the fudgsicles, written to the Calgary weights and measures office and the minister's office, and hired an independent laboratory to weigh the fudgsicles. They averaged 2.516 ounces, not three ounces as the label stated. She labelled it fraud. Significantly, Grace pointed to the ownership of Woodland Dairy Ltd. "It is an affiliate of Palm Dairies Ltd., which itself in turn is an affiliate of Burns Foods Ltd." This time the parliamentary secretary to the minister of consumer affairs took the matter seriously enough to have an up-to-date history of the complaint on his desk. He promised "special checks" by the dairy products division.

A few days later Grace got a publicity windfall. Basford named the members of the new Canadian Consumer Council, a research group which Grace suspected was designed to study consumer issues to death instead of dealing with them. One man named to the council was A.J.E. Child, president of Burns Foods Ltd. of Calgary. Grace rose in the House on a point of privilege. Since Child's company, Burns Foods, was under investigation for defrauding the public by selling underweight fudgsicles, she argued, his appointment should be held in abeyance until the investigation was completed. The Speaker ruled there was no point of privilege. Child took his place on the council.

The whole incident did get people talking. The *Toronto Daily Star* reported: "Underweight Fudgsicle Case Turns Out To Be A Sticky One." The *Calgary Herald* wrote: "Fudgsicle Problem Hard To Lick." The *Albertan* headline writer had a field day with "Lady MP Spanks Child in Commons," and the subhead was almost as good: "Consumer Council Post . . . Fouled in Fudgecicle [sic] Fuss." The staff-written story led off, "The furious fulminations of a fiery female Fudgsicle fan filled the House of Commons Thursday. Would Mrs. Grace MacInnis take a job away from a child? You bet your sweet fudgsicle she would."

Grace was on a roll that first week of November 1968. The government had brought down its first budget and debate in the Commons was underway. She called it a "frightening" budget. The people had put this government in power "because they were in trouble and needed desperately to believe in Santa Claus," she lampooned the Prime Minister. "This is a streamlined version in modern dress of Santa Claus with Superman under the hood." The budget had failed Canadians, Grace declared, by placing new taxes on moderate and low-income citizens, failing to step up "production and the jobs and wages that go with production," and making no provision to increase the incomes of pensioners. One in every five Canadians was living in poverty, according to that Economic Council of Canada report less than two months ago. What was the government going to do?

On her way home to Vancouver for spring break 1969, Grace stopped in Winnipeg to address a Winnipeg and District Labour Council banquet, part of a labour institute at the University of Winnipeg. It was a joyous weekend. When she was proclaimed an honorary citizen of the City of Winnipeg in a presentation March 29, 1969, Grace's feelings about her home town came full circle. The city where she had grown up, the city she had first left as part of a family of pacifist pariahs, welcomed her back.

The effect of the rising cost of living on low-income Canadians continued to be Grace's number one priority throughout 1969. Grace would even side with BC's Social Credit government if she thought it would result in lower prices for consumers. She got into a tangle with the BC pharmacists when she backed BC Welfare Minister Dan Campbell, a Socred, in protesting a new one-dollar surcharge the pharmacists had slapped on every prescription filled for a social welfare recipient in BC. The manoeuvre was part of a pay-raise dispute, and the complaint was turned over to the Combines Investigation Branch.

In late spring a 9.4-percent rise in Toronto-area beef prices set boycotters marching once again. Grace was first to draw the matter to the attention of MPs, and it became the centre point of a controversy over the broad wave of price increases that sent the cost of living up 4.7 percent over 1968. In line with the Trudeau government strategy of putting off action in favour of information gathering, Consumer Affairs Minister Basford announced the establishment of a Prices and Incomes Commission that would operate alongside the Canadian Consumer Council.

Grace was highly critical from the first. "Apparently the commission is to provide a sort of rarefied study seminar . . . empowered to publish information as to how price stability can be achieved." She pointed out that its sessions would be held in private, and that its function was purely educative. "It has no power to act as a policeman in defence of the consumer. It has no power to intervene in individual price and income decisions. It has no power to launch inquiries into rising living costs. In short it has no power except to use moral suasion, a weapon which was already proved a broken reed in the carnivorous jungle of the marketplace." Grace demanded again, as she had since 1966, a prices review board with teeth and guidelines for all forms of income, including profits, rents, interest and professional fees.

Trudeau's next budget, in June 1969, did nothing to assure Grace that the people she was fighting for would get a better break. She kept a can of meat paste hidden diplomatically in her desk on June 16, obeying the Speaker's ruling against exhibits in the chamber. But she used the can to good effect, as she had used the fudgsicles. "I have here in my desk a tin of sandwich paste," she said with a flourish, to dramatize how the price had nearly doubled in two months. A trade unionist had complained about this price increase, she told the MPs. He wanted to know why trade unionists could not raise their wages at will, while food packers raised prices at will. Later, she had the can of meat paste delivered to Basford's office as a symbol of her fight.

For months Grace had been urging a reopening of joint Senate–Commons committee hearings into the cost of living spiral, but when Basford announced in June that these hearings would take place, it seemed like just one more stalling tactic to Grace. It reminded her of a story her father used to tell about a family crossing the Russian steppes in a sled, with wolves in close pursuit. "As the wolves drew closer, a coat was thrown to them, and this allowed the tiring horses to open the gap. But when the wolves found that the coat was not edible they quickly renewed their chase. Then a blanket was thrown from the sled, and then another coat, always slowing the wolves just enough. It seems that Mr. Basford is always throwing coats and blankets," she remarked. "It's just a question of whether his boards and commissions and white papers and committees will divert the consumers long enough to save their budgets."

At the end of July, Grace got some support. A federal Trade Commission report accused supermarkets of driving up the grocery bills of the poor, then handing out game prize money to their more affluent suburban neighbours. Poor downtown residents wound up paying as much as ten percent more for groceries than suburbanites. The report said grocery bills were higher in city areas because the markets were competing less aggressively than in suburban areas, and providing smaller supplies of weekly specials. It sounded all too familiar to Grace.

She was somewhat encouraged when Basford announced a nine-point plan for enforcement of criminal laws against misleading advertising. The crackdown on deceptive use of contests, "free" offers that were not in fact free, and bait and switch advertising, amounted to a few crumbs thrown in the direction of consumer protection. Grace was more hopeful in August, when the Economic Council of Canada came out with a report urging greater federal powers to deal with combines and monopolies, measures she had been urging since the 1930s.

Grace was now thoroughly disenchanted with the Trudeau government, particularly with one provision of the new set of rules by which House of Commons business was conducted. Whatever respect she might have retained for the Prime Minister's intellect, whatever hope she had that he might sponsor new measures of social justice, vanished in the anger over the rule limiting opposition debate. The rule gave the government power to pilot a controversial bill through the House in a minimum of four days of debate over a period of ten sitting days, regardless of any objections. Opposition members gave up the holiday month of July to fight this rule. They negotiated hopefully until the Cabinet suddenly broke off discussion, closure was imposed, and the measure was adopted on division in its original form.

Grace's speech protesting the closure evoked images of a fiery J.S. Woodsworth and an indignant Angus MacInnis standing in that same green chamber arguing against closure in their day. "Last Tuesday [July 22, 1969] we who sit opposite the government witnessed something very disturbing as the government house leader gave notice of closure," Grace pronounced. "The mask of democratic leadership slipped suddenly from the face of the Prime Minister who sat revealed as a man of supercilious arrogance with mockery in his face. He sat there while the three opposition leaders made their statements. Then, in a house dazed by the shock of the government's action, he rose and, turning his back on parliament in an ultimate gesture of contempt, he made his nonchalant way out of the chamber. Those of us who witnessed it will not forget it. It will take many, many oceans of words to sweep away that expression. It will take much more than words; it will take a great deal of action to obliterate that."

All opposition members were angry; some shouted "fascist tendencies" and "Heil Hitler" at the Prime Minister. Trudeau snapped, "When they are fifty yards from Parliament Hill, they are no longer honourable members—they are just nobodies." The closure rule was forced through; the honeymoon was over.

The attention of the Canadian public was not focussed only on parliament that summer; too many other exciting events were going on. Young North Americans made counterculture history when an estimated 500,000 gathered in southern New York state for the three-day Woodstock rock festival. On July 20, Neil Armstrong and Buzz Aldrin made the first human footprints on the moon, and hundreds of millions of earthbound humans were there via television. "No one can ever again look at the moon without seeing in it the symbol of the incredible stamina of man and the equally incredible power of his technology," Grace announced to the Federation of Women Teachers' Associations of Ontario a few days later. "The leap to the moon has become the incontestable proof of man's ability to dominate the universe. Or has it? The moon walk and the subsequent pictures from Mars have underlined for some of us the inescapable fact that man is biologically bound to our planet earth, with its vital and vulnerable supplies of air, soil and water. It has underlined also the frightening fact that these supplies are diminishing rapidly under the impact of man's voracious technology. Exhaustion of natural resources, overpopulation, pollution, nuclear war, are mounting threats to the continued existence of man as a species."

Grace argued that instead of spending a hundred billion dollars on the Vietnam conflict, that sum and more must be spent on "providing the kind of environment that will produce fine human beings." Instead of spending another hundred billion dollars on space exploration, "we must first plan to explore the human resources of earth and provide ways and means by which they can develop their full potential so as to enrich the world with beauty and goodness and kindness." In the words she had learned literally at her father's knee, Grace told the teachers, "You can't develop the fine flower of civilization on the rotten root of poverty."

The contemporary cry "power to the people" was an old maxim for Grace. She had been working to place more economic and social power in the hands of the least advantaged Canadians since she first came to Ottawa in 1931. "People power can begin almost anywhere," she told delegates to the annual Saskatchewan NDP convention in July. "The main ingredients for making people power are these: a specific problem needing solution, a group of ordinary folk prepared to work together to solve it, the help of an expert willing to give of self and time. After that comes organization . . . . Knowledge is the rock upon which the structure of people power must be founded."

On July 25, 1969, Grace turned sixty-four. She marked the day by clipping the astrology column from the *Toronto Star* headlined "People Born Under Leo Are Sure To Rule." Grace was mentioned in the *Star*'s listing of famous Leo personalities, along with Jacqueline Kennedy Onassis and Princess Margaret. Grace found the revival of interest in astrology in the late 1960s mildly intriguing, and recognized in herself the characteristics of a Leo: a ruler and teacher, dignified, proud, yet friendly and cheerful, with a flair for dramatic presentation.

Back in British Columbia in time to campaign for the August 27 provincial election, Grace lent her name and the aura of her success to the cause of NDP candidates Dennis Mulroney, her stalwart sign captain in 1968, and Mickey Rockwell in Little Mountain, a two-member provincial riding within Vancouver–Kingsway. But BC did not choose an NDP government led by Tom Berger, a moderate, responsible lawyer. On election day, Mulroney and Rockwell were defeated along with all but twelve NDP candidates. W.A.C. Bennett and his Social Credit government, who campaigned to defeat "Marxist Socialism," remained in power.

Grace relaxed on a cruise to Alaska before travelling to Jasper, Alberta, for a meeting of the France–Canada Association of Parliamentarians, the Association Interparlementaires Canada–France, with parliamentarians from both countries. House of Commons Speaker Lucien Lamoureux was president of the Canadian section and Grace was treasurer. Lamoureux was speaker during Grace's entire parliamentary term, 1966–74, and she said that on the whole he was very good to her, although she made a nuisance of herself "bouncing up and down like a yo-yo" in the House. Serving together on this political, nonprofit body facilitating exchanges on scientific, cultural and commercial matters deepened the understanding between them.

When the Waffle movement arose within the NDP in 1969, Grace had seen it all before. By now manoeuvres by self-styled "true" socialists to take over the party were almost to be expected. The Waffle looked remarkably like the party-within-a-party the Socialist Fellowship had tried in the 1950s. There was even a confidential Waffle mailing list people had to get on to receive Waffle materials, just as Rod Young had done for the Socialist Fellowship with the anonymous Box 16.

Although the Waffle episode proved traumatic for the party and Grace was decidedly on the establishment side, she avoided emotional involvement of the kind which embroiled her for decades with the communists and the Socialist Fellowship. Her primary effort now centred in the Commons on obtaining a better legal position for Canada's disadvantaged. She was now able to take a longer view of these periodic struggles with the party's left wing.

The 1969 NDP federal convention took place in Winnipeg in October, three months after Manitoba elected its first NDP government led by Premier Ed Schreyer. The Waffle Manifesto was introduced there. This controversial document had been written largely by University of Toronto economist Mel Watkins, who in 1968 had headed a task force on foreign investment in Canada under Liberal Cabinet minister Walter Gordon. The essential message of Watkins's report was that since "multinational corporations run this country, why don't we get them to run it better. Why don't we leave them the power but get more benefits for Canadians?" By spring of 1969 Watkins was more involved with grassroots radicalism on the campus. He and colleagues James Laxer, Ed Broadbent and Gerald Caplan, gathered their ideas into the "Manifesto for an Independent Socialist Canada," the Waffle Manifesto. It echoed some of the anti-capitalism language of the Regina Manifesto, but Grace contrasted the Waffle statement of socialism with that of the NDP old guard. "The 'Waffle Manifesto,' as it came to be known affectionately," she wrote, "was couched in anti-American, anti-imperialist, rather old-fashioned, doctrinaire language. Further, it advocated two Canadas instead of one. [In contrast,] the [federal] Council statement, it seemed to me, appeals to modern socialists. It outlines concrete measures to free this country from economic control both from outside and from corporations at home. Its language is rather stodgy but its ideas are dynamic, at least in the opinion of two-thirds of the delegates." Grace voted with the majority in favour of the federal council statement to defeat the Waffle Manifesto, yet she seemed to enjoy the greater degree of passion and participation the Waffle's activities had generated within the NDP. It showed there was life in the old party yet.

But she antagonized the young radical feminists by saying there was a proper way for females to advance within the party, and it was not by a quota system. She wrote, "Of course I did not agree with the girls when they wanted twenty-five positions on Council set aside for women on a non-elective basis. They regarded this as a power base. I told them it would be a crutch which, if they got it, they must kick aside at the first opportunity. They didn't get it." Merit should be the only criterion for election to the council or any position, in Grace's view. Had she not proved herself electable to the federal council time and again, over factional resistance, without an enforced quota? She believed other women should be able to do the same. She appeared at times to ignore the great advantage she enjoyed in her position as J.S. Woodsworth's daughter. Because she wanted to see herself as making her career independently on her own, Grace had tried to discipline herself not to trade on her family connections, and she minimized this advantage when comparing herself with other women.

Nor did Grace want to see women spend their energy organizing solely women as many radical feminists were doing. "I tried in the early years of women's lib to get those women to see that if they wanted to get their measures through legislatures which were nearly one hundred percent male-dominated the only hope they had was to get male spokesmen on their delegations to show that it wasn't solely a women's issue, but the silly things, frequently they kept their conferences shut even to men sitting in and seeing what it was about. Now, of course," Grace said in 1980, "women are getting far more wisdom on this matter."

The Winnipeg convention might have attracted more young people and women than previous conventions, but Grace noted sadly the very few delegates from Quebec and from trade unions. After all the upheaval of ten years before to create a new party that would embrace trade unionists, she was disappointed at their lack of participation.

As 1969 drew to a close, for the first time in eighteen years editors of women's sections in daily newspapers were unable to name a Canadian Woman of the Year. Grace was named most newsworthy in the category of public affairs, with this remark: "Although she does not consider herself a champion of women's causes, Mrs. MacInnis campaigns steadily for such things as maternity leave and more nursery care facilities. As a member of the Commons Health Committee she supported the move to more lenient laws on birth control and abortion." It was not the only news report that trivialized Grace's contribution, even while recognizing her work. She did not merely "support" more lenient laws on birth control and abortion; Grace in fact led these fights. She took positions that were far more radical than those held by Trudeau, and she pushed both the Pearson and Trudeau governments much further toward actions safeguarding the rights of women than they would otherwise have moved. It may be tempting to hang labels on Grace's attitude such as "pragmatic feminist," "socialist feminist" or "theoretical feminist," but Grace saw issues of home and family, birth control, abortion, child care and income security for women simply as human issues. If anything, she could be called a socialist and a humanist.

CHAPTER 15

Fast Forward

Harsh winds keened over the Hill in late October 1969 as Parliament resumed for the second session of the twenty-eighth Parliament under Prime Minister Trudeau. For the first time, a throne speech touched on Canada's "befouled water, despoiled beaches, rotting marine vegetation, and diminished fishing" along with "pollution in the Arctic Seas" as matters requiring legislation. The United Nations had resolved, on a Swedish–Canadian initiative, to hold the First International Conference on the Human Environment in Stockholm in 1972. Around the world a small group of people in many countries and varied walks of life had picked up the planet's alarm signals warning of a rapidly deteriorating environment.

The issue of water quality rose to the top of Grace's agenda for this session. Though an opposition politician and a member of a small party, she mobilized the Canadian public by focussing on the single narrow issue of phosphates in detergents. Grace's campaign for a ban on phosphates was a classic example of her style of action. Her work with the Canada Water Act formed a pattern of success she would employ throughout her parliamentary career.

As early as June 1967 Grace had become alarmed at the contamination of Lake Erie. In Welland, Ontario, she told a meeting how shocked she was to see the extent of pollution in the nearby lake. She noted that the US government was spending 3.9 billion dollars for lake cleanup, but "our government is doing almost nothing while Lake Erie is being turned into an open cesspool."

In fall 1969 the International Joint Commission (IJC), charged with monitoring and investigation of waters spanning the Canada–US border, issued a report on Lake Erie, Lake Ontario and the international section of the St. Lawrence River. It confirmed Grace's early warnings of phosphate buildup. Phosphate compounds, then a major ingredient of detergents, provide a nutrient to algae, causing the microscopic plants to bloom in great clouds and consume oxygen that would otherwise nourish fish. And the phosphate problem was not confined to the Great Lakes. Grace knew in May 1969 that the waters near Long Harbour, Newfoundland, were in trouble. A constituent wrote to alert her that toxic waste was being dumped into Long Harbour by the Electric Reduction Company of Canada (ERCO), the only Canadian manufacturer of phosphates and a company wholly owned by Albright and Wilson Ltd. of England. Officials closed the plant temporarily. In answer to Grace's questions in the House, Eugene Whelan, parliamentary secretary to the minister of fisheries and forestry, promised that Long Harbour would be reclaimed for fishing. The restoration would be paid for entirely by ERCO.

In early November the government introduced the Canada Water Act, which proposed to fine polluters up to five thousand dollars a day and force them to halt operations until pollution control systems were in place. But there were no sections dealing with limitations on the dumping of nutrients such as phosphates.

Grace would consider this law in detail during the first half of 1970; she was named to the Standing Committee on National Resources and Public Works where the Water Act went for clause-by-clause review. Under Trudeau's reforms, detailed debate on virtually all legislation now took place in committees.

As an opening volley, Grace introduced her own water quality bill in late January with stiff penalties for manufacturers and stores selling detergents containing phosphates. Then she peppered the government with questions on the issue. By February 27 she squeezed an announcement from Energy Minister Joe Greene that "we are going to ban phosphates." The soap companies claimed there was no safe, effective, practical substitute for phosphorus, and warned that "a cleanliness crisis would be created by banning detergents [containing phosphates] from the market." They appeared to ignore the existence of a non-phosphate detergent compound being used in Sweden. Early in November 1969 this argument collapsed when Dr. Philip Jones of the University of Toronto announced he had created a detergent, Formula N, which contained no phosphates whatever. Lever Brothers promised to research the new compound without delay.

Awareness of environmental issues surged to the forefront of the Canadian consciousness in the winter and spring of 1969–70. Articles about pollution in the news media roused public awareness, and prompted investigations of dump sites by government authorities. On November 4, the first conference of users of the Great Lakes met in Toronto to discuss pollution.

When Grace delivered her first major speech on the Canada Water Act in January 1970, she complained that nationwide standards of water quality were missing from the Act although water is constantly in motion across political boundaries. She objected that the legislation failed to spell out federal–provincial cost-sharing arrangements for the three to four billion dollars the minister estimated would be needed to handle Canada's water problems during the next decade. Nor was there funding to help municipalities put in sewage treatment facilities. Beyond these shortcomings, Grace noted that a Canada-wide ban on phosphates had not been written into the law. She accused the government of drafting the legislation completely in line with the thinking of the big detergent companies.

Significantly, she said, University of Toronto Chancellor Dr. Omond M. Solandt had been "very cool and sceptical" in response to the discovery of a phosphate-free detergent at his own university. She pointed out that Solandt was not only "the vice president of the Electric Reduction Company, the firm which manufactures all phosphates for detergents in Canada, the same firm which has been pumping pollution into Placentia Bay, killing the fish and taking away the livelihood of the Newfoundland fishermen, [but he] also happens to be the Chancellor of Toronto University and the president of the Science Council of Canada."

This was the opening move in Grace's campaign to force Solandt's resignation as president of the science council for conflict of interest, and there was even more at stake. "This is not a matter of party politics," she stressed. "It is a matter of whether we are likely to survive in our own environment." Grace was doing battle with the same old enemies, who now threatened environmental destruction in addition to spiralling prices, inadequate wages and opposition to social security measures. Five days later she renewed her attack on Solandt in the House with the help of Ran Harding and David Lewis, but Treasury Board President Charles Drury expressed confidence in "the ability of Dr. Solandt to rise above this type of conflict."

Yet, when questioned at a Toronto news conference about the Formula N discovery, Solandt had admitted to reporters that his views on the subject might be "slightly biased" because of his connection with ERCO. Solandt stated his position on phosphates in December, saying, "It is too much to expect an industry using a harmless ingredient to go out and see if that ingredient is having any effect on the environment."

During question period on January 30 Grace again called for Solandt's resignation, only to be ruled "argumentative" by the Speaker. But her campaign to ban phosphates was winning support. In one week Grace received five hundred letters on the subject, one from Dr. L. Yaffe, chairman of McGill University's Department of Chemistry. W5, an investigative CTV program, aired an item on Formula N which showed it cleaning as well as detergents with phosphates. In vain Grace suggested that a Crown corporation be formed to manufacture and market the new formula. Industry spokesmen and some government MPs still professed doubt that phosphates were even a problem.

Soon after the Canada Water Act went to committee, Energy Minister Joe Greene responded to Grace's repeated demands for a nationwide ban by promising to suggest, on a province-by-province basis, a reduction in phosphates of twenty-five percent in 1970, an additional cut of ten percent in 1971 and an outright ban in 1972, though he seemed none too sure of the timetable for a ban. Grace was convinced that only public pressure would bolster the minister's resolve. She began to instruct people in the techniques of effectively pressuring the government. She had a new tool: a detailed laboratory analysis of the phosphate content of the twenty-four most common detergents, carried out by Pollution Probe, a newly formed anti-pollution group at the University of Toronto. It showed a variation from 52.5 percent phosphate content in the Amway product to only 8 percent in the Swedish product, and less than 1 percent in soap products such as Ivory Snow. Grace distributed copies of these reports far and wide.

Consumer boycotts are not enough now, Grace advised the Quebec section of the Consumers' Association of Canada and its president Thérèse Casgrain. "The consumer is up against well-trained, well-prepared lobby groups representing the detergent manufacturers." She suggested the housewives of Canada must "help" the Energy Minister achieve the ban with an intensified letter-writing campaign to give him the ammunition of public pressure, but she told the Montreal meeting not to waste time writing to Prime Minister Trudeau; he was under the influence of Dr. Solandt, whose advice was tainted by conflict of interest. Not until January 1971 did Dr. Solandt resign as vice-chair of the ERCO board of directors, and then he announced that the resignation was not due to conflict of interest. His term as chairman of the science council expired in May 1972.

Grace worked with the CAC as she worked with other citizens' groups, courteously. But she never hid her belief that the CAC was too pliant beneath government pressure; too concerned with well-fed, middle-income people and neglectful of the poor. Grace had formed this opinion years ago, and her memory was long. "Right at the end of the war," she recalled, "when things were returning to so-called normal, Thérèse Casgrain and I were members of the CAC. One of the issues was whether controls on housing should be lifted. We opposed lifting controls because of the effect on low-income people. The CAC seemed lukewarm on the matter. A wire was received from Prime Minister St. Laurent, advising the CAC the government wanted to lift the controls. At the crack of the whip, the CAC went on record in favour of lifting the controls. That is the reason [Thérèse and] I left the organization rather promptly, and neither of us returned for many years. When I was elected in 1965 I decided it would be a good idea, as I was concerned with consumer affairs, to rejoin the CAC."

Similarly, Grace saw increased government grants to the group in the Trudeau years as "a definite way of nailing the CAC to the government cart." Still, CAC members joined the national letter-writing campaign to ban phosphates, and Grace valued their participation. Energy Minister Joe

Greene was feeling the pressure. That week he told the detergent companies to reduce the phosphate content in their products twenty-five percent by August 1, and warned that a total ban on phosphates could be imposed by 1972.

In committee hearings from February through the first week of May, Grace hammered away at the government's position. Broadly representative public hearings were a democratic right, she insisted, and underlined the public's right to be informed of all government research on water pollution. She pointed to London's successful clean-up of the Thames River. She reminded committee members and witnesses that a Swedish non-phosphate detergent was already available. Listening from the back of the room at almost every hearing were representatives of major soap manufacturers. Grace contended that a single national water quality standard, rather than a range of provincial standards, was the only way to ensure clean water for Canadians. In her evidence to the committee Casgrain agreed; her view was contradicted later that day by spokesmen for the Quebec Association of Water Technicians, who favoured provincial jurisdiction. But by then the dispute was a dead letter, as Energy Minister Greene had achieved agreement with the provinces for a phosphate ban by the end of 1972.

Emphasizing the dangers of pulp mill pollution on the Fraser River, oil drilling in the Georgia Strait and sewage problems everywhere, Grace told the House indignantly, "Our beaches in British Columbia around Vancouver have been closed whole seasons because it was not considered safe for the health of people to let them bathe there. Surely we are foolish to be permitting waste to get into waterways to the detriment of human beings." Her goal was real environmental cleanliness, rather than sparkling white detergent-washed clothes and dishes which resulted in filthy lakes and oceans. Industry would not really suffer if they had to stop making and selling phosphate cleaners, she claimed.

Grace found many shortcomings in the Canada Water Act, which she claimed began "with the idea that you pollute water first before anything can be done about it." She favoured a preventive approach. She wanted the principle of "polluter pays" written into the bill, and she wanted a Federal Pollution Control Board which would investigate complaints by any six Canadians. Curiously, her greatest difficulties with the Canada Water Act arose over the simplest issues. She asked that the word "phosphate" should be included somewhere in the law, and that manufacturers be required to state the phosphate content of their products on the packages. But government officials called her efforts a "public relations facade" and found seemingly endless reasons why these simple measures could not be taken.

In late May Grace got a break from the intense pace of parliamentary work. As a member of the Canadian delegation to the France–Canada Association of Parliamentarians, the Association Interparlementaires Canada–France, she attended a conference in France's Loire valley. The delegates considered problems common to Canada and France, "the most important of which was pollution," she noted. Delegates from France's National Assembly introduced Grace to the concept of bio-degradability as a standard for detergents.

When she returned to Canada, Grace found that her phosphate letter-writing campaign had been successful. By the time the Canada Water Act came to the floor of the House for final debate, the government had received 1,678 letters advocating a phosphate ban.

In the end, the Canada Water Act included few of the provisions Grace had worked for, but she did get a ban on phosphates by 1972. In this achievement Grace demonstrated a recipe for securing government action. She shared it with a group of teachers from the US and Canada at their July 1970 convention in Victoria. "The ingredients are important," she said. "A real community need strongly felt, accurate knowledge, wise leadership, a simple, single demand, and an overwhelming deluge of public pressure directed to the right place."

As 1970 unreeled, Grace's life seemed to accelerate. Driven by an inner sense of urgency, she packed more into each hour than ever before and skillfully juggled environmental, consumer, youth, labour, women's and party concerns. Grace's parliamentary work had become her entire life; there was no time for anything else.

A heavy load of committee work occupied her from early morning to late at night, for she was diligent about attending hearings. On April 7, 1970, a typical day, work began in her parliamentary office at 8:00 a.m. where she fielded constituents' problems with the assistance of her valued secretary Betty Irwin. At 9:30 Grace attended a session of the Committee on National Resources and Public Works on the Canada Water Act. When it adjourned at 12:50 p.m., Grace had two hours and forty minutes to eat lunch and handle other business. Then at 3:30 she went to the Committee on Health, Welfare and Social Affairs where Minister Ron Basford appeared to justify spending estimates for the Combines Investigation and Competition Policy Program. This committee recessed for dinner at 6:05 and reconvened for an evening sitting at 8:20, when Grace was one of only eight members present. Very often she appeared in the House for the "late show," the 10:00 p.m. proceedings on adjournment, when private members had a short window of time to speak. She arrived home near midnight, to grab a few hours of sleep before the next day brought another round of equally demanding tasks. About this time Grace began wearing dark-rimmed reading glasses to protect her eyes from the strain of the mountains of printed material she saw daily.

Despite this punishing schedule, Grace did not believe MPs deserved special treatment, especially not when across Canada income security measures were falling far behind the cost of living. In reply to Trudeau's budget, Grace accused the government of diverting attention away from measures to help low-income people by enticing the public to focus on, in her words, "a Prime Minister who can divide his Christmas holiday between scuba diving in the West Indies and skiing in the Alps and to hell with the people . . . a Prime Minister . . . taking the place of the Queen, the flag and whatever other symbols you like." In her eyes the sin of "contempt for Parliament and contempt for the people" lay squarely on the shoulders of the Prime Minister.

Money and power continued to flow to the highest levels rather than being shared with the people. Early in 1970 the government introduced a single bill to increase pensions for government employees, MPs and senators. Grace was entirely in favour of increasing pensions for civil servants. But she felt MPs and senators should not get a pension increase until the needs of low-income Canadians had been met. She pressed this point in the Health, Welfare and Social Affairs Committee, where the bill was debated, and in the House.

When the NDP put forward a motion to increase old age and veterans' pensions in May, Grace had just returned to Ottawa from a week in her constituency "particularly indignant" over the plight of "elderly people in their pitifully small places trying to keep themselves dignified, neat and clean . . . trying to save a few cents on grocery items here and there." She scolded the government for failing to increase an old age pension plus supplement when the cost of living had risen "more than two and a half times as much as the increase in the pension and supplement together" The government said nothing could be done about pensions until the white paper on social reform was complete, likely not in time to take any action in the current session.

When a government bill was introduced in December to add but forty-two cents to old age pensions, then freeze them at eighty dollars a month and increase only the supplement, Grace told the House, "this bill has the sour smell of poverty about it." She was especially angry because the supplement hike was to be financed by not giving the two percent annual increase to pensioners who had other income. This eroded the principle of universality. Grace called these arrangements "refinements of torture which . . . make the poor finance the destitute." She still believed a universal pension and supplement should be paid out and taxed back from higher-income recipients.

Closer to Christmas 1970, when the report of the government's Advisory Committee on Parliamentary Salaries and Expenses recommended pay increases for MPs of up to seven thousand dollars a year, Grace, along with Douglas and Knowles, opposed them. But she declined to return the increase to the government as former Prime Minister John Diefenbaker had done in 1963 because, she said, "I could put the money to better use than the government could."

She faulted the government for side-stepping poverty with councils, commissions, studies, white papers and boards of inquiry. Grace was thoroughly aware of the value of obtaining accurate, complete information before policy became legislation; she herself had an enviable reputation for doing her homework. But she objected to research as a tactic to delay action.

Grace took aim at David Leighton, professor of business administration at the University of Western Ontario, the recently appointed chairman of the twenty-four member Canadian Consumers' Council which promised to target US investment and control over business. By December 1969 council members were publicly criticizing their own body for doing nothing. Grace rose in the House to ask for a government investigation of charges by members "that the council has spent a year in almost total idleness, torn by bitter internal dissension and gagged by the chairman." Not satisfied with the response of the minister, Ron Basford, who accused her of using the issue for "personal publicity," Grace sent a letter to the editors of many major daily newspapers across the country repeating the charges. She added one by council member Beryl Plumptre, a former president of the Consumers' Association of Canada, that Dr. Leighton could not be effective when he held down two other jobs in addition to the chairmanship. In closing, she said the public had a right to know what was being done with the council's 100,000-dollar annual budget.

This letter brought a defensive response from Leighton. He had given up his consulting practice, he said, and held the chairmanship as an unpaid, part-time position. He denied he had ever "gagged" council members; he had told them that only the chairman could act as official spokesman for the council. An increasingly angry exchange of letters between Grace and Dr. Leighton ran into February. He called her "irresponsible"; she maintained the council had done nothing to deserve its budget allotment. In the end, Grace sent a letter apologizing to Leighton only for repeating the charge that he held down three jobs. It was a rare letter of apology.

By March 1971 Basford was disenchanted enough with Leighton's leadership to appoint a new chair and new members of the consumers' council. At once Grace objected that the new council again included no representatives of low-income consumers. Basford defended his appointments, and she had to leave the matter there.

Sub-zero winds sliced through the Ottawa night of February 20, 1970, as Grace and Stanley Knowles, with several members of the working press and youthful supporters, marched in front of the Skyline Hotel carrying picket signs. Their messages, "Male Chauvinists Your Days Are Numbered" and "Type Stories, Not Women," were aimed at the journalists attending the National Press Club Ball inside.

Allowing women into the National Press Club as members was the subject of endless debate among the reporters and editors, both at the club bar and at a series of long annual meetings. A month before the club had voted fifty-eight to fifty-three to keep its men-only membership policy. The opposing camps had degenerated into acronyms. AMEN stood for the Ad Hoc Movement to Encourage Non-Discrimination, the pro-female voters; while SCREW stood for the Society for the Continued Rejection of the Equality of Women. The club had sent invitations to the ball addressed "Gentlemen" to all MPs and senators, including Grace and the female senators. Grace knew that Canadian women could never achieve full equality as long as the reporters and editors who shaped public awareness still would not accept women as truly equal. The press club membership was moved to change, in part by Grace's demonstration. Soon after the incident the club called a special meeting to decide on the admission of women, and on April 24, 1970, women were admitted as active members. Today about twenty percent of the membership of the National Press Club is female.

This action was the closest Grace ever came to considering herself a feminist. Recounting the protest in a letter to her brother Charles, Canadian ambassador to Ethiopia, Grace described the picketers as "some of us feminists of both sexes."

Canadians were still bitterly divided on the question of abortion. There were those who sent Grace lurid, bloody photographs of fatalities they claimed were abortions and letters blaming her for these deaths. Catholics, their tradition of opposition to abortion and birth control fortified by the 1968 papal encyclical "Humanae Vitae," demanded that Grace consider the repercussions if Jesus had been aborted. Old CCFers called her to account for the consequences to Canada if her grandmother had aborted J.S. Woodsworth.

Some women, reasonably satisfied with the principles of the new law, were still distressed at lack of access to the medical procedure. Of Canada's 948 general hospitals, only 143 had established abortion committees in the year following passage of abortion reform. But there were many women who were outraged by the Trudeau government's halfway measure of abortion law reform that left them at the mercy of panels of doctors, invariably male, before whom they could not appear, but who held them to a standard of proof that did not admit of personal circumstances. These women believed that their wombs were not government property.

On April 28, 1970, a caravan of cars and vans left Vancouver for Ottawa bearing seventeen of those women. One was Grace's cousin Ellen Woodsworth. Ellen's grandfather Harold was J.S. Woodsworth's brother. Her father was Ken Woodsworth, with whom Grace had tangled over communist influences at the Canadian Youth Congress in 1940. When Ellen was growing up in Toronto, Ken helped establish the social planning council, while her mother Jean was active in the United Church and the YWCA. In Ellen's words, they were "left-thinking socialists" who were persecuted for their beliefs. "I think my father got really smashed by the McCarthy era. My parents were both persecuted for signing the Stockholm Peace petition, and my mother was thrown off the local PTA. People went to her at various jobs and tried to get her fired. It was a bad time.

"I remember my brothers getting beaten up. I remember we had a CCF sign out front and people going by the house and screaming at us. It was like having the Klan right outside. And I remember my father, who was a member of the Legion, running for alderman, and a whole smear campaign against him.

"We suffered, and a lot of people I know suffered, and I think it was really despicable that the CCF joined in that. I think they should have had a broader sense of who was on their side than they did."

Of course, Ellen knew that her cousin Grace MacInnis had been part of the CCF establishment which rejected the actions of radicals like her parents. Although each woman was working in her own way for the liberation of Canadian women from the tyranny of gender, this resentment stood between them; they had never met.

Ellen had become politically involved against the Vietnam war and for Native rights. She was head of the Speakers' Bureau at UBC, and set up the first women's centre in her office at the Student Union Building. She was part of one of the first women's liberation groups in Canada, the Vancouver Women's Caucus. They wanted abortion removed entirely from the Criminal Code. At a Women's Caucus meeting in February 1970 the idea arose for an abortion caravan that would drive across Canada to confront the federal government at Ottawa.

Through Ellen's eyes the abortion caravan was an experiment in public education. "It was tremendously exciting," she recalled. "Four cars left from Vancouver, a truck and a Volkswagen van, and we travelled all across Canada—stopping. We sang our way across, we spoke our way across, we did street theatre, we gathered women all across the country and ended in Toronto with a big rally.

"Then we went to Ottawa where women from Quebec, the Maritimes and eastern Ontario joined us, and discussed about how we would proceed. It was finally decided. We had one march right up, [to the Parliament Buildings] but none of the leaders would meet with us." The headline in the Ottawa Citizen read, "Pleas for abortion greeted by silence." Trudeau had told the Commons on Friday that he had no intention of changing the abortion law and immediately departed on a tour of the Pacific.

On Saturday May 9 after the march, 450 pro-choice women crowded into the railway committee room in the Centre Block to read their demands. Grace, accompanied by Deputy NDP Leader David Lewis and NDP MP Lorne Nystrom, as well as Conservative House Leader Gerald Baldwin, met with the demonstrators. In the crowd was abortion caravan organizer Ellen Woodsworth, who saw her famous cousin Grace in action for the first time that day. A few members of the anti-abortion group Alliance For Life squeezed in at the back of the room, among them Sheila Copps, later a Liberal MP but then a high school student and daughter of Hamilton's mayor. Grace asked the anti-abortionists to leave. The group took up the chant, "Out, out, out!" Some left. Copps, in what would become her characteristic fashion, refused, shouting, "It's a public meeting, isn't it?"

Grace was the only MP to address the group, supporting their views and reminding them that since the inadequate Trudeau reform became law she had introduced resolutions to remove abortion from the Criminal Code in 1969 and in 1970. "A fundamental freedom for every woman is the right to decide whether or not she shall bear a child," Grace proclaimed. "To compel her to do so is a crime against the woman, the child and society. It is intolerable that women of wealth can go to Japan, England and New York and secure a legal abortion, while women without means must face dangers of mutilation and death at the hands of an unskilled bungler."

Canadian abortions were archaic, Dr. Henry Morgentaler told the rally, emphasizing that more than a thousand Canadian women died annually after back alley abortions.

Grace warned they would get nowhere unless petitions demanding abortion law repeal were signed and presented to the government, a two-year process. Grace had been urging a letter-writing and petition campaign since 1967. Cries of "That's too late" and "We can't wait" from the protesters greeted this proposal. Carrying a black coffin memorializing Canadian women who had died from botched abortions, the demonstrators then marched to the Prime Minister's residence at 24 Sussex Drive to place the coffin on the front steps, decorated with a wreath and the instruments of quack abortionists.

On Monday Ellen Woodsworth and thirty-five other women dressed conservatively, placed thick locks and chains in their handbags, and were admitted to public galleries and the east and west members' galleries of the House of Commons. According to Hansard, some forged the signatures of MPs on passes to gain entry. The women stationed themselves at intervals overlooking the Commons and chained themselves to the chairs. One connected a microphone to the simultaneous translation system attached to each gallery chair. During question period they stood up one at a time and deliberately disrupted the proceedings, making speeches and shouting "We want abortion on demand." According to one demonstrator, "The MPs became increasingly disturbed. Shouting cries of 'whores,' and 'sluts,' some rushed up into the galleries and the Speaker was finally forced to adjourn parliament." Guards with bolt cutters released the women, and they were not charged. The House resumed its sitting forty-five minutes later.

Such a disturbance was unprecedented. The demonstrators had disrupted the House for less than an hour, but they had forced the country to sit up and take notice. As it happened, Grace was not in the House to witness this protest. She was on a fact-finding trip to Nova Scotia related to the Canada Water Act.

On June 14 Trudeau met with sixty-two members of the Vancouver Women's Liberation Front and promised to introduce an abortion repeal bill before June 26. His only condition—an absolute impossibility—was that the Opposition agree to pass the law to remove abortion from the Criminal Code in one day.

Grace and Greenwood MP Andrew Brewin secured NDP caucus consensus for participation in the one-day debate, but the caucus was by no means united behind abortion law repeal. MP John Burton of Regina East sent a letter to Trudeau distancing himself from MacInnis and Brewin. The one-day debate on abortion was never held. On June 25, Grace and Brewin received a letter from Trudeau informing them that the French Catholic Créditistes had refused to participate.

It was during this time that Grace began working more closely with Dr. Morgentaler, with whom she had renewed her acquaintance at the abortion caravan rally. He furnished her with examples of horrors caused by not repealing the abortion law equally as vivid as the worst cases paraded by the other side; she put these horror stories on record in the Commons.

Grace was fearless when it came to confronting angry opponents, and particularly courageous in defending the right of young people to dissent and to have opportunities to become productive members of society. She saw behind the long hair and wild clothes to the yearning within for a better world, as the Beatty Street Armoury incident in fall 1970 revealed.

The Trudeau government had made an effort to deal with the waves of young summertime travellers rolling across the country to the Pacific beaches. Federal government buildings were opened as hostels; in downtown Vancouver the Beatty Street Armoury adjacent to the bus depot was selected. After Labour Day, when government funding for hostels ran out, notice was given that the armoury hostel was closing. Grace received a copy of an apprehensive telegram to three cabinet members from the Metropolitan Council of the United Church of Canada. The church requested continued funding as there were still three hundred people living there and no sign that the number of transients in Vancouver was declining. Grace wired support of the church's request to the three ministers. They agreed to keep the hostel open for a limited time over the objections of Liberal MP Ray Perrault of Burnaby. Generally supportive of the hostel program, Perrault had been appalled when visiting the armoury unannounced to find men and women in bed together at noon and belongings strewn about. A red flag hung from the Vimy Ridge memorial; a clenched fist was drawn on one Maple Leaf flag and a hammer and sickle on another; the walls were emblazoned with images of North Vietnamese leader Ho Chi Minh.

The next day Grace walked right into the middle of a fight at the armoury. Long-haired youths were confronting a group of a hundred angry veterans and dockworkers demanding that they be evicted for desecrating the armoury and the memorial. Reporters and TV cameras were on the scene; another hundred people watched from across the street. Grace faced down the hostile crowd. The main question was "whether work could be found for the people in the hostel," she declared. "While one might be concerned with desecration of the flag, I'm more worried about the deterioration of our young people." She was loudly booed, but Grace stood her ground. "You can't bully me or frighten me," she said and called for the government to keep the armoury open until an alternative was found.

Vancouver was divided. Mayor Tom Campbell wanted the hostellers out. Trade union leaders dissociated themselves from the actions of the dockworkers. Grace received abusive phone calls and angry letters accusing her of political grandstanding. The cabinet moved the hostellers to the army base at Jericho Beach on the western outskirts of town. Their colourful costumes and flippant attitude drew open hostility from army families also housed on the base.

Grace defended the young people to comfortable suburbanites at the NDP Burnaby–Richmond–Delta constituency meeting September 29. "Today's young people . . . are a generation raised to be passive consumers of food, fashions, fun at a time when what the world needs desperately is active creators. What young people want and must have today is a chance to do their own thing. To give of themselves to the process of living on this earth, of pushing evolution a notch higher. If they can't get this chance, they and we are doomed," she proclaimed, showing a depth of understanding rare in sixty-five-year-old women of that era.

On October 3 the Jericho Beach hostel was closed. Through government and private charities rental housing was found for the 350 hostellers. On October 5, the day Parliament resumed after summer break, Grace asked what the government would do to employ these young people, but all at once the issue seemed irrelevant. On that day peaceful Canada was transformed into a country under siege. The government and all MPs had an incendiary crisis on their hands that would put Grace's courage to the test.

In Montreal on October 5 the British Trade Commissioner to the Province of Quebec, James Cross, was kidnapped by a cell of the Quebec nationalist revolutionary group Front de libération du Quebec. Two days later Prime Minister Trudeau closed the second session of the twenty-eighth Parliament, having passed, among other laws, the Canada Water Act and the Textile Labelling Act that bore the imprint of Grace's thinking.

On October 8, the Prime Minister formally opened the third session. His throne speech did not mention Quebec, but Quebec overwhelmed his thoughts, his heart and the attention of his government. That night External Affairs Minister Mitchell Sharp authorized the French CBC radio network to broadcast the entire FLQ Manifesto, one of the group's demands for the release of James Cross.

The FLQ Manifesto raged at "patronizing 'big bosses' and their henchmen who have made Quebec their hunting preserve for 'cheap labour' and 'unscrupulous exploitation'." Most of the issues raised in the diatribe were matters of money, jobs and anglophone control of the French economy, problems acknowledged by many Quebec residents. But the FLQ's method of change was not politics but violence.

Trudeau was furious that the broadcast had been allowed. His first concern was that there be no surrender to terrorist demands, no sign of weakness. The next day Sharp told the House that the FLQ demands could not be met.

On October 10 Quebec Justice Minister Jerome Choquette announced the province would not meet the FLQ demands, but the federal government would exchange safe conduct to a foreign country for the release of James Cross. Quebec Labour Minister Pierre Laporte listened to Choquette on the radio at home in the Montreal suburb of St. Lambert, then went outside for a pickup football game. A car screeched up and two armed men abruptly muscled the labour minister in.

Pierre Laporte was a friend of Trudeau's from Brébeuf school days. They had written together in the 1950s for the landmark magazine *Cité Libre*. In the language of the Quebec question Laporte and Trudeau were federalists, not nationalists. Four agonizing days of negotiations with the two FLQ cells holding Cross and Laporte failed. Frightened, Premier Robert Bourassa and Montreal Mayor Jean Drapeau pressured Trudeau for help. When Quebec's final deadline was ignored by the FLQ, the two governments of Quebec and Canada, often bitter antagonists, chose a common course of action. Trudeau could not yield to terrorist demands even to save his friend Laporte.

At 4:00 a.m. on October 16 the federal cabinet proclaimed the War Measures Act to meet the perceived threat of "apprehended insurrection." While invoked in both world wars, this act had never been used before in peacetime. Canadians, accustomed to civil liberties enjoyed by few peoples in the world, got a nasty jolt. Regulations accompanying the War Measures Act banned the FLQ and made attendance at an FLQ meeting a crime, much as the Communist Party had been banned in the past. Police were granted extraordinary powers of search, seizure and arrest. The Crown acquired powers of detention that, in the words of former justice of the BC Supreme Court, Thomas Berger, "effectively disposed of the right of habeas corpus as we know it." Prisoners could be held incommunicado, thus denied the right to legal counsel.

On national television October 16 Trudeau told the shocked country that he had taken this action to "root out the cancer of an armed, revolutionary movement." Only three reasons have ever been given publicly for this unprecedented use of the War Measures Act: two government officials, Cross and Laporte had been kidnapped; large amounts of dynamite had been stolen in Quebec; and premier Bourassa had requested rescue by "emergency powers." Yet, in Quebec and across the country, public and media support for Trudeau's move was overwhelming. In Berger's words, "To question the propriety of invoking the War Measures Act was to side with the kidnappers."

Grace was selected by the NDP caucus as one of four to speak to the issue, along with Douglas, Lewis and Brewin. On October 17 she told the Commons why, in her view, the War Measures Act should never have been invoked.

First, Grace objected, Parliament had been circumvented. She called for a complete briefing on the facts in a special closed meeting, with opportunity for debate since Parliament was already in session. "In my opinion this is just another example of this tendency to downgrade the authority of Parliament," she warned. Grace believed that the existing Criminal Code, perhaps with amendments, was powerful enough to handle the FLQ crisis without need for the War Measures Act.

She had many unanswered questions about the instant disappearance of civil liberties, especially as it applied to her own home town where, she told the Commons, "Not more than thirty-six hours after invoking the Act the mayor of my own city of Vancouver, a city where no one has yet heard of a state of insurrection existing, showed himself to be very eager to take action under the Act . . . . The fact is that he is running for election."

But no questions were being answered, Grace charged. "The only answer we got was that we must have faith in the Prime Minister. The Prime Minister is a fine man, an upstanding man, a lover of his country—Why cannot we rest our confidence there? I want to say that if the angel Gabriel appeared to me in person and asked me to turn over the functions of Parliament to him because he was a clean-living, fine angel, my answer would be, no. To do so would be to negate our very reason for being here as representatives of the people." That comment was quoted as far away as Australia.

She cautioned the House: "My memory goes back to days [of 1919] when I was a very young girl and Section 98 was placed on the statute books of this country . . . . It was before the House for two or three hours and received Royal Assent quickly; it was put through in a panic situation. People at that time—nobody believes it any more—believed firmly that we were in the midst of a red revolution on the banks of the Red River . . . . That section, section 98, was on the statute books of this country for seventeen long years."

She worried too that Trudeau could extend the powers he had under the War Measures Act beyond April 30, the date authority for the law was set to expire. "Once you move into the area of calling organizations illegal," Grace warned, "heaven alone knows where this will end."

Less than twelve hours later, at the St. Hubert Air Base near Montreal, a police bomb squad gingerly pried open the trunk of a green Chevrolet to find the corpse of Pierre Laporte.

The NDP caucus meeting that followed was "very dramatic," said federal NDP secretary Cliff Scotton, who attended. "It was a harrowing experience. I mean, people didn't say, I'll go for it or, I won't go for it. They agonized about it in a context which was terribly frightening. There was a lot of pressure. Grace would probably have less trouble in coming to a conclusion about it because of her sense of civil liberties, her whole understanding of what had happened to the Japanese Canadians and the Padlock Law in Quebec."

Panic stalked the land. Vast amounts of explosives were rumoured to be in FLQ hands. Parliament Hill was surrounded by armed forces. "You had Gallup polls saying that 87.9 percent of the Canadian people agreed with the removal of their civil liberties," Scotton said. "People are prepared to accept authority, even in a non-totalitarian state. But there were some people who you would not believe who wavered in favour of going along with it. I mean people who later turned out to be heroes of the occasion for having opposed it."

NDP MP Mark Rose was one of the waverers. Reliving that agonizing caucus meeting, he visualized how Grace had stood firm. "She was very big on principles—the principle of the thing. I was very contemptuous of principles, I said, 'I've got principles I haven't even used yet.' And I remember she just looked at me, and said, 'And probably never will.' But not in anger, almost in sorrow. I don't mind saying that I was wavering until the last minute, but I saw people stand up, such as Tommy and Grace, and I thought aw hell, if you can't even support your own people. Because we weren't sure about the issue, it was apprehended insurrection."

In the end only sixteen MPs, all NDP, voted nay. Mark Rose joined Grace in this group. Four NDP members voted with the government: Frank Howard, Barry Mather, Max Saltsman and Harold Winch. Lorne Nystrom explained that it was touch-and-go right down to the wire. "Two of the MPs notified the caucus that they couldn't go with us, and two changed their mind on the floor. There were two or three others who almost did. Going in we had eighteen, but we could have been down to eleven or twelve. On the floor pressure was so immense it is hard to describe."

The vote was taken during the day of October 19. That night Grace spoke in reply to the throne speech. She expressed deep sympathy for Madame Laporte and her family in their grief, and for all Quebec citizens "as they attempt to root out the cancer of violence and terrifying hatred which is threatening them and all Canadians." But then she addressed the underlying cause of the FLQ disruptions, which she believed to be the root cause of all social rebellions. "Terror does not flourish and cannot flourish in those countries where there is a fair and even sharing of the economic and social benefits available," she affirmed.

But a number of Grace's Quebec colleagues supported Trudeau's action. Frank Scott wrote, "A shock treatment was needed to restore the balance. It was given, and it worked. There was only one death and it was not caused by the forces of law and order." Nor was Thérèse Casgrain prepared to accept Grace's concept of civil liberties. "I can hear Thérèse now," Grace said, mimicking her friend, "Well, if you get your mailbox burnt up and your cabinet minister is shot, you too would be concerned about this."

On October 21, under "awesome" security, the Laporte funeral was held in Montreal with former Prime Ministers Diefenbaker and Pearson present, as well as Prime Minister Trudeau. That day Grace presented to the House the retraction of a statement made by NDP MP Andrew Brewin. Evidently Brewin had not intended for publication comments accusing Conservative MPs and the four New Democrats of reneging on their principles when they voted with the government on the War Measures Act.

Grace did not make that mistake. The rift with her father over pacifism had taught her that intimate colleagues could differ intensely on important questions of principle and still continue loving one another and working together, as long as each was convinced of the other's sincerity.

On November 2 the Trudeau government introduced a replacement for the War Measures Act, the Public Order (Temporary Measures) Act. Police would have to bring charges sooner, but the attorney general's consent was still needed for bail. Grace reluctantly voted for the alternative law in order to move it into committee where amendments to widen civil liberties could be made. "As Mr. Douglas said, our choice is not between this measure and a measure that we might prefer," she wrote to an Ottawa fan. "Our choice is between this measure and the War Measures Act. I have learned that a great many choices one has to make are not between good and bad, but between bad and worse."

Grace told the House November 12, "I say quite seriously that if you were to arrest every FLQ member in the province of Quebec tonight and were to apply capital punishment to them, there would be a fresh crop there tomorrow morning until and unless you get rid of the economic conditions which make it possible for these people to flourish. They flourish in an atmosphere of social insecurity and social despair." She noted trenchantly that in October thirty-eight percent of all Canada's unemployed lived in Quebec.

All this time British Trade Commissioner James Cross was still missing.

Then, on November 21, a letter from Cross with a photo of him sitting on a case of dynamite was received. This time negotiations produced the release of Cross on December 4 in exchange for the safe passage of seven people to Cuba.

The Public Order (Temporary Measures) Act expired on April 30, 1971, and was not renewed. In all police rounded up 497 people in Quebec. Only sixty-two were ever charged; of these eighteen were convicted. Just two of those convictions were for offences under the War Measures Act. Eventually two men were convicted and sentenced to life in prison for the murder of Laporte. Two more got prison terms for their parts in the Laporte kidnapping. Cross's kidnappers returned to Canada to plead guilty one by one during the late 1970s and early 1980s.

For her vote against the War Measures Act, Grace was subjected to a torrential wave of negative public sentiment. In answer to one critical constituent she wrote, "I can assure you that those of us who did so were not politicking. We knew perfectly well that our stand would be exceedingly unpopular across the country, and that many of our constituents would be deeply disturbed and indignant. We believe strongly that the FLQ and other terrorists must be rooted out like a deadly cancer. But we also believe that the unlimited power of the War Measures Act is far too dangerous to the civil liberties of the people of this country to be used if any other means are available . . . . I could not have voted otherwise. To have done so would have been to betray all the beliefs I cherish most and to have acted dishonestly with those I represent."

Inevitably, Christmas appeared on the horizon with the welcome opportunity for some fun. At the NDP Christmas party the MPs were invited to do skits and take-offs on other caucus members. Grace played the part of David Lewis costumed with heavy black-rimmed glasses and a floppy man's suit. For MPs Doug Rowland and David Orliffe, David portraying the bra-burning "feminist movement at its most outrageously noisy stage," Grace brought one of her old bras with a pack of matches tied to the strap. The terrible tension of the War Measures Act controversy having dissolved somewhat in merriment, the divided NDP caucus bound its wounds with laughter.

CHAPTER 16

Status—What Status?

Florence Bird and the Royal Commission on the Status of Women completed their three-and-a-half year, three million dollar study on September 28. Canadians had filed 468 briefs and over a thousand letters of opinion. The findings were printed and bound in one easy-to-read volume, ready for release. Eclipsed by the crisis in Quebec, however, the report remained on the shelf until December 7, when the Public Order (Temporary Measures) Act had been passed and the country had settled down somewhat.

In the interim Grace turned up the volume on women's issues. She introduced yet another bill to repeal the abortion section of the Criminal Code. In support of the proposed bill she circulated a private survey to her 263 male colleagues containing only one question: "Would you favour legislation at this session of Parliament to repeal those sections of the Criminal Code having to do with abortion?" Only seventy-seven bothered to respond. Of these forty said yes, thirty-five said no, and two were undecided. She had replies on both sides from all parties, but very few MPs signed their names. "They were scared to come out of the woodwork," she explained later. "It wasn't important in their lives . . . they got past the sniggering stage but they were at the stage where it [abortion] was still very much under wraps."

A federal Liberal policy convention in Ottawa in late November passed a resolution to remove abortion from the Criminal Code. The next day, Grace was on her feet in the House, urging the government to introduce such legislation. Slowly, the climate of public opinion was changing. Before Grace introduced her first abortion law reform bill in 1967, abortion was rarely if ever discussed in mixed company. By raising the issue in every imaginable public forum, Grace had not only helped to legitimize it as a topic of discussion, but had roused a considerable section of middle-class public opinion in support of decriminalizing the operation.

When the Report of the Royal Commission on the Status of Women was tabled December 7, Grace saw with satisfaction that all of her hard-fought points had been endorsed. Six of the 167 recommendations dealt with day care, including one for a federal-provincial cost-sharing agreement under a proposed national Day Care Act.

The report recommended the right to an abortion on "the sole request of any woman who has been pregnant twelve weeks or less," and abortion on request after twelve weeks, "if the doctor is convinced that continued pregnancy would endanger the physical or mental health of the woman, or if there is a substantial risk that if the child were born, it would be greatly handicapped, either mentally or physically."

Affirmative action programs were recommended for Crown corporations, the armed forces and the public service to foster greater balance of male and female personnel. The report said the Royal Canadian Mounted Police should be open to female enlistment. Changes to bring equality to tax and family allowance laws were recommended, as well as changes to the Unemployment Insurance Act. A long list of changes to federal and provincial laws governing equal pay, pensions, insurance, housing and education, including sex education, were recommended, all in accord with Grace's thoughts on these matters.

The "poverty of women" came as a shock to the RCSW, chairperson Bird recalled. The Commission's analysis of tax returns showed that women received only twenty percent of all income earned in Canada. Despite equal pay laws women were paid less than men even when employed at jobs of equal value and responsibility. "The fact is that nearly two-thirds of all welfare recipients are women," said Bird.

In line with Grace's insistence that half-day work was sensible for women with young families, the report recommended a further study on a greater use of part-time work in the Canadian economy. And, in line with Grace's bills on occupational training, the RCSW recommended that the federal law be amended so that "full-time household responsibility be equivalent to participation in the labour force in so far as eligibility for training allowances is concerned."

There were only two points on which Grace took issue with the findings of the report. First was the recommendation that two women from each province be summoned to the Senate as seats became vacant, and that women continue to be summoned until the numbers of men and women were closer to parity. The NDP wanted the Senate abolished. Besides, Grace saw this proposal as a token solution "inconsistent with the principle that women should have equal status, not special status." Second, she felt the report had failed to cover the special concerns of women between fifty and sixty-five years of age. Still, this historic document was the best tool she had ever possessed to pry additional rights for women from an all-too-often indifferent government.

Grace was disappointed and frustrated that Trudeau tabled the RCSW report without comment, thus effectively blocking debate on its contents. "When a three-million-dollar commission is brought to the House, the minister in charge usually makes some comments in order to open discussion on the subject. Mr. Trudeau didn't even bother," she observed. Grace tried to spark debate that day by asking Trudeau if he was ready to implement the recommendations on a national Day Care Act and to ease restrictions on abortion. He put her off; the cabinet needed more time for study. The next day she bounced up again. Would the Prime Minister consider designating one minister to handle implementing the recommendations? This time Trudeau was more forthcoming. A pending government reorganization bill would allow "great flexibility," and he would consider handing the job to one minister.

Grace did not believe the Prime Minister was particularly interested in advancing the status of Canadian women. "I think Mr. Trudeau believed that there were two rooms of a home which were suitable for women," she suggested cynically. "One was the kitchen and the other was the bedroom. In other words, I don't think he really understood the idea of equality in a practical way." Her greatest fear was that the Commission's report would be lost in the shuffle, and this seemed likely when the Davey Report on the Mass Media, tabled two days after the RCSW report, diverted the attention of MPs and the media. But Grace had one great advantage. The eyes of Canadian women were upon her, the sole woman in the House, and she lost no time creating a wave of public interest. She urged thirty-five of the largest women's groups to participate in a national write-in campaign that would inundate the Hill with mail. This tactic had worked in getting phosphates banned from detergents; Grace believed it would work again.

At a news conference in Ottawa December 11, Grace sent out a nation-wide appeal to women to flood the Prime Minister's office with "thousands and thousands and thousands" of letters and petitions. They were to focus on two simple issues, the designation of a single cabinet minister to get action on the recommendations and a national day care program. Tommy Douglas and Toronto MP John Gilbert flanked her at the news conference because, Grace said, "in the NDP we consider the status of women a matter of equal concern to men and women."

Thousands of letters did pour in to the Prime Minister's office over the next few months. The atmosphere of ridicule which had surrounded the commission in its early days had vanished. Within the NDP, Grace formed a Federal Caucus Committee on the Status of Women in Canada. In accord with her strategy of getting and keeping men involved in the fight for women's rights, she took the role of vice-chair, handing the position of chair to Andrew Brewin. By early 1971 the caucus had selected a list of fifty RCSW recommendations and approved a campaign to get them implemented. At the top of the list was a national Day Care Act.

Sometimes Grace's insistence on day care was misunderstood by people who thought she cared more for the free time of mothers that she did for the well-being of children. But Grace saw it was financial necessity that drove women with young children into the workplace. She knew that for them quality, affordable child care was essential, while at the same time she upheld the advantages of family nurture. "Having been brought up by a mother who believed that her first concern was to give care and attention to her six children, I have no doubt at all about the necessity of enabling mothers to spend a great deal of time with their children," she wrote to a woman who had heard her expound the virtues of day care on CBC radio. "I honestly believe that unless one can do some part time service outside the home—whether paid or not—one cannot be a whole person in the full sense of the word."

When the Commons reconvened early in 1971 Grace had an unexpected treat for her colleagues and the media. Over the holidays she had fitted herself with a silvery wig. She wore it like a helmet as she marched into the first sitting January 11.

Moments after the sitting commenced Grace adjusted her new curls and rose on a point of privilege concerning her allegation that the Commons Health committee, of which she was a member, was mishandling its study of a bill on product packaging. That, she told a Canadian Press writer, showed the men that she was "still the same old battle-axe" underneath. The House erupted with a round of desk-thumping approval. She assured everyone that her new hair was harmless. But a few seconds later Conservative MP Robert McCleave walked by wisecracking, "Hello, cool and sexy."

Instead of being overwhelmed by sexist remarks, Grace used the novelty of the wig to her advantage. She asked Acting Prime Minister Mitchell Sharp what the government was doing about designating a federal cabinet minister for women's affairs. Sharp joked, "I don't know whether anyone in cabinet wants to be responsible for women." Outside the Commons, he denied the RCSW report was a political hot potato in cabinet.

The centrepiece of the day came when Grace introduced a motion restating her personal definition of socialism. In fine Woodsworth style she moved that the government "abolish poverty by redistributing income and planning productive resources so that the wealth created by modern technology may provide a much more equal standard of living for Canadians . . . . We need a new ethic to bind us together if we are to keep Canada in one piece . . . . My resolution," she concluded, "embodies the absolutely essential first step to achieving a united country which will be of some use in bringing about a harmonious and united world."

At the parliamentary "late show" that night Grace hounded the government to remove abortion from the Criminal Code. The Canadian Medical

Association Journal, the Canadian Psychiatric Association, and the federal Liberals had all publicly declared they were in favour of repeal. When would the government act? A parliamentary secretary promised "a special debate on abortion to be held later this session."

A few days later the smooth flow of Commons business was again disrupted by the hairpiece. When Grace rose to ask a question of Transport Minister, Donald Jamieson, the House erupted with comments and catcalls. Jamieson said, "Mr. Speaker, I am going to have to insist that the delightful honourable member—" Another MP interjected, "Also irresistible." Jamieson: "—revert to her former status, because I cannot even hear what she is saying." Grace, in an unintended double entendre, replied, "I am not going to take it off to please you, but I will repeat my question." Some members chanted enthusiastically, "Take it off, take it off!" The Speaker ruled her question out of order and suggested Grace put the matter to the House at ten o'clock during the "late show." Jamieson, with mock gallantry, said, "Mr. Speaker, the best offer I have had today is to meet with the honourable member at ten o'clock."

Her colleagues razzed Grace unmercifully about her new hair, but she did not seem to mind or react to the comments as sexist. In fact, she enjoyed being the centre of attention. She had adopted the wig for practical reasons; her own hair was thinning, and she had lost patience with even the minimal amount of fussing demanded of her in the morning to keep it groomed. But she did not deny there were fringe benefits.

Yvonne Cocke, a friend and active BC party organizer, said she will never forget when Grace decided to wear the wig. "She had kept it in the boy's bob and never learned to deal with her hair," Cocke commented. "So when she decided that she wanted to change her appearance, it surprised everybody, but she bought a wig instead of letting her hair grow and getting a perm. And then, of course, made no bones about it. In the House of Commons it was quite the joke, but she almost preened herself with this new wig. It was not very typical of the way we all looked at her, as a no-nonsense kind of person."

Letters arrived with compliments and jokes on the wig. Grace replied to an Ontario man, "Thanks ever so much for your flattering comments about the wig. I certainly intend to follow your advice and keep my hair on!"

As the only female MP, Grace devoted all her free time to advocating laws to give effect to the RCSW recommendations. She spoke to business and professional groups, students, women's groups and political meetings. She told the McGill Alumni in February that the report "is not a feminine document, not a female document . . . but a human document . . . . Today more and more women want to be whole persons—the baby and the book, the life and the career, private life and public life."

There was no lack of inequities for Grace to address. For the 1971 census year the questionnaire declared the head of the household to be the husband. Grace caused an uproar in the House by complaining about this "antediluvian" statement. The 1971 census form was not changed but, by the time the 1981 census was taken, such designations were seen as sexist. As was often the case, Grace had anticipated a shift in public opinion and pushed it forward.

Prime Minister Trudeau was undergoing an apparent burst of interest in advancing the rights of women. At a Liberal fundraiser in Toronto March 3 his entire address reconsidered "the role of women in a modern community." "Would we, for example, be experiencing today the same threat of environmental pollution, which is largely attributable to a male-dominated technology?" he asked. "Would it have taken so very long for governments to have become aware of the need for extensive protection of the consumer?" In this speech Trudeau dismissed Grace's repeated demands for salaries for housewives, but he did support her initiative for family planning and promised federal–provincial co-operation on day care.

"I pledge the full support of the Liberal government to the removal of discrimination and the provision of opportunity to women in all fields of Canadian life," Trudeau declared. The following day the fifty-year-old Prime Minister married twenty-two-year-old Margaret Sinclair of North Vancouver, daughter of former Liberal cabinet minister James Sinclair. What Trudeau had ringingly pledged on the eve of his marriage was a range of opportunity for Canadian women that he refused his own wife. Margaret, a university graduate, was frustrated because her new husband would permit her neither to undertake post-graduate studies nor to hold a job. "He is an old-fashioned man when it comes to the position of women in the home, and he wanted me dependent on him," Margaret wrote in her autobiography, *Consequences.* After the 1974 election campaign she wrote: "Pierre was not interested in my mind, or my personality, or my maturation. What he wanted was a decorative child-making machine, a plastic wife to rear his children and decorate his home, a symbol, not a person." She complained that the millionaire Trudeau, "so loving and understanding in many ways, has one blind spot: he is mean about money." In an earlier book, *Beyond Reason,* Margaret revealed: "Pierre objects passionately to birth control, and had persuaded me to give up the pill within months of our meeting."

This, then, was the man who had the power to grant or deny all of Grace's earnest, ambitious plans for the advancement of women.

Five days after the Trudeau wedding, the House debated the RCSW report, a topic chosen by the NDP for opposition day debate. Grace urged a national day care act to allow women to become "fully rounded individuals . . . just as men have been able to do for a long time." About 32 percent of the Canadian paid labour force was composed of women, and of those 57.6

percent were married women, Grace told the House, outlining the enormous need for day care centres. "Not long ago the Minister of National Health and Welfare (Mr. Munro) estimated that in Canada more than nine hundred thousand children of working mothers might need day care, but only nine thousand are getting it in day care centres." She warned that the rest were at risk, and so were their mothers. Why did Canada lag so far behind England, Sweden, France and Denmark in the provision of day care? she asked. "I think that behind every objection is the expense."

But cost was certainly not the only factor. Men of all parties still felt as Conservative Saskatchewan MP Frederick Bigg did. A lawyer and former RCMP sergeant with three daughters, Bigg was frank in this debate. "Housewives generally are not classified as labourers," he began. "Their rewards are not in the form of money. They do not receive pensions . . . . They are dedicated women. They are the backbone of the nation." Then he scolded, "It may well be that if we got back to those basic principles, instead of whining about Women's Lib, we would be better off . . . . You cannot expect morality in school and hard work if your only reason for existence is have bigger and better abortions so you can spend more time in the beauty parlour."

Such opposition only seemed to strengthen Grace. A week later, she was on her feet again, pressing the government to designate one cabinet minister for the RCSW recommendations. Trudeau said he was "surprised at my suggestion that we downgrade the report to the level of one minister, adding: 'I say the full cabinet is concerned with it.'" "Having learned from my childhood that what is everybody's business is nobody's business," Grace noted acidly, "I was not impressed with this reply."

Two weeks later a debate on government reorganization gave her another chance. Women were becoming impatient, she warned. "Women are sick and tired of tolerant smiles and a superior look on the faces of government members." By the end of May she could chalk up a modest success. Trudeau handed the responsibility for the recommendations of the RCSW to Minister Without Portfolio Robert Andras. But Grace never let up the pressure to allow free and easy access to sex education and birth control information, especially for sexually active and mobile young women. She shocked the self-satisfied smiles right off the faces of government MPs a few weeks later when, in the Health and Welfare Committee, she urged that the locations of family planning clinics and sexually transmitted disease (then called venereal disease) treatment centres should be posted in washrooms, "in hotels, at airports, railway stations and gasoline stations." Her comments, as usual, received wide publicity.

In late May her unrelenting efforts were recognized by the university community, as Grace received the first of her eight honorary Doctor of Laws degrees from Brock University of St. Catharines, Ontario. Her convocation address to the graduates played on the themes closest to her heart, the urgent need to rescue a world at risk from overpopulation and pollution, and the prospect of building a world based on human, not materialistic values. Ever the optimist, in early July Grace spoke of progress to 1400 women from forty-nine countries and all walks of life at a conference of the International Federation of Business and Professional Women (IFBPW) in Edmonton. "I believe Canadian women are on the edge of making a real advance in politics, thanks to advancing technology, pioneer women in various fields, young folk who reject today's materialistic values, women's liberation, and innate common sense."

Across Canada that sultry summer of 1971 Grace spoke at national, regional and local conferences on family planning, parenting and child care, urging Canadians to express their views in writing to the government. As autumn approached she intensified her push for repeal of the abortion law. Trudeau had allowed one chink in his armour: in the throne speech he had promised a special debate on abortion. Now Grace demanded it.

On September 7, soon after the new sitting began, she insisted the government set a date for the debate. Prime Minister Trudeau replied that tax reform was top priority for this part of the session, and the debate would take place if there was time for it. She waited. Then one day during question period a few months later, she demanded the date again. "In view of the fact that last year 1,649 Canadian women went to the state of New York to have abortions performed, will the government now—" The honourable members convulsed with laughter. "As usual, Mr. Speaker," Grace fumed, "we get the snickers."

The following Friday at a high school in Dartmouth, Nova Scotia, Trudeau referred to the "upcoming debate on abortion." Grace was ready for him Monday morning, asking when. Trudeau said when there was time. Grace pushed her luck; she asked if Trudeau now planned abortion repeal legislation. She pushed too far. Trudeau growled, "No, Mr. Speaker; that is not what we said we would do in the Speech from the Throne to which the honourable member is constantly referring."

Not deterred, Grace popped up again that night. "Last year 1,649 Canadian women had to seek such help in New York State," she repeated. "I understand that forty-four percent of them were from the province of Quebec alone. It [the current law on abortion] is forcing uncounted other women to run from hospital to hospital in Canada trying desperately to find one that will help them." Pointing out Trudeau's hypocrisy, she noted, "Last Friday the Prime Minister told a high school class in Nova Scotia that women should be the ones to decide whether they should have the legal right to have an abortion if they want one. The young folk applauded loudly, quite unaware of the fact that the Prime Minister is unwilling even to have a debate on abortion in this House this session, as he promised a year ago."

Each year Grace spoke to the United Auto Workers (UAW) Leadership School headed by her old friend Alan Schroeder in Port Elgin, Ontario. There she was always greeted by the portrait of American socialist Eugene Debs which had hung in her father's office for years until she presented it to Schroeder in recognition of his work to drive communists from the UAW. In commenting to the UAW in 1971 on the theme of men and women growing into a liberated future "together," she criticized the "women's lib" approach to defining a new role for Canada's women as too one-sided.

This attitude placed Grace at odds with the new radical wave of feminists. Despite her work in Parliament for freedom of reproductive choice and other goals she had in common with the feminists, Grace could never go far enough to please them. It was a cultural and generational gap: many young feminists didn't trust anybody over thirty, certainly nobody who wanted to work hand-in-hand with men. Regardless, Grace pushed on alone in the House and successfully placed the issue of family planning in the spotlight. The government announced Canada's first government-sponsored national conference on family planning for February 1972.

Grace's position was strengthened by the public demonstrations of the Ontario Women's Abortion Law Repeal Coalition. Five hundred people gathered November 20 in Ottawa to show support for two private members' bills for abortion repeal, Grace's and that of Ontario Liberal MP Hylliard Chappell, chair of the Comparative Law section of the Canadian Bar Association. The demonstration gave her demands greater clout, and in turn Grace worked with the coalition to prepare its petition to Parliament.

Grace, almost alone among MPs, was speaking up for more than half the population of Canada. By the end of 1971 Canadians were asking Grace why there had been so little action on the recommendations in the Status of Women report. She urged her correspondents to pressure their MPs, and so many letters came in that Grace needed two secretaries. "We have noticed that, with the exception of yourself, there has seldom been a mention of the report," wrote the chair of the Canadian Federation of University Women's Committee on the Status of Women. "We wonder how many MPs actually have read the report or even a summary of its 167 recommendations."

If the Canadian government did not entirely appreciate Grace's efforts to implement the RCSW recommendations, women around the world did. In its December 1971 edition the distinguished Paris magazine *Marie-Claire* named Grace among "Les 50 Femmes les Plus Importantes du Monde," the fifty most important women in the world. The article listed three heads of government: Sirimavo Bandaranaike of Ceylon (now Sri Lanka), Indira Gandhi of India and Golda Meir of Israel. Quite a few elected legislators were included: Shirley Chisholm, the first black woman elected, in 1964, to the State of New York Assembly; US Senator Margaret Chase Smith; socialist Italian Senator Angelina Merlin and two members of the Swedish government, Minister of Disarmament Alva Myrdal and Minister of Family Planning Camilla Odhnoff. The radical Catholic feminist Bernadette Devlin, elected as an Irish deputy to Westminster in 1969, was listed. In other spheres, the list included *Washington Post* publisher Katharine Graham, celebrated feminist writer Betty Friedan, anthropologist Margaret Mead, cosmonaut Valentina Tereshkova and British Nobel Prize-winning chemist Dorothy Hodgkin. Grace, the only Canadian on the list, shone in that company.

The years 1970 and 1971 seemed to speed by in a blur of action. Grace's work on women's rights also stressed the needs of Canada's children and men; her work on behalf of consumers, especially of low income, was even more universal. While only half the population is female, everyone old enough to spend a penny for candy is a consumer. In Grace's eyes the basic issue was simplicity itself—large corporations, often foreign-owned, took advantage of their customers. Means of redressing the balance had to be found.

Parliament was at least paying lip service to an attempt to eradicate poverty in Canada. The Senate Commission on Poverty, set up in November 1968 and chaired by Senator David Croll, was midway through its public hearings. These gathered evidence, not from people living in poverty, but from federal and provincial government departments, professional agencies, and secular and religious community groups.

From her earliest days in Parliament, Grace and the NDP caucus had been working toward a prices review board with real power to control the cost of living that would include all forms of income—"prices, profits, salaries, professional fees, rents, wages, interest rates"—and regulate prices of basic goods and services. The Trudeau government created the Prices and Incomes Commission in May 1969, with a limited mandate: to gather facts that would persuade business and labour to voluntarily keep their demands within bounds to help slow down inflation. In Grace's view it was another toothless body, a screen for inaction, little better than the useless consumer council. She zeroed in on Dr. John Young, who had come from British Columbia to chair the commission.

Early in 1970 the commission invited 250 business leaders to what the government heralded as a conference on price stability. The business leaders announced they would raise prices less than they might have, if other sectors of society also showed restraint. "It should more correctly have been called a conference on profit maintenance," Grace declared in a February speech. "We have over and over again said that these reviews should be made in public . . . [but] this communiqué states that business has agreed to having these reviews made in secret." In her view, the taxpayers had a right to know how their money was being spent.

Business leaders were blaming organized labour for boosting prices with incessant wage demands, but labour had a protectress in Grace. "Organized labour has said it is willing to sit down and discuss an incomes policy, provided all forms of income are included in that discussion," she told the House. "But it is not prepared to be the whipping-boy of the government so that attacks can be made on wage increases gained by organized labour."

At a conference of the Religion Labour Council of Canada in Ottawa a few weeks later, Grace tangled with fellow panelist Dr. Young. When he claimed that the commission represented the interests of consumers, she snorted, "That is a big assumption." But she became even more indignant when Young said holding investigations in public would take too much time. "Surely we have reached the stage where democracy implies participation," she scolded.

In March, Dr. Young appeared before the Commons Health, Welfare and Social Affairs Committee to justify program expenditures of a million dollars. Grace patiently waited her turn and then pounced. First she demanded a target date by which price stability would be accomplished. Dr. Young provided all kinds of numbers, but no date. She asked for a list of community sectors from which the commission had obtained co-operation. Dr. Young was able to list only business and government.

What about the professional community? asked Grace. Doctors' average income had increased a third in the two-year period 1967–68. Consumer Affairs Minister Basford praised the commission for increased provincial vigilance against further increases in doctors' incomes. Grace was not satisfied. "They already are so far out of line . . . . Really what you are doing is freezing an inequitable situation," she complained. The usually cool economist raised his voice in anger at Grace's persistent assertions that he had known his policies would cause unemployment. But Grace cited a speech in Vancouver in which Dr. Young had said, "We knew that the burden of our policy would fall primarily and personally on the unemployed."

Young's insistence on holding secret inquiries seemed to Grace the most unfair part of the entire commission. In another committee hearing in early April she hammered away at Young's "star chamber" approach to investigating industry price increases. But she could not get him to conduct hearings publicly, take evidence from other sectors in addition to industry or allow the public to cross-examine industry on the price increases.

In October Young publicly called recent wage settlements of grocery store chains "excessive, unjustified and inflationary," and blamed organized labour for rising food prices. Liberal appointee Young had a poor relationship with organized labour, and the unions would not go along with voluntary wage restraints. Grace demanded Young issue a corrective statement. Saying that the Steinberg's chain did not raise prices after wage settlements, Grace went to bat for labour and for one of her customary adversaries, a major grocery chain. She told the Commons the firm "has lived up to the terms of the guidelines and in addition has enabled its employees to get a fair deal without harming the consumer." But the government would not demand a correction from Young.

When Young came before the Health and Welfare committee to justify his estimates in 1971, Grace aired her impatience with the commission's endless study. She wanted action to justify the commission's budget. She tried to prod Young toward replacing voluntary controls, which even he admitted had not been successful, with real controls on a selected few basic necessities of life. It was a testy session, and she did not succeed.

In July 1971, the Commission received a six-month extension of the deadline for its inquiry. By November the Ottawa *Citizen* reported that the Prices and Incomes Commission had spent $3,455,527 in the two years of its existence, making it the second costliest commission in Canadian history. Grace was on her feet in the House protesting this waste of public money and reminding an increasingly embarrassed government of the remorseless rise in the cost of living. But her protests were to no avail.

At last the Prices and Incomes Commission wound up its costly exercise on June 30, 1972, with ten reports still pending. The government was not obliged to make the final report public. A commission spokesman, who declined to be named, predicted: "Inasmuch as it contains a contingency plan for price and wage control, a strategy, if you like, it wouldn't make much sense to make it public. Then the people it affects could start taking action to circumvent it."

But to Grace it was the same old story of taxes wasted on studies not available to the taxpayers.

Grace was happier with the government for the Canada Co-operatives Association Bill introduced in 1970. It won approval from the co-operative movement and from Grace in her speech to the House. Flourishing co-operatives for producers and consumers were essential to Grace's vision of socialist economic justice. The Regina Manifesto had encouraged them; over the years Grace herself had written many a resolution, article, pamphlet and report championing co-ops.

Since the late 1960s the co-op movement had enjoyed a renaissance in North America. "Co-operatives are not ordinary business concerns in any sense of the term," Grace told the House in the debate on this bill. "Their motivation is not competition, it is co-operation . . . . Their purpose is not to make a profit for those people who engage in them. Their purpose is to provide goods and services at cost to their members. In addition, they have a whole different set of values. Their idea is that people develop and grow, and society develops and grows harmoniously and well, through people working together to achieve a purpose which is in the interests of all of them."

Grace told the MPs that this legislation would help people acquire valuable skills in directing their own affairs all the way from the local to the federal level. She noted, "the co-operative movement can become an even greater force than it is now in helping people become intelligent consumers." Such compliments from Grace on government legislation were rare indeed. Her speech earned letters of praise from across Canada written by people deeply involved in the co-op movement.

In December the government dropped an amendment to the Income Tax Act that would subject co-operatives to taxation similar to that imposed on competitive businesses. Grace was unusually laudatory in the House, but described her speech in a letter to Morden Lazarus, managing editor of the NDP's Co-operative Press Association, as "a love feast served with arsenic." Grace took some credit for pressuring the government to drop the threatening amendment, and protested irritably when her name was left off a list, published by the BC Co-operative Union, of MPs who had worked for special co-op legislation.

Grace argued for the protection of the consumer in the marketplace in every case—interest rate hikes on department store charge accounts, safety standards for toys, ingredients listed on baby foods, the high cost of prescription drugs, proliferation of junk mail advertising, wastefulness and hazard of non-returnable bottles and cans, textile care labels in garments—and against industry's convenience and profit-taking. Frequently she urged that low-income consumers themselves be included on decision-making panels. Consumers appreciated her ideas, but the government, caught as it was between the competing interests of corporations and consumers, reacted with annoyance.

Grace's fight for unit pricing of groceries gave rise to one of the most amusing incidents of her parliamentary career. When the government introduced the Consumer Packaging and Labelling Act in late 1970, no uniform laws required the listing of ingredients on food packages and no nationwide law required bilingual labelling. Canadians could have little or no idea of what they were actually purchasing in their packages of food, let alone the cost of each unit. But unit pricing was no new concept. The Consumers' Association of Canada was asking for unit pricing; the Steinberg's grocery chain had adopted the practice in the late 1960s; experiments with unit pricing were taking place in the United States.

Early in 1971 the Health, Welfare and Social Affairs Committee decided on detailed consideration of the act. Grace carefully laid her plan for the January 19 hearing, when she would have the opportunity to question executives of the Grocery Products Manufacturers of Canada. She enlisted the help of Les Benjamin from Winnipeg, the other NDP member of the committee. The freshman MP was an enthusiastic Grace MacInnis fan.

"Gracie was one of the most persistent people I've ever run into. When she was trying to get something accomplished she wouldn't take no for an answer. I sat with her in the health committee, when we were doing the Packaging and Labelling Act. I'll never forget. Grace phoned my office and instructed me, ordered me, to come and help her. So I went over there. And she'd got another MP and one of her staff and had us pick up a whole bunch of cardboard boxes and haul them over to the West Block for the committee meeting."

The first witness was the head of the Grocery Products Manufacturing Association. Grace emptied the boxes, Benjamin recalled. "She's got a grocery store sitting there. Three different sizes of bottles of ketchup, four different sizes of breakfast cereal." Grace asked the reason for fourteen- and nineteen-ounce cans. Why couldn't they be ten-, twenty- and thirty-ounce cans so consumers could calculate the price per ounce? The manufacturing representative said the cans had always been those sizes. Then Grace produced three different sized ketchup bottles and demanded that he work out the best price per ounce. He began his calculations on paper.

Benjamin said, "'No, no, no, no,' she says. 'Don't figure it. Don't write it down. Imagine that you're a mother dragging two squalling kids through the supermarket with a cart full of groceries, and she's trying to shop economically. Which one is the best price per ounce?' Turns out the middle-sized one is the best. But he didn't know the answer. And then when she got into breakfast cereals, it was funny! And the TV cameras could come in and take pictures of this crazy grocery store she had. She slaughtered them."

G.G.E. Steele, president of the Grocery Products Manufacturers of Canada, passed the buck to the retailers. "Mr. Basford cannot legislate for end retail prices. We cannot make such a recommendation as a manufacturers' association." But he acknowledged that unit pricing might be of benefit under some conditions. When she finally relinquished the floor, Grace was satisfied that her demonstration had made a strong case for unit pricing, but she did not hold her breath waiting for Basford to bring it in.

Two months after her grocery test, when the Consumer Packaging and Labelling Act came up for third reading in the House, Grace introduced a motion for unit pricing. "The consumer today is being bamboozled, deceived and completely bewildered by the juggling of prices and quantities," she said. She introduced additional motions to require that storage conditions and "best before" dates be printed on packages of perishables. But all of her amendments were defeated, and on March 24 the House unanimously passed the Act.

Most consumers respected Grace's work and enjoyed the entertaining manner she used to make her points, but there were always critics. A Toronto man called her grocery price test "absolute poppycock." As old-timers often did, he tried to use guilt to force Grace into his view of her proper role. "When I recall that famous picture of those dedicated few in the early '30s: Woodsworth,

Coldwell, Douglas, MacInnis . . . a picture that suggests supreme dedication almost saintliness, what a come down it is to read of one connected with that revered memory quibbling about the size or labelling of catsup bottles and soap boxes . . . . Size of catsup bottles?—it is to laugh."

Grace replied defensively, "I would suggest that the dedicated figures to whom you referred were also dedicated to trying to improve the day to day conditions of people in low income groups who needed champions in such matters as unemployment, health care, housing and all the other things that private business would not and could not provide."

Eight months after Grace's grocery test committee hearing Basford asked supermarket chains to voluntarily introduce unit pricing. Today unit pricing remains a voluntary practice in the grocery retail industry.

Precisely because unemployment was so high and poverty seemed inescapable for so many, consumer issues remained high on Grace's agenda during winter 1970 and spring 1971. As the early April thaw sent slushy snow and ice down the steep hillsides of the West Coast, Grace and Margaret Mitchell negotiated forty miles of treacherous mountain road to Squamish for a conference of BC's poor people.

Grace advised the conference to concentrate on one single achievable goal to present to government; she suggested a guaranteed income. The conference, conducted by political novices, was split by a fierce personal power struggle, but the three-day meeting did produce one resolution: that all low-income community groups in BC should work together for a "guaranteed flexible income, equal or above the poverty line set by the Economic Council of Canada."

One evening in Squamish they went to a pub for a beer. "Of course," Mitchell recalled much later, "most of the people had maybe money for one beer if that, so they weren't expecting to have a very heady night out. And Grace, of course, rarely took a drink. She'd probably take one just to appear to be one of the crowd but she certainly wasn't a drinker. But as we sat at these tables beer began to come from everywhere, great mounds of it, trays of glasses of beer came to the table, and people thought they were in heaven—all this free booze. I looked up, and I could see there were a lot of IWA members who recognized Grace, and of course to them she was quite a heroine, so it was really in recognition of her that they were sending all this free booze over to the table."

In those days Mitchell was a community development worker raising her two children on $1,970 a year. Now a four-term NDP MP, Mitchell credits Grace with getting her interested in politics. That trip to Squamish, Mitchell said, was "the beginnings of a friendship, but Grace was somewhat formal in a way. It was really once I got into politics that she became a mentor and a very good friend."

In late April 1971 more than 1600 NDP delegates gathered in Ottawa for a leadership convention that turned out to be the most acrimonious in recent memory. The party's beloved leader Tommy Douglas was retiring, and was honoured once more at a special banquet April 23; the House of Commons suspended its evening sitting to allow NDP MPs to attend. As soon as the speeches and toasts were over, the leadership battle, brewing for months, began in earnest. There had been only one real leadership fight in the previous history of the CCF and NDP, the 1961 contest in which Douglas easily bested Argue, less by ideology than by force of personality. The 1971 leadership fight was to be much more competitive, and would include both ideological and personality components.

The Waffle had not been idle during the two years since its rejection by a majority of delegates at the 1969 NDP convention in Winnipeg. Young 1960s revolutionaries and old CCF Marxian socialists saw their radical banner rise again. This coalition was not going to submit to the moderate party establishment without a fight. Waffle leader Mel Watkins had been elected an NDP party vice-president in 1969, and had continued his campaign to move the party in what he saw as a more socialist direction. As then NDP federal secretary Cliff Scotton put it, "To them, if you nationalized something, that meant you were a socialist. There's nothing inherent about public ownership, public control, that made it saint-like. But these people said the basic tenet of [socialist] belief is ownership of the means of production and distribution." Other central planks in the Waffle platform were Quebec self-determination and a Canada free from American economic and cultural domination.

Watkins and many other economists were seriously concerned about the effect of foreign investment in Canada. As Watkins wrote in 1971, "About two-thirds of our resource and primary manufacturing industries are controlled by foreigners and about three-fifths of our secondary manufacturing industry; of this foreign control about four-fifths is American . . . . To lose control of the economy is to lose control of the essence of our modern technological society." Watkins saw democratic socialism as Canada's only hope of standing against the US-dominated multinational corporations.

While many NDPers, including Grace, shared the Waffle goal of Canadian economic independence and more autonomy for Quebec, most did not endorse the Waffle's means of reaching these goals. Scotton said, "It was a question of degree, it was a question of speed." Grace was opposed to the Waffle movement because "It was being used by people who had never been good strong NDP supporters. Never. They wanted to make these things into big issues regardless of what the higher command in the party wanted or if that was wise. We weren't supportive of the way they wanted to do it and their strategy. They were young men in a hurry, if you will. And they wanted to go far faster and farther and in a different way. Our people are political and our people realize that you can't move any faster than people are prepared to go. The job of a political person is to judge what can be done in the climate and under the conditions that you've got to work with."

Ed Broadbent was the first to declare his candidacy for the leadership, but the front-runner was veteran David Lewis. Credited by most for his central role in bringing the NDP to birth a decade before, Lewis at sixty-one was seen by some as too old. He bore scars of the many bitter battles he had fought over the years to keep the party moving down his chosen track; each scar represented at least one adversary. He was by no means universally loved within the party. Lewis's main rival was Watkins's Waffle compatriot, James Laxer, an articulate young man with an aura of knowingness that appealed to many younger delegates. Frank Howard, a former IWA logger from northern BC, an MP since 1957 and one of the four who voted with the government on the War Measures Act, was also in the race. John Harney, former secretary of the Ontario NDP and fluently bilingual, rounded out the field.

Broadbent's biographer, Judy Steed, quoted one observer of this "horrible" 1971 leadership contest. "There was intense bitterness among the [leading] candidates, dirty dealings, backstabbing and a sort of psychological violence to it." Lewis finally emerged as leader, defeating his closest rival Laxer only after four agonizing ballots. Harney came third, Broadbent fourth. The party was by no means prepared to entrust its fortunes to Laxer, a man whom political historian Alan Whitehorn described as a "young and largely inexperienced Marxist-leaning Waffler." Whitehorn, commenting on this leadership election in his book *Canadian Socialism*, noted: "It is likely that a significant number of delegates voted not so much for Laxer or the Waffle (he got less than twenty-three percent of the vote on the first ballot) as against Lewis."

Because she rejected the Waffle completely, Grace's decision was between Lewis and Broadbent. "For various reasons I wasn't too happy about having Lewis as the leader at that stage because he'd been there—he was older. He had certain characteristics that I didn't like much. But he was a very able person. I made up my mind that I'd rather have him because he hadn't betrayed us on any of our policies at all, and in fact he'd been outspoken and very good. I made up my mind that I was going to vote for Lewis. And then we had the convention where we had this bearpit session with all the candidates having a little while to outline their own ideas. Here to my astonishment, when it came Broadbent's turn, he was trying to satisfy both sides. No, I thought, if you're that kind, I'm glad I'm backing Lewis. And Lewis was elected. Broadbent had his Waterloo over the Waffle at that convention.

"Well, it came the next session [of Parliament]. I saw Broadbent grow. He said very little. But he devoted himself specifically to two topics: the auto pact and housing. He made a thorough job of both. He knew what he was talking about and doing, and there was no more waffling, no more trying to catch favours from this side or the other side. By the time the next election for a leader rolled around, I voted for Broadbent. He recovered from that earlier mistake. He was trying to conciliate two groups that weren't able to be conciliated. The Waffle has disappeared."

Yet, despite her vote for Lewis, Grace had some serious problems with his leadership. For instance, "Lewis was inclined to interfere in provincial matters. In my case in Kingsway, he sent along a trade unionist who was going to show us how to run the campaign. Kingsway people were exceedingly able in running the campaigns. We made up our mind, there was no reason for falling out with Lewis. Let him come. He came along. Each of our people assumed his or her station in the committee room. The poor soul had not a thing to do but pace the pavement outside and hope that he'd meet people. Now, Lewis did that kind of thing . . . . Lewis enjoyed power, tremendously enjoyed power."

Besides the leadership contest, this 1971 NDP convention featured passage of a comprehensive resolution on gender equality. It included clauses on abortion law repeal and free-standing clinics in addition to hospital facilities for abortion. Many of Grace's other points were included: wages for homemakers, a national Child Care Act and a long list of measures to ensure equality in the workplace.

While she was the standard-bearer for women's equality in Parliament, Grace herself was the target of negative feelings from younger, more hard-core radical NDP women such as Hilda Thomas, a UBC English professor. She was at the leadership conference in Ottawa, but felt that none of the candidates represented her views. "In 1971, we started to organize a women's movement," she said, "a feminist movement in the party, because the fact is that the Waffle was just as chauvinist as every other structure in the party and a lot of women came very rapidly to see this."

From its opening in November 1988 Thomas was president of the Everywoman's Health Centre Society, the governing body of the Vancouver Abortion Clinic, the city's only free-standing abortion clinic. Her goals with regard to reproductive rights and freedoms matched Grace's, but there was friction between them. Thomas believed that Grace had inherited her husband's seat in the House, and this privileged position kept her out of touch with women without such an advantage. "There is a certain extent to which Grace was one of the boys," Thomas observed. "Because of her father and her husband, she had a place made for her in that largely male circle in the back room. That's not to say that she didn't constantly lend support around things that she felt strongly about, and the abortion issue was certainly one of those things. She was pro-choice. She didn't say abortion is evil or wicked or shameful or there should be limitations or restrictions. She also understood the solution is, in so far as there is one, is to prevent unwanted pregnancy."

It was close to the time of the 1971 federal convention that Grace was heckled by Waffle members and feminists during a speech at an Ottawa school. Elaine Bernard, later president of the BC NDP and currently executive director of the Trade Union Studies Program at Harvard University, was in the audience. Grace was advising compromise, this time with regard to feminist goals of more power and autonomy for women. "We have to cut a deal here. If we can't get the whole loaf, we must settle for half a loaf," Grace attempted. A Waffler shouted from the audience, "What if it's poisoned?" Grace was used to heckling by political opponents; now evidently some NDPers were in that category.

After the 1971 defeat of their candidate Laxer the Waffle did not vanish, but centred its efforts in the Ontario NDP. There it grew stronger. Vigorously opposed by the Ontario NDP leader, David's son Stephen Lewis, still the Waffle provided what one social historian called "a platform for labour malcontents of every political persuasion." During early 1972 the battle intensified until, as Grace put it, "It has reached the stage of being a party within a party, seeking to undermine and destroy both the democratically decided program and officers." In a letter to an Ontario Waffle supporter, Grace explained, "It is at this point that such an organization tears our Party to pieces and makes it ineffective . . . . If there is a party within the NDP which is so different in its objectives and methods from the NDP that it is continually attacking the Party, then I say quite decisively that such an organization out to be out on its own, building its own party with its own ideas and objectives."

Grace had formed her opinion as a result of her years of struggle with the communists, Trotskyists and the Socialist Fellowship. It would never change. In the end, following several bitter battles, the Waffle left the NDP to form the Movement for an Independent Socialist Canada. There were no electoral successes, but it served as an important example to would-be radicals in Canada.

December 6, 1971, was a red letter day for Grace—the fiftieth anniversary of J.S. Woodsworth's election to Parliament. Stanley Knowles, as his successor in Winnipeg North Centre, brought the occasion to the attention of the House. He asked for greetings to be sent to Lucy Woodsworth, now ninety-seven and still a resident of Saint-Vincent Hospital in Ottawa. The members responded with gratifying approval.

That same month Canadian editors voted Grace as the Most Newsworthy Woman in Public Affairs. When Christmas rolled around, her monthly "Report from Ottawa" was a classic piece of Grace MacInnis family prose. "Dear Friend," she wrote. "The approach of Christmas brings childhood memories of sending a letter up the chimney to Santa and feeling confident as we watched the flames licking the paper that our dearest wishes would come true on Christmas morning.

"Grown up wishes are much more difficult and it's harder to get Santa Claus to listen, particularly when he's having his ear bent by powerful business lobbies who want legislation to help them, and who, up to this point at least, appear to have the necessary muscle to get it.

"Those of us who represent plain people with families have no choice but to keep on trying to get more action on bread and butter needs like jobs, housing, pensions, day care centres, a guaranteed income and above all the right to be considered a full human being who wants to do his or her share if only the chance is made possible."

CHAPTER 17

For the Love of the Common People

G race's heart was touched by the letters that poured into her office asking
help in dealing with every conceivable area of life. No request was too
trivial, no part of Canada too remote from Vancouver–Kingsway to receive
Grace's personal and painstaking attention.

She earned a national reputation as "a universal mother-figure," despite
her childless life. Some called her "Mrs. Everywoman's MP." One retired
RCMP Staff Sergeant from Victoria dubbed her "Mrs. Parliament." She
replied, "I do not know that I can measure up to your title, Mrs. Parliament,
but it is certainly encouraging to get a letter like yours from time to time. It
makes one feel that our work down here is not all being done in a long dark
tunnel."

Correspondents would scrawl illegibly, enclose messy batches of grocery
receipts, address her as "Dear Sir," indicate that she was the MP for Richmond
or some other riding, and usually spell her name wrong, but they knew Grace
was someone who would take action on their behalf. Whether she could
count on their votes or not, Grace could not turn away from people with
problems. She could not bear to see the little incomes pinched still more, the
precious human lives eroded by the lack of a few dollars.

The Alberta man who had tipped her off to the underweight fudgsicles,
George Strong, kept up a correspondence with Grace until her retirement.
A veteran living in hospital, Strong prided himself on being a consumer
watchdog and sent numerous clippings and information about non-returnable bottles, misleading cigarette advertising, race track regulations and fad
diets. Each Easter and Christmas he sent Grace luxury chocolates, and over
the years he became a friend.

Grace gave her sincere attention to everyone who wrote, whether they
presented tiny irritations or life-shattering circumstances. She replied to even
the most lengthy and desperate requests with courteous, respectful advice
and was often able to interest a cabinet minister enough to get results. When

338

prisoners and their families complained to Grace that their letters to MPs were opened and censored by prison officials, Grace passed the complaints on in a forceful manner to then Solicitor General Jean Pierre Goyer. Soon after, partly due to her intervention, Goyer changed the rules to permit correspondence between federal prisoners and MPs to be delivered unopened.

A teenaged constituent wrote when his girlfriend's parents refused to let him see her because he was not Catholic. He wanted the national age of adulthood lowered to seventeen. Grace responded quickly and with respect. His note of thanks gave her a lift. "Your interest in the concerns of the 'little people' of this country has caused me to open my eyes somewhat."

Grace's own eyes were opened by some correspondents, like the sixty-year-old South Burnaby pensioner who was physically handicapped and blind. She asked Grace to work for a boost in the handicapped pension. "My basic pension is seventy-five dollars per month while the OAP is eighty dollars. I could do a lot with that extra five dollars. We are a minority group and therefore get no hearing from any of the government parties," she wrote. Grace could not promise any improvement, but she replied, "Letters like yours make me feel more determined than ever to continue to push for justice—especially for people who are in such a helpless position as yourself." A middle-aged constituent wrote for help in finding affordable housing for his family, as one landlord after another raised the rent beyond the reach of his modest earnings. A British World War Two veteran, he hoped to buy a small home. Grace wrote five cabinet ministers on his behalf, and advised him to contact the owner of a large Vancouver real estate firm. When the real estate executive personally found him a place, the grateful man wrote Grace that her "prompt and positive action . . . surely has amended my feeling toward members of parliament."

Her compassion for US draft dodgers and deserters evading Vietnam service by entering Canada was made crystal clear to correspondents. One Ontario man complained that a Toronto citizens' group was mailing into the US information on how to immigrate to Canada, together with quotes from Prime Minister Trudeau about admitting draft dodgers and deserters to the country. She dictated a curt but courteous reply, "I believe that most Canadians value our British tradition of providing a haven for people who are being persecuted for religious, political and social convictions. I regret exceedingly that material such as you enclosed should be put to the purpose of trying to stir up Canadian citizens to oppose young men who recognize that war today is futile and completely degrading to the human spirit."

Regardless of ethnic or national origin of a frustrated applicant to enter Canada, Grace extended help if she could. A widowed constituent with a crippled son wanted to bring her sister-in-law from Hong Kong to care for the boy so she could hold her bank job. She appealed to Grace when she feared the application would be refused. Grace contacted a Vancouver immigration official and replied kindly to the distraught woman, "I realize that you have already been to the Immigration Department. But there are officials and officials, and also it helps for a member of Parliament to show an interest in a case."

Early in 1972 it was evident that the generous mandate Canadians had granted Trudeau in 1968 had eroded. Dissatisfaction was rife, especially on cost-of-living issues, and election date speculation was building. At her Vancouver–Kingsway nominating meeting January 31, 1972, Grace was again chosen by acclamation. This solid show of support boosted her spirits as nothing else could.

She learned that Harold Winch, suffering the effects of ill health, would not stand for re-election. For everyone who had known and worked with him during the more than thirty-eight years he had represented Vancouver East federally and provincially, Harold Winch's retirement was the passing of an era in Canadian socialism. There had been a Winch at the very centre of socialist activity in British Columbia since Harold's father Ernie was elected to the Legislature in 1933. When they were young socialists together in the 1930s and 1940s, Harold undoubtedly held more radical opinions than Grace. But by the time he retired, that was reversed. He voted with the Trudeau government on the War Measures Act, while Grace opposed it. Winch told a reporter upon retirement: "We are in a very difficult position because emotionally and psychologically we are fast heading into a permissive society which is becoming anarchy and not democracy . . . . What I see developing today is a divergence from an understanding of social conscious-ness and responsibility to individualism and irresponsibility." Winch said in the same interview that he would not favour legalizing marijuana and LSD. Grace was in favour of legalizing and taxing marijuana, though not LSD, a sharply more permissive attitude than Winch's.

This man, who had been radicalized by police action at a demonstration in 1930s, now spoke against demonstrations. "There's a psychosis of demon-strationitis," Winch opined. "Sometimes it is worthwhile and responsible, but in the majority of cases it is not." Grace, on the other hand, repeatedly encouraged citizens to demonstrate peacefully so that the pressure of public opinion could be brought to bear on a reluctant government. She spoke at many a demonstration, always from a handful of notes rather than a prepared speech, as she enjoyed the spontaneity of the moment when she could expand on her theme.

About the women's liberation movement Winch would only say, "I don't think they should take it to extremes. I think women are doing pretty well in our society. There are still some things to be overcome, like equal pay." Grace, knowing from experience how far women had to go, was far more radical on women's rights than her old friend.

A federal election was on the horizon, but first Parliament reconvened in Ottawa. When the members returned to the ice-bound capital, Prime Minister Trudeau ended the third session of the twenty-eighth Parliament, the longest session in Canadian history, lasting 496 days from October 8, 1970, to February 16, 1972. The next day he opened a new session with a freshly shuffled cabinet on deck.

The throne speech promised to combat social isolation and create jobs by co-operating with business and industry. Yet the government intended to reintroduce a stiff competition bill governing price fixing and monopolies bucked by business in the last session. Promises of development for resource and energy industries, price supports for wheat farmers, a new Canada Labour Code, and "policies to ensure the equality of women" were included, as well as a new social insurance arrangement, the Family Income Security Plan (FISP).

Predictably, Grace's speech in reply was disapproving. She pictured Trudeau taking refuge from the dual monsters of unemployment and inflation by soaring above all domestic matters to assume the heroic posture of Horatius on the International Bridge, a charming millionaire hero of world affairs sublimely ignoring the misery of the one Canadian in every five living below the poverty line beneath his feet. The government's plans for income security did not impress Grace. She called it "doubletalk where a means test is dignified by the title of 'guaranteed income.' What we need," she insisted, "is a genuine guaranteed income coupled with a genuine guaranteed opportunity for useful work."

But her speech was not unrelieved censure. She endorsed the Opportunities for Youth program introduced the previous summer to fund projects initiated by young people. And a compliment went to Ron Basford, now minister for urban affairs, on the government's decision to block a Four Seasons Hotel development at the entrance to Stanley Park. Grace had worked to foil the plan with a coalition of Vancouver groups including radical young people who occupied the land as a "people's park" and more conventional NDP, civic and labour organizations. She had made their objections clear to the federal government, which then decided to kill the development.

In this speech Grace gave notice that food would be her future point of focus. She pleaded that the government find ways to help "the undernourished elderly people who fill the garrets and basements of our cities and have to exist on tea, toast and cat food in far too many cases." She assured the House her concern was "based on the many personal interviews, telephone calls and letters that I have had with my constituents and many others across Canada during recent weeks and months."

At the end of February Grace introduced four private member's bills, all covering her perpetual interests: the repeal of abortion from the Criminal Code; an amendment to the Adult Occupational Training Bill to permit housewives to qualify for training allowances; a bill requiring listing of phosphate content on detergent packages; and her Human Rights Code.

Her next big battle was in March against the Trudeau government's Family Income Support Programme (FISP). The plan was to take family allowances away from about one million middle- and upper-income mothers for redistribution as increased payments to lower-income mothers. The intent of the bill was clearly to help the people Grace always said deserved help the most, those who had least. But it was drafted with a means test, which destroyed the principle of universality, one of Grace's cherished principles. In opposing the FISP plan Grace fought for two of her most crucial issues at once, the advancement of women and the escalating cost of living. She attacked in the FISP debate on March 27. The universal distribution of pension and allowance cheques must be combined with taxation to recover funds from the wealthy because, she declared, "It is simple, it is uncomplicated, it is fair and it works."

To Grace a universal benefits system meant freedom, independence and human dignity for Canadians. She knew the vast majority did not abuse the system. "Over the years there has been practically no case of cheating or dishonesty," she told the House. "I know this is a fact because each year we question the officials before the Health and Welfare committee and this is what they tell us." Grace begged Health Minister John Munro to allow Canada's mothers to keep the "small badge of status" family allowance cheques conferred. Most important, Grace wanted to communicate the very real need that existed among women of all classes for these tiny cheques, less than ten dollars a month per child. "Many of them . . . have had to use these allowances for urgent things such as food, clothing and rent," she attested. "A great many mothers in the low and middle income groups have, by sacrifice, set aside the whole or a part of the family allowance cheque to pay for the educating of their children . . . . For far too many women of either the high or low income group, the family allowance cheque has been the only source of ready cash which they could call their own."

When the bill came back from committee for second reading, Grace objected even more strongly. "We are told there is no money for family allowances. But we hear estimates of up to ten billion dollars for the Mackenzie Valley pipeline and ten billion dollars for the James Bay hydro . . . . There is plenty of money for pipelines and things like that, but no money for people." She charged that only two of the 167 recommendations of the Royal Commission on the Status of Women had been implemented in the seventeen months since the report was tabled. She reminded the MPs of her proposal of government-funded salaries for mothers. "The government would not go for that," she cried. "The government is not satisfied with insulting women . . . it is prepared to snatch away the only bit of money that is paid directly to women . . . . This is not a war on poverty that the government is conducting; it is a war on women. It is a war against the family." She wound up with a stern warning. "One million angry mothers represent trouble for the government . . . . What the government is trying to do is dangerous . . . for the homes of this country and dangerous for the government, if it wants to survive."

This much the government now recognized. Liberal members' offices had been flooded with irate calls and letters from middle-class women distressed at the prospect of losing their family allowance cheques. In view of an impending election, the government could not afford to alienate so many women. While over half of Canadian families would have received an increase in benefits under FISP, seventeen percent would have faced a reduction and fully thirty percent would have lost their allowances completely.

The bill came up for final reading in July 1972, on the last day before the summer recess. As the sitting had extended past 4:00 p.m., unanimous consent was required to continue. Unanimity was denied by Paul Hellyer, now an independent MP but a former leadership candidate for the federal Liberals in 1968 who later joined the Tories.

During the 1972 election campaign, voters made their opposition to the FISP legislation unmistakable. Shortly after the election the minority Trudeau government brought in a plan directly in line with Grace's thinking. They tripled family allowance benefits and retained universality while making the benefits taxable. Universal family allowances were finally abolished by the Conservative government of Prime Minister Brian Mulroney. An income-based child benefit, not unlike the earlier FISP proposal, was passed by Parliament and came into effect in 1993.

In spring 1972 US President Richard Nixon came to Ottawa for talks with the Prime Minister. In this pre-Watergate year Vietnam was in the forefront of Grace's thoughts. She asked in the House, "In view of the recent bombing of Haiphong and other events escalating the war in Vietnam, was there any discussion . . . of the use of the war in Vietnam and the possibility of bringing it to a conclusion quickly?" Trudeau replied only "that he was committed to a policy of a negotiated settlement in Vietnam with continued withdrawal of US troops."

Canada's part in the Vietnam conflict was damaging to the Trudeau government in the eyes of some voters. But Trudeau was not about to change Canada's long-standing defence production sharing arrangements with the US as Grace and others were demanding. The Prime Minister's Office replied to written protests with a form letter saying, "It is not entirely accurate to state that Canadian military equipment is being supplied to the United States designated specifically for use in Vietnam, although some of it is undoubtedly being used there."

Grace repeatedly attempted to highlight the government's complicity with the US in this conflict that was not officially a war by requesting that the government table the report of Dr. Alje Vennema, head of Canadian medical services in South Vietnam from 1964 to 1968. She was turned down in March 1972 but renewed her requests in June after Dr. Vennema published an article about the suppression of his attempts to expose the use of napalm and poison gas by the US. Grace wanted to impress upon the MPs that Canadian personnel in Vietnam were engaged in a futile exercise of "caring for the victims while helping to cause the casualties." Grace never did obtain the Vennema Report, but the Trudeau government's support for the US in Vietnam lost it a substantial number of voters who hoped an NDP government would deal with this conflict differently.

In mid-March 1972 a cross-country conference on abortion was held in Winnipeg to generate public support for abortion law repeal. Grace and Laura Sabia, now chair of the National Ad Hoc Action Committee on the Status of Women in Canada, co-signed the fundraising letter. Unable to attend, Grace sent greetings. In them she noted a recent New Jersey court ruling that the state law allowing abortion only to save the mother's life was unconstitutional, as it violated a woman's right to privacy. Grace told the delegates, "Things are moving . . . . Join forces with birth control groups who share our belief that every child should be a wanted child."

In May the BC Women's Abortion Law Repeal Coalition took a petition bearing fifteen thousand signatures to Ottawa, to join similar petitions of groups from across Canada. The signatures were presented to the government in support of the bills of Grace and Hylliard Chappell (L–Peel South) for repeal. The petitioners could not have known that personally Pierre Trudeau was absolutely opposed to birth control, let alone abortion, as his wife Margaret later revealed. Did personal attitudes influence his handling of the abortion repeal movement? Almost certainly, but there was another crucial reason why Trudeau shied away from the question and held off the promised debate. Facing an election, he could not antagonize his largely Catholic caucus by forcing them to defend a policy that was not openly popular in most Quebec ridings. Repeal was out of the question.

Still, Grace knew there was "a long, slow battle going on in the minds of people everywhere on this issue," and she kept up pressure in the House. Media recognition was some compensation for government inaction. The May 1972 issue of *Chatelaine* magazine picked fourteen key MPs and rated them based on their motivation to act on women's concerns. Only five, including Grace and Stanley Knowles, were given the honour of the title "Today" MP; the others were "Out of Touch" or "Yesterday" MPs.

The warm spring afternoon of May 4, 1972, marked nearly five years to the day from that May afternoon in 1967 when Grace had introduced Canada's first abortion bill. It was more than five years since the Royal

Commission on the Status of Women had been struck; an election was now in the offing. The Trudeau government, eager to attract women to the Liberal fold, was busily buffing its image. From her seat in the NDP corner Grace listened to Bryce Mackasey, the minister responsible, praise the government's response to the RCSW recommendations. He listed Liberal accomplishments: new jobs for women in four ministries as consultants on dealing with women; a family planning division in the Ministry of Health to co-ordinate federal–provincial programs; ninety new day care centres created under the Local Initiatives Program (LIP); child care allowances now a deductible expense for tax purposes; better occupational training allowances for women; an equal employment opportunity office for the Public Service; maternity leave provisions in the Unemployment Insurance Act. Each measure was one Grace had goaded the government to implement. To her the list seemed pitifully short.

Replying to Mackasey, she began to chide the government for moving so slowly. "Some pious hopes have been expressed about how the government intends to encourage the appointment of more women to senior posts in the public service," she commenced. The background chatter began to rise. "However," Grace continued, "apart from token positions where women have been so outstanding that they could not be ignored, these hopes have not been anything more than expressed." The conversational din grew louder.

Exasperated, Grace said, "One of my colleagues has just made the rather regrettable suggestion that even at this stage there are many members— 'MCPs' they might be called—not paying the attention they might at this time. On behalf of the women of Canada, I ask them to listen." Some honourable members called, "Explain 'MCPs'." Grace retorted, "I will not compete with the Prime Minister in that department. As far as the major recommendations of the Royal Commission on the Status of Women are concerned, there has been no action or only microscopic action taken to this point." In French she rebuked a Créditiste MP for talking instead of listening. "I am afraid the government has laboured mightily in its mountain of red tape," she concluded, "and given birth to a very small mouse indeed compared with what is necessary. Women are grateful for what they have got but, like Oliver Twist, they intend to keep on asking for more."

A press scrum greeted Grace as she emerged from the chamber. Reporters clamoured to know what she meant by MCPs. One challenged, "You called them male chauvinist pigs, didn't you?" Then Grace had a sudden brain wave. "You said that, I didn't," she shot back. "MCPs could mean Members of the Canadian Parliament." The reporters were silenced. She called it her one moment of triumph in Ottawa.

The next day Charles Lynch wrote, "If he [Mackasey] had been born a woman, he wouldn't have become a cabinet minister . . . or the great blarney artist that he is as minister of woman power. He had an all male audience

Grace, wearing her wig and sensible shoes, canvasses the issues with voters at Kingsway and Knight streets in Vancouver during her last parliamentary campaign. September 1972.

The consumers' champion compares produce prices during the early days of the Food Prices Review Board. Vancouver, 1973.

The five women elected to Parliament in 1972, framed by stone arches along the gallery overlooking the foyer of the House of Commons. From left: Flora MacDonald, Grace, Jeanne Sauvé, Albanie Morin, Monique Bégin. Ottawa, April 1973.

for his performance on Thursday except for Mrs. Grace MacInnis, our only female MP, who was applauded by all sides of the House for the sole reason that she is a woman." But Lynch did not mention the MCP remark.

Eric Downton of the *Vancouver Sun* Ottawa bureau was not so circumspect. He opened with: "Members of Parliament were called Male Chauvinist Pigs Thursday by the only woman in the Commons." Grace had left for Vancouver by the time Downton called her office; he quoted Grace's secretary, Betty Irwin, as saying, "she had 'definitely meant' Male Chauvinist Pigs when she used the letters MCP." But was he in error there, as he was in his next sentence? "The taunt was not reported by Hansard, the official record of House proceedings." In fact, the entire exchange is found in Hansard.

Grace loved telling this MCPs story and told it to most interviewers. She acknowledged that the current popular phrase "male chauvinist pigs" had been the first meaning of her double entendre, but she never really explained the reference to Prime Minister Trudeau. We can speculate that she referred to him as the prime example of an MCP in both senses.

As Parliament rose for summer recess, Grace could take pleasure in one real accomplishment. The government accepted her amendment to the Adult Occupational Training Act of 1967 defining housekeeping as bona fide employment. This allowed women employed in the home to qualify for all forms of employment training assistance.

Grace returned to Vancouver to campaign for the NDP simultaneously on two levels, federal and provincial. A BC provincial election was gearing up for August 30. NDP Leader Dave Barrett, a former social worker with a genial, informal style, created a fresh image for the NDP as the party that cared. From the new BC Status of Women Council Rosemary Brown was nominated as an NDP candidate. Alex Macdonald was in the race, as were Bob Williams, Dave Stupich, Dennis Cocke and other strong NDP candidates who had survived the disastrous 1969 BC contest.

Although Grace had urged a single cabinet minister be appointed to deal with the RCSW report, she blasted the notion of a provincial women's ministry proposed by a group of Vancouver NDP women. "To segregate us into a Women's Ministry I feel would be wrong," she wrote. "It would be like giving women a crying towel and we don't need that. We need to face these social injustices head on and not hide behind anything." Sounding remarkably like Trudeau holding off her demand for a single cabinet minister, Grace argued, "There are ministries now established. We should utilize them and make them consider new ideas to integrate women into all fields."

Despite all her high-intensity work since entering Parliament, Grace had not suffered with arthritis, except for some pain and weakness in her hands. But at the end of July her right knee, one of the joints most affected earlier, had become inflamed. Some friends recommended an acupuncturist in her neighbourhood, Dr. Kok Yuen Leung of the North American College of Acupuncture. Born to a Chinese medical family and practising since 1941, Dr. Leung had been president of the Chinese Acupuncture Institute of Hong Kong for more than a decade when he came to Vancouver. Dr. Leung had a lengthy waiting list, but because Grace was afraid her campaign plans would be curtailed by arthritis, he fitted her in for fifteen acupuncture treatments over six weeks. Dr. Leung made no extravagant claims for the efficacy of his treatment, but Grace felt she did improve.

While undergoing acupuncture in late August, Grace was canvassing BC by car, bus and plane. The provincial NDP conducted a vigorous campaign, but after an unbroken string of election losses since 1933 few dared to believe the party could win. On election night old-timers like Grace refused to get excited until the final returns were in. But then euphoria reigned. Thirty-eight ridings went NDP, Social Credit took ten, Liberals five, and Conservatives two. Grace watched the returns in Ottawa, where the Trudeau government had recalled MPs for dissolution of the twenty-eighth Parliament. She wrote Premier-Elect Dave Barrett a delighted note of congratulation: "Although you have now become as inaccessible as Mars or Jupiter, it's fun following you and Shirley through the media." Fun was at a premium now; the federal election date was set for October 30.

Back home in mid-September, Grace hosted a meeting of core campaign workers at her apartment. Roy Cummings, newly elected MLA in Vancouver–Little Mountain, was campaign manager; Dennis Mulroney was back on sign detail. They printed twenty-five thousand leaflets with the slogan "? Food Prices Too High ?—Vote Grace MacInnis." At NDP rallies and all-candidates meetings Grace made key points of the urgent needs: a federal probe of high food prices, a prices review board with teeth, government-funded food aid for low-income people, government help for single parents with housing, health care, income support and child care. And she assured people that the unions would accept wage controls, "if such controls include controls on prices, profit, interest, rent, wages, salaries and any other form of income."

A very hot campaign issue for Grace was Canada's involvement in the Vietnam conflict. Newspapers during the campaign ran headlines such as "$458 Million Awarded Firms Making War Parts." Speaking to a conference sponsored by the Vietnam Action Committee she promised that an NDP government would cancel defence sharing agreements with the US. "The US will not pull out of the war," she said, "because it is necessary for the manufacturers of weaponry and munitions, and if it did there would be a revolution from the corporate welfare bums they keep down south of the border as well as the ones we have up here." This condemnation of the armament makers echoed her 1937 pronouncements in *Canada Through CCF Glasses.*

The climax of the campaign for Grace came when she appeared in Victoria with David Lewis and Tommy Douglas to a standing ovation of a thousand loyal NDPers. The piano rang the chords of "O Canada"; no more embarrassing renditions of "The Red Flag" or "God Save the King" as in the past. Douglas spoke first, reminding Grace of their years with the first federal CCF caucus in 1935, he as an MP and she as caucus secretary, and how people had mocked their youthful idealism. Grace stressed the urgency of electing an NDP government to assure social justice for Canada's common people. Finally Lewis gave his "corporate welfare bums" speech that across the country was drawing the kind of media and public attention usually reserved for the Liberals and Conservatives. In a historic breakthrough, the NDP now held power in three provinces under premiers Dave Barrett in BC, Ed Schreyer in Manitoba and Alan Blakeney in Saskatchewan. The future looked promising.

Election night brought a stunning personal victory for Grace. She won by a margin of 11,356, forcing all the other candidates to forfeit their deposits. Characteristically, she credited her campaign team. "My one boast is thanks to the committee that I had, their hard work and intelligent work, we managed in that final election to take every single poll in the riding. That was unparalleled! I could have been elected again I know, but I had to stand down because of the arthritis." But for the moment, Grace held the demon arthritis at bay, and retirement was the last thing on her mind as she accepted a victory kiss from Barrett, BC's first NDP premier.

Nationally, the NDP under Lewis's leadership captured a record 31 seats. Trudeau's Liberals slipped to a minority position with 109 seats to 107 for Stanfield's Tories, and 15 for the Créditistes. The NDP held the balance of power. Four other women would join Grace in the green chamber. Perhaps at last, Grace, thought, she might accomplish her long-term goals: a national day care system, repeal of the abortion law and control of the cost of living.

In November *Canadian Magazine* ran an article on acupuncture that mentioned how Grace had used it to control arthritis, and she received a flood of letters from arthritis sufferers who were eager to obtain help too. Grace had contacted the new BC health minister, Dennis Cocke, about legalizing acupuncture. Cocke appointed a committee of doctors to investigate, and invited a Chinese acupuncturist to demonstrate, teach and set standards for the ancient healing art in BC. But in December, before the evaluation could be completed, pressure from the medical establishment caused Dr. Leung to close his clinic and move it to Seattle. Grace was angry at the medical profession for blocking the treatments she needed in their fear that acupuncturists "might provide stiff competition to the regular doctors." There was a surge of public interest in acupuncture, but it was too weak to force legalization in time for Grace to continue her treatments.

Right after the federal election, Grace travelled to Toronto for two days of NDP meetings, then to Ottawa, then finally, exhausted with pain, she headed home. There she collided again with the provincial NDP's left wing. The newly formed NDP Vancouver Area Council had decided to field candidates in the December 13 Vancouver civic election. A faction within the provincial NDP wanted to run a joint slate with a civic left-wing party, Committee of Progressive Electors (COPE). At a Vancouver Area Council meeting in early November, Grace was adamant that no coalition should take place. "We've got a policy for civic government," she told them. "Let us go ahead!"

Hilda Thomas was one of those in favour of the joint slate with COPE. "It was absolutely squashed by the provincial executive with Grace as one of those most actively opposed. I think it had something to do with the players," Thomas speculated. "As far as she was concerned, we were left-wing nuts. We were feminists. We were not any of the things we were accused of being, but we were routinely accused of being Trotskies, CPers, you name it." Thomas saw Grace's position as imperious and dictatorial. "She was one of the people on the executive at that time who absolutely forbade us to go into any kind of alliance with COPE."

At home Grace's telephone rang from early morning to late at night. Each caller had a problem, political or personal, for her to solve. Finally a friend offered a house where she could hide away and relax before "a euphoric and very satisfying provincial convention" in late November.

The upcoming session of Parliament now absorbed her attention. In a letter to Lewis, she urged in-depth research and discussion on the NDP cost-of-living policy which she thought inadequately prepared to face Stanfield's Tories.

Four women would join Grace in the Commons: Monique Bégin (L–St. Michel), Albanie Morin (L–Louis Hebert), Jeanne Sauvé (L–Ahuntsic) and Flora MacDonald (PC–Kingston and the Islands). But the female MPs would not form a bloc even on women's issues. "All of us feel that essentially we are here primarily as Members of Parliament, belonging to three different parties with different approaches," Grace replied to a request from the National Action Committee on the Status of Women for a joint meeting with all five. "We feel that now, when we have a minister specifically charged with implementing the recommendations of the Report of the Royal Commission on the Status of Women, the place for women's organizations to begin is with that Minister, Hon. John Munro."

Before Parliament opened in January, David Lewis announced that to earn NDP support the Trudeau government would have to increase old age pensions, take immediate steps to create jobs and halt rising food prices. Accordingly, the throne speech reflected these goals.

As the thirty-one-member NDP caucus was larger than ever, co-operation was crucial to keep things running smoothly. Grace played the role of peacekeeper, according to first-term MP Stuart Leggatt from New Westminster, later Justice of the BC Supreme Court. "I recall the caucus very well. To the great credit of Tommy Douglas and Grace, who were great friends, they had this feeling that they should never undercut the leader, certainly in a caucus meeting, and they didn't do that. They allowed David to be the leader, and they really kept any disagreements that they had away from an open rift. Most of those that were elected in the 1972 Parliament were Tommy Douglas socialists, you see. They weren't David Lewis socialists. There was respect for Lewis who was a fine leader, but he comes from Ontario, and there's a regionalism in Canada. Grace never let people forget the long view every time we started to debate things. A lot of the reason I respect her and love her a great deal is that she would never allow the short-term view to overcome the long-term goals."

Mark Rose, re-elected in Fraser Valley West, said that Grace loved the social conviviality as well as the serious side of working in Parliament. "She had a very optimistic attitude. You would knock on her door, and she would say, 'Come on in.' There was nothing haughty about her at all. It was the common touch."

Shortly after Parliament opened, Grace, as the NDP's consumer affairs critic, called for the establishment of a special committee to investigate rising food prices. Her similar resolutions had been ignored in past sessions, but this time the government accepted her challenge.

The Food Prices Inquiry of 1973 was a fight from the start. The government motion proposed a Joint Senate–Commons committee. The NDP was against a joint committee with senators, in Lewis's words, "not only because they are an unrepresentative group of political appointees, but also because many of them hold directorships in the huge food stores and processing chains which dominate the industry."

The Commons Special Committee on Trends in Food Prices was appointed January 25. In its new, chastened mood, the government agreed to leave senators out and accepted an NDP amendment for a sixty-day interim report aimed at preventing the government from pigeonholing the committee's findings. Grace was one of three NDP members. From the outset Grace pushed her issues: inclusion of co-operatives in the study, detailed investigation of the profits and financial control of supermarket chains and monopolies, how to guarantee the basics of a healthy diet to low income Canadians, and the establishment of a review board with power to roll back prices.

Grace called the twenty-five-member committee a "schizophrenic" group. A tug of war developed between producer-oriented and consumer-oriented MPs. The Liberals slipped behind a screen of studies to put off action of any kind, while claiming to act expeditiously. The Conservatives, who wanted a wage and price freeze like that in force in the US, were unco-operative, calling the committee "a witch hunt" and "a circus."

During the hearings, Grace tangled with supermarket executives who could not account for profits that rose, in one case, 47.4 percent in one year on a 10 percent increase in sales. In vain she demanded figures on how much of the meat packing industry was dominated by the five largest companies. She charged that the Canadian consumer was "paying through the nose" for supermarket price wars and for the construction and maintenance of too many food stores. Grocery executives and conservative economists blamed the labour unions for soaring food prices, a position Grace believed was unfair and untrue. She looked forward to the appearance of witnesses from the Canadian Labour Congress (CLC) to refute this argument. Just before the sixty-day interim report was due, the CLC witnesses appeared: Jean Beaudry, executive vice-president; Russell Bell, research director and Seppo Nousiainen, assistant research director. From Grace's viewpoint their testimony was a disaster: to her amazement, there was no reference to wages in the CLC brief. She asked about the proportion of unionized workers in various sectors of the food industry; the three CLC men could do no more than guess. She asked about the average weekly wages of union workers. They referred her to Statistics Canada. She asked about non-union wages; they could not supply the numbers. She asked for their opinion of a food prices review board; they had no answer thought out. The atmosphere grew hostile; committee members began drifting out. Grace cut her questioning short in disgust.

Two days later Grace and NDP committee member Alf Gleave received an angry letter from Beaudry, Bell and Nousiainen copied to all NDP federal caucus members. "We were utterly appalled by your performance," they wrote. "We object to your interrogation methods, which were strongly reminiscent of the late United States Senator McCarthy, who pre-judged his witnesses as guilty before they even took the stand . . . . We were also astonished . . . to hear you and other members of the Committee asking for information which is readily available from Statistics Canada . . . . [This] can only reflect on the competence of the Committee itself."

Grace replied, "Frankly, my questioning methods were the same as they have always been in committees . . . . This is the first time I can recall being criticized for them, publicly or privately. For months the trade union movement has been under fire by opposition critics as being the chief cause of rising food prices. Had you studied the evidence already before the Committee, you would have realized that the questions to your witnesses would centre about wages and wage levels.

"I tried to help you by asking questions about the wages of workers in the food industry where they are deplorably low. I followed through with questions designed to bring out the fact that the great percentage of workers in the food industry are unorganized and hence at the mercy of low wages and poor conditions . . . . You had practically no information with you . . . . To meet with this response from the Canadian Labour Congress on the very points where we were hoping to be able to defend them was disastrous."

Grace felt the incident as a personal slap in the face. She explained later, "I felt here was one of my babies, the Prices Committee, and I was getting little enough support from the other members. I looked forward for a long time to getting a real good lift when the Labour Congress people came. I was all set for it. And here they acted just like they had six other meetings that day. They weren't prepared for any decent kind of questioning. I got annoyed."

Meanwhile, food prices skyrocketed; meat and poultry prices were up seventeen percent in one year. The Department of Agriculture, claiming that families could halve their grocery bills by bargain buying, released three "nutritionally adequate" weekly menus. While others attacked them for their reliance on starchy foods, Grace dubbed the menus "a snow job," and calculated that to buy even the cheapest of the three would cost people living on incomes of under $3000 almost fifty percent of their income.

The food prices committee's interim report called for an independent food prices review board, but without power to reverse price increases. The Liberal and NDP committee members supported this halfway measure; the Tories were opposed. Despite strong reservations, Grace voted for it. The other important recommendation was federal–provincial co-operation on programs to get basic foods on the tables of low-income people.

A week later Consumer Affairs Minister Herb Gray announced the formation of a Food Prices Review Board. Grace, speaking with confidence for the NDP in this minority Parliament, told the House, "We have no intention in this party of accepting any such toothless wonder. We want legislation with teeth in it and we are satisfied that the consumers want such legislation." The NDP list of essentials was stiff. As Grace put it: "steps to ensure that prices be not increased; rollback where necessary for the public welfare and, support prices and subsidies to the farmers . . . . The board must be able to summon witnesses and require production of papers, books, records, financial statements, agreements, contracts, leases . . . . The minister should be required to announce within fifteen days of receiving the board's recommendations what specific measures he plans to take . . . . Finally, these hearings must be public and reports and recommendations must be made public without delay . . . . Anything less than those . . . and we will not support such legislation."

But they did. In the recorded vote 129 Liberals, New Democrats and Social Credit MPs defeated 90 Conservatives to accept the majority report of the Commons Special Committee on Food Prices. The Food Prices Review Board (FPRB) commissioners would be appointed under the Federal Inquiries Act, Gray announced, giving them the powers Grace had called for: to summon witnesses, take evidence under oath and require the production of documents. The board would produce a quarterly report and make recommendations to cabinet.

Beryl Plumptre, president of the Vanier Institute of the Family and former head of the Consumers' Association of Canada (CAC), would chair the five-member board. She had been on the Wartime Prices and Trade Board and the Economic Council of Canada, but Grace had no confidence that she could make the FPRB effective. In fact, with the appointment of Plumptre as chair, Grace suspected the Food Prices Review Board would behave for Trudeau the way the Consumers' Association of Canada twenty years earlier had obediently heeded Prime Minister St. Laurent.

She was proved correct. The new board was merely an investigative body. Few were fooled. In the *Toronto Star*, Dennis Braithwaite dubbed it "a cream-puff outfit" set up to respond to complaints with "typical bureaucratic evasion." Allan Fotheringham in the *Vancouver Sun* pronounced the FPRB a "con job on housewives . . . a sham battle."

Food prices continued to rise, and corporation profits surged fifty-three percent in the first quarter of 1973. The oil crisis hit in May and deepened through the summer as the Arab oil-producing nations cut back production. There was concern that skyrocketing fuel prices would drive food prices still higher. The government lifted the twelve percent federal sales tax on children's clothes and shoes, cosmetics and confectionary products. That was some help, but in the Commons Grace popped up almost daily demanding implementation of the food prices committee recommendation that low-income people be provided with proper food. "What I was really after," she explained, "was a basket of food prepared which would be a certain price and limited to people of a certain income, so that there would be a proper balance of nutrition available for people. I never could get that, but I tried it over and over again."

"I agree completely with your frustration and your disappointment about the Food Prices Review Board," she wrote an Ontario man. "All I can tell you is that I fought harder for a proper Board than I have ever fought for anything in my life. And I have made no secret, privately or publicly, of the fact that I am bitterly disappointed by what we have got."

On January 22, 1973, the US Supreme Court released its famous Roe v. Wade decision that a woman's right to abortion is protected by the constitutional right to privacy. This ruling instantly set off renewed demands in Canada for removal of abortion from the Criminal Code. On March 16 in Toronto, at another Cross Canada Conference for Abortion Law Repeal, Dr. Henry Morgentaler publicly announced for the first time that he had been doing abortions at his Montreal clinic for years. Claiming the moral high ground, he told the conference, "I believe the Canadian abortion laws are in violation of the Canadian Bill of Rights," and urged that his clinic be taken as a prototype. Morgentaler mailed Grace a copy of his speech with a letter complaining that his revelations received "almost no publicity due to a Press black-out."

Abortion rights activists turned up what pressure they could. Eleanor Wright Pelrine, a journalist and author of the 1972 book *Abortion In Canada*, moved to mount an abortion test case in the Canadian courts. On April 5 Grace's question in the House requesting abortion repeal and the establishment of abortion clinics was rudely rejected by Justice Minister Otto Lang, and her request for a debate on the question was denied. Lang was applauded by Conservative and Liberal MPs.

Still, public opinion on abortion was slowly changing. In February nationally recognized journalist Peter Newman editorialized in *Maclean*'s weekly news magazine in favour of making abortion an accepted right of women, which drew an approving letter from Grace. In May CTV's news program *W5* televised Dr. Henry Morgentaler performing an abortion. He faced an additional thirteen charges after the show, but such a program would never have aired in 1967 when Grace introduced Canada's first abortion law reform bill.

On July 6 Grace introduced yet another bill for repeal. Contraception was the first line of defence, she argued, but birth control pills were still not widely available. Though ably seconded by her new ally in caucus, lawyer Stu Leggatt, it was not adopted.

In late July the federal NDP convention in Vancouver featured a stormy session on women's issues, including abortion. Yvonne Cocke, a BC vice-president, took the party to task for failing to come to grips with the problems of women. By this time the party's feminists were better organized with a strong women's caucus.

Women's caucus member Hilda Thomas recalled Grace's pivotal role in that 1973 convention. "Part of our agenda was to reactivate the federal Participation Of Women Committee, to have a conference on women's issues funded by the party, which we got in Winnipeg in 1974, and to make women's issues a major item on the agenda of the 1975 convention. We got through all of those in the time allotted to us, and still there was the resolution in defence of Henry Morgentaler. So our time was up [when] our floor manager went to the microphone and said, 'Well, Mr. Chairman, our one woman MP is here and wishes to speak on this resolution.' Of course to say that our one woman MP had been denied the right to speak on a woman's issue in the convention was politically impossible. So David Lewis, who was just fit to be tied, went to the microphone and moved that the time be extended. It was a real triumph in manoeuvring for the women. Grace spoke very strongly in defence of Morgentaler."

Grace painted Dr. Morgentaler as "someone who couldn't bear to pass by on the other side when confronted by the fact that women were suffering misery and mutilation and death," and called on the convention to defend him. The delegates responded with unanimous approval. Grace, Hilda Thomas and eight other high-profile NDPers signed a declaration urging that charges against Morgentaler be dropped. Thomas got what she wanted, but the incident left her with a sour memory of Grace's attitude. "I'm sorry to say that, although we made it absolutely clear to her what we were up to and how we planned to get through these issues, she expressed some distress about having been used," Thomas explained later. "I thought she should have been very happy to be used in such a cause."

Grace had a knack for unintended double entendre that made for instant publicity. In November she inadvertently got family planning headlined even above the walkout of union CBC newsmen. In question period she challenged Manpower Minister Robert Andras as to why the Family Planning Association of BC had been turned down for a Local Initiatives Project (LIP) grant. She attempted to quote figures: "8,200 abortions, 11.2 percent out of wedlock births, and 11 percent increase in gonorrhea, 5,000 new cases of children in care in 1972 in BC." Amidst the bellowing din the Speaker admonished her to "ask a question and not convey information."

"Thank you, Mr. Speaker," said Grace, "I was laying the groundwork for the question." The members fell about their desks laughing. "A schoolboy type of tittering goes on when these questions are raised," Grace scolded. Wiping the grin from his face, Andras promised to reconsider. The grant was not forthcoming, but the photo of Grace shaking her finger at the errant MPs was front page news.

If her fellow MPs could only have seen Grace the morning of June 18 buying *Penthouse* magazine! George Strong, her Alberta watchdog, had written objecting to the presence of the sex magazine on local newsstands and sent her a dollar to purchase a copy and see for herself if the material was objectionable. After perusing the magazine, Grace replied, "I quite agree with you that it is straight pornography and its only purpose can be to titillate and inflame the male." To arouse public opinion against "this type of mental filth" Grace sent the magazine to Helen Frayne, an Ottawa radio personality, asking her to raise the issue on the air. She explained, "The anatomical details of the women involved did not bother me particularly, but evidently the same could not be said for males, young and old, whose imaginations are apt to get a bit out of hand in such matters." To Grace limiting pornography was a matter of respect for women, the most basic expression of status.pornography

While she did not support censorship, Grace wanted to ensure that good taste ruled the airwaves and respect for women was the norm. When the Vancouver Status of Women Council complained to Pierre Juneau, director of the Canadian Radio and Television Commission (CRTC), about sexist treatment of women's personal problems on a local radio station, Grace received a copy and wrote to support the women's group. The complaint was about a CJOR program, "Female Forum", hosted by then sportscaster Denny Boyd, later the writer of a long-running popular column in the *Vancouver Sun*. Boyd's attitudes on the show, the women complained, were "insensitive and paternalistic. Women are labelled 'chicklets, fillies, darling and doll.' We find these labels analogous to chink, wop or frog, and just as offensive." The CRTC agreed with Grace and the Status of Women Council and banned radio talk shows on sex. CJOR dropped the show.

At the beginning of June 1973, Labour Minister John Munro appointed a twenty-eight-member (twenty-six women and two men) Advisory Committee on the Status of Women, chaired by Dr. Katharine B. Cooke. It represented a cross-section of groups—Native people, the Royal Canadian Legion and the National Action Committee on the Status of Women—but no left-wing feminists. Grace was satisfied to see a Human Rights Commission at the top of the new committee's priority list. On December 10, 1973, the twenty-fifth anniversary of the UN Universal Declaration of Human Rights, Justice Minister Otto Lang announced the intention of the Canadian government to establish a Commission on Human Rights and Interests.

Just before Christmas recess the government presented a second report on the status of women. While cautiously approving its recent moves, Grace blasted the Trudeau regime for failing to deal with some of the most urgent problems: day care, labour code changes, runaway husbands, the Indian Act and property rights for married women. Her speech was delivered in the fiery MacInnis form to which the Commons had become accustomed, but Grace herself felt handicapped: her arthritis was getting worse. The one-mile walk from her apartment to Parliament Hill had become torture. Brother Charles began to pick her up for work in the morning on his way to the Department of External Affairs. Late at night, Ran Harding of Kootenay West, the party's environment critic, gave Grace a ride home. She was relieved to get home to Vancouver for a Christmas rest.

Monday, January 14, 1974, was Lucy Woodsworth's one-hundredth birthday. Grace and Charles gathered with other family members and friends for a celebration at Saint-Vincent's Hospital where Lucy had lived for the past ten years.

After Charles returned from his tours of duty as Canadian ambassador to South Africa and later to Ethiopia, he visited his mother frequently. "Although for a long time she read a lot and enjoyed visitors," Charles observed, "her mind gradually weakened until in the end she found difficulty in recognizing even members of the family. Saint-Vincent's is a Catholic institution, and although my mother was not a Catholic the treatment she was accorded by the staff there was really wonderful." Her hundredth birthday was a "memorable occasion," and "quite a few old friends including Stanley Knowles were present."

Sitting in his parliamentary office in 1988, a slow, sweet smile broke over Knowles's face as he recalled that hundredth birthday party. "Grace was very much in love with her mother. As much as age ninety-five she [Lucy] was very bright." But on that day, he said sadly, Lucy did not recognize her guests, only the nurses.

Grace told no one at the party, but privately she had decided Lucy's hundredth birthday marked the end of an era for her. Proudly she had carried the socialist banner her father had floated aloft more than sixty years ago. Now the burden had grown too heavy, not for her heart and mind, but for her body. The following day, January 15, 1974, Grace announced her retirement from politics due to arthritis.

The announcement triggered an outpouring of affection and honour from across Canada. Even the conservative *Ottawa Journal* wrote, "The *Journal* has often disagreed with Mrs. MacInnis during her nine years in the Commons. For all that, we and others have respected her ability, hard work and zeal in advocating consumers' and women's rights . . . . So ends a parliamentary dynasty of more than a half century that has seen many governments rise and fall."

Many bouquets arrived by mail, like the one on Parliamentary Press Gallery stationery from J. Alex Hume, former reporter with the Ottawa *Citizen,* who had covered her father and her husband too. "What I always admired most about Mr. Woodsworth, Mr. MacInnis and you as well is that you always put forward your political conviction without falling into the trap which all found so personally objectionable of being sanctimonious." There were commendations from opposition MPs, including Annapolis Valley Conservative Pat Nolan: "I wanted to write extending my congratulations on your outstanding contribution to Canadian Parliamentary life. I know you fought some lonely battles and at times it could not have been easy, but your determination and quiet dignity impressed all, even though there was not total capitulation!"

Grace was gratified by the sheer numbers of people writing to express disappointment at her retirement, and to share their cures for arthritis. But there was no remedy; the crippling disease had begun its onslaught.

On February 26, 1974, Parliament was prorogued. The Chief Justice of Canada, Rt. Hon. Bora Laskin, Acting Deputy Governor General, summed up the events of the past session, and as Grace listened she could feel the walls of pain within her body rising up to close her off from this Parliament she had known and loved since she was a girl. Despite the warm red carpeting in the Senate chamber, Grace was chilled to the bone.

Laskin recounted Trudeau's visit to the People's Republic of China last autumn, a first for a Canadian Prime Minister. In addition to a trade agreement, a health services agreement had been signed under which a team of Canadian anaesthetists would study acupuncture in China. The rest she knew: the introduction of the National Energy Program for energy self-sufficiency forced by the recent oil crisis; the passage of some additional measure of social security, though not enough; the Foreign Investment Review Act; a housing measure with many shortcomings; another five-year restriction on capital punishment.

The next day MPs and Senators were back in the Senate chamber for the opening of the second session of the twenty-ninth Parliament, with newly sworn Governor General Jules Léger presiding. This, Grace suspected, would be the last time she would be present for the opening of a session of Parliament. The NDP was restive under the government's reluctance to bring in legislation the party favoured; some NDPers were just waiting for the right moment to bring the government down. The throne speech placed the supply and price of oil at the top of its legislative list, followed closely by control of food prices which, the governor general said, had risen sharply again "as a result of the growth of world population on which has been superimposed serious crop failures in a number of countries." Grace had warned of this very situation since she entered Parliament. Now, for the first time in a throne speech, Grace heard mention of her most basic goal "for the consumer, in not requiring an undue proportion of income for Canadians to secure a sufficient and balanced diet."

Finally, at the end of the speech, Grace was pleased to learn that the Human Rights Commission would proceed and would include protection against discrimination for women. Crown corporations would be encouraged to hire and promote more women, and federal government regulations governing gender equality would be implemented. It was not the whole loaf, nor even half a loaf, but Grace had managed to slice a piece from the loaf of power and privilege to enrich the lives of Canadian women.

In her last parliamentary session Grace led the NDP charge against the embattled Liberal government. David Lewis called the party's latest set of demands the NDP's cash-on-delivery policy, and all the demands were Grace's urgent issues. She outlined them in her address in reply to the throne speech. "First, we need a Food Prices Review Board with power to act and power to apply selective controls on the basis of nutritional need," she declared. "That means a subsidy where necessary and justified. I am thinking of bread and milk . . . . There would need to be export controls for other things, such as have been imposed with regard to oil . . . . It will mean rollbacks in price. The price of bread should be rolled back without further fuss.

"Second, the government ought to pass legislation giving the Food Prices Review Board power to compel the books of the big food chains and other parts of the food distribution system to be opened. The board should have power to lay bare the industrial and financial connections of the food chains . . . . Third, we need court action where indicated . . . . Fourth, the government should consider imposing an excess profits tax . . . . Fifth, . . . the government should take the initiative in bringing about international agreements [for] sugar . . . [and] grains . . . . Sixth, . . . the formation of co-operatives as one means of standing up to the big giants . . . . Consumers cannot be fobbed off with talk . . . consumers know the Food Prices Review Board as presently constituted is as a weak reed in a violent storm."

Three days after this speech, Grace introduced a motion to invest the Food Prices Review Board with the powers she had outlined. Grace also wanted new people on the board so that, as she put it in her motion, "its members may consist of persons who are aware that the distribution of food should become an essential service to the public rather than a series of profit-making enterprises." In March the Food Prices Review Board produced a report on the price of bread of which Grace approved because it recommended a maximum two-cent increase instead of the four cents the industry wanted. But the Bakery Council ignored the board directive. It was the board's first real test, and it failed to keep down the price of bread. Grace was not impressed with the performance of board chair Beryl Plumptre, as she told one Richmond couple. "The only exception I take in your letter is your phrase 'your fond admiration pour Madame Plumptre.' She has never been one of my favourite people."

Yet regardless of her personal opinion, when Plumptre's salary came up in the Miscellaneous Estimates Committee of which Grace was a member, she and NDPer Terry Grier sided with seven Liberals to out-vote the eight Tories supporting a motion to reduce Plumptre's annual salary from forty thousand dollars to one dollar. Grace saw the motion as a political manoeuvre which would not lower the price of food. She knew that both Liberals and Conservatives wanted the present system of food production and distribution for profit to continue. But Grace never gave up. She believed, as she had for decades, in a cradle-to-grave social safety net as a prerequisite for higher civilization. In a February 1974 interview she said, "You see the welfare state business, we have a lot of those bricks in place now, I'm not worried about that. But in order to hold it we have to get the resources to do it. We're realizing that what we've got to do is to get deeply involved in the battle for the control of these resources that are essential for human survival . . . . Even before the oil we were involved in the food battle. We lost that round because neither of the big parties would go for a Food Prices Review Board that had any power. But I don't consider that a failure. To me that is unfinished business."

Grace never backed away from the abortion battle either. On March 7 she appeared with MP Stu Leggatt at a press conference called to announce an abortion tribunal and Parliament Hill rally. About four hundred women, a few men and the two MPs attended the rally that windy Saturday in March. All 264 MPs had been invited, but only Grace and Leggatt showed up. Leggatt emphasized that only 247 of Canada's 1422 hospitals had abortion committees. "There is abortion for the rich and trauma and horror for the poor," he declared. The two MPs accused the government of subjecting Dr. Morgentaler to "unjust and scandalous intimidation." A shrinking minority stands in the way of legal abortion in Canada, Grace told the crowd. "It is a shameful situation when a minority's dogmatic belief makes it impossible for the majority to get the care they need," she said. "Dr. Morgentaler is carrying the torch—he must be supported. I cannot see why fair-minded Canadians do not rally and insist that the campaign of harassment now going on against him and his colleagues cease."

Broadcast through loudspeakers, Grace's big voice boomed out across the Hill. Too few MPs were willing to stand up for women's rights, she charged. "A lot of men believe abortion is strictly a woman's problem—a dirty, messy business. 'Leave it to the women,' they say, as they leave all the other dirty messes to women. About all MPs know is the horrible, exaggerated picture of abortion. It turns them off, they don't even want to hear the word. But it's not a female problem, it's a human problem."

After the rally, Grace boarded a plane for Vancouver where she was scheduled to speak the next day at a conference on the status of women hosted by the BC Teachers' Federation at Simon Fraser University. Significantly, Grace told the five hundred teachers she would not select a woman for nomination to political office simply because she was a woman, but would choose the person with the best qualifications.

As spring unfurled across the country, election speculations sprang up as thick as crocuses. In Vancouver–Kingsway, considered a safely NDP seat, party organizers spoke of importing a high-profile candidate such as novelist Pierre Berton or historian-broadcaster Laurier LaPierre. By the middle of April Grace knew an election was imminent. Although many urged the NDP to continue supporting the minority Liberals, Grace thought it was time to bring down the government. "When the NDP found itself in a balance-of-power situation after the last election," she wrote one constituent, "we decided that we would support the Liberal Government as long as we could get measures of legislation from it that would be of value to the Canadian people. As you say, we have managed to get quite a few things forced out of the Government—measures like improved Old Age and Veterans Pensions, tax cuts for people in the lower income brackets, Family Allowances at twenty dollars a month. However, the time has come when we must face the fact that we are no longer able to get the other things that people need. The Government will not set up a Food Prices Review Board with any power to deal with the spiralling cost of living. They will not take measures to tax the huge profits that big corporations are making. We need this revenue for all kinds of things that people require.

"If we were to continue propping up the Liberal Government, we would, in my opinion, lose all credibility as a Party and we would lose our very reasons for existence. It will be only a short time before people come to realize that the Government is no longer doing anything to help them. They will turn savagely on the Government and if the NDP is still supporting the Government, it will go down the drain as well. I do not want to see this happen and this is why I believe we must fact the prospect of an election."

The final dissolution of the working partnership between the NDP and the Liberal government occurred over the budget introduced Monday, May 6, by Finance Minister John Turner. Grace, in her riding, immediately began to scramble for plane reservations to return to Ottawa. She sent NDP House Leader Stanley Knowles a note making her position clear, just in case she failed to get back for the Tuesday morning caucus meeting. "I want you to know that when the vote comes on whether or not to bring down the Government I would be in favour of doing so at the earliest possible opportunity." The NDP caucus agreed.

In the Commons that Tuesday, Trudeau called the proposed opposition vote against the budget "irresponsible." He pointed to provisions for a cut in personal income tax, strengthening of the Combines Investigation Act, and a ten-percent surtax on some corporate sectors which would, even by NDP estimates, bring in $800,000,000 for the year. The budget contained a measure allowing price rollbacks on food, and another to beef up the Agricultural Products Co-operative Marketing Act. Finally, Trudeau reminded the House, first reading had just been given to an omnibus bill on equal rights for women. Would the opposition throw all this away? It would, and it had its reasons.

Just before the final vote, Tommy Douglas outlined those reasons. "We asked for selective price controls. The government said no . . . . We asked the government for a two-price system . . . to keep the prices of Canadian products and raw materials at levels lower than world levels . . . . But the Minister of Finance . . . said it would not work . . . . We asked for legislation to curb excess profits. What did we get? . . . an absolute farce . . . on one hand he [the Finance Minister] imposed a ten percent surcharge on certain corporations while with the other he gave them a one percent reduction in taxation . . . . It is a budget that will perpetuate a situation in which the real income of the wage earner and salary earner is going down $5.50 a week." Through NDP glasses this budget was way off the mark.

Moments later the question was called, and Grace voted with 136 NDP and Conservative members to defeat the government. It was her final vote in the House of Commons.

CHAPTER 18

The Trail is Ready

It all changed so quickly. On May 5 Grace was an MP accepting an honorary Doctor of Laws degree at Notre Dame University in Nelson, BC. Her convocation address foreshadowed the question of sustainable development in the exact words used thirteen years later by another socialist leader, Mrs. Gro Harlem Brundtland, chair of the UN Commission on Sustainable Development. Far ahead of her time, Grace saw three interrelated problems in the one issue: "The problem of the production of goods and services on a world-wide scale to meet the needs of all the world's inhabitants without exhausting the resources essential for future needs; the problem of doing this without the pollution of air, soil and water to the stage where it endangers the health, well-being and existence of our own and other species; and the problem of population on a world scale which is now occurring at a rate which will leave standing room only in the rapidly advancing future." Grace knew she was one of the few to see the crucial importance of this issue. "In our Parliament at Ottawa, none of these problems is as yet receiving urgent attention," she warned. "The time of reckoning is near."

On May 7 the Vancouver–Kingsway NDP held its nominating meeting. Grace was to have been there and Stu Leggatt was to have been the keynote speaker, but both were in Ottawa for the crucial vote that would precipitate the election. Grace sent a greeting, "May the best man or woman be chosen! And then let us get behind our candidate and start the drive to victory." These commonplace words were precisely directed to the internal friction that had developed over the nomination.

Hilda Thomas, the feminist folksinger and UBC English professor from the west side of Vancouver, was up against Dennis Mulroney who had deep Vancouver–Kingsway roots. He had been Grace's campaign organizer in 1965 and her sign captain in other campaigns. A maintenance foreman with the Greater Vancouver Water District, president of his union, and a member of the NDP provincial executive, Mulroney was not well known to the general public.

Thomas, frustrated because Grace insisted on disregarding gender, reasoned, "The number of women in the House was just minuscule and likely to remain so. The Liberals nominated a woman, Simma Holt, but Grace refused to take a position that a woman should replace her. I tried very hard to get a woman from the riding to run and was unable to find anyone, so I took a flyer at it myself, and actually came second to Dennis, although I was a parachute candidate coming in at the last minute, without any support from Grace. I always felt that was a mistake on her part."

On May 8 the second Trudeau government was history, and Grace was no longer an MP. Now she was plain Grace MacInnis, political volunteer. With arthritis in knees, hands and wrists plaguing her, she bravely campaigned for Dennis Mulroney in the July 8 general election. Mulroney faithfully supported her positions on the issues, including abortion law repeal, but he was less than charismatic, and the public mood had tilted again in Trudeau's direction. Simma Holt, a *Vancouver Sun* reporter, captured Vancouver–Kingsway for the Liberals.

It was a fiasco for the NDP. Only Tommy Douglas and Stu Leggatt won in BC. The party took but sixteen seats nationally; David Lewis was defeated. Trudeau's Liberals won a majority government with 141 seats, the Tories captured 95; there were 11 Créditistes. Grace was disappointed, but relieved that she could now rest and deal with her arthritis.

At her retirement, Grace's work was noted with distinction throughout Canada; she was showered with honours. The *Vancouver Sun,* not always a supporter, wrote respectfully: "The voice of this province in the Commons will never be the same." The walls of her apartment were crowded with plaques, scrolls and framed degrees from Laurentian, Notre Dame, Trent, Simon Fraser and Brock universities. In November the University of Toronto presented her with an LL.D. It was a proud day for Grace when she delivered the convocation address to the newest graduating class of the university from which her mother had graduated nearly eighty years before. Grace's own alma mater, the University of Manitoba, presented her with an honorary LL.D. in November 1975, and the University of British Columbia followed suit in June 1977.

July 24, 1974, the day before Grace's sixty-ninth birthday, the Vancouver City Council voted to make her the first female recipient of the city's highest honour, freeman of the city. Mayor Art Phillips quipped, "It has been established that Mrs. MacInnis will be a freeman and not a freewoman or freeperson." At the ceremony in December she received a medal, a scroll and, most valuable, free lifetime meter parking privileges.

In honour of the hundredth anniversary of her father's birth on July 29, 1874, Grace's biography *J.S. Woodsworth: A Man to Remember* was reprinted.

Grace with two colleagues in February 1975. Left to right: David Lewis, Grace, Dave Barrett. {Ian Lindsay/Vancouver Sun}

Grace at age seventy-nine, Ottawa, 1985.

While she was still mobile, Grace often lectured about her father's life. Younger NDP members viewed J.S. Woodsworth as a remote figure whose opinions they rarely considered when making decisions, but hearing Grace speak of his religious and political development inspired them. Her fragility in contrast with her powerful voice and great courage awakened respect, even awe. J.S. Woodsworth was a great symbol of moral force, she affirmed, the Canadian parallel to figures such as Abraham Lincoln, Martin Luther King and Chairman Mao Zedong.

Just before Christmas, Grace was named an officer of the Order of Canada. At the investiture ceremony October 1975 at Rideau Hall, her dear colleague, Thérèse Casgrain, was made a companion of the Order of Canada. She was now entitled to be known as Dr. Grace Woodsworth MacInnis, OC.

One of the most thrilling nights of Grace's life was February 8, 1975. A testimonial banquet and dance in her honour hosted by the Vancouver–Kingsway NDP, drew 650 people. A giant banner emblazoned "Amazing Grace," flanked by two Canadian flags, stretched across one wall of the BC Institute of Technology Student Activities Building. The piper played "Amazing Grace" as he led in the head table guests: Stanley Knowles, Harold Winch, David Lewis, BC Premier Dave Barrett, Manitoba Premier Ed Schreyer, Saskatchewan Premier Alan Blakeney, Donald C. MacDonald, MPs Max Saltsman, Lorne Nystrom, Andrew Brewin, Les Benjamin, Ed Broadbent, and SFU president Pauline Jewett. In the crowd were Grace's secretary Betty Irwin, her old friend Daisy Webster, and a future BC premier, Mike Harcourt, then deputy mayor of Vancouver.

BC Premier Dave Barrett told the cheering crowd, "Many people condemn socialists as too radical, that they don't understand the times. But Grace MacInnis and others like her have been proven right all along." David Lewis called her "one of a half-dozen truly great parliamentarians to serve in the House .... Grace MacInnis represents the most decent that there is in the behaviour of human beings. She never ceases to think not of humanity in the large but of human beings in their daily lives."

Grace's own speech was tough and forward-looking. First she assured her well-wishers that she would not desert them. "You never retire from politics if you're an NDPer," she consoled them. "You're in it for life." She reminded the younger members of the audience, "It took forty years to give Dave [Barrett] the toe-hold he has now .... This thing is a long continuous fight. We're not going to win in our generation."

When Vancouver was at its bone-chilling coldest, on February 23, 1975, Grace took off for the warmth of the South Pacific on a glorious sixty-nine-day day cruise. From the first night in Moorea, green jewel of the Pacific, Grace dined at the captain's table. In Tonga they feasted on the beach and in New Zealand they strolled through luxurious rose gardens. In Australia a couple from the cruise ship flew Grace in their small plane on a tour of Sydney and Canberra.

As she cruised Grace snapped photos to fill her new white album, a gift from her namesake NDP Club in Victoria, BC. She photographed the Carmelite monastery in Singapore where she visited through a grillwork screen with Sister Marguerite, a nun she had befriended when they were both seventeen-year-olds at the Congregation de Notre Dame French language school in Ottawa. She snapped jade treasures at the National Museum in Taipei; shops stuffed with electronic goodies in Hong Kong; Tokyo skyscrapers beside the Imperial Palace; Diamond Head at Waikiki. At the farewell party in Honolulu, Grace celebrated in a red and black floor-length dress patterned with tropical leaves. The delightful cruise had fulfilled her dreams. Too soon it was all over.

Back home Grace had to watch the BC NDP government of Dave Barrett self-destruct. Problems establishing government auto insurance, rumours of wild overspending and Barrett's habit of springing legislation on his cabinet an hour before it was to be introduced had set the stage with distrust and ignorance. On October 7 the BC Legislature passed emergency measures forcing 60,000 striking forest, railway, propane and food industry workers back to work. Len Guy, secretary-treasurer of the BC Federation of Labour, cried that Barrett's government should be replaced by one "true to the honourable traditions of J.S. Woodsworth, Angus MacInnis, and Tommy Douglas." Grace countered that the premier's action was in line with CCF founding principles. "I think J.S. Woodsworth and Angus MacInnis would feel very strongly in favour of what Mr. Barrett is trying to do, and that is to get the powerful groups to realize that the whole community is more important than only one section of it."

A few weeks later, citing the need for a mandate to apply recently announced federal wage and price controls, Premier Barrett called a snap provincial election. Though he still had twenty-one months left in his term and Christmas was approaching, the date was set for December 11. In hindsight it was a grave mistake. The voters rejected the NDP in favour of a Social Credit government under Premier William Bennett, son of W.A.C. Bennett. Grace's hopes were dashed, but she never blamed Barrett. "I must give great credit to Dave Barrett," she said. "He has always taken the attitude that the NDP is an umbrella organization under which sectional interests in the community can become members and participants . . . . We in BC have never had the idea that the NDP is a compact between the trade unions and the CCF. Gradually we must realize there is no other way but compromise. This is the basic principle of the co-operative commonwealth. If you lose sight of that I don't think you can really have faith in a gradual transition to a new society. Socialism is about equality."

The first weekend of July brought more than 1600 delegates to the 1975 NDP leadership convention in Winnipeg. Grace's tribute to outgoing Leader David Lewis in the convention book glossed over their differences and centred on Lewis's crowning achievement. "I'll always remember why I decided to vote for him as leader," she wrote. "It was because he had the vision and the courage to speak out against the imposition of the War Measures Act in a Parliament and a Canada that was being driven through fear and lack of information to jeopardize priceless civil liberties."

The NDP leadership race shaped up as Ed Broadbent against MP Lorne Nystrom, former MP John Harney and BC MLA Rosemary Brown, who ran a grass-roots campaign emphasizing women's rights issues of day care, abortion and income security for housewives—Grace's issues. But Grace voted for Broadbent, not Brown. She liked the way Broadbent had strengthened after the party's rejection of his equivocal attitude toward the Waffle in 1971. On the fourth ballot Broadbent defeated Brown by three hundred votes.

When speaking of Grace, Broadbent's eyes light up; there is power and enthusiasm in his voice. For him Grace is an inspiration, the model of a dedicated, hard-working, practical social democrat. Broadbent appreciated Grace's support and welcomed her occasional advice to the federal caucus over his fifteen years as leader.

When the Supreme Court ruled on January 28, 1988, that Canada's abortion law was unconstitutional, leaving abortion decisions to the pregnant woman and her physician, Grace wrote a triumphant letter to Broadbent encouraging him to stand fast against the anticipated backlash. It was read aloud at the next meeting of the federal caucus. "When I heard that the Supreme Court had stricken down those sections of the Criminal Code dealing with abortion, I was jubilant," Grace wrote. "Now, I thought, NDP convention policy has been vindicated . . . . The fight will be bitter, but we can win, incontestably. Writing to you in this way, Ed, may be akin to teaching my grandmother, but this whole issue has been an investment of time and emotion and thought for me for so long that I find it hard to sit idly by while Mr. Mulroney, who knows no law but his own, searches for ways and means to defeat the Supreme Court."

After the federal election of November 21, 1988, returned another Mulroney Conservative government, Broadbent was considering resigning. The NDP had won a record total of forty-three seats, but Broadbent felt the party needed a change and so did he. Grace thought he should remain as leader. She wrote him explaining that the situation was too chaotic for a new leader to emerge. Broadbent was pleased with her support but announced his resignation nevertheless.

On March 1, 1976, Lucy Woodsworth died in hospital at the age of 102. Charles was the only one of her children who was in Ottawa at the time. Her remains were cremated and the ashes interred May 15 in the cemetery at Cavan, Ontario. Stanley Knowles conducted the memorial service in the presence of Belva and Ralph Staples, Bruce and Howard and their wives.

Grace's arthritis-ravaged body was undergoing treatments at the G.F. Strong Rehabilitation Centre in Vancouver that sunny May morning, but in spirit she was with her family. She dearly loved and admired her mother, and was grateful for the lessons in living Lucy had taught. She wrote, "Mother used to tell us: 'Life is just like the leaves that bud in the spring, grow green and healthy in the summer, turn to brilliant colours in the autumn and finally fall from the trees to die in the winter. We should not mourn for the leaves that fall because they will always be replaced the following spring . . . . Mother's great serenity has lasted right through her illness. She has been and is an inspiration to me."

In honour of Lucy, Grace established a memorial fund for the children of Vancouver's east side to supply the small essentials that make the difference between developing creativity and neglecting it: piano lessons, ice skates, group field trips. "My mother was always greatly concerned about low-income people, families and children," Grace explained. "She left us each a little legacy. I took it with some of my own savings and together with Margaret Mitchell and the head of Cedar Cottage Neighbourhood House we created the Lucy L. Woodsworth Fund for Children."

The Neighbourhood Services Association handled administration of the Fund, and Grace personally selected the children who would benefit. Over the years she developed a cross-Canada list of donors. The Fund became her vocation until just before she left Vancouver in 1987 for a retirement home. The "Lucy Fund" continues to help children under the direction of the Neighbourhood Services Association.

At the end of August 1976 Grace was well enough to travel to Winnipeg for the unveiling of a bust of J.S. Woodsworth created to adorn the lobby of a new provincial government office building named the Woodsworth Building by the Schreyer NDP government. Charles, Stanley Knowles and Winnipeg MP David Orlikow joined the celebration. Continuing her work with the party, that year Grace took the chair of the three-member BC NDP Honorary Life Membership Committee, a job she held until 1981. It was a time of honours and leave-taking for the old guard. On November 29, 1976, when his home riding of Nanaimo honoured retiring MP Tommy Douglas with a testimonial dinner, Grace delivered invigorating words on the highlights of her old friend's career.

Grace's contribution to low-cost housing was to be recognized with a project named for her. On May 23, 1975, she beamed with pleasure as NDP Housing Minister Lorne Nicolson ceremoniously pressed a time capsule into the fresh concrete at 9200 Government Road in Burnaby. The 216-unit project was named MacInnis Place. But with Social Credit back in power, affordable rental housing was not the priority it had been under the NDP. In March 1976, with the project partly built, the government discouraged rentals, and proposed to sell the units instead. Grace and others protested unsuccessfully; Burnaby municipal council approved the strata title conversion in April 1976.

A year later MacInnis Place won a Canadian Housing Design Council award, but the new owner-residents complained that condensation in the units had caused mould and mildew. In December the government sold MacInnis Place to a Vancouver businessman for ten million dollars, exactly what it cost to build. The new owner called it Glenrobin, a name unintentionally connected with Grace: Glenrobin was the town where she had first taught school.

In 1975 Grace served as honorary campaign chair for the Canadian Arthritis and Rheumatism Society (CARS) fundraising drive. She began by speaking at the CARS Centre near Vancouver General Hospital where arthritis sufferers, herself included, learned ways of handling simple tasks such as combing their hair, putting on their socks or pouring a cup of tea so as to place the least stress on swollen, twisted joints.

Medical articles describe rheumatoid arthritis as a chronic, destructive, deforming collagen disease with an autoimmune component. Synovial tissue inside the joints produces too much fluid, leading to stiffness, swelling and soreness. Joints become unstable and limited in their range of motion. There are periods of remission alternating with attacks. Rheumatoid arthritis is more common in women than in men. Recent studies suggest that women who have early pregnancies or have taken birth control pills are at lower risk of this type of arthritis. Because Grace had never been pregnant or taken oral contraceptives, she was at greater risk of arthritis than many women. Some researchers suggest genetic links in rheumatoid arthritis, and it may be that the genetic pattern for this disease existed in Grace's family. Her youngest brother, Howard, also suffered from rheumatoid arthritis and was confined for years to a wheelchair.

Between April 20, 1976, and December 19, 1980, Grace spent four periods of six to eight weeks in the G.F. Strong Rehabilitation Centre recuperating from operations on her joints. During this time she had both knees and one hip replaced with artificial joints that gave her a greater range of motion with less pain. She employed a housekeeper and learned to use special tools for ordinary tasks. She had a door key with an extra large handle, thick cushions on each chair so that, by rocking back and forth, she could stand up under her own power, and frictionless covers over her car seats.

Until 1985 she still had a car, which gave her some measure of independence, but she had trouble steering with her painfully deformed hands.

Friends recall many near misses. Yvonne Cocke said, "She drove that doggone car until she was a hazard on the road. I always remember when she finally decided that she had to give it up. Her grip was not very good. One day she got parked and couldn't get out of the parking spot. So she had to ask a complete stranger to get her car out of this parking spot because she didn't have enough strength in her hands to turn the wheel. At that point she decided. That was one of the hardest things for her to do, to give up that independence."

When asked to speak about living with arthritis, Grace would always say, "The secret is to learn to accept oneself at each stage . . . to give oneself the care needed . . . and to live as fully as possible at every stage of life." She advised a simple diet, a regular exercise program, and techniques to deal with the side-effects of medications. But most important, she said, was "watching my thoughts, learning to confront my fears and take life in stride, always striving to reach a plateau of well-being, stay there and watch for possibilities to reach a higher one."

In 1978 Canadians began to anticipate a federal election call. In Vancouver–Kingsway the nomination battle pitted Phyllis Young, a minister in the Barrett cabinet, against Ian Waddell, who had served as legal counsel to Thomas Berger's Mackenzie Valley Pipeline Inquiry. Waddell courted Grace. "I took Grace out to lunch with the hope that she might at a bare minimum remain neutral," Waddell recalled. "She was worried that we had to have a candidate that could win. We had lost the riding in 1974 to Simma Holt and she did not like that." When Waddell won the nomination, Grace wrote an endorsement for his campaign leaflet, but active campaigning was out of the question.

Grace helped another first-time NDP candidate find her feet in the 1979 election. A movement to draft Margaret Mitchell arose in Vancouver East, and she consulted Grace before making a decision. Mitchell recalled: "She wasn't one to come out and take sides because it was a very competitive nomination, but she was very supportive behind the scenes and helped me a lot afterwards too. It was a very tough nomination, there was quite a split between the factions within the riding afterwards. She advised me, 'Just go ahead and be positive with everyone and pretty soon that will look after itself. Don't take sides, you just stay above it.'

"I was confronted during the campaign with the anti-choice people demonstrating, and it would get a little nasty. She would say, 'Now just remember that even though we have a lot of Catholics in the riding who feel strongly about this issue, they will see you as a person who is concerned about many issues. Always be a multi-issue person.' I think that helped put it in perspective, because it was a pretty emotional confrontation. You think that it [abortion law repeal] is a major political block, too, which it turned out not to be."

On election day, May 22, 1979, with Grace's support and encouragement, Ian Waddell won Vancouver–Kingsway by a healthy margin. Margaret Mitchell took Vancouver East. Across Canada the NDP won 26 seats, up 10 from their previous standing. The Conservatives under Joe Clark came to power with 136 seats to the Liberals' 114. The Créditistes held six seats. After Waddell went to Ottawa, he considered Grace his mentor. "I used to try and keep in touch with her, and get advice. We had our annual lunches, and I would always take her to a trendy restaurant, she appreciated that. I could just go and talk to her. We would drive in the evening in my little sports car. She wouldn't seek out people to give advice, but she would press some of her causes, like the Japanese Canadian redress."

In October 1979 Grace's work on behalf of Canada's women was recognized in a significant way. Newly installed Governor General Ed Schreyer created the Governor General's Awards in Commemoration of the Persons Case. The honour would celebrate the fiftieth anniversary of the 1929 British Privy Council ruling that Canadian women were "qualified persons" under the British North America Act. Each year a small group of women would be selected from nominations by the public.

Grace was chosen that first year along with four women who had been part of her life: Thérèse Casgrain; Mary Two-Axe Early of Caughnawaga, founder of Indian Rights for Indian Women, whom Grace and Thérèse had accompanied to a public hearing of the Royal Commission on the Status of Women; Sophia Dixon, delegate to the CCF Regina convention of 1933; and Eileen Tallman Sufrin, leader of the drive to unionize the T. Eaton Company in the 1940s and 1950s who had stood with Grace on the moderate side of the CCF–NDP. The other two women selected were Dr. Elizabeth Bagshaw, a birth control pioneer, and Marion Royce, first director of the Women's Bureau in the federal Department of Labour, and member of the UN Commission on the Status of Women. Grace attended the awards ceremony at Rideau Hall and visited the House of Commons in time to hear Ian Waddell make a statement in her honour.

At a ceremony in Winnipeg in May 1982 came recognition that Grace felt it a special honour to receive, the Canadian Labour Congress Award for Outstanding Service to Humanity, also awarded that day to Stanley Knowles.

Some of the wisest socialist thinkers in Canada gathered for the Frank Scott symposium at Simon Fraser University in February 1981 to honour the great lawyer, teacher and poet. Scott, now eighty-two, was in attendance. Grace served on the conference planning committee headed by Thomas Berger, currently a Justice of the BC Supreme Court. Impetus for the event came from SFU English professor Sandra Djwa, who was writing a biography of Scott. The symposium awakened interest in strengthening the university's program in humanities. This stimulus, coupled with the realization that little recognition had been given to J.S. Woodsworth in the colleges and universities of Canada, gave rise to the idea of a teaching chair in his name at Simon Fraser University.

The J.S. Woodsworth Chair in the Humanities was formally established in 1983. Berger chaired the Leadership Committee of the J.S. Woodsworth Endowment Fund, and Grace was on the committee with a diverse all-party group that included Tommy Douglas, Maurice Strong, Jack Munro, Bishop Remi De Roo, Eugene Forsey, Gordon Fairweather, Pauline Jewett and Harold Winch. Their funding goal was one million dollars.

As campaign director, Yvonne Cocke worked with Grace on brochures and correspondence for the national campaign drive. By February 1990, with more than 1500 individual gifts, the endowment fund stood at over $1.2 million, and the idea had expanded to include a Humanities Institute as well as the teaching chair. The J.S. Woodsworth Chair will be filled for the first time in 1994 by Alan Whitehorn, professor in the Department of Politics and Economics at Royal Military College, Kingston, Ontario.

Grace viewed the J.S. Woodsworth Chair as a counterweight to the dehumanizing computerization of society. She hoped that the institute and the chair would direct students toward the core questions of life: "Why are people here? What is important in the way our organization works? What are the important goals? Is it to build a place where people are in harmony with their environment and where wanted children can be born and brought up and developed? A big frontier we still have to deal with is children. We haven't got any children's lib movement at all going yet. Father would have liked to see it used that way. The best memorials to him are always the living things that are done in his memory."

Not long before Frank Scott died in March 1985, a letter from Grace told him of the J.S. Woodsworth Chair, a loving memorial which Scott had helped to inspire. His wife Marian replied, "Frank was still able to be delighted."

The NDP's fiftieth anniversary celebration in Regina July 2–3, 1983, a few weeks before Grace's seventy-eighth birthday, was the last, great emotional event she would share with the party as a whole. "It was a time when we thought the party was almost on the way out," said MP Margaret Mitchell. "We were way down in the polls, the media were predicting our demise. Grace, in her introduction of Tommy Douglas, was a great inspiration. Many of the younger women as well as the party generally would have revived much of their awareness of what she stands for, not just as a woman, but within the party as a pioneer."

It was a glorious night for Grace. In her own words, "As we survivors of the Founding Convention looked out over the scene of happy fellowship ... we were struck by the differences between the two conventions.

Instead of the 131 delegates in 1933 there were now some 1800. They now represented all ten provinces with a few from the northern territories. Instead of being mainly from the big farm organizations, the assorted local labour and socialist parties, the sprinkling of young university professors and the members of the Ginger Group in the House of Commons, these 1983 delegates represented a well-integrated, nationwide political party with policies forged by the biennial conventions of fifty years, and with outstanding achievements, both legislative and in the fundamental thinking of the Canadian community."

Grace recalled the electrifying effect Tommy Douglas had upon that audience, discouraged as they were, frustrated and facing huge problems. "Tommy, inspired by the audience and his memories, gave one of the greatest speeches of his life. It was all there—his humorous, light-hearted opening, a few political references, then into his subject, the building of a society for people, where people were at once the central concern and the motivating force. Before their eyes the listeners saw the picture of a real participatory democracy organized for people, by people.

"They saw human and environmental resources employed in creating conditions where each individual would have a chance to fulfil his or her potential while contributing to the common life . . . . The audience listened intently. And, as they listened, their doubts and fears and frustrations fell away. It could be done. It was being done all over the world by groups of men and women who saw the vision and were prepared to make it come true. Of course there would be backsets, periods of bleak reaction. But the dream would not die."

The dream was very much alive, but death touched Grace closely that July. A few days after the convention, her dear sister Belva died of a heart attack on the Cavan farm. Ralph arranged for a memorial gathering November 13 at the J.S. Woodsworth house, his birthplace, Applewood. Grace could not attend, but she was there in spirit.

About this time Grace's cousin Ellen Woodsworth, with whom she had never been close, took a step to close the distance. Ellen was a radical feminist working on such issues as wages for housework, pensions for homemakers, day care and abortion rights. These were Grace's issues too, but the two women had been estranged. Ellen realized, "Maybe some of the gap between us was because we were both such stubborn strong-minded people. I wasn't going to admit my connection to her because I was going to make my own way. She probably saw me as a young wide-eyed radical. I was hired to do an analysis of the needs of the Kingsway riding and to try to bring together some organizations in Kingsway for social change. So I called her and said, 'I would really like to talk to you about that community, what is it historically and where is it going?'

"And I went over and met with her at her place, and we had a really good talk. I continued to work in that riding, so I just kept going to see her. I started to have more and more respect for her. I realized that she wasn't as uncritical of the NDP as I had thought. She's definitely a party person all the way, but she has got a lot of criticism. We just started to like each other." Grace too found pleasure in the new understanding with her cousin, but declined to compare their work. "She wouldn't make any connection there," Grace said, "and I wouldn't either, particularly. I'm thoroughly sympathetic with what she's trying to do, but that's her job. We are not ones for mixing or interfering or even commenting on the jobs of our relatives. We were pleased that everybody had the courage to go their own way."

In the federal election of September 4, 1984, Brian Mulroney was Conservative leader and Ed Broadbent still led the NDP. Ian Waddell, Vancouver–Kingsway incumbent, relied on Grace's help, grateful she could still command a restless crowd.

"It was Broadbent's first western meeting," recalled Waddell, "kicking off the 1984 campaign at St. Jude's Church in East Vancouver. The national media was there, and they are pretty fierce with the cameras. Ed comes in right at the end to a fanfare, very much the modern politician. I remember Grace was pretty crippled then and had to be helped to the podium, but she stayed out there just bashing it out to the crowd over that great big group of microphones."

On voting day the party survived with thirty ridings. Both Waddell and Mitchell were re-elected. The Mulroney Conservatives took a decisive 211 seats; the Liberals were reduced to forty. As usual Grace viewed the setback stoically, but she found it harder to be philosophical about a calamity that struck without warning about two months later.

On the evening of October 29, 1984, the old Woodsworth home at 60 Maryland Street in Winnipeg broke out in flames. Police suspected arson, but the cause of the blaze was never determined. At the time the house was owned by the Woodsworth House Historical Society, but the foundations and interior walls were cracked, and estimates for renovation were up to $110,000. The house was on Winnipeg's Building Conservation List, but the tab was too high for the city, and Manitoba's NDP government seemed to fear public criticism if it spent tax dollars preserving the house of a socialist pioneer. It seemed certain that the 1907 building would be razed to make way for a parking lot.

But $40,000 had been raised toward restoration and work was underway when the fire broke out. From the ashes arose a new determination to save the Woodsworth House. Plans emerged to rebuild the structure partly as a museum and partly as a modern centre for meetings and research. Another fundraising team went into action. Charles and Bruce Woodsworth contributed drawings and memories of the house to supplement the original plans. Now the community uses the kitchen and meeting rooms, the exterior is restored, and the living room, dining room and study appear as they did on Grace and Angus's wedding day.

Increasingly disabled, Grace did little travelling in 1985. She went to Ottawa April 18 for a special NDP caucus of all present and former MPs to celebrate the equality provisions of the new Canadian Constitution. Six months later she spoke at a riding association supper in Winnipeg North Centre, where Cyril Keeper had replaced the ailing Stanley Knowles. Keeper's socialist faith was revived by Grace's inspiring speech that brought J.S. Woodsworth's vision of the co-operative commonwealth to life. He wrote, "I felt a link through you to your father and into the future. Personally I admired your gutsy bluntness and your self-assured assertiveness. You are a very generous person and your kind comments about me were as raindrops in the desert. Flowers sprouted and blossomed where days before the land was barren . . . . Your statements of principle found an echo in the core of my being."

Grace's eightieth year brought an especially satisfying honour. On February 15, 1986, the Japanese Canadian Citizens Association Redress Committee held a testimonial dinner for Grace in the midst of their national campaign for monetary compensation for losses suffered during internment in World War Two. Thomas Berger gave the keynote speech, and among the guests were several friends from the old days, particularly Hide Hyodo Shimizu, one of the Japanese franchise delegation Grace and Angus had received in Ottawa fifty years before. In 1989 Grace was delighted when the government agreed to provide financial redress to these Japanese Canadians.

On Vancouver's hundredth birthday, April 6, 1986, Grace was among one hundred senior citizens honoured with a Distinguished Pioneer Award. Socialist colleagues Tom Alsbury, Mildred Fahrni, Daisy Webster and Harold Winch were also honoured as well as Evelyn Lett, who had worked with Grace on the 1943 Subcommittee on the Postwar Problems of Women. As Vancouver Mayor Mike Harcourt opened the ceremony, Grace smiled into a familiar face from her last term in Parliament, Jeanne Sauvé, Canada's first woman Governor General.

In mid-February 1987 a federally appointed Electoral Boundaries Commission recommended that the Vancouver–Kingsway riding be eliminated in order to create four new ridings in rural and suburban areas of British Columbia. Immediately a movement sprang up to resist elimination of the riding. Grace naturally objected, but she was not in a position to influence the outcome. Outraged public meetings and court hearings did not reverse the recommendation. When the 1988 federal election was called, the riding of Vancouver–Kingsway did not exist.

Grace's arthritis was getting worse. Even with the help of a homemaker, daily tasks were overwhelming. She began to look forward to the relief of being cared for at the same time as she feared giving up what independence she still had. In March 1987 Grace moved to Shorncliffe, a nursing home in the town of Sechelt near Gibsons (the new name of her old home, Gibson's Landing), where she had hoped to spend her last years close to friends and family. She now used a cane for short distances, but she also had a motorized wheelchair. Much as Grace hated to admit it, her world was shrinking. She kept abreast of political events by listening to the radio, reading the *Manchester Guardian Weekly* and receiving visits from friends and family members.

November 12, 1987, brought the sad news of Howard Woodsworth's death in Ontario. The eldest Woodsworth sister and the youngest brother had never been particularly close, but there was much love and respect between them.

Political friends visited frequently. Margaret Mitchell vividly recalled her trip to Shorncliffe with Stanley Knowles, who was continuously grieving for his lost intellectual faculties after a brain operation. Mitchell said, "I was amused at the way she dealt with Stanley, because the lead question always is, 'How are you, Stanley?' That's pretty natural, but Stanley always tells you, over and over again about the brain operation. Well, we got up to visit Grace, and he told her about this. She tolerated it maybe twice, and then she said to him, 'Stanley, we're just not going to talk about brains this afternoon.' And he didn't. We had a wonderful time. He was able to tune in to almost everything. He was running around taking pictures just like a kid."

Through the years Grace collected the wisdom of sages including Confucius, Gautama Buddha, St. Francis of Assisi, Reinhold Niebuhr and Mahatma Gandhi. Late in life she became interested in the life story of the Dalai Lama and his Buddhist philosophy. One of her homemakers in Vancouver was a Tibetan exile; across the language barrier they spoke of Buddhism. Grace enjoyed studying these peaceful faiths which enriched and deepened her faith in the co-operative commonwealth.

On December 2, 1989, at the NDP leadership convention in Winnipeg, Audrey McLaughlin, the MP from Yukon Territory, was chosen the first woman leader of a Canadian political party. The climate of public opinion that in her own day had barred Grace from becoming the party's leader had changed. McLaughlin now stood atop a pyramid of public readiness for a woman leader that Grace's work had helped to build. Grace appreciated McLaughlin's accomplishment and wished her well.

Physically, Grace was deteriorating despite her faithful exercising. Just before her eighty-fourth birthday she moved from the relative freedom of Shorncliffe to Totem Lodge at St. Mary's Hospital in Sechelt. There she tried to continue her reading and correspondence, but her hands were so shaky that writing became impossible. For a while she had an amanuensis to take dictation, but later Grace was very frustrated, trapped within her pain and disability. One day she fell while negotiating a hallway with her walker, and she was then confined to the wheelchair and the bed. Her body was weakened, but her mind remained keen and her heart compassionate. On July 10, 1991, after suffering a stroke, Grace died. She was two weeks short of her eighty-sixth birthday.

In the Commons, MPs rose to pay tribute to this outstanding socialist humanitarian. The memorial service at Vancouver's Unitarian Church was overflowing with family, friends and political colleagues. Mike Harcourt, then BC NDP leader, attended, as did MP Dave Barrett. Harold Winch delivered the eulogy, recounting how Grace had worn his hand-me-down boots in the years when his father and hers argued socialism versus religion until the walls trembled. He evoked Grace's dedication to principle, her determination and her optimism in the face of setbacks, and closed with a rousing declaration that socialism is still the way to the future glory of civilization.

More than sixty years earlier, Grace wrote "To One of Them," defining her father in words that through conscious and fearless living she earned for herself. "The very few keep their eyes fixed on the summits of experience. They follow the steep trails which lead directly to the peaks. But they do not remain there . . . . They push on alone into this pathless solitude . . . . And so, when the great mass of humanity arrives, the trail is ready."

Appendix

List of Delegates Attending the First CCF National Convention in Regina, Saskatchewan, July 1933

Until now there has been no list of delegates to this historic convention. As I researched Grace's life, I was able to compile an incomplete listing. There were 131 delegates in total; I have identified 100. Even this partial list reveals that there were many delegates from provinces east of Manitoba, contrary to the assertions of some historians that the CCF was primarily a western Canadian group. In fact, more than one-third of the accredited delegates were from Ontario and Quebec. Ontario had 45 delegates present, the largest delegation of any province. There were 26 from CCF Clubs, 5 from the labour section, and 14 from the United Farmers of Ontario.

The absence, or presence, of one delegate is particularly interesting. T.C. (Tommy) Douglas, the first CCF premier in Canada (Saskatchewan, 1944–1962), stated publicly on several occasions that he had attended the Regina convention. At the 1956 national convention in Winnipeg, for instance, he said, "I went to my first national convention in Regina in 1933, and I have attended every national convention since." Yet in taped interviews with me, Grace emphatically denied that Douglas was there, and I have seen no newspaper report of the Regina Convention referring to his presence.

In a more recent book, *Tommy Douglas: The Road to Jerusalem*, Thomas H. McLeod and Ian McLeod state, "Tommy Douglas did not register as a delegate at the Regina convention of 1933 . . . . The registrar, Clarence Fines, did not see Douglas there." It seems likely that Douglas, as president of the Weyburn Independent Labour Party, was tied down with local commitments and travelled to Regina City Hall only on Friday, the third day of the convention, where he observed the afternoon session. That evening McLeod and McLeod state, Douglas drove two convention delegates to a public meeting in Weyburn, where he is quoted as saying the convention was "the finest thing I have ever seen."

It is possible that Grace, busy on the convention floor, did not see Douglas seated in the visitors' area that afternoon. Yet could it be that Grace, who worked closely with him from 1934 on, never spoke with him about the events of that Friday? Did he never mention to her that he was seated as a visitor and that he was inspired by the closing ceremonies of the convention? Yet Douglas tried to give the impression, especially as he assumed leadership of the NDP, that he had been present during the entire Regina convention. In 1961 he told CBC broadcast journalist Paul Fox, "In 1933 when we had our first founding convention of the CCF I still recall the opening address which was given by Mr. J.S. Woodsworth." Woodsworth's opening address was given on Wednesday, July 19, 1933, not on Friday, July 21, the only day during which any source suggests Douglas could have been there. Douglas could easily quote from Woodsworth's speech, which was widely reproduced in print, but that is not the same as having witnessed Woodsworth's original delivery.

However, by the time of the last CCF national convention August 9–11, 1960 in Regina,

Douglas had created enough belief in his attendance at the 1933 Regina convention that he was introduced as part of a group of seventeen people who had been there. And in the introduction to *Essays On the Left* published in 1971, M.J. Coldwell wrote, "Both Tommy and I were delegates to this convention which launched the CCF." Still, Grace insisted Douglas was not there, and that he was certainly not a delegate.

Any reader with evidence that someone not on this list did attend, or with fuller information on listed delegates, please send it to the publisher so that subsequent editions of this book can be updated. Thank you.

A–E: Almond, Lloyd—Montreal, PQ, national council; Barefoot, George—Norwood, MB; Blackburn, Mr. M.—St. James, MB; Blumberg, Mr. J.—N. Winnipeg, MB, alderman; Brigden, Beatrice—Winnipeg, MB,national council; Campbell, Archie—Alvinston, ON, United Farmers of Ontario; Campbell, Mr. M.D.—St. Vital, MB; Campbell, Milton, N.—MP, MacKenzie, SK (probable); Campbell, William—MB, organizer Manitoba delegation; Carmichael, Archibald, M.—MP, Kindersley, SK; Ching, Clarence; Coldwell, Major J.—Regina, SK, national council, president Saskatchewan Labour Party, 2nd CCF national leader; Coote, George G.—MP, Macleod, Alta. United Farmers of Alberta; Cotton, Lorna H., Ph.D.—Toronto, ON, resolutions committee; Cruden, Thomas—Toronto, ON, national council, president Socialist Party of Canada; Cunningham, Mrs. B.—N. Winnipeg, MB; Dixon, Sophia—Unity, SK, national council; East, James—socialist, nurse on WWI hospital ships; Eliason, Frank—Saskatoon, SK, secretary United Farmers of Canada, Saskatchewan Section; Ellston, W.—person whose copy of the resolutions committee report is held by the national archives (MG 28 IV 12 vol.7).

F–J: Farmer, Seymour J.—MLA, Winnipeg, MB, national council, minister of labour in Manitoba coalition government of John Bracken 1940–1942; Feeley, Myron—Saskatchewan minister, early CCF candidate; Fines, Clarence, M.—Regina, SK, convention registrar, credentials committee, president Western Conference of Labour Political Parties, Saskatchewan provincial treasurer in CCF government, 1944; Forsey, Eugene—Montreal, PQ, professor economics and political science McGill University, resolutions committee, League for Social Reconstruction; Fries, Hans; Gardiner, Robert—MP, Acadia, AB, president United Farmers of Alberta, national council; Garland, Mr. E.J. (Ted)—MP, Bow River, AB, chairman, later CCF national organizer, still later Canadian High Commissioner to Ireland and Minister to Norway; Good, Mr. W.C.—Paris, ON, United Farmers of Ontario, former MP, president Canadian Cooperative Union, vice-president the *Weekly Sun*; Goodale, Mr. W.H.—Winnipeg, MB; Gordon, J. King—PQ, Chair Christian Ethics McGill University, League for Social Reconstruction; Gray, Mr. M.A.—N. Winnipeg, MB, alderman, Independent Labour Party, later CCF MLA; Hammond, Lloyd—Montreal, PQ, national council; Hannam, H. Herbert—ON, educational secretary of United Farmers of Ontario; Heaps, Abraham A.—MP, Winnipeg North, MB; Hewlett, Mr. A.W.—Brandon, MB; Irvine, William—MP, Wetaskiwin, AB, national council; Johnson, Mr. H.G.—Manitoba delegation general secretary; Jones, Owen L.—Vancouver, BC, later mayor of Kelowna, BC, CCF MP 1948–57, president BC CCF 1960.

K–0: Kennedy, D.M.—MP, Peace River, AB (probable); Kristiansen, Mr.—United Farmers of Canada; Latham, George—Edmonton, AB, national council; Lebourdais, Donat, M.—Toronto, ON, constitution committee, originator of CCF Clubs, former Liberal; Lucas, Louise—Mazenod, SK, United Farmers of Canada, Saskatchewan Section, national council; Lucas, William T.—MP, Camrose, AB (probable); Luchkovich, Michael—MP, Vegreville, AB (probable); MacInnis, Angus—MP Vancouver South, national council; MacInnis, Grace—Ottawa, ON & Vancouver, BC, BC CCF Clubs, audit committee, ways & means committee; Macphail, Agnes, C.—MP, Grey South East, ON, United Farmers of Ontario, chair Ontario CCF council; McKenzie, Frank—Vancouver, BC, later president BC

CCF; **McLean, John**—Camlachie, ON, United Farmers of Ontario; **Maund, Mr. C.G.**—Toronto, ON, credentials committee; **Mentz, Walter**—Edmonton, AB; **Miller, Mrs. E.G.—S.** Winnipeg, MB; **Moriarty, William**—Toronto, ON, 1st executive secretary of the first Central Committee Workers Party of Canada (Communist, Trotskyite), Marxian Education League; **after 1924, member Communist Party of Canada Central committee, business manager of** *The Worker*, represented CPC at 5th ECCI Plenum in Moscow, 1925; **Morton, Elizabeth**—Toronto, ON, Socialist Party of Canada; **Mosher, Aaron R.**—Ottawa, ON, national council, president Canadian Brotherhood Railway Employees, later president All-Canadian Congress of Labour (ACCL); **Nicholson, W.G.**—ON, vice-president United Farmers of Ontario; **Osterhout, Mildred**—Vancouver, BC, later Vancouver School Board trustee, Mrs. Mildred O. Fahrni.

P–T: Parkinson, Joseph F.—Toronto, ON, University of Toronto, League for Social Reconstruction; **Philpott, Capt. Elmore**—Bronte, ON, national council, former Liberal, later a syndicated columnist; **Pielak, Joseph; Pratt, Mrs. O.; Priestly, Norman**—Calgary, AB, first secretary CCF; **Pritchard, William A.**—Vancouver, BC, national council, Marxist, Vancouver Labour council, first president Associated CCF Clubs of BC (Aug. 1933); **Queen, John**—MLA, Winnipeg, MB, national council, later mayor of Winnipeg; **Rathwell, Marshall**—Navan, ON, United Farmers of Ontario; **Robinson, Bert**—Toronto, ON, former leader Canadian Labour Party, Marxist, resolutions committee; **Romer, Dr. J.**—Toronto, ON, Dovercourt CCF Club; **Roper, Elmer**—Edmonton, AB, editor/publisher the *People's Weekly,* national council, later mayor of Edmonton, CCF leader Alberta, CCF MLA; **Schubert, Joseph**—Montreal, PQ, alderman, national council; **Scott, Frank R.**—Montreal, professor of law, McGill University, constitution committee, League for Social Reconstruction, co-drafter Regina Manifesto, later national chairman CCF; **Scott, Mr. R.J.**—Ontario, president United Farmers of Ontario; **Sinkinson, R.P.; Skilling, Gordon**—Toronto, ON; **Skinner, Robert**—Vancouver, BC, first BC CCF president; **Smily, Powell**—Toronto, ON; **Spafford, Mr. H.**—Brandon, MB, alderman; **Speakman, Alfred**—MP, Red Deer, AB, United Farmers of Alberta, audit committee, ways & means committee; **Spencer, Henry E.**—MP, Battle River, AB; **Spencer, Zella**—Comox, BC (perhaps only a visitor); **Spry, Graham**—Toronto, ON, United Farmers of Ontario, president & editor, the *Weekly Sun,* (formerly the *Farmer's Sun*), national secretary, League for Social Reconstruction, later secretary to Sir Stafford Cripps, MP, British Labour Party; **Steeves, Dorothy Gretchen**—Vancouver, BC, first woman CCF MLA in BC 1934–45; **Stewart, Mrs.; Stirling, George, F.**—Salmon Arm, BC, later CCF MLA; **Stubbs, Lewis St. George**—Norwood, MB, Independent Labour Party, former Manitoba County Court Judge, in July 1933 CCF candidate federal by-election Mackenzie, defeated; Manitoba MLA 1936–48; **Sutherland, J.K.**—Hanna, AB, resolutions committee, United Farmers of Alberta; **Swailes, Robert Blatchford**—BC, elected CCF MLA 1933; **Toothill, Mr.**—Regina, SK; **Turner, Amelia**—Calgary, AB, credentials committee, later Mrs. Norman Smith.

U–Z: Underhill, Frank—Toronto, ON, president League for Social Reconstruction, University of Toronto history professor, co-drafter Regina Manifesto; **Waters, Benjamin**—Vernon, BC, CCF Club; **Webber, Mr. H.G.**—S. Winnipeg, MB; **White, Fred J.**—Calgary, AB, constitution committee, leader Alberta Labour Party provincial caucus, later Prairie Regional Director Unemployment Insurance Commission; **Whitty, Mr. J.L.**—Montreal, PQ, alderman, national council; **Williams, George H.**—Semans, SK, president, United Farmers of Canada, Saskatchewan Section, national council, constitution committee; **Williams, Mr. G.R.**—Kamloops, BC, national council; **Wilmott, W.H.**—Brigden, ON, United Farmers of Ontario; **Winch, Ernest E.**—Vancouver, BC, Socialist Party of Canada, Marxian, resolutions committee, later CCF MLA Burnaby, BC 1933–57; **Woodsworth, James Shaver**—MP Winnipeg North Centre, MB 1921–42, president, founder CCF; **Young, Byron**—Brigden, ON, United Farmers of Ontario; **Woodsworth, Lucy**—observer.

Notes

The following chapter notes identify some of the source materials which are specific to given chapters. More generally, sources which were used throughout include the archival collections, interviews, newspapers and periodicals listed under primary sources below. Other frequently used sources were personal correspondence between the author and Grace MacInnis, Charles Woodsworth's unpublished memoir, "A Prophet at Home," and interviews conducted by Peter Stursberg, Mary Bishop, Ann Scotton and Joy Trott. Books referred to throughout include: Gad Horowitz, *Canadian Labour in Politics*; David Lewis, *The Good Fight*; Grace MacInnis, *J.S. Woodsworth: A Man to Remember*; Kenneth McNaught, *A Prophet in Politics*; Doris Shackleton, *Tommy Douglas*; D.G. Steeves, *The Compassionate Rebel*; and Walter Young, *The Anatomy of a Party*. All speeches quoted from the BC legislature and the Canada House of Commons were taken from the *Journals of the British Columbia Legislature* and the *House of Commons Debates* respectively, while speeches quoted from parliamentary committees were taken from *Minutes of Proceedings* for the appropriate committee.

Chapter 1: A Prairie Lily

For history of the Woodsworth and Staples families see Mollie Gillen's articles in *Chatelaine* magazine. For Woodsworth's view on immigration, see his *Strangers Within Our Gates*; for his views on social problems, see *My Neighbor*. For church background see Rupert E. Davies, *Methodism*. A useful survey of the social position of women can be found in Alison Prentice et al, *Canadian Women: A History*; for an overview of business conditions see Michael Bliss, *Northern Enterprise*. For information on the social gospel see R.J. Campbell, *Christianity and the Social Order*; for a survey of socialism see G.D.H. Cole, *A History of Socialist Thought*; Margaret Cole, *The Story of Fabian Socialism*; Anne Fremantle, *This Little Band of Prophets: The British Fabians*; and *Fabian Essays in Socialism*, edited by G.B. Shaw; particularly useful was Daniel Bell's article, "Socialism." The Tommy Douglas material is drawn from Doris Shackleton's biography, *Tommy Douglas*. The Leon Edel incident is taken from the author's interview and personal correspondence with Edel.

Chapter 3: Dreams and Discipline

Material for this chapter comes from Olive Ziegler's biography, *Woodsworth, Social Pioneer*; the biography of Agnes Macphail, *Ask No Quarter*, by Margaret Stewart; and Doris French and Alison Prentice et al, *Canadian Women: A History*, particularly Chapters 9 and 10. The material on the MacInnis lineage comes from Robert Bain, *The Clans and Tartans of Scotland*.

Chapter 4: Back Home and Broke

Facts about the Persons Case are found in a brochure available from Rideau Hall, "The

Governor General's Awards in Commemoration of the Persons Case," and the case is generally mentioned in histories of Canada. For Grace's post-Europe years in Winnipeg see *University of Manitoba Quarterly*, Autumn 1930.

Books include Anthony Mardiros' biography *William Irvine: The Life of a Prairie Radical*; Irene Howard, *The Struggle for Social Justice in British Columbia: Helena Gutteridge, the Unknown Reformer*; and Agnes Macphail's story by Doris French and Margaret Stewart, *Ask No Quarter*. Andrew MacLean's fawning portrait of his boss, *R.B. Bennett*; Lewis Thomas's interviews with Tommy Douglas, *The Making of a Socialist*; Susan Trofimenkoff's portrait, *Stanley Knowles*; Leo Heaps' biography of his father, *The Rebel in the House: The Life and Times of A.A. Heaps, MP*; and Dennis Guest's *The Emergence of Social Security in Canada*. The manifesto for the League for Social Reconstruction is from Frank R. Scott, *A New Endeavour*. The views of various prominent socialists are found in the collection of articles, *Forum: Selections from the* Canadian Forum, edited by J.L. Granatstein and Peter Stevens. See also J. King Gordon's "The Politics of Poetry," in Djwa and Macdonald's *On F.R. Scott*; and Sandra Djwa's biography of Scott, *The Politics of the Imagination*. See Gerald Caplan's *The Dilemma of Canadian Socialism* for facts about the CCF in Ontario. For an overview of Canadian business conditions see Michael Bliss's *Northern Enterprise*.

For facts on the changing role of Canadian women see *Dreams of Equality*, by Joan Sangster; Veronica Strong-Boag's *The New Day Recalled*; and Prentice et al, *Canadian Women: A History*. For a detailed survey of early history of the birth control movement in the United States and Europe see Ellen Chesler, *Woman of Valor*.

For material on the Communist Party of Canada (CPC) see Tim Buck's books, and the CPC's *Canada's Party of Socialism: History of the Communist Party of Canada 1921–1976*. William Rodney's *Soldiers of the International* is a close-up study of Canada's communists in this era. Particularly valuable is Alan Whitehorn's article, "The Communist Party of Canada." For an examination of human rights with reference to the Communist Party of Canada, see Chapter 5 in Thomas Berger's classic, *Fragile Freedoms*. Also see Norman Penner's *The Canadian Left*.

Newspaper articles of particular interest are the Grace Woodsworth and Grace MacInnis columns published in a group of weekly labour and socialist papers, such as the *Weekly News*, Winnipeg, Manitoba, on file at the National Archives of Canada. Issues of *The Challenge* are found in the Grace MacInnis Papers, University of British Columbia Library, Special Collections. The *Weekly Sun*, earlier called the *Farmer's Sun*, is found only at the University of Guelph Library. The *U.F.A. Weekly* was also consulted.

Chapter 5: Advance and Defend

Facts about the work of J. King Gordon come from his unpublished paper, "The Imperatives of Social Democracy: Then and Now," courtesy of Grace MacInnis. The Communist Party of Canada's reaction to the CCF is contained in G. Pierce, *Socialism and the CCF*. For a participant's view of the On To Ottawa Trek see Ronald Liversedge's book of that title, and for the general views of Canadian communists see Tim Buck, *Yours in the Struggle*. For a reporter's view of the times see *The Winter Years* by James Gray. See also *Social Planning For Canada*, published by the League for Social Reconstruction. For a quick overview of the government's position see *Mr. Prime Minister* by Bruce Hutchison. A more complete exploration of Canada's international relations is found in Soward, Parkinson et al, *Canada in World Affairs: The Pre-War Years*. For a thorough survey of Canada's preparations for World War Two see James Eayrs, *In Defence of Canada*.

The section on CCF summer camps is based on Grace MacInnis, "Summing Up the Summer School," in the BC *Federationist*, September 9, 1937; a *Vancouver News Herald* article, July 15, 1939; a report by William Mandale, 1945; the Camp Woodsworth Program 1950, and the author's interviews with Grace MacInnis and Mildred Osterhout Fahrni.

Chapter 6: World at War

Material for this chapter is drawn from James Eayrs, *In Defence of Canada*; Bruce Hutchison,

Mr. Prime Minister; Aloysius Balawyder, *Canadian–Soviet Relations between the World Wars*; and Patricia Strauss, *Cripps: Advocate Extraordinary*. Also useful was Soward et al, *Canada in World Affairs: The Pre-War Years*; Norman Penner, *The Canadian Left*; Doris Shackleton's *Tommy Douglas*; and Susan Trofimenkoff's biography *Stanley Knowles*. Leo Zakuta, *A Protest Movement Becalmed*; the BC *Federationist*, and the *Canadian Tribune* were also helpful.

Chapter 7: Wartime MLA

Some details of memorial ceremonies for J.S. Woodsworth were provided by Mildred Osterhout Fahrni's biographer, Nancy Knickerbocker. Books include C. Cecil Lingard and Reginald Trotter, *Canada in World Affairs: September 1941 to May 1944*. Particularly helpful for understanding the history of Japanese Canadians during World War Two is Ann Gomer Sunahara, *The Politics of Racism*. Also see Susan Walsh, "The Peacock and the Guinea Hen," found in Prentice and Trofimenkoff, eds., *The Neglected Majority*.

Chapter 8: A House Divided

Books of note include Gerald Caplan, *The Dilemma of Canadian Socialism*; Barry Broadfoot's collection of interviews with and about Japanese Canadians, *Years of Sorrow, Years of Shame*; Ann Gomer Sunahara's *The Politics of Racism*; and Cameron Nish, *Quebec in the Duplessis Era*. See also Michiel Horn, *The League For Social Reconstruction* and Alison Prentice et al, *Canadian Women: A History*. For a short history of Canada's social security network see Dennis Guest, *The Emergence of Social Security in Canada*.

Chapter 9: Citizen of the World

This chapter is based on material in the Rodney Young Papers at the University of British Columbia Library, Special Collections; material from the Franklin D. Roosevelt Library in Hyde Park, New York and interviews conducted by the author.

Books consulted include *The Politics of Racism* by Ann Gomer Sunahara, and Lester Pearson's autobiography, *Mike*, vol. 2.

Chapter 10: Intimate Enemies

Books consulted include, for material on the 1950 CCF convention, Dwja and Macdonald, eds., *On F.R. Scott*; for a view from inside the Liberal power structure, *Mike* by Lester Pearson and *Pearson: His Life and World* by Robert Bothwell. Facts about the "Red Scare" in the United States are detailed in Thomas C. Reeves, *The Life and Times of Joe McCarthy*. For a personal view of events inside the United Nations during this time, see Eleanor Roosevelt's *On My Own*. For an exploration of the ethics of free speech see Thomas Berger, *Fragile Freedoms*, Chapter 5, "The Communist Party and The Limits of Dissent." For biographical information about Thérèse Casgrain see her autobiography, *A Woman in a Man's World*, and also Isabel Bassett, *Women In Quebec*.

The section on the 1952 BC election is based on material from Roger Keene and David Humphreys, *Conversations With W.A.C. Bennett*; and Ivan Avakumovic, *Socialism in Canada*. See also Lorne Kavic and Garry Nixon, *The 1200 Days: A Shattered Dream*, and for the mechanics of the transferable vote see T. Patrick Boyle, *Elections British Columbia*.

Chapter 11: Policy-Maker Behind the Scenes

Books that were useful include Dennis Guest, *The Emergence of Social Security in Canada*; J.W. Pickersgill, *My Years with Louis St. Laurent*; Arthur Turner, *Somewhere—A Perfect Place*; Doris French and Margaret Stewart, *Ask No Quarter*; Morden Lazarus, *Years of Hard Labour*; and Thomas C. Reeves, *The Life and Times of Joe McCarthy*.

Chapter 13: Ambition Fulfilled

For an analysis of the election, see Alan Whitehorn, *Canadian Socialism*; *Report of the Royal Commission on the Status of Women in Canada*; Thérèse Casgrain, *A Woman in a Man's World*;

Pierre Trudeau, *Approaches to Politics*; and George Radwanski, *Trudeau*. For a discussion of abortion, see Eleanor Pelrine, *Abortion in Canada*.

Chapter 14: One Woman, 263 Men

Books consulted include Thomas Hockin, ed., *Apex of Power*; George Radwanski, *Trudeau*; and Richard Gwyn, *The Northern Magus*. Further useful information about Pierre E. Trudeau in this period is found in these articles: Paul Fox, "The Liberals Choose Trudeau," *Canadian Forum*, May 1968, and "Why They Can't Burst the Trudeau Balloon," in *Maclean's*, January 1969. The material about the Royal Commission on the Status of Women in Canada is drawn from the Commission's report, the autobiography *Anne Francis* by Florence Bird, and the author's interview and personal correspondence with Florence Bird. For a first-person account of the emergence of the Waffle movement see Dave Godfrey and Mel Watkins, *Gordon to Watkins to You*.

Chapter 15: Fast Forward

The section on the abortion caravan is based on the author's interview with Ellen Woodsworth, *House of Commons Debates*, the *Report on Parliamentary Security Incidents Since 1962* prepared by the Parliamentary Library, reports in the *Ottawa Citizen*, the *Globe and Mail*, Gwen Hauser's article, "Parliament Forced To Listen," in the *Pedestal*, June 1970, and Sharon C. Hager, "The Campaign for Legal Abortion in Canada 1970–1978," a draft manuscript sent to Grace MacInnis for comment.

The War Measures Act section is drawn from correspondence in the Grace MacInnis Papers at the National Archives of Canada and the author's interviews with Grace MacInnis, as well as newspaper reports. The following books were also useful: Malcolm Levin and Christine Sylvester, *Crisis in Quebec*; Thomas Berger, *Fragile Freedoms*; Robert Bothwell et al, *Canada Since 1945*; Richard Gwyn, *The Northern Magus*; George Radwanski, *Trudeau*; and Djwa and Macdonald, eds., *On F.R. Scott*.

Chapter 16: Status—What Status?

Books consulted include the Grace MacInnis booklet, *Toward Freedom*; David A. Croll, *Poverty in Canada*; and Ian Adams et al, *The Real Poverty Report*.

The 1971 NDP leadership convention section is based on the author's interviews with Grace MacInnis and Hilda Thomas; Mel Watkins's article "The Multi-National Corporation and Socialism," in Laurier LaPierre, ed., *Essays on the Left*; John Bird's article "Lewis the Inevitable Choice," in the *Financial Post*; Alan Whitehorn, *Canadian Socialism*; Desmond Morton, *NDP: The Dream of Power*; Doris Shackleton, *Tommy Douglas*; and Judy Steed's biography, *Ed Broadbent*. The NDP Resolutions Reference was also useful.

Chapter 17: For the Love of the Common People

Books consulted include Keith Bantine, *The Welfare State and Canadian Federalism*; Christopher Leman, *The Collapse of Welfare Reform*; Eleanor Pelrine, *Abortion in Canada*; and Marian Faux, *Roe v. Wade*. Periodicals consulted include Leonard Shifrin, "Family Income Security Issues," Social Planning Council of Metropolitan Toronto, 1976; *Chatelaine*, May 1972; *Canadian Magazine*, November 11, 1972; *Western Producer*, March 15, 1973; *Farm & Country*, March 27, 1973; the *Fisherman*, May 13, 1973; and the *Martlet*, February 21, 1974.

Chapter 18: The Trail Is Ready

Facts about the Governor General's Award winners are found in "The Governor General's Awards in Commemoration of the Persons Case," Rideau Hall, Ottawa, 1991; "Partners in Action," a pamphlet issued by the Status of Women Canada, Ottawa, n.d.; and a list, "Recipients of the Governor General's Awards in Commemoration of the Persons Case," Status of Women Canada, Ottawa, 1992.

The section on arthritis is drawn from: *Mosby's Medical and Nursing Dictionary, 2nd ed.* (C.V. Mosby Co., 1986); Kathryn L. Sewall and David E. Trentham, "Pathogenesis of rheumatoid

rheumatoid arthritis," *The Lancet* (January 30, 1993), pp. 283–4; "Arthritis: the facts," *Independent Living* (May–June, 1991), p. 55; Robert Winchester, "Genetic determination of susceptibility and severity in rheumatoid arthritis," *Annals of Internal Medicine* (November 15, 1992), p. 869; J.M.W. Hazes, B.A.C. Dijkmans, J.P. Vandenbroucke, R.R.P. de Vries and A. Cats, "Pregnancy and the risk of developing rheumatoid arthritis," *Arthritis and Rheumatism* (December 1990), p. 1770.

The section on the J.S. Woodsworth Chair was compiled from "The man, the chair, the endowment fund," Simon Fraser University pamphlet, c. 1983; J.S. Woodsworth Chair in the Humanities Program, SFU, 1990; and the *Institute for the Humanities Newsletter*, Spring, 1988.

Facts about the Woodsworth House can be found in "Protecting Woodsworth House," "Restoring Woodsworth House" and "Woodsworth House Museum," pamphlets of the Woodsworth House Historical Society, n.d.

The list of 100 Distinguished Pioneers is contained in the *Vancouver Centennial Program*, vol. 2, no.1.

Facts about the elimination of the Vancouver–Kingsway riding are drawn from the "Report of the Electoral Boundaries Commission for the Province of British Columbia," 1987; a press release from Vancouver Mayor Gordon Campbell, July 8, 1987; and interviews conducted by the author.

Books consulted include Judy Steed's biography, *Ed Broadbent*; Alan Whitehorn, *Canadian Socialism*; and Lorne Kavic and Garry Nixon, *The 1200 Days: A Shattered Dream*.

Primary Sources

Archival Materials Used

Colin Cameron Papers. University of British Columbia Library, Special Collections.
Communist Party of Canada Papers, National Archives of Canada.
Co-operative Commonwealth Federation and the New Deomocratic Party Papers, National
    Archives of Canada.
Paul Fox Collection, University of British Columbia Library, Special Collections.
Angus MacInnis Memorial Collection, University of British Columbia Library, Special Col-
    lections.
Angus MacInnis Papers, University of British Columbia Library, Special Collections.
Angus MacInnis Papers, National Archives of Canada.
Grace MacInnis Papers, University of British Columbia Library, Special Collections.
Grace MacInnis Papers, National Archives of Canada.
New Democratic Party Papers, University of British Columbia Library, Special Collections.
James Shaver Woodsworth Papers, National Archives of Canada.
Dorothy Gretchen Steeves Papers, University of British Columbia Library, Special Collections.
Vancouver–Kingsway New Democratic Party Constituency Association Papers, University
    of British Columbia Library, Special Collections.
Ernest Winch Papers, University of British Columbia Library, Special Collections.
Rodney Young Papers, University of British Columbia Library, Special Collections.
Walter Young Papers, University of British Columbia Library, Special Collections.

Newspapers consulted include the *Albertan*, the *Calgary Herald*, the *Christian Science Monitor*, the *Edmonton Journal*, the *Express* (Vancouver), the *Globe and Mail*, the *Hamilton Spectator*, the *Intelligencer* (Belleville, ON), the *Kelowna Daily Courier*, the *Kingston Whig-Standard*, *La Presse*, *Le Devoir*, the *London Evening Free Press*, the *London Times*, the *Montreal Gazette*, the *Montreal Star*, the *Nanaimo Free Press*, the *Nelson Daily News*, the *North Shore Press*, the *Oshawa Times*, the *Ottawa Citizen*, the *Ottawa Journal*, the *Sault Daily Star*, the *Seattle Post-Intelligencer*, the *Telegraph-Journal*, *The Age* (Melbourne, Australia), the *Toronto Star*, the *Toronto Telegram*, the *Ubyssey*, the *Vancouver News Herald*, the *Vancouver Province*, the *Vancouver Sun*, the *Victoria Colonist*, the *Victoria Times*, the *Welland Tribune*, the *Windsor Star*, the *Winnipeg Free Press* and Canadian Press reports.

Periodicals consulted include the *Bulletin* (Greater Vancouver Japanese Canadian Citizens Association), *Canadian Labour*, *Canadian Magazine*, the *CCF News*, *Chatelaine*, the *Commonwealth*, the *Democrat*, the *Federationist*, the *Fisherman*, *Industry*, the magazine of the Canadian Manufacturers' Association, *Maclean*'s, *Marie-Claire* (Paris, France), the *Pacific Tribune*, *Saturday Night*, *Time*, and *Vancouver Life*.

Interviews

Les Benjamin, MP
Gertrude Bennett
Thomas R. Berger
Elaine Bernard
Florence Bird
Ed Broadbent
Hilary Brown
Yvonne Cocke
Leon Edel
Mildred Osterhout Fahrni
Kathleen Inglis Godwin
Cyril Keeper
Stanley Knowles
Hilda Kristiansen
Justice Stuart Leggatt
Stephen Lewis
Charles Lynch
Lynn McDonald
Grace MacInnis
Jim McKenzie
Margaret Mitchell
Marjorie Nichols

Lorne Nystrom
David Orlikow
Barbara Porter
Mark Rose
Doug Sabourin
Clifford Scotton
Opal Skilling
Evelyn Grey Smith
John Smith
Peter Staples
Dave Stupich
Hilda Thomas
Arvena Tokarek
Ian Waddell
Harold Winch
Jessie Mendels Winch
Bruce Woodsworth
Charles Woodsworth
Ellen Woodsworth
Jean Woodsworth
Jerry Zaslove

Index

Cole, G.D.H., 124
Committee of Progressive Electors (COPE), 350
Commons Special Committee on Trends in Food Prices (1973), 351–354
communism, 83, 97, 124, 191, 198, 201, 209–210, 225–227, 231. *See also* socialism versus communism; versus socialism, 204
Communist Party of Canada (CPC), 93, 97, 100–102, 105, 117, 141, 144–145, 149, 170–171, 183–184. *See also* Labour Progressive Party (LPP)
Conroy, Patrick, 225
conscription, World War One, 50; World War Two, 141, 158–159, 162
Consumer Affairs, Department of, 273–276, 278
consumer prices, 202
consumer protection, 260–261, 272–273, 275–276, 278–281, 292–295, 327–330, 348. *See also* advertising, packaging practices; Canadian Consumers' Council; Consumer Affairs, Department of; food prices; Joint Senate–Commons Committee on Consumer Credit; unit pricing; food prices, 294–295; fudgsicles, 292–293
Consumer's Bill of Rights, 273
Consumers' Association of Canada (CAC), 303, 307, 354
convention, 1933 CCF national, 98–100; 1934 CCF national, 110, 199; 1936 CCF national, 126; 1937 CCF BC, 199; 1937 CCF national, 126; 1938 CCF national, 132; 1939 CCF BC, 137; 1940 CCF national, 146; 1942 CCF BC, 159–160; 1942 CCF national, 164; 1943 CCF BC, 170, 172; 1944 CCF BC, 172, 175; 1944 CCF national, 176; 1946 CCF national, 187, 196; 1948 CCF national, 197, 208; 1949 CCF BC, 200; 1950 CCF national, 204–210; 1951 CCF BC, 214; 1952 CCF national, 216, 219; 1954 CCF BC, 226–227; 1954 CCF national, 227–228; 1955 CCF BC, 229; 1956 CCF national, 233–234; 1957 CCF BC, 237, 238; 1958 CCF BC, 240–241; 1958 CCF national, 242; 1959 CCF BC, 242, 244; 1960 Canadian Labour Congress (CLC), 245; 1960 CCF BC, 245; 1960 CCF national, 245; 1961 NDP BC, 250; 1961 NDP federal, 249; 1965 NDP BC, 257; 1965 NDP federal, 257; 1967 NDP BC, 268, 272; 1967 NDP federal, 277–278; 1967 NDP Quebec, 276; 1969 NDP federal, 297, 299; 1969 NDP Saskatchewan, 296; 1971 NDP federal, 333–335; 1972 NDP BC, 350; 1973 NDP federal, 355; 1975 NDP federal, 368; 1983 NDP federal, 373; 1989 NDP federal, 377
Cooke, Katharine, B., 357
Cooper, Minerva, 184
Coote, George, 82, 91
Copps, Sheila, 310
Cornett, Jack, 201–202
Cowan, Ralph, 270
Criminal Code of Canada, birth control, 264. *See also* Section 98
Croll, David, 327
Cross, James, 312–314, 316–317
Cruden, Thomas, 102
Cummings, Roy, 348

D

day care, 179, 260, 263, 265, 268, 276, 282, 299, 319–321, 323–324, 335, 345, 374
de Gaulle, Charles, 277
De Roo, Remi, 373
Debs, Eugene, 326
Del Vayo, Alvarez, 121
Denmark, 120
Dickson, Jim, 260
Diefenbaker, John, 194, 238, 241, 250, 262, 288, 306, 316
divorce law in BC, liberalizing, 182
divorce, grounds for, 279
Dixon, Fred, 31, 55
Dixon, Sophia, 372
Djermanovic, Rojko, 224–225
Djwa, Sandra, 373
Dodge, William, 219
Douglas, A. Vibert, Dr., 178
Douglas, Thomas C. (Tommy), 31, 100, 126, 132, 137–140, 142, 173, 175, 199, 228, 232–233, 248–249, 258, 261, 267, 273, 277, 280–281, 284–285, 288, 306, 314, 316, 320, 332, 349, 351, 362, 364, 367, 369, 373–374
Doukhobors, franchise for, 220
Downton, Eric, 347
Drapeau, Jean, 313
Drew, George, 184, 203
Drury, Charles, 302
Duplessis, Maurice, 176, 178

E

Early, Mary Two-Axe, 372

Scotton, Clifford, 282, 315, 333
Section 98, Criminal Code of Canada, 52, 68, 84, 101, 111, 314
Segur, Vincent, 168
sexually transmitted disease, 324
Sharp, Mitchell, 313, 321
Shaver, Esther Josephine (Woodsworth), 25, 28, 33
Shearwood-Stubbington, D., 189
Shimizu, Hide Hyodo, 376
Showler, Birt, 197
Simon Fraser University Institute for the Humanities, 373
Sinclair, James, 201
Sissons, Charles, 24
Skinner, Robert, 102
Smith, Evelyn G., 208–209, 211
Smith, John, 208, 210
Smith, Stewart, 106
Social Democratic Party (SDP), 31
social fascism, 105
social gospel, 22–23, 116
social insurance, 166, 220
socialism, 98, 367; Canadian type, 101; in Scandinavia, 117, 120; Marxian, 230; versus communism, 219, 226, 231
Socialist Fellowship, 211–214, 218, 220
Socialist International, 228
Socialist Party of Canada (SPC), 94, 102
Socialist Party of Great Britain, 208
Solandt, Omond M., 302–303
Sommers, Robert, 235–236
Soviet Union, 85, 87, 99, 117–119, 153, 170, 198, 230
Spanish Civil War, 121, 123
Speakman, Alfred, 82
Special Select Committee of the House of Commons on Price Spreads and Mass Buying, 107, 109
Spencer, Henry, 82, 91
St. Laurent, Louis, 203, 222, 303
Stalin, Joseph, 66, 99, 118, 184
Stanbury, Robert, 269
Stanfield, Robert, 281
Stanley Park Club, 226
Stanley Park Four Seasons development, 341
Stanley Park Open Forum, 211
Staples, Belva (Woodsworth), 27, 29, 33, 38, 65, 71, 76, 161, 247, 250, 253, 262, 275, 369, 374
Staples, Hannah, 24, 65, 247
Staples, Lucy, see Woodsworth, Lucy, 26
Staples, Maureen, 247

Staples, Ralph, 247, 253, 262, 275, 369
status of women, 265. See also Royal Commission on the Status of Women
Stauning, Thorvald, 120
Steeves, Dorothy Gretchen, 46, 93, 106, 129, 141, 151–152, 158, 167, 193, 199, 203, 205, 209, 211–214, 219–220, 228, 250
Stevens, Henry Herbert, 107, 109, 114
Stirling, George, 102
Strachan, Robert, 235, 242, 250, 260, 272
Strong, George, 292, 338, 356
Strong, Maurice, 373
Stubbs, Lewis St. George, 90, 102
Stupich, David, 213, 220, 228, 238, 347
Sufrin, Eileen Tallman, 372
sustainable development, 363
Sweden, 118–119

T

tax changes, for working women, 265
Taylor, Charles, 282
Telford, Florence, 95
Telford, Lyle, 94–97, 109, 152
Textile Labelling Act (1970), 313
Thatcher, Ross, 231
Thayer, Harold, 229, 238
Thomas, Hilda, 335, 350, 355–356, 363
Thorson, J.T., 69
Tolmie, S.F., 117
trade unions, 216, 225–226, 231, 233, 238–242, 244–245, 294, 312, 326–328, 332, 348, 352, 367. See also BC Federation of Labour; Canadian Labour Congress; Meany, George
Trades and Labour Congress (TLC), 105, 242
transferable ballot, 217
Trotsky, Leon, 21, 66, 118
Trotskyists, 213–214
Trotter, W.R., 58
Trudeau, Margaret (Sinclair), 323
Trudeau, Pierre Elliott, 235, 262, 267, 272, 277, 279–281, 283–284, 288, 291–293, 295–296, 300–301, 303, 306, 308–309, 311–316, 319–320, 323–325, 327, 341, 343–344, 362, 364
Truman, Harry S., 184, 209
Turner, Arthur, 152, 238, 260
Turner, John, 275, 288, 362

U

Underhill, Frank, 93
unemployment insurance, 87